Professional Design Patterns In VB.NET: Building Adaptable Applications

Tom Fischer
John Slater
Pete Stromquist
Chaur G. Wu

Professional
Design Patterns in VB.NET:
Building Adaptable Applications

ISBN (pbk): 1-59059-274-3

Printed and bound in the United States of America 2345678910

Distributed to the book trade in the United States by Springer-Verlag New York, Inc., 175 Fifth Avenue, New York, NY, 10010 and outside the United States by Springer-Verlag GmbH & Co. KG, Tiergartenstr. 17, 69112 Heidelberg, Germany.

In the United States: phone 1-800-SPRINGER, email orders@springer-ny.com, or visit http://www.springer-ny.com. Outside the United States: fax +49 6221 345229, email orders@springer.de, or visit http://www.springer.de.

For information on translations, please contact Apress directly at 2560 Ninth Street, Suite 219, Berkeley, CA 94710. Phone 510-549-5930, fax 510-549-5939, email info@apress.com, or visit http://www.apress.com.

The source code for this book is available to readers at http://www.apress.com in the Downloads section.

Credits

About the Authors

Tom Fischer

Tom Fischer's career spans a broad range of technologies, working with some of the most prestigious consulting firms in the Twin Cities. His certifications include the Sun Certified Java Programmer (SCJP), Microsoft Certified Solution Developer (MCSD), and Microsoft Certified Database Administrator (MCDBA).

As a Microsoft Certified Teacher (MCT), Tom also helps teach other developers about the latest .NET tools and technologies.

I would like to dedicate my contributions to Theresa, Ali, and Kate. They are the greatest! – TF

John Slater

John Slater is a project manager at Management Reports International in Cleveland, OH. At MRI he is currently developing applications for the property management industry. Right now, he is working on several projects using .NET development tools and .NET Enterprise servers.

In his free time John enjoys outdoor activities and playing with his children Rachel and Nathan. He can be reached at jr_slater@hotmail.com.

Pete Stromquist

Pete Stromquist is a consultant at Microsoft Technologies (one of the nation's premier Microsoft Certified Solution Providers), specializing in web-enabled application development using Microsoft tools and technologies. He has spent the last several years architecting and developing the following types of applications: intranet content management, web-enabled training and testing software, B2B and B2C e-commerce, and web-based telemetry and logistics. He has complemented his VB skills with several other technologies such as: XML, XSL, COM+, IIS, ASP, and of course .NET.

Pete also enjoys teaching and presenting on .NET technologies. He has a Mechanical Engineering background, and received his Bachelor of Science from the University of Minnesota.

Chaur G. Wu

Chaur Wu currently works for Trend Micro Inc. as a senior software engineer. He started software programming before he was old enough to qualify for a driving license. The first program he wrote was a bingo game – in assembly code on an 8051 single chip. To capitalize on the program, he ran a small casino in the lab – he developed primitive game boxes that connected his pals and allowed them to place bets.

He's also been involved in much larger projects. For example, he developed a program in C++ to simulate the movement and geographical coverage of GPS satellites. As a research assistant in his graduate study, he implemented a wavelet-based video compression algorithm for a traffic surveillance system sponsored by Boston City Department of Transportation. He also helped solve a blurred image problem using inverse filters and other image processing algorithms for a client who designs fiber optics components in San Jose, CA.

His technical interests include distributed software systems in Java, COM, and .NET, generative programming, software design, and neural networks. Outside of work, his favorite vacation combines a one-night gambling trip to Reno followed by a day of skiing at some resort near Lake Tahoe.

You can email Chaur at cha_urwu@hotmail.com.

I would like to dedicate my efforts in this book to my two-year-old daughter, Sarah.
– CGW

Table of Contents

Table of Contents

Table of Contents

Table of Contents

Introduction

It is perhaps easiest to think of a design pattern as a template for a solution. When presented with a problem, the first thing we do is identify the defining characteristics of the problem. Then, we examine our armoury to see whether we have a generic solution that solves the problem we've characterized. If so, we apply the solution template and hence solve the problem.

The design pattern itself describes both the defining characteristics of the problem and the characteristics of the solution. The solution template is tried and tested, which means that once we've correctly identified which pattern to use, we can apply it without the need to do research and proof-of-concept testing.

This process is one that applies in all walks of life – architecture, medicine, furniture restoration... Not all disciplines use the term "design pattern", but in any case the process is the same. This book is about design patterns in object-oriented programming (OOP).

So, a design pattern in OOP is a solution template – it describes the *characteristics* of the problem and of the solution, but leaves you (the developer) to implement the *details* of the solution. Design patterns are not about programming "tricks"; rather, they penetrate to the heart of the problem at hand, and allow you to break things down into constituent parts. Design patterns help you see the path toward the overall solution, without dictating it.

This book draws on the work of the Gang of Four (or GoF) – Erich Gamma, Richard Helm, Ralph Johnson, and John Vlissides – whose seminal book *Design Patterns: Elements of Reusable Object-Oriented Software* (Addison-Wesley, ISBN 0-201-63361-2) describes the fundamentals of design patterns in OOP and catalogs 23 design patterns in significant detail.

Design patterns rely on true OO capability in the production language. Unlike previous incarnations of Visual Basic, VB.NET is truly object-oriented and requires a rather different mindset. In this book we will put the focus on using design patterns with VB.NET, and on how to put the GoF patterns (and other patterns) to use in that context.

Who is This Book For?

This book is primarily targeted at developers and architects who wish to see **discussion and functional examples of design patterns, coded in VB.NET**. The concepts behind design patterns are language-independent; therefore, the concepts described in this book can be applied in any truly object-oriented language. The book's examples are all coded in VB.NET.

The book does not assume that you have any knowledge of design patterns, but it does assume familiarity with **Visual Basic .NET**. Some knowledge of **OOP** and/or **UML** will also help the reader to appreciate this book, because most of the design patterns are built on OO principles and described using UML diagrams.

This book does contain a *UML Primer* (in Appendix A), and thus is not intended to exclude readers who are not well-versed in OOP and UML. For those readers, this book uses UML to describe some fascinating and generic applications of OO principles, and should make a good companion to a "first principles" book on OOP or UML. We do not explain the basics of OOP or UML during the course of the chapters themselves – instead, we expect that the reader is already armed with some experience or is willing to fill in the gaps.

This book is also targeted at:

❑   Readers who are familiar with VB.NET and wish to use OO techniques like design patterns to get more from the language and from their application architecture

❑   Readers who have seen the GoF *Design Patterns* book, and wish to see some of the GoF patterns and other patterns demonstrated in VB.NET

❑   Readers who have tried implementing design patterns in Visual Basic, and wish to learn how the true OO nature of VB.NET makes the whole thing much easier

This is a fundamentally practical book, and for the VB.NET developer it makes a good companion to the more theoretical GoF *Design Patterns* book.

What Does This Book Cover?

Chapter 1 begins with a definition of design patterns, and a discussion of what design patterns mean to VB and VB.NET programmers. It also contains working demonstrations of about a dozen of the GoF design patterns, with commentary and comparison.

In Chapters 2–4, we examine three case studies, each of which examines the role of design patterns in one of the three tiers of a classical 3-tier application. **Chapter 2** takes the data tier, **Chapter 3** takes the middle (business logic) tier, and **Chapter 4** takes the presentation tier. These case studies provide us with a number of lessons. For example:

- We discuss the process of recognizing the characteristics of a design pattern within a given problem, and hence design a solution architecture that is based on that pattern

- We examine implementations of GoF patterns and other patterns (in isolation and in combination)

- We look at how to translate patterns into code

- We highlight the advantages gained by applying patterns to particular problems

Although they are similar, each of these case studies is a stand-alone study designed to focus on the relevance and implementation of design patterns in the context of one particular tier.

To complement the main three case studies, **Chapter 5** examines .NET Remoting – a candidate technology for tying together the distributed tiers of a .NET application. Chapter 5 is not an introduction to .NET Remoting, but looks at the subject of .NET Remoting from a design patterns point of view. In it, we look at how design patterns have been built into the principles of .NET Remoting from the start, and how .NET Remoting also supports the developer who uses design patterns in his remoting implementations.

Chapter 6 rounds off the book by suggesting some related areas and subjects that follow on naturally from a study of design patterns. It also includes a selection of resources, references, and further reading.

What This Book Does Not Cover

This book is *not* a catalog of design patterns. Rather, its subject is the application of design patterns in real world scenarios. During the course of the book, we will discuss most (although not all) of the GoF patterns. We will also make use of some other non-GoF patterns (such as Store and Forward, Model/View/Controller, and Asynchronous Programming).

The book also does not teach VB.NET, OOP, or UML; it is assumed that the reader has some familiarity with these subjects or is willing to fill in the gaps where necessary. However, as we've already mentioned, there *is* a *UML Primer* contained in the back of the book, in Appendix A – this is intended as a quick tutorial or reference in UML.

What You Need to Use This Book

The examples in this book are coded in VB.NET. If you wish to build the examples for yourself, then you will need some or all of the following:

- A suitable operating system. Either **Windows 2000 Professional, Server** or **Advanced Server Edition** (at the time of writing, the latest service pack is SP2), or **Windows XP Professional Edition**.

- The **.NET Framework SDK**.

- In Chapters 1–4, we use the **Visual Studio .NET** IDE to build and compile applications. In fact, VB.NET ships with both the .NET Framework SDK and Visual Studio .NET; it is possible to buiild and compile these applications without VS.NET, using the command-line tools that ship with the .NET Framework SDK. We use the command-line compiler only in Chapter 5.

❑ Chapters 2 and 3 make use of a **SQL Server 2000** database server. If you don't have access to a SQL Server installation, you can run the examples using the SQL Server Desktop Engine (also known as **MSDE**).

MSDE is shipped with the .NET Framework SDK, and also with VS.NET. To install it, execute the file InstMSDE.exe (which is found in the \Program Files\Microsoft.NET \FrameworkSDK\Samples\Setup\MSDE folder). MSDE does not offer the same admin tools as SQL Server, but there are some useful command-line utilities detailed in the file \Program Files\Microsoft.NET\FrameworkSDK\Samples\Setup\html \ConfigDetails.htm. Moreover, note that VS.NET provides an arguably better UI to a SQL Server database.

❑ Chapter 3 makes use of a "legacy" class library application. We provide both the source code and the compiled DLL for this application. You don't need to build it yourself. However, if you *want* to compile the DLL for yourself, you'll need **Visual Basic 6.0** to do it.

❑ Chapter 5 makes use of **MSMQ**, and Chapters 2 and 4 make use of **IIS 5.0**. These Windows Components ship with all versions of Windows 2000 and also with Windows XP Professional Edition. Some editions do not install MSMQ and IIS as part of the default OS installation – you can install them manually from the Control Panel | Add/Remove Programs dialog.

Style Conventions

We have used certain layout and font styles in this book that are designed to help you to differentiate between the different kinds of information. Here are examples of the styles that are used, with an explanation of what they mean.

As you'd expect, we present code in two different ways: in-line code and displayed code. When we need to mention keywords and other coding specifics within the text (for example, in discussion relating to an `if...else` construct or a class or object) we use the single-width font as shown in this sentence. If we want to show a more substantial block of code, then we display it like this:

```
Public Shared Function GetInstance() As MySafeSingleton
  If m_Instance Is Nothing Then
    m_Instance = New MySafeSingleton()
  End If
  Return m_Instance
End Function
```

Sometimes, you will see code in a mixture of gray and white backgrounds, like this:

```
Public Shared Function GetInstance() As MySafeSingleton
  m_Mutex.WaitOne()
  If m_Instance Is Nothing Then
    m_Instance = New MySafeSingleton()
  End If
  m_Mutex.ReleaseMutex()
  Return m_Instance
End Function
```

In cases like this, we use the gray shading to draw attention to a particular section of the code – perhaps because it is new code, or it is particularly important to this part of the discussion. We also use this style to show output that is displayed in the console window.

Advice, hints, and background information comes in an indented, italicized font like this.

> **Important pieces of information (that you really shouldn't ignore) come in boxes like this!**

Bulleted lists appear indented, with each new bullet marked as follows:

❑ **Important Words** are in a bold type font.

❑ Words that appear on the screen, or in menus like the File or Window, are in a similar font to the one you would see on a Windows desktop.

❑ Keys that you press on the keyboard like *ctrl* and *enter* are in italics.

Customer Support and Feedback

We value feedback from our readers, and we want to know what you think about this book: what you liked, what you didn't like, and what you think we can do better next time. You can send us your comments by e-mailing support@apress.com. Please be sure to mention the book's ISBN and title in your message.

Source Code and Updates

As you work through the examples in this book, you may choose either to type in all the code by hand, or to use the source code that accompanies the book. Many readers prefer the former, because it's a good way to get familiar with the coding techniques that are being used.

Whether you want to type the code in or not, it's useful to have a copy of the source code handy. If you like to type in the code, you can use our source code to check the results you should be getting – they should be your first stop if you think you might have typed in an error. By contrast, if you don't like typing, then you'll definitely need to download the source code from our web site! Either way, the source code will help you with updates and debugging.

Therefore all the source code used in this book is available for download at http://www.apress.com. Once you've logged on to the web site, simply locate the title (either through our Search facility or by using one of the title lists). Then click on the Source Code link on the book's detail page and you can obtain all the source code.

The files that are available for download from our site have been archived using WinZip. When you have saved the attachments to a folder on your hard drive, you need to extract the files using a de-compression program such as WinZip or PKUnzip. When you extract the files, the code is usually extracted into chapter folders.

Errata

We have made every effort to make sure that there are no errors in the text or in the code. However, no one is perfect and mistakes do occur. If you find an error in this book, like a spelling mistake or a faulty piece of code, we would be very grateful to hear about it. By sending in errata, you may save another reader hours of frustration, and of course, you will be helping us provide even higher quality information.

To find known errata and submit new errata, simply go to the appropriate book page on the Apress website at http://www.apress.com.

forums.apress.com

For author and peer discussion, join the Apress discussion groups. If you post a query to our forums, you can be confident that many Apress authors, editors, and industry experts are examining it. At forums.apress.com you will find a number of different lists that will help you, not only while you read this book, but also as you develop your own applications.

To sign up for the Apress forums, go to forums.apress.com and select the **New User** link.

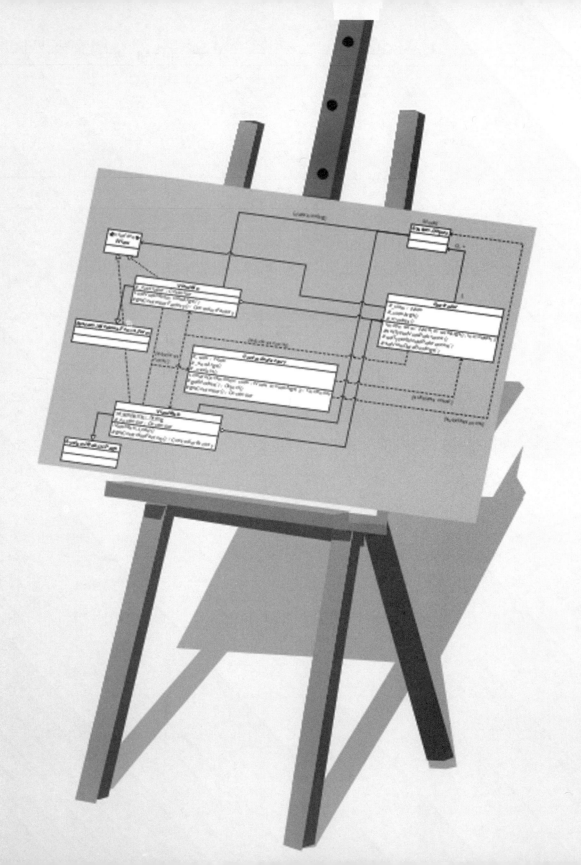

1

Introduction to Design Patterns

In the time since developers first began to apply object-oriented techniques, something quite fascinating has occurred. As the development community gained a better and better understanding of the implications of OOD, it became increasingly obvious that certain types of problem were appearing over and over again – and that similar types of problem could be solved using similar types of solution.

Around the world, experienced software engineers were independently finding that they could recognize certain specific structural (and object-related) requirements in their project design. Moreover, each time they recognized a certain requirement, they could apply a certain object pattern to achieve the required solution.

Over time, and by its very nature, OO programming has spawned a common set of recognizable problems and solutions. Thus, when a developer begins to design an application and discovers certain problems or structures are required, they often find that that *type* of problem or structure has already been identified elsewhere, and that a suitable, well-tested solution already exists.

This phenomenon has earned its own nickname – **design patterns**. In this chapter we will present an introduction to design patterns by tackling the subject from three different angles:

❑ First, we'll take a look at what design patterns are, and what they mean to Visual Basic developers.

❑ Second, with the help of a fictional payroll application, we'll compare two designs and see how the use of a design pattern can improve a VB.NET application.

❑ Finally, we'll explore some basic design patterns – focusing in particular on some very common patterns and some that are relevant to this book.

What is a Design Pattern?

Essentially, a design pattern is a combination of two things: a description of a *problem* and a description of its *solution*. It describes the problem in terms of its defining characteristics, and then describes the solution in terms of the elements involved, how they work together and what they do.

Design patterns are used in many walks of life. In Town Planning and Architecture, design patterns are used to describe the characteristics of generic problems in civic and building design, and standard solution patterns that can be applied to the problem in order to solve it. The challenge of civic designers and architects is to recognize the patterns in real life problems, match them up to the theoretical problems of one of the standard design patterns, and then solve the problem by applying the prescribed solution.

> *Note that the solution doesn't describe details of a particular implementation. Instead, it is like a* ***template***: *it describes all the necessary elements and characteristics of the solution in generic language, and forms the basis for many implementations.*

In this book, we're thinking about the concept of design patterns as applied to object-oriented programming (OOP). In the OOP context, the principles of design patterns are similar. Each pattern consists of:

❑ A description of a common programming **problem**, stated in general terms.

❑ A description of a tried and tested **solution** to the problem. The solution is in template form, describing each of the participating classes, the roles and responsibilities they have, and their relationships to one another.

For the programmer involved in an OO analysis and design task, the challenge is to recognize each generic problem pattern in their project, match it to an established design pattern, and apply the solution template to their project within their project design.

Catalogs of Patterns

This leads us to the question of where design patterns come from. Is there a definitive list of design patterns that no OO programmer should be without?

It's probably impossible to produce an exhaustive list of all possible design patterns, but as time goes on, it gets harder and harder to find new, fundamental ones. While this is an interesting academic challenge in its own right, the real purpose of design patterns is to help us build applications, and over recent years, many of the most common patterns have been identified and documented.

There is one particularly important and famous work in this area, which we'll meet in this section.

The Gang of Four

In the early 1990s, this new design practice was taking the software building business by storm. There was a proliferation of technical papers, conferences and communities that provided vehicles for programmers to exchange their latest ideas and patterns. But at first, as in any new science, information was not well cataloged or easily consumed. In 1994, four people – Erich Gamma, Richard Helm, Ralph Johnson, and John Vlissides – remedied that deficiency. They wrote what would become the pattern "bible" – *Design Patterns, Elements of Reusable Object-Oriented Software* (Addison-Wesley, ISBN 0-201-63361-2). The success of this book earned them the affectionate nickname, *the Gang of Four* (or *GoF*) – and the patterns described in the book are often referred to as the **GoF patterns**.

The GoF's *Design Patterns* book catalogs 23 design patterns. They're not just a bunch of ideas that piqued the authors' interest. These patterns represent a collection of design motifs that occur regularly in many well-built object-oriented applications. For example, their Adapter pattern constitutes a blueprint for converting the interface of an existing class into a different one with minimal effort. Any software engineer who knows about the Adapter pattern knows that there is at least one tried-and-tested way to accomplish this task without prototyping or proof-of-concept testing.

Each GoF pattern is given in terms of:

❏ A statement of the problem, in generic language, in the form of the pattern's **intent**, its **motivation**, and its **applicability**.

❏ A description of the solution, in terms of its **structure**, a list of its **participants** and the **collaborations** between them, the **consequences** of applying the pattern, **implementation** notes, some **sample code**, some **known uses** and a list of **related patterns**.

Other Catalogs and Resources

The 23 GoF patterns are not the only OO design patterns in existence. However, this book does form the single largest printed catalog of design patterns. There are many other references on the Web that you may find helpful when looking for more information. The list of web sites below is by no means exhaustive:

http://www.cetus-links.org/oo_patterns.html – An excellent listing of other links

http://hillside.net/patterns/ – The unofficial "home" of the patterns community

http://c2.com/cgi-bin/wiki – Another unofficial "home" of the patterns community

http://www.xmlpatterns.com/ – Patterns for XML (these are definitely not GoF patterns!)

http://www.dofactory.com/patterns/patterns.asp – This site is written for C# programmers, but the principles are all translatable into VB.NET

Design Patterns and Visual Basic

Despite the general applicability of design patterns, the capabilities of the underlying target language are very important. In their *Design Patterns* book, the GoF demonstrate their ideas using C++ and Smalltalk – and both of these languages are about as object-oriented as a production language can be.

In fact, this is indicative of an important consideration when applying design patterns in an object-oriented environment: namely, that the production language must be *truly* object-oriented. The reason for this is that OO design patterns are built on the foundations of OO theory – abstraction, encapsulation, polymorphism, and (implementation) inheritance. If your intended target language is one that lacks the key features associated with true object-oriented development, then this jeopardizes your chances of being able to apply a pattern in that language.

This presented a problem to anyone who wanted to apply design patterns to Visual Basic application. No version of Visual Basic (up to and including version 6.0) is truly object-oriented – in particular, VB does not directly support implementation inheritance. The task of employing patterns in VB is tedious at best, and any VB6 application that relies on a complex inheritance scheme requires quite a few workarounds.

The Arrival of VB.NET

Given this situation, it is easy to see why most Visual Basic developers were inclined to snub design patterns. While many recognized the benefits that design patterns brought to the design table, the complexity and risk involved with shoehorning the resulting designs into a Visual Basic application negated these benefits. Experienced Visual Basic developers did the cost/benefit analysis and found that design patterns did not pay.

The arrival of the .NET Framework and VB.NET has dramatically changed the analysis. VB.NET is truly object-oriented, and therefore is a good choice of production language for OO applications whose designs are based on design patterns.

Overnight, Visual Basic developers have acquired one of the most powerful object-oriented languages there is. However, they've also discovered that migration from VB6 to VB.NET is more difficult than their migrations to earlier versions of VB. While they're armed with a mastery of strange API calls and undocumented tricks, this doesn't provide much insight into crafting sound object-oriented applications. VB.NET programming requires a shift in mindset, to accompany the more object-oriented nature of the language.

Fortunately, the wealth of activity that was directed at other OO languages now provides some answers for the VB.NET programming community. From the work done to support the application of design patterns in languages like C++ and Smalltalk, there is a huge body of lessons learned and best practices in the form of design patterns in all OO languages.

When Should we use Design Patterns?

Sometimes, it *is* difficult to evaluate whether it's worth using design patterns in a particular situation – that is, when the application of design patterns will constitute a net gain. Like the VB6 developers who avoided design patterns because it was difficult to shoehorn the results into their chosen language, there are situations in which design patterns aren't right.

It's probably helpful to list some situations in which a developer might *not* want to use design patterns. After all, you wouldn't want to use a tool that adds a level of complexity unless it gives you some discernable benefit. If any of the following applies to your current situation, then you might find that it's not suitable to try to apply design patterns within that project:

- ❑ When the application being built today will not change, the code accurately captures all requirements, and there are no planned enhancements or features. The application you're building will be the first and last release. (Yeah, right.)

- ❑ Your application's code requirements are unique. No software engineer has ever built anything like it. The program does not deal with any of those routine issues like object creation and event notification. (Just what *does* it do, then?)

- ❑ There is plenty of time to prototype all of your new design ideas. Alternatively, you are so confident of your ideas that they do not require any proof-of-concept testing.

- ❑ Everyone on your team has worked together for twenty or so years. If you ask Bill to try the "thing-a-ma-jig" trick, he knows exactly what to do. The team already possesses a common design vocabulary, so you don't need to learn someone else's.

If your situation is described in any of the above, please pass this book on to a friend. Otherwise, keep reading.

There are two questions to keep in your head when you're trying to work out the value of design patterns in your project. First, can you justify the presence of the pattern, even when you consider the extra complexity and potential performance hit that it brings? Second, will the added value of a proven design and lower maintenance bills cover the upfront investment?

How a Design Pattern can Improve a Design

Before we begin to step through our description and examples of some of the GoF patterns, let's look at a sample of the design work surrounding a fictitious payroll application. We'll look at two different design proposals: one of them employs a design pattern, and one does not. We'll see how the one with the design pattern turns out to provide a significantly more extensible and flexible design.

The Fictional TakeHomePay Application

The preliminary requirements have been gathered for the WantaBeBig Corporation's new "Take Home Pay Calculator" application, hereafter known as TakeHomePay. WantaBeBig has invited two software companies (N and P) to propose designs for the application, and each hopes to win the coding phase contract.

WantaBeBig have specified that the target language for the application is VB.NET. They have not stated any application design expectations.

In a requirements document, they have:

- ❑ Outlined that the purpose of the TakeHomePay application is to estimate the amount of money that a WantaBeBig employee can expect to see in their next paycheck, immediately after submitting timesheets

- ❑ Stated that calculating this amount would involve several complex calculations, based on varying country taxes, local taxes, and retirement plan contributions

- ❑ Included details of all of the business rules for these cumbersome calculations

- ❑ Noted that WantaBeBig currently operates in London and New York City and may open up other offices over the next few years

- ❑ Predicted that the Personnel Manager had plans for the introduction of a second retirement plan

Unsurprisingly, the lead architects of the two consulting companies take different approaches. One architect designs TakeHomePay in the style of a number of previous applications that his team had built using Visual Basic 6.0. The other architect, with similar experience, elects to employ some recently acquired pattern knowledge in his design. We'll look at each of these designs in turn.

The Non-Pattern Design

Since the lead architect at Company N had constructed a payroll-like application before, he takes little time modeling the application. He produces the following object model:

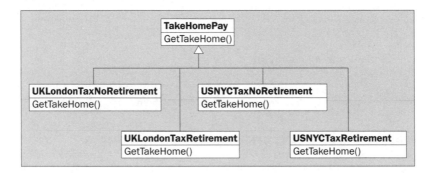

This figure is a standard UML class diagram. If you're not sure how to translate it, or if you would appreciate a quick UML refresher, please refer to the UML Primer in the Appendix A.

The design is simple and straightforward, and contains just five classes in total:

❑ The main driver class, `TakeHomePay`

❑ Four supporting classes (representing the two offices and the fact that an employee either belongs to the retirement plan or doesn't)

The Pattern Design

As it turned out, the lead architect at Company P has also built payroll applications in the past. But he is worried. He doesn't like the idea of creating a bunch of specialized classes to handle every combination of country, locality, and retirement option for an employee. Moreover, he is concerned about the potential for new offices and retirement plans! After considerable thought, he thinks that maybe a design pattern known as *Decorator* could be used to manage the required functionality of the `TakeHomePay` application – and it will also be able to cope with additional requirements in the future:

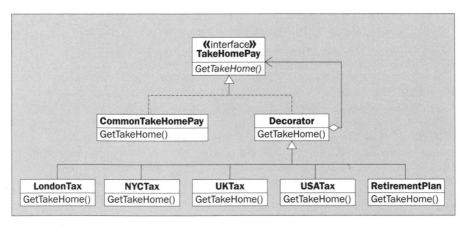

If you're curious about how the Decorator pattern works, but you don't want to jump ahead, you'll be pleased to know that the mechanics of this pattern are surprisingly simple. All of the derived classes from Decorator operate on a concrete object (CommonTakeHomePay in this example) that gets passed around like a hot potato. For example, an instance of a CommonTakeHomePay object might first be passed as a parameter into LondonTax. That entire object could then be passed as a parameter into UKTax, and so on. Throughout the entire process, the derived class objects (UKTax, LondonTax, etc.) all operate on the single original CommonTakeHomePay object.

A Change in the Requirements

After the software consulting companies submitted their proposals, the WantaBeBig Company started offering a second retirement plan and opened an office in Miami. They decide that, in the light of this business development, it would be foolish to award the TakeHomePay contract immediately. Instead, they ask the consulting companies to resubmit their designs in the light of the new information.

Both lead architects decide simply to extend their existing designs to take in the new structure. At Company N, the lead architect finds that he can model the new requirements like this:

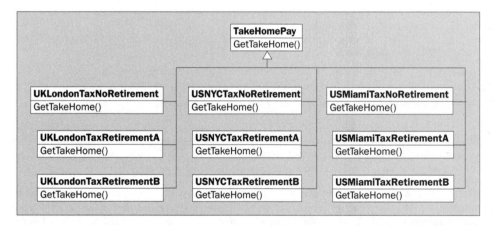

As you can see, they have to add no fewer than five new classes to the existing design. There is still one main driver class, TakeHomePay; but now there are *nine* supporting classes (representing the three offices and the fact that there are now three retirement plan options – A, B and none). It's becoming clear that further additions to the business empire will cause rapid growth in the size of this object model.

At Company P, lead architect finds that his revised model is almost identical to the original:

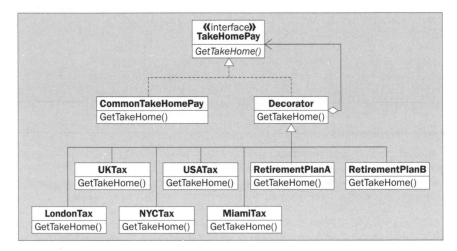

One of the objects represents the new Miami office, and the other represents the new retirement plan. This is clearly a more extensible design.

Which Design Won the Contract?

The difference in the ability of each design to handle additional requirements is dramatic. The pattern-based design only needed two new classes, while the non-pattern design experienced a type of "class multiplier" effect.

Which `TakeHomePay` application would you want to build or maintain? The choice is between one with a sophisticated pattern-based architecture and one with an astronomical number of classes. Of course, most experienced Visual Basic developers could think of several improvements for the non-pattern design. But why bother? The Decorator pattern already solved the problem.

Remember, too, that this wasn't an exercise in finding the best way to tackle this particular problem, but a demonstration of how a pattern could make a profound difference in the ability of your solution to adapt to changing requirements. We'll return to this example later in this chapter, and give an implementation of the `TakeHomePay` application using Company P's Decorator-based design.

Now that we've seen an example of patterns in action, let's take a tour of the different patterns documented by the GoF.

The Building Blocks

In their *Design Patterns* book, the GoF classified their 23 patterns into three broad categories: **creational patterns**, **behavioral patterns**, and **structural patterns**. Within these categories, each of the patterns has a name that is chosen to reflect the purpose of the pattern. The names of the patterns and their categories provide designers with a useful handle for thinking about which type of pattern may solve a particular high-level problem. For example, if you need a pattern that describes object creation, then you're likely to need one of the five creational patterns.

In this section we're going to take, as a starting point, these three categories of patterns. We'll explain the common characteristics of each category, and we'll examine in more detail some of the most commonly used patterns in each category.

As I mentioned earlier, the GoF describe each pattern by using a standard template. (That is, they state the problem in terms of the intent, motivation, and applicability, and the solution in terms of structure, participants, etc.) This template is based on standards for documenting and describing designs that have been developed over years; while it borders on being academic in nature, its features are useful without exception. In particular, the **intent** constitutes a brief and insightful synopsis of the pattern. Here, for each pattern we discuss in depth, we'll include a statement of the GoF's intent for that pattern quoted from their *Design Patterns* book.

Note that we won't examine *all* 23 of the GoF patterns in depth. The aim of this book is not to cover ground that has already been laid by *Design Patterns*, but to help put things into a VB.NET perspective with real examples. Once you've seen these more common patterns in action, you will be well equipped to investigate and appreciate the others.

Running the Examples in this Chapter

All the code for this chapter is contained in a Visual Basic .NET console application called `Wrox.ProDPA6985.Ch01`. Each pattern's demonstration code resides in its own VB file, executed via a `Main` routine on that file.

To execute the demonstration for a pattern, open the `Wrox.ProDPA6985.Ch01` solution in Visual Studio .NET. View the properties for the project (by typing *Shift+F4*) and set the corresponding module as the **Startup object**. For example, if you set the **Startup object** to **Singleton**, as shown below, and then execute the application, it will run the `Main` routine that demonstrates the Singleton pattern:

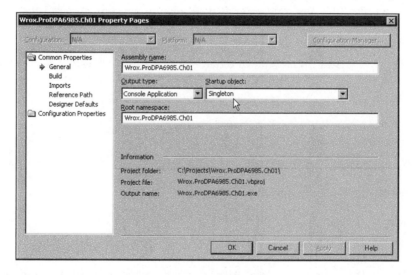

Let's start our discussion with the family of creational patterns.

Creational Patterns

Creational patterns make applications less dependent on the vagaries of simplistic object construction and class referencing. They provide a more flexible approach towards the four Ws of object creation – Who, What, Where, and When.

Two of the creational patterns we discuss – Abstract Factory and Factory Method – exemplify the subtlety and difficulty of properly applying patterns. Their names are similar, and fundamentally they do the same thing – they both create objects. However, it's *how* each pattern achieves its task that makes all the difference. Abstract Factory uses *objects* to manage object creation, while Factory Method relies on *class inheritance* to create the right object.

The GoF cataloged five creational patterns: Abstract Factory, Builder, Factory Method, Prototype, and Singleton. We'll be covering the Singleton, Abstract Factory, and Factory Method patterns.

The Singleton Design Pattern

> **GoF Intent**: Ensure a class only has one instance, and provide a global point of access to it.

The most humble of patterns, **Singleton** ensures that an application creates exactly one instance of the class in question. One classic application of Singleton is the management of scarce database connections – this was particularly true before the advent of built-in pooling. Many other applications are still relevant today – including the management of printer objects and TCP/IP connection objects.

In the old days of Visual Basic 6.0 and earlier, VB did not support explicit object creation. Instead, VB hid object creation and developers were usually forced to control object creation with the aid of class events and global variables. With the advent of VB.NET, the days of implicit object creation are gone. We now have an accessible New constructor method, and this means that we can employ the Singleton pattern in our VB.NET code.

> *In fact, the introduction of the default constructor into VB.NET is more than an object-oriented nicety. One leading cause of VB6 bugs was the fact that developers could not always control object creation. In particular, problems arose when declaring a variable using the New keyword, like this:*
>
> ```
> Dim objSomeObject As New SomeObject
> ```
>
> *In such circumstances, the developer could never be certain if or when the Visual Basic runtime engine instantiated the object.*

Singleton is so simple that a diagram doesn't help to explain it. The mechanics are straightforward:

1. Hide the default class constructor

2. Add a shared member referencing the solitary, instantiated object

3. Create a public function that creates/returns the referenced object

> *To emphasize the importance of applying design patterns accurately, let me recount a little story. A programmer once implemented his own Singleton-like pattern by ignoring Step 3 and using the default constructor instead. The idea made sense, and to a point, it worked. Only one problem – each execution of New meant that a second instance of the class would be created!*
>
> *The moral of the story is that you should think twice before reinventing the wheel. One of the benefits of using an existing design pattern is that its consequences are known and documented. As soon as you change the specification of the design pattern, you can no longer be sure of the behavior and consequences.*

An Example

Here's an example of a class called `MySingleton`, which is implemented using the Singleton design pattern. The default constructor, `New()`, has been hidden (by making it `Private`). The `Shared` member, `m_Instance`, represents the single shared instance of the object, and the public function `GetInstance()` returns the object reference (but only creates it if it doesn't already exist):

```vb
Public Class MySingleton
  ' Private members
  Private Shared m_Instance As MySingleton
  Private Shared m_TimeOfBirth As String

  ' Private New constructor
  Private Sub New()
    Console.WriteLine("Creating Singleton at " & Now.ToLongTimeString)
    m_TimeOfBirth = Now.ToLongTimeString
  End Sub

  ' Public method for "creating" the instance
  Public Shared Function GetInstance() As MySingleton
    If m_Instance Is Nothing Then
      m_Instance = New MySingleton()
    End If
    Return m_Instance
  End Function

  ' Public property
  Public ReadOnly Property TimeOfBirth() As String
    Get
      Return m_TimeOfBirth
    End Get
  End Property
End Class
```

Just because `New` is not publicly unavailable, this doesn't mean we don't need to create a `MySingleton` object instance. The trick is to make sure that `GetInstance` only creates it when the object does not exist!

Here's a little routine to show the design pattern in action. We create two object variables, `objTest1` and `objTest2`, and use our public `GetInstance()` method to instantiate them:

```vb
Sub Main()
  Dim objTest1 As MySingleton
  Dim objTest2 As MySingleton
  Dim i As Integer

  ' call GetInstance()
  objTest1 = MySingleton.GetInstance()
  Console.WriteLine("GetInstance() called at " & _
                    Now.ToLongTimeString & "; " & _
                    "objTest1.TimeOfBirth()=" & _
                    objTest1.TimeOfBirth())
```

```
         ' wait a while
         For i = 1 To 500000000
         Next

         ' call GetInstance() again
         objTest2 = MySingleton.GetInstance()
         Console.WriteLine("GetInstance() called at " & _
                           Now.ToLongTimeString & "; " & _
                           "objTest2.TimeOfBirth()=" & _
                           objTest2.TimeOfBirth())

         MessageBox.Show("Click OK to end")
      End Sub
```

Of course, we can't use the New *constructor to create them, because it's private. If you try using code like this:*

```
      Dim objTest1 As New MySingleton()
```

...then you'll get an IntelliSense error message notification.

When you run this example, you should get output like this:

```
Creating Singleton at 16:43:51
GetInstance() called at 16:43:51; objTest1.TimeOfBirth()=16:43:51
GetInstance() called at 16:43:57; objTest2.TimeOfBirth()=16:43:51
```

What does this show? First, there's only one Creating Singleton... line, which shows that during the course of this execution, the private New() constructor only runs once – so only one instance is created. The subsequent lines show that the two object variables objTest1 and objTest2 are references to the same singleton object – the one that was created the first time GetInstance() was called.

Singletons in Multithreaded Applications

There is one *gotcha* worth mentioning. When creating singletons for multithreaded applications, you need to make sure they are thread-safe. In the example below, a Mutex object does the trick, but many other techniques exist. That's the beauty of patterns – it's the idea that counts, not the code!

```
Public Class MySafeSingleton
   ' Private members
   Private Shared m_Instance As MySafeSingleton
   Private Shared m_TimeOfBirth As String
   Private Shared m_Mutex As New System.Threading.Mutex()

   ' Private New constructor
   Private Sub New()
      Console.WriteLine("Creating Singleton at " & Now.ToLongTimeString)
      m_TimeOfBirth = Now.ToLongTimeString
   End Sub

   ' Public method for "creating" the instance
   Public Shared Function GetInstance() As MySafeSingleton
      m_Mutex.WaitOne()
      If m_Instance Is Nothing Then
         m_Instance = New MySafeSingleton()
```

```
      End If
      m_Mutex.ReleaseMutex()
      Return m_Instance
   End Function

   ' Public property
   Public ReadOnly Property TimeOfBirth() As String
      Get
         Return m_TimeOfBirth
      End Get
   End Property
End Class
```

The Abstract Factory Design Pattern

> **GoF Intent:** Provide an interface for creating families of related or dependent objects without specifying their concrete classes.

Suppose we have to write an interactive storybook application, which tells the story about a family of three bears – Daddy Bear, Mommy Bear, and Baby Bear. Suppose also that the program must also be able to tell this story using one of two bear families – either golden bears or brown bears. (Users ask for the strangest things.) Of course, we will not know which family to use for the story until run time; some users like to hear the story told with brown bears, others prefer to hear it told with golden bears.

Our application will need to create three objects in the implementation of this storybook application – either GoldenDadBear, GoldenMomBear, GoldenBabyBear or BrownDadBear, BrownMomBear, BrownBabyBear. What is the best, most flexible way for our code to instantiate all of the necessary bear objects, based on the user's choice of "golden" or "brown"? This far-fetched design requirement occurs more frequently than you might imagine, and matches the **Abstract Factory** design pattern.

A classic application of Abstract Factory involves the creation of entire families of GUI widgets. If you ever build an application running on Windows and some future Linux-based shell, then you just might need to manage the creation of toolbars, textboxes, dialog boxes, etc, based on the choice of operating system. Here, as in our bear story application, the Abstract Factory pattern provides the solution.

A Simple Non-OO Solution

For the sake of comparison, before we examine the Abstract Factory solution let's take a look at a more basic approach. We might consider begetting our bear family by using a simple decision structure. We'd use a Select Case statement whenever we needed to decide which bear version of the desired family member to create. We'd need a global variable (something like gBearFamily) that would remember the user's preference for Golden or Brown bears. Then, when building an objBabyBear, we'd first read the gBearFamily global variable; and based on its value we'd call the associated family's BabyBear constructor within a Select Case:

```
Select Case gBearFamily
   Case "Golden"
      objBabyBear = New GoldenBabyBear()
   Case "Brown"
      objBabyBear = New BrownBabyBear()
End Select
```

I am not going to rant about the evils and dangers of relying on global variables, because I have used them too. Despite the honored membership of the global variable in the Spaghetti Code Club, the fact is that VB6 developers were often hard-pressed to find a more efficient alternative.

Aside from the reliance on global variables, and the many `Select Case` statements now littering the application, more significant problems could surface after the first release of the application. For example, maybe we forgot that `objDadBear` really came in three flavors, not two. And how easy is it to keep those little changes in the `BrownBabyBear` class synchronized with its `GoldenBabyBear` counterpart?

A More Flexible Design Pattern Solution

It is with such depressing prospects in sight that we bite the bullet and apply the Abstract Factory pattern. After all, it was conceived for this exact situation – managing object creation given multiple families of related objects.

Let's look at the UML for our solution, based on the Abstract Family pattern. It might be easier to appreciate this pattern if you think of it in two parts – the "bear creation managers" and the "bear implementers". In our storybook application, the three `BearFactory` classes (on the left) serve as the object creation managers. The other classes implement the bears:

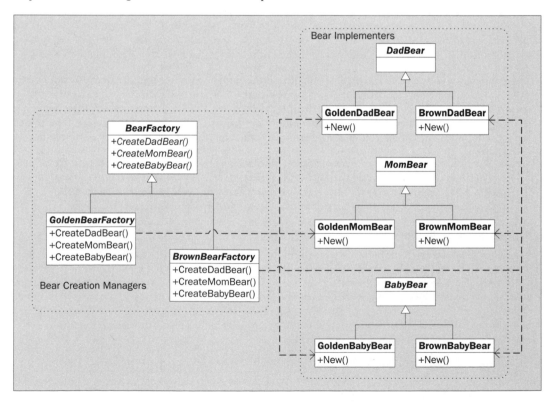

Let's see how this translates into code. We'll start by building the bear creation managers. First, here's the `BearFactory` interface:

```
MustInherit Class BearFactory
   Public MustOverride Function CreateDadBear() As DadBear
   Public MustOverride Function CreateMomBear() As MomBear
   Public MustOverride Function CreateBabyBear() As BabyBear
End Class
```

Next, we use this to build the two bear creation managers, GoldenBearFactory and BrownBearFactory:

```
Public Class GoldenBearFactory : Inherits BearFactory
   Public Overrides Function CreateDadBear() As DadBear
      Return New GoldenDadBear()
   End Function

   Public Overrides Function CreateMomBear() As MomBear
      Return New GoldenMomBear()
   End Function

   Public Overrides Function CreateBabyBear() As BabyBear
      Return New GoldenBabyBear()
   End Function
End Class
```

The colon (:) notation in the first line of this class is a line continuation character. The VB.NET engine expects the Inherits BearFactory *clause to be on a new line, like this:*

```
Public Class GoldenBearFactory
   Inherits BearFactory
```

I just prefer using the colon line continuation character – it makes the inheritance relation more obvious.

The BrownBearFactory creation manager is very similar to the GoldenBearFactory creation manager we've just seen:

```
Public Class BrownBearFactory : Inherits BearFactory
   Public Overrides Function CreateDadBear() As DadBear
      Return New BrownDadBear()
   End Function

   Public Overrides Function CreateMomBear() As MomBear
      Return New BrownMomBear()
   End Function

   Public Overrides Function CreateBabyBear() As BabyBear
      Return New BrownBabyBear()
   End Function
End Class
```

Now, we'll construct the bear implementers. We will use interfaces again, to ensure that all of our bear family members act accordingly. For example, the interface BabyBear guarantees that BrownBabyBear and GoldenBabyBear are good kids:

```
MustInherit Class DadBear
End Class

MustInherit Class MomBear
End Class

MustInherit Class BabyBear
End Class
```

Having created the generic `DadBear`, `MomBear`, and `BabyBear` classes, we can describe the specific `Golden` and `Brown` specializations that inherit from these classes. Here are the `GoldenDadBear` and `BrownDadBear` classes that inherit from `DadBear`:

```
Public Class GoldenDadBear : Inherits DadBear
   Public Sub New()
      Console.WriteLine(TypeName(Me).ToString & " Created")
   End Sub
End Class

Public Class BrownDadBear : Inherits DadBear
   Public Sub New()
      Console.WriteLine(TypeName(Me).ToString & " Created")
   End Sub
End Class
```

In order to keep the example simple, we've made these classes very small. We'll need four more classes for `GoldenMomBear`, `BrownMomBear`, `GoldenBabyBear`, and `BrownBabyBear`:

```
Public Class GoldenMomBear : Inherits MomBear
   Public Sub New()
      Console.WriteLine(TypeName(Me).ToString & " Created")
   End Sub
End Class

Public Class BrownMomBear : Inherits MomBear
   Public Sub New()
      Console.WriteLine(TypeName(Me).ToString & " Created")
   End Sub
End Class

Public Class GoldenBabyBear : Inherits BabyBear
   Public Sub New()
      Console.WriteLine(TypeName(Me).ToString & " Created")
   End Sub
End Class

Public Class BrownBabyBear : Inherits BabyBear
   Public Sub New()
      Console.WriteLine(TypeName(Me).ToString & " Created")
   End Sub
End Class
```

It is worth noting how any Abstract Factory pattern rests on the strategic application of interfaces. It is through interfaces that all of our "Bear Creation Managers" communicate with all of the "Bear Implementation" classes.

Now we can write a little routine to test this. We'll use a simple message box to ask the user whether they want to create a family of golden bears or a family of brown bears. The result is captured in the object variable `objGoldenPreferred` (which evaluates to either `DialogResult.Yes` or `DialogResult.No`):

```
Sub Main()
  Dim objBearFactory As BearFactory
  Dim objDadBear As DadBear
  Dim objMomBear As MomBear
  Dim objBabyBear As BabyBear
  Dim objGoldenPreferred As DialogResult

  ' choose one of these
  objGoldenPreferred = _
      MessageBox.Show( _
          "Click Yes for Golden Bears. Click No for Brown Bears", _
          "Storybook Application", MessageBoxButtons.YesNo)
```

Then we use the value of `objGoldenPreferred` to create the appropriate `BearFactory` object:

```
  ' create a BearFactory, depending on user's selection
  If objGoldenPreferred = DialogResult.Yes Then
    objBearFactory = New GoldenBearFactory()
  Else
    objBearFactory = New BrownBearFactory()
  End If
```

Finally, we can use the following generic code to create `DadBear`, `MomBear`, and `BabyBear` objects. This code will use the `BearFactory` object selected above, and hence create members of the desired bear family:

```
  ' use the BearFactory object to create DadBear, MomBear, BabyBear
  objDadBear = objBearFactory.CreateDadBear
  objMomBear = objBearFactory.CreateMomBear
  objBabyBear = objBearFactory.CreateBabyBear

  MessageBox.Show("Click OK to end")
End Sub
```

The object constructors report to the console at the time they are executed, noting the object type being created. So, when you run this application you should see a message box like this:

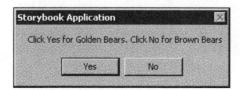

If you click **Yes**, then the application will go ahead and tell the story using golden bears. You'll see this output at the console:

```
GoldenDadBear Created
GoldenMomBear Created
GoldenBabyBear Created
```

If you click **No**, then the application will tell the story using brown bears, and you'll see this output at the console instead:

```
BrownDadBear Created
BrownMomBear Created
BrownBabyBear Created
```

We had to create a foundation of 12 classes in order to be able to write such a generic piece of code in the `Main()` routine. But with that foundation in place, the application as a whole is immensely scalable and extensible. Abstract Factory not only manages existing families of objects, but also easily handles the addition of new families.

However, there is one caveat. The constraining influence of the `BearFactory` class means that if you create a new family, it must look very much like the existing families. If you wanted to add a new bear family with teenagers, then things would get a little more complicated – it can't be done using the Abstract Factory pattern alone. In fact, you might save the situation by using the Abstract Factory pattern in conjunction with the Adapter pattern – but that discussion is for another time…

The Factory Method Design Pattern

> **GoF Intent:** Define an interface for creating an object, but let subclasses decide which class to instantiate. Factory Method lets a class defer instantiation to subclasses.

Don't blink when watching **Factory Method** in action for the first time. If you do, you stand a good chance of missing the subtlety of its magic. The underlying premise is rather simple. A common requirement in applications is for an object factory class that creates an array of similar objects, like this:

```
Public Class InflexibleDwarfFactory
  Private m_Dwarfs As New ArrayList()

  Public Sub New()
    m_Dwarfs.Add(New Dwarf("Bashful"))
    m_Dwarfs.Add(New Dwarf("Doc"))
    m_Dwarfs.Add(New Dwarf("Dopey"))
    m_Dwarfs.Add(New Dwarf("Grumpy"))
    m_Dwarfs.Add(New Dwarf("Happy"))
    m_Dwarfs.Add(New Dwarf("Sleepy"))
    m_Dwarfs.Add(New Dwarf("Sneezy"))
  End Sub

  Public Sub ShowDwarfs()
```

```
        Dim aDwarf As Dwarf
        Console.WriteLine("Created by " & TypeName(Me).ToString & ":")
        For Each aDwarf In m_Dwarfs
          Console.WriteLine(aDwarf.Name)
        Next
      End Sub
   End Class
```

This is a perfectly functional class, up to a point. However, what happens when we want to adapt this object factory to create the Dwarf objects in a different order? Or when we want the object factory to create a different set of Dwarf objects? Using the model above, we would be forced to revisit the DwarfFactory itself and re-code it.

We can achieve a much more flexible situation by applying Factory Method. Here, we replace the default constructor, New(), with our own custom constructor method, AddDwarfs():

```
   Public Class DwarfFactory
      Protected m_Dwarfs As New ArrayList()

      Public Overridable Sub AddDwarfs()
        m_Dwarfs.Add(New Dwarf("Bashful"))
        m_Dwarfs.Add(New Dwarf("Doc"))
        m_Dwarfs.Add(New Dwarf("Dopey"))
        m_Dwarfs.Add(New Dwarf("Grumpy"))
        m_Dwarfs.Add(New Dwarf("Happy"))
        m_Dwarfs.Add(New Dwarf("Sleepy"))
        m_Dwarfs.Add(New Dwarf("Sneezy"))
      End Sub

      Public Sub ShowDwarfs()
        Dim aDwarf As Dwarf
        Console.WriteLine("Created by " & TypeName(Me).ToString & ":")
        For Each aDwarf In m_Dwarfs
          Console.WriteLine(aDwarf.Name)
        Next
      End Sub
   End Class
```

Now, the array of Dwarf objects is Protected, rather than Private – thus, any object that inherits from DwarfFactory has access to the array. Just as significantly, the AddDwarfs() constructor method is Overridable, which means that an inheriting object can implement its own AddDwarfs() constructor method.

> *It is not possible to make New() overridable, and this is another reason why the InflexibleDwarfFactory class really is so inflexible.*

So let's use our DwarfFactory class to build an application to illustrate its newfound flexibility. We haven't created the Dwarf class yet, so let's do that next. This simple class contains an implementation of the default constructor, New(), which sets the dwarf's name. It also has a read-only Name property. All of our fairy tales will need this little helper class:

```
Public Class Dwarf
  Private m_Name As String

  Public Sub New(ByVal Name As String)
    m_Name = Name & " the " & TypeName(Me).ToString
  End Sub

  Public ReadOnly Property Name() As String
    Get
      Return m_Name
    End Get
  End Property
End Class
```

We'll write a little application that tells two stories: first, it tells the story of *Snow White* (which, as we all know, features seven dwarfs). Then, it will tell a new story, *Snow White II The Sequel,* in which Dopey travels to visit his Scottish cousins Morag and Murdo. For the second story, we'll create a new object factory based on `DwarfFactory`, like this:

```
Public Class SnowWhiteIIDwarfFactory : Inherits DwarfFactory
  Public Overrides Sub AddDwarfs()
    m_Dwarfs.Add(New Dwarf("Dopey"))
    m_Dwarfs.Add(New Dwarf("Cousin Morag"))
    m_Dwarfs.Add(New Dwarf("Cousin Murdo"))
  End Sub
End Class
```

Now we can tell the two stories:

```
Sub Main()
    Dim objSnowWhiteDwarfFactory As New DwarfFactory()
    objSnowWhiteDwarfFactory.AddDwarfs()
    objSnowWhiteDwarfFactory.ShowDwarfs()

    Dim objSnowWhiteIIDwarfFactory As New SnowWhiteIIDwarfFactory()
    objSnowWhiteIIDwarfFactory.AddDwarfs()
    objSnowWhiteIIDwarfFactory.ShowDwarfs()

    MessageBox.Show("Click OK to end")
End Sub
```

When you run the application, you should see the following output. Admittedly, the plot of these two stories is not strong, but you can see that the character list is different:

```
Created by DwarfFactory:
Bashful the Dwarf
Doc the Dwarf
Dopey the Dwarf
Grumpy the Dwarf
Happy the Dwarf
Sleepy the Dwarf
Sneezy the Dwarf
```

```
Created by SnowWhiteIIDwarfFactory:
Dopey the Dwarf
Cousin Morag the Dwarf
Cousin Murdo the Dwarf
```

Thus, although we have added a little complexity in the way the `Dwarf` objects are created (inserting an extra constructor method in addition to the existing constructor), we have gained flexibility by encapsulating object creation without encumbering the default constructor. In fact, this feature is invaluable in situations when the superclass's default constructor is more complex than that of the `DwarfFactory` constructor. For example, what if the `DwarfFactory` constructor included a user authentication mechnaism? Would you (or could you) include that logic in your new constructor?

Some programmers consider Factory Method to be a default coding style. Indeed, many developers feel that the ability to take explicit control of object creation is so important that it should never be left sitting in the middle of some arbitrary method. The power and flexibility gained by taking control via Factory Method (and indeed Abstract Factory) are quite significant, as we've seen here.

At this point, we will leave the subject of creational patterns, and move on to look at some structural patterns.

Structural Patterns

Structural patterns govern how objects and classes work together. The most common feature of these patterns is that they all work by inheritance. Each pattern applies the principles of inheritance in quite different ways to accomplish its ends. Some patterns, like Adapter, apply inheritance with incredible simplicity, while others require a little coffee and serious thought.

> *Before we go crazy with inheritance, it's worth noting a warning expressed by the GoF in relation to the question of object inheritance versus object composition. In brief, they expressed a strong preference for composition when faced with a choice between it and inheritance. If you ever built an application relying on a superclass that someone changed without your knowledge, then you probably have an idea why they said that!*

The GoF cataloged seven structural patterns: Adapter, Bridge, Composite, Decorator, Façade, Flyweight, and Proxy. We'll cover all but Flyweight here.

The Adapter and Façade Design Patterns

GoF Intent for Adapter: Convert the interface of a class into another interface clients expect. Adapter lets classes work together that couldn't otherwise because of incompatible interfaces.

GoF Intent for Façade: Provide a unified interface to a set of interfaces in a subsystem. Façade defines a higher-level interface that makes the subsystem easier to use.

The purpose of the **Adapter** pattern is not ambitious. It is designed simply to *adapt* the interface of a class so that it is compatible with the client that needs to use it. This requirement may be as trivial as changing method names to fit your application's conventions.

By contrast, the **Façade** (pronounced "fa-*sahd*") pattern does a little more work. It creates a "façade class", which acts as a layer between the client and a set of service classes. The client then sends its requests to an instance of the façade class, which acts as an agent – manipulating the requests as necessary and sending them on to the set of service classes. The purpose of the façade class is to eliminate the difficulties that the client would otherwise have in sending requests to a complex set of service objects.

From these initial descriptions, it's rather difficult to tell these two patterns apart. Indeed, in practice they can often be used interchangeably, because both patterns deal with the task of changing classes' interfaces in order to make them easier for the client application to use.

However, as we'll see in the examples that follow, the structure of these two patterns is different, and they do solve two subtly different problems. In particular, we'll include a UML diagram that describes how the following two applications implement the two patterns – the difference between Adapter and Façade becomes clearer when you compare these two diagrams.

The Adapter Pattern – an Example

Suppose we are designing a restaurant ordering system. It will make use of two classes:

- ❑ A class that handles orders for a fast food restaurant. This class will be called `FastFoodOrderer`, and we'll write it in-house.
- ❑ A class that handles orders for a fancy French restaurant.

However, at the time of the first release, the second of these classes will not be available to us. In fact, this class is to be coded by a third party and we don't even know its interface yet. Therefore, the first release of the application will *only* allow the user to order food from a certain no-frills fast food restaurant. For the second release, we want to be able to adapt the third party class and insert it seamlessly into the existing application.

In order to do this, the client application will have a single object called `objFoodOrderer`, which is capable of ordering both fast food and French food. Food will be ordered through the method `objFoodOrderer.Order()`. Our `FastFoodOrderer` class will also have an `Order()` method. We don't know whether the French restaurant class will have an `Order()` method, but it doesn't matter. We'll design the application in such a way that we'll be able to adapt its interface to fit our application.

Here is the UML diagram for our application. It includes the implementation of the third-party class, which (as it turns out) is called `FrenchRestaurant`, and has a method called `OrderFromMenu()`:

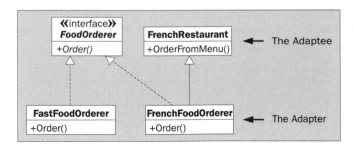

This pattern allows us to use polymorphism in our client application to create an instance of a FoodOrderer class, and use its Order() method. What happens next depends on what the user has asked for:

- ❏ If the user is ordering French food, the application will use the implementation of Order() provided by the FastFoodOrderer class.

- ❏ If the user is ordering fast food, the application will use the implementation of Order() provided by the FrenchFoodOrderer class. This class is the **adapter** class – it adapts the OrderFromMenu() method of the FrenchRestaurant class (the **adaptee**), allowing the client application to use it indirectly.

Without this adapter/adaptee pattern, recoding our second release would be rather more difficult. In order to facilitate calls to FrenchRestaurant, it might be possible to convert FoodOrderer to an abstract class, perhaps add some new, specialized methods to FrenchRestaurant. Either way, these are rather less than desirable options.

Let's see how our application develops. First, here's the FoodOrderer interface:

```
Public Interface FoodOrderer
  Sub Order(ByVal Request)
End Interface
```

Now, here's the FastFoodOrderer class that implements the FoodOrderer interface:

```
Public Class FastFoodOrderer : Implements FoodOrderer
  Public Sub Order(ByVal Request) Implements FoodOrderer.Order
    Console.WriteLine(Request & " coming up. ")
  End Sub
End Class
```

And here's the first version of the client application. It includes some simple test code in which we use the FoodOrderer object to order some fast food:

```
Sub Main()
  Dim objFoodOrderer As FoodOrderer

  Console.WriteLine("Let's order from the Fast Food restaurant: ")
  objFoodOrderer = New FastFoodOrderer()
  objFoodOrderer.Order("1 Cheeseburger")

  MessageBox.Show("Click OK to end")
End Sub
```

When you run this, you can see (in the console output) that the FastFoodOrderer object has handled the request for a cheeseburger:

```
Let's order from the Fast Food restaurant:
1 Cheeseburger coming up.
```

After this first release, the third party delivers its implementation of the French restaurant class. This is what they deliver:

```
Public Class FrenchRestaurant
  Public Sub OrderFromMenu(ByVal Request)
    Console.WriteLine(Request & "? Oui, monsieur. Bon appetit. ")
  End Sub
End Class
```

The rules of polymorphism won't allow the objFoodOrderer object to be instantiated to type FrenchRestaurant, because they're not related. So, we now build our FrenchFoodOrderer class:

```
Public Class FrenchFoodOrderer : Inherits FrenchRestaurant
                              : Implements FoodOrderer
  Public Sub Order(ByVal Request) Implements FoodOrderer.Order
    OrderFromMenu(Request)
  End Sub
End Class
```

The first line of the adapter class of the application, FrenchFoodOrderer, is quite busy – it inherits and implements simultaneously. This is not an unusual OO construction. It appears quite often within the .NET Common Language Runtime (CLR) itself.

Now we can add some extra code to the client application, to demonstrate that objFoodOrderer is indeed capable of ordering food from either establishment:

```
Sub Main()
  Dim objFoodOrderer As FoodOrderer

  Console.WriteLine("Let's order from the Fast Food restaurant: ")
  objFoodOrderer = New FastFoodOrderer()
  objFoodOrderer.Order("1 Cheeseburger")

  Console.WriteLine("Now let's order some French food " & _
                    "from their fancy restaurant menu: ")
    objFoodOrderer = New FrenchFoodOrderer()
    objFoodOrderer.Order("Moules Mariniere")

    MessageBox.Show("Click OK to end")
End Sub
```

Here's the output:

```
Let's order from the Fast Food restaurant:
1 Cheeseburger coming up.
Now let's order some French food from their fancy restaurant menu:
Moules Mariniere? Oui, monsieur. Bon appetit.
```

While we've tried to avoid unnecessary code here, the main structure of the pattern is clear. We can now use a similar technique to add more classes, which communicate orders to other restaurants. In each case, we'd simply add the third-party object and an adapter object. In our application, the objFoodOrderer object would be able to assume the role of any of the adapter objects, and pass food orders to any eaterie in town!

The Façade Pattern – an Example

To demonstrate the Façade pattern, we'll continue on the theme of food, this time but present a different problem. This is another application that orders food – but this time, the order involves a number of calls to the methods of three service classes (`SupermarketVisit`, `Cleaner`, and `MealPreparer`). Overall, we think that the complexity of these method calls is too much. Our developers can certainly all figure out how to make all these calls, but why should they all waste time learning a complex API? This is where the Façade design pattern comes in.

To solve this problem, we create a new class or interface that manages all the calls to the methods of the three service classes. At the cost of one class, we will make it very easy for any developer to order some food without navigating a bunch of some potentially complex interfaces!

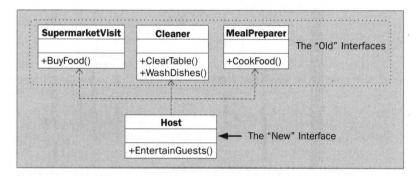

Let's start at the top of our UML diagram with the three service classes. For the sake of brevity, we'll use three simple service classes. You'll need to pretend that they have horribly complex interfaces:

```
Public Class SupermarketVisit
  Public Function BuyFood(ByVal Food As String)
    Console.WriteLine("Buying some " & Food & "...")
    Return Food
  End Function
End Class


Public Class MealPreparer
  Public Function CookFood(ByVal Food As String)
    Console.WriteLine("Cooking the " & Food & "...")
    Return Food
  End Function
End Class


Public Class Cleaner
  Public Sub ClearTable()
    Console.WriteLine("Clearing the Table...")
  End Sub

  Public Sub WashDishes()
    Console.WriteLine("Washing the Dishes...")
  End Sub
End Class
```

Now we'll write our façade class, which acts as an agent – making the use of these service objects very easy for the client application:

```
Public Class Host
   Public Function EntertainGuests(ByVal Entree As String)
      Dim objSupermarketVisit As New SupermarketVisit()
      Dim objMealPreparer As New MealPreparer()
      Dim objCleaner As New Cleaner()

      objMealPreparer.CookFood(objSupermarketVisit.BuyFood(Entree))
      objCleaner.ClearTable()
      objCleaner.WashDishes()

      Console.WriteLine("What a pleasant evening. ")
   End Function
End Class
```

As you can see, the `Host` class performs all the necessary roles in one simple function call: buying the food, preparing it and cleaning up afterwards. The interface for the `Host` class is much simpler than the combined API of the three service objects, and this makes the code in the client application extremely simple:

```
Sub Main()
   Dim objHost As New Host()
   objHost.EntertainGuests("Pasta")

   MessageBox.Show("Click OK to end")
End Sub
```

This is what you will see in the console window when you run this application:

```
Buying some Pasta...
Cooking the Pasta...
Clearing the Table...
Washing the Dishes...
What a pleasant evening.
```

Notice how all we had to do was call `EntertainGuests()` and the rest was all done for us. Much easier than having to put in all those different calls every time our program wanted to throw a dinner party!

Comparing the Adapter and Façade Patterns

Finally, note that an Adapter pattern would not have helped us much here. The problem is not that we cannot call the `SupermarketVisit`, `Cleaner`, and `MealPreparer` interfaces as they exist. Rather, it is that having to use them at all is a pain! It is this observation that *really* highlights the difference between the Adapter and Façade patterns.

The Bridge Design Pattern

> **GoF Intent:** Decouple an abstraction from its implementation so that the two can vary independently.

The **Bridge** pattern attempts to remove the need for developers to write adapter classes for an application. You may recall how the Adapter pattern is used to adapt the interface of an existing class, when its own interface is incompatible with the client that needs to use it. When we use a Bridge, it's because we want to build our application in such a fashion that we can easily add different interfaces to our application.

But that's not all. After abstracting the interface, Bridge proceeds to abstract the implementation as well. Ultimately, it allows interfaces *and* implementations of an application to vary independently of one another. With interfaces on one side, and implementations on the other, the Bridge pattern acts as the middleman linking the two sides.

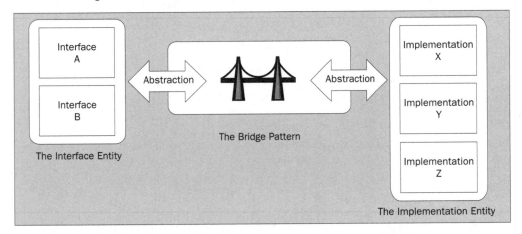

To demonstrate, we'll consider an application that concerns itself with a typical enterprise purchasing application. Within the enterprise, users can issue purchase orders (POs) for either office supplies or raw manufacturing materials; their POs can be sent to either a retail store or a wholesaler for completion. Initially, it looks like we could implement this by creating one class for each permutation of order – so you would have four classes:

- ❑ `OfficeSuppliesRetailPO`
- ❑ `OfficeSuppliesWholesalePO`
- ❑ `ManufacturingMaterialsRetailPO`
- ❑ `ManufacturingMaterialsWholesalePO`

This design would certainly solve the problem we've presented. However, like the first example in this chapter, this design would suffer from "class multiplication" if we ever needed to extend the application. For example, if we subsequently needed to extend our purchasing system to accommodate another type of supply and another type of supplier (say, computer equipment supplies and an online supplier) then we'd suddenly need nine classes instead of four.

The Bridge pattern is quite appropriate in this situation. In the solution we described above, we'd need a class for each *interface–implementation combination* – where an "interface" is an interface to the purchasing system (a purchase order) and an "implementation" is a mechanism uses to fulfill that order (a supplier). In following the pattern, we separate interface from implementation by creating an abstract generic class of purchase order and another abstract generic class for the suppliers. These two classes, and the interaction between them, form a **bridge** between the two sides of the system, allowing them both to vary independently:

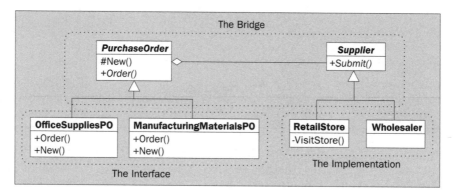

Now, if we come across a situation in which we need to extend the solution to accommodate a new type of purchase order or a new supplier, the developer simply needs to add an extra interface class (deriving from PurchaseOrder) or implementation class (deriving from Supplier).

The Interface Side: Purchase Orders

Let's start by looking at how the Bridge pattern allows us to have two different types of purchase order. On the interface side of the bridge, we have the generic PurchaseOrder class:

```
Public MustInherit Class PurchaseOrder
  Protected m_ProductID As Integer
  Protected m_Supplier As Supplier

  Protected Sub New(ByRef s As Supplier, ByVal ProductID As Integer)
    m_ProductID = ProductID
    m_Supplier = s
  End Sub

  Public MustOverride Function Order(ByVal Quantity As Integer) As String
End Class
```

The PurchaseOrder's New() constructor is a protected method, which prevents all but inherited classes from instantiating it. This is a common OO technique. VB.NET supports this behavior in classes that are defined using the MustInherit class modifier, as this one is. Moreover, the Order() method is given here using the MustOverride modifier. So, in this case, we can't create instances of the PurchaseOrder class directly – we can only create more specialized objects that inherit from PurchaseOrder. Any such class can make use of the superclass's New() constructor, but must provide its own implementation of the Order() method.

We can see these implications take their course by looking at the classes that implement the specific types of purchase order. First, the OfficeSuppliesPO class:

```
Public Class OfficeSuppliesPO : Inherits PurchaseOrder
  Public Sub New(ByRef Vendor As Supplier, ByVal ProductID As Integer)
    MyBase.New(Vendor, ProductID)
  End Sub

  Public Overrides Function Order(ByVal Quantity As Integer) As String
    If Quantity < 10 Then
```

```
          Return m_Supplier.Submit(m_ProductID, Quantity)
      Else
          Return TypeName(Me).ToString & _
                              " only handles small quantity orders!"
      End If
   End Function
End Class
```

As you can see, the `OfficeSuppliesPO` class inherits from `PurchaseOrder`. Its constructor makes use of the `PurchaseOrder`'s constructor. It also provides its own implementation of the `Order()` method.

We can also look at the `ManufacturingMaterialsPO` class and make the same observations here:

```
Public Class ManufacturingMaterialsPO : Inherits PurchaseOrder
   Public Sub New(ByRef Vendor As Supplier, ByVal ProductID As Integer)
      MyBase.New(Vendor, ProductID)
   End Sub

   Public Overrides Function Order(ByVal Quantity As Integer) As String
      If Quantity > 1000 Then
          Return m_Supplier.Submit(m_ProductID, Quantity)
      Else
          Return TypeName(Me).ToString & _
                              " only handles large quantity orders!"
      End If
   End Function
End Class
```

Thus, effectively we have created two different `PurchaseOrder` implementations. Specifically, each has a different implementation of the `Order()` method.

The Implementation Side: Suppliers

Now let's look at the "implementation" side of the bridge – the generic `Supplier` class:

```
Public MustInherit Class Supplier
   MustOverride Function Submit(ByVal ProductID As Integer, _
                               ByVal Quantity As Double) As String
End Class
```

The `Supplier` class, like the `PurchaseOrder` class, is defined using the `MustInherit` class modifier. Its single method, `Submit()`, is also given using the `MustOverride` modifier.

Representing the specific types of supplier, we have the `RetailStore` and `Wholesaler` classes. First, here is our `RetailStore` implementation:

```
Public Class RetailStore : Inherits Supplier
   Public Overrides Function Submit(ByVal ProductID As Integer, _
                                   ByVal Quantity As Double) As String
      Return VisitStore(ProductID, Quantity)
   End Function
```

```
        Private Function VisitStore(ByVal ProductID As Integer, _
                                ByVal Quantity As Double) As String
      If Quantity < 5 Then
        Return Quantity.ToString & " x Product #" & ProductID.ToString & _
                          " is on your desk."
      Else
        Return Quantity.ToString & " x Product #" & ProductID.ToString & _
                          " is due tomorrow."
      End If
    End Function
  End Class
```

We have a new departure here – the interface of the `RetailStore` class is different from that of the `Supplier` class. This represents the fact that we might visit a retail store to purchase supplies. We wouldn't visit a wholesaler, so the `Wholesaler` class doesn't support such a method:

```
Public Class Wholesaler : Inherits Supplier
  Public Overrides Function Submit(ByVal ProductID As Integer, _
                                ByVal Quantity As Double) As String
    Return Quantity.ToString & " x Product #" & ProductID.ToString & _
                        " will be shipped next week."
  End Function
End Class
```

OK, now let's test this pattern. Here's a little client application in which we use a few different combinations of purchase orders and suppliers, using the same pair of objects (`objPurchaseOrder` and `objSupplier`) in each case:

```
Sub Main()
  Dim objPurchaseOrder As PurchaseOrder
  Dim objSupplier As Supplier

  Console.WriteLine("Order some office supplies from the retail store:")
  objSupplier = New RetailStore()
  objPurchaseOrder = New OfficeSuppliesPO(objSupplier, 544628)
  Console.WriteLine(objPurchaseOrder.Order(5000))

  Console.WriteLine("Now order some manufacturing materials " & _
                "from the wholesaler:")
  objSupplier = New Wholesaler()
  objPurchaseOrder = New ManufacturingMaterialsPO(objSupplier, 7791028)
  Console.WriteLine(objPurchaseOrder.Order(5000))

  MessageBox.Show("Click OK to end")
End Sub
```

The attempt to order 5000 items of Product #544628 ends in a warning that we can't order such large supplies using an `OfficeSuppliesPO`. Then the attempt to order 5000 of Product #7791028 ends in a more successful outcome:

```
Order some office supplies from the retail store:
OfficeSuppliesPO only handles small quantity orders!
```

```
Now order some manufacturing materials from the wholesaler:
5000 x Product #7791028 will be shipped next week.
```

Comparing the Bridge and Abstract Factory Patterns

The Bridge and Abstract Factory patterns actually have a lot in common. The major difference lies in how the implementation classes are conjured up. In the Bridge pattern demonstration that we just observed, there's no factory object. The client application creates the supplier and purchase order classes explicitly:

```
Sub Main()
   ...
   objSupplier = New Wholesaler()
   objPurchaseOrder = New ManufacturingMaterialsPO(objSupplier, 7791028)
   ...
End Sub
```

By contrast, consider the bear application, which we used earlier to demonstrate the Abstract Factory pattern. In that application, there were a number of similar factory objects. The implementation objects were determined by the selection of the appropriate factory object:

```
Sub Main()
   ...
   If objGoldenPreferred = DialogResult.Yes Then
      objBearFactory = New GoldenBearFactory()
   Else
      objBearFactory = New BrownBearFactory()
   End If
   ...
   objDadBear = objBearFactory.CreateDadBear
   objMomBear = objBearFactory.CreateMomBear
   objBabyBear = objBearFactory.CreateBabyBear
   ...
End Sub
```

The Composite Design Pattern

> **GoF Intent:** Compose objects into tree structures to represent part-whole hierarchies. Composite lets clients treat individual objects and compositions of objects uniformly.

The **Composite** pattern applies to a common problem, in which we need a set of objects to model and manipulate a tree structure. A tree structure consists of a collection of hierarchical container and leaf objects, in which a container can contain other containers and leaves, but a leaf cannot contain either.

A classic example of this container-and-leaf structure is in a file system. The folders are containers (they can contain files and other folders). The files are leaves (they cannot).

So, imagine an application that needs to list the entire contents of a folder (including all its subfolders and files). To do this, we would need systematically to look at each of the items (files and subfolders) contained in the named folder, and list them. Obtaining the size of a *file* is easy, but obtaining the size of a *subfolder* is a little more subtle: we'd also need to examine all the items (subfiles and subsubfolders) in the subfolder and list the names and contents of those.

So, this seemingly simple task requires some pretty sophisticated code work:

- ❑ Part of the challenge is in representing the recursive relationship correctly.

- ❑ It would also help if we had a reliable way of iterating through all the objects in a container, and working with each one in the same way regardless of whether it was a container or a leaf.

The Composite pattern exists for just this kind of task. We will explore a very simple implementation of it. Our demonstration supports a customizable set of leaf and container objects. Each leaf and container object will have a name property. It will support a method that returns the name of the object, and it will also support a method that returns the names of any contained objects.

Composite provides an excellent example of how design patterns provide well-proven remedies without a lot of fretting and guessing. While many experienced developers would know that recursive programming can juggle container and leaf objects, would they also know how to code it?

Here is the UML diagram for our simple application:

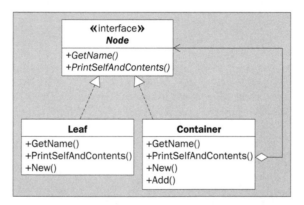

This simple diagram captures the essence of Composite. First, note that the `Node` interface contains two methods (`GetName` and `PrintSelfAndContents`), and that the `Leaf` and `Container` classes both implement the `Node` interface. This ensures that *both* classes possess these required common behaviors.

Second, as indicated by the line with a clear diamond at one end and an arrow at the other, a `Container` object may "contain" `Node` interface-derived objects. This is crucial to the pattern's success. It cements the relationship between the `Leaf` and `Container` classes. While the interface *relates* `Leaf` and `Container`, the specified containment feature tells exactly *how* they are related – that a `Container` object may contain `Leaf` objects and other `Container` objects.

Let's see what this looks like in code. First, here is the `Node` interface. Remember that this describes the methods that must be implemented by both the `Leaf` and `Container` classes:

```
Public Interface Node
  Function GetName() As String
  Sub PrintSelfAndContents()
End Interface
```

Each `Container` object has two member variables: a `String` to store its name and an `ArrayList` to store any nodes that it contains. For convenience, it has an `Add()` method that allows us to add other `Leaf` and `Container` objects to this `Container` object. The `GetName()` method returns the `Container`'s name:

```
Public Class Container : Implements Node
  Private m_Name As String
  Private m_Nodes As New ArrayList()

  Sub New(ByVal Name As String)
    m_Name = "Container_" & Name
  End Sub

  Sub Add(ByRef Item As Node)
    m_Nodes.Add(Item)
  End Sub

  Function GetName() As String Implements Node.GetName
    Return m_Name
  End Function
```

More interestingly, its `PrintSelfAndContents()` method outputs the name of the `Container`, followed by the names of all the nodes it contains. This is the recursive element of the Composite pattern in action:

```
  Sub PrintSelfAndContents() Implements Node.PrintSelfAndContents
    Console.WriteLine(m_Name)
    Dim tmpNode As Node
    For Each tmpNode In m_Nodes
      tmpNode.PrintSelfAndContents()
    Next
  End Sub
End Class
```

Each `Leaf` object, by contrast, has just one member variable: a `String` to store its name. It has no `Add()` method, because (by definition) you can't add other objects to a `Leaf`. Again, the `GetName()` method returns the `Container`'s name. This time, the `PrintSelfAndContents()` method is implemented differently – it *just* outputs the name of the `Leaf`:

```
Public Class Leaf : Implements Node
  Private m_Name As String

  Sub New(ByVal Name As String)
    m_Name = "Leaf_" & Name
  End Sub
```

```
    Function GetName() As String Implements Node.GetName
      Return m_Name
    End Function

    Sub PrintSelfAndContents() Implements Node.PrintSelfAndContents
      Console.WriteLine(m_Name)
    End Sub
  End Class
End Class
```

OK, now it's time to put together a short application to test these objects. We'll put together a simple hierarchy of `Leaf` and `Container` objects, and then output the contents of the root container to the console window:

```
Sub Main()
  ' create some arbitrary heirarchy of containers
  Dim objRoot As New Container("Root")
  Dim objChild1 As New Container("Child1")
  Dim objGrandChild1 As New Container("Grandchild1")
  Dim objChild2 As New Leaf("Child2")

  objRoot.Add(objChild1)
  objRoot.Add(objChild2)
  objRoot.Add(New Container("Child3"))

  objChild1.Add(objGrandChild1)
  objGrandChild1.Add(New Leaf("GreatGrandchild1"))
  objGrandChild1.Add(New Leaf("GreatGrandchild2"))

  ' output the contents of the root (including all subcontainers)
  objRoot.PrintSelfAndContents()

  MessageBox.Show("Click OK to end")
End Sub
```

When you run this application, you should get output like this:

```
Container_Root
Container_Child1
Container_Grandchild1
Leaf_GreatGrandchild1
Leaf_GreatGrandchild2
Leaf_Child2
Container_Child3
```

Before we leave the Composite pattern, here is a little teaser. In this pattern, where do you think is the best place for the node manipulation methods, `Add` and `Delete`? In this application, we have placed them in the `Container` class. This does raise an issue, because in this solution, the `Leaf` class does not support these methods: therefore, the client application must be careful that it's calling the `Add` or `Delete` method of a `Container` object, not a `Leaf` object.

The alternative is to include the `Add` and `Delete` methods in the `Node` interface, so that both the `Container` and `Leaf` classes must implement these methods. This resolves the issue described in the previous paragraph – but what code should the `Leaf.Add` and `Leaf.Delete` methods contain? It's not at all obvious, and even the experts are divided on this one! In practice, it's best to resolve this issue with some sensible use of error-raising techniques.

The Decorator Design Pattern

> **GoF Intent:** Attach additional responsibilities to an object dynamically. Decorators provide a flexible alternative to subclassing for extending functionality.

If you read about our fictional `TakeHomePay` application earlier in this chapter, then you should already have some idea of what's going on with the **Decorator** pattern. In that example, we saw how the lead architect of Software Company P was able to adjust the design of the `TakeHomePay` application to take account of additional functionality requirements, without adding a plethora of new classes. The original design was based on the Decorator pattern, which made it more extensible – and consequently, the new features required just two more classes.

The extensibility of the design is the main byproduct of the Decorator pattern. Its purpose is to make it easy to add new pieces of functionality (or responsibilities) to the application at any time during or after the completion of its construction.

In this section, we'll demonstrate the Decorator pattern by building a version of the `TakeHomePay` application. Here's the UML diagram for the version we'll build here:

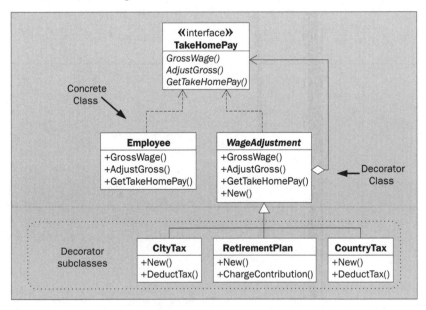

This diagram is identical in shape to the diagrams developed by Company P (in the design phase discussion earlier in this chapter). The UML clarifies the different key roles of the demonstration code, as well as the buzzwords of the pattern:

- The `Employee` class represents the Decorator pattern's **concrete class**. Its purpose is to house all of the required employee methods.

- The `WageAdjustment` class represents the Decorator's **decorator class**. Its purpose is to contain a reference to the concrete class instance (an `Employee` object).

❑ The `CityTax`, `RetirementPlan`, and `CountyTax` classes are the Decorator pattern's **decorator subclasses**. These classes contain the additional methods and properties required to work with an `Employee` object – each one represents a different piece of functionality.

The Interface

Let's take a look at the code required to build this application. First, the `TakeHomePay` interface:

```
Public Interface TakeHomePay
   Property GrossWage()
   Sub AdjustGross(ByVal Adjustment As Double)
   Function GetTakeHomePay() As Double
End Interface
```

This interface will be implemented by the concrete class (`Employee`) *and* by the decorator class (`WageAdjustment`). As we'll see, the concrete class contains the true implementations; the decorator class will use them. All will become clear when we look at these two classes.

The Concrete Class

First, let's examine the concrete class. The `Employee` class contains two private members, which represent the employee's gross and net wage. Also, it implements the `TakeHomePay` interface:

```
Public Class Employee : Implements TakeHomePay
   Private m_GrossWage As Double
   Private m_NetWage As Double

   Public Property GrossWage() Implements TakeHomePay.GrossWage
     Get
       Return m_GrossWage
     End Get
     Set(ByVal Value)
       m_GrossWage = Value
       m_NetWage = Value
     End Set
   End Property

   Public Sub AdjustGross(ByVal Adjustment As Double) _
                            Implements TakeHomePay.AdjustGross
     m_NetWage -= Adjustment
   End Sub

   Public Function GetTakeHomePay() As Double
                            Implements TakeHomePay.GetTakeHomePay
     Return m_NetWage
   End Function
End Class
```

The purpose of the one property and two methods in the interface can be described as follows:

❑ The `GrossWage` property is a read/write property that represents the current value of the employee's gross wage. When we set the gross wage, it also resets the net wage.

❑ The `AdjustGross` method accepts a double-point numeric value, and calculates the net wage by deducting the given amount from it.

❑ The `GetTakeHomePay` method returns the employee's net wage.

The Decorator Class

Now let's look at the decorator class. It also implements the `TakeHomePay` interface, but as the code here shows, it does so in a rather different way:

```
Public MustInherit Class WageAdjustment : Implements TakeHomePay
  Protected m_TakeHomePay As TakeHomePay

  Public Sub New(ByRef thp As TakeHomePay)
    m_TakeHomePay = thp
  End Sub

  Public Property GrossWage() Implements TakeHomePay.GrossWage
    Get
      Return m_TakeHomePay.GrossWage
    End Get
    Set(ByVal Value)
      m_TakeHomePay.GrossWage = Value
    End Set
  End Property

  Public Sub AdjustGross(ByVal Adjustment As Double) _
                         Implements TakeHomePay.AdjustGross
    m_TakeHomePay.AdjustGross(Adjustment)
  End Sub

  Public Overridable Function GetTakeHomePay() As Double _
                         Implements TakeHomePay.GetTakeHomePay
    Return m_TakeHomePay.GetTakeHomePay
  End Function
End Class
```

How does this work? First, note that `WageAdjustment` uses the `MustInherit` access modifier. This is because in the Decorator pattern, the decorator object itself cannot be instantiated directly. Rather, we create instances of the decorator subclasses (`CityTax`, `RetirementPlan`, and `CountyTax`) that we'll see in a moment.

Second, note that each of these decorator subclasses contains a constructor. For example, this one is taken from the `CountryTax` decorator subclass:

```
Public Sub New(ByRef thp As TakeHomePay, ByVal CountryName As String)
  MyBase.New(thp)
  m_CountryName = CountryName
End Sub
```

When the client application uses the constructor, it passes a reference to an `Employee` object as the first parameter, like this:

```
Dim objEmployee As New Employee()
Dim objCountryTax As CountryTax
...
objCountryTax = New CountryTax(objEmployee, "USA")
```

When you follow this sequence of constructor calls, you can see that thp (the private object variable defined in the WageAdjustment class's constructor) is a reference to objEmployee (the Employee object created by the client application). Thus, every instantiation of the WageAdjustment class contains a reference to the concrete Employee object at the center of the operation.

That's the structure that lies at the heart of the Decorator pattern. Now we understand this, we can add the individual decorator subclasses, and then we'll be ready to write a little client application to test it out.

The Decorator Subclasses

So, let's briefly run through the three decorator subclasses in this example. Each of the decorator subclasses inherits from the decorator class, WageAdjustment. First, here's the CountryTax class:

```
Public Class CountryTax : Inherits WageAdjustment
  Private m_CountryName As String

  Public Sub New(ByRef thp As TakeHomePay, ByVal CountryName As String)
    MyBase.New(thp)
    m_CountryName = CountryName
  End Sub

  Public Sub DeductTax()
    If m_CountryName = "USA" Then
      m_TakeHomePay.AdjustGross(0.4 * m_TakeHomePay.GetTakeHomePay)
    ElseIf m_CountryName = "UK" Then
      m_TakeHomePay.AdjustGross(0.3 * m_TakeHomePay.GrossWage)
    End If
  End Sub
End Class
```

Here, you can see the constructor that we mentioned above. Each decorator subclass can also contain other methods and properties that relate to the specific functionality of this class. This class just contains the DeductTax method, which is used to deduct country tax from the employee's wage.

Now here's the RetirementPlan class. Its structure is very similar to the CountryTax class, and only the specific functionality is different:

```
Public Class RetirementPlan : Inherits WageAdjustment
  Private m_PlanName As String

  Public Sub New(ByRef thp As TakeHomePay, ByVal PlanName As String)
    MyBase.New(thp)
    m_PlanName = PlanName
  End Sub

  Public Sub ChargeContribution()
    If m_PlanName.StartsWith("D") Then
```

```
        m_TakeHomePay.AdjustGross(0.02 * m_TakeHomePay.GrossWage)
    Else
        m_TakeHomePay.AdjustGross(0.1 * m_TakeHomePay.GrossWage)
    End If
  End Sub
End Class
```

Finally, here's the `CityTax` class. Again, its structure is very similar to the `CountryTax` class:

```
Public Class CityTax : Inherits WageAdjustment
  Private m_CityName As String

  Public Sub New(ByRef thp As TakeHomePay, ByVal CityName As String)
    MyBase.New(thp)
    m_CityName = CityName
  End Sub

  Public Sub DeductTax()
    If m_CityName = "NYC" Then
      m_TakeHomePay.AdjustGross(0.05 * m_TakeHomePay.GrossWage)
    End If
  End Sub
End Class
```

A Sample Application

Now, here's a simple client application that demonstrates how all these classes work in perfect harmony. First, we create an `Employee` object and set its gross wage. Then, we create a sequence of decorator subclass objects (`CountryTax`, `RetirementPlan`, and `CityTax`) and use each one in turn to adjust the employee's wage. At each stage, the methods of the decorator subclass objects are working with the single instance of the `Employee` class (as described above) to adjust its wage value:

```
Sub Main()
  Dim objEmployee As New Employee()
  Dim objCountryTax As CountryTax
  Dim objRetirementPlan As RetirementPlan

  ' set employee's gross wage
  objEmployee.GrossWage = 1000D
  Console.WriteLine("Employee's gross wage: $" & objEmployee.GrossWage)

  ' pass objEmployee object to objCountryTax, and deduct tax
  objCountryTax = New CountryTax(objEmployee, "USA")
  objCountryTax.DeductTax()
  Console.WriteLine("Wage after Country Tax: $" & _
                    objEmployee.GetTakeHomePay)

  ' pass objEmployee object to objRetirementPlan,
  ' and deduct retirement plan contribution
  objRetirementPlan = New RetirementPlan(objCountryTax, "Defined Benefit")
  objRetirementPlan.ChargeContribution()
  Console.WriteLine("Wage after Retirement Plan Contribution: $" & _
                    objEmployee.GetTakeHomePay)
```

```
    ' pass objEmployee object to objCityTax,
    ' and deduct retirement plan contribution
    Dim objCityTax As New CityTax(objEmployee, "NYC")
    objCityTax.DeductTax()
    Console.WriteLine("Wage after City Tax: $" & _
                      objEmployee.GetTakeHomePay)

    MessageBox.Show("Click OK to end")
End Sub
```

After each one, we report the adjusted wage by writing it to the console. When you run this demonstration, your output should look like this:

```
Employee's gross wage: $1000
Wage after Country Tax: $600
Wage after Retirement Plan Contribution: $580
Wage after City Tax: $530
```

In Chapter 5, we'll see another implementation of the Decorator pattern, which uses the decorator subclasses in a slightly different way.

Cascades of Decorator Classes

There's one final point to note in relation to the Decorator pattern. In this pattern, the purpose of a decorator class is to decorate the top-level interface (TakeHomePay) by adding extra functionality to it. The restriction imposed by the Decorator pattern is that a decorator class can only decorate classes that implement that top-level interface.

What this means, in practice, is that we can have as many levels of decorator subclasses as we like – with each level decorating the previous level by adding more and more functionality. The logic is this:

> **Assertion 1:** By definition, a decorator class can decorate *only* classes that implement the top-level interface.
>
> **Assertion 2:** By design, every decorator (sub)class implements the top-level interface.
>
> **Conclusion:** A decorator can decorate a decorator. In other words, we can **cascade** as many layers of decorator subclasses as necessary.

How does this relate to our application? Well, it's like this:

❑   The Employee class implements the TakeHomePay interface, and this is the reason we can decorate Employee using a decorator class, WageAdjustment.

❑   Also, the WageAdjustment class implements the TakeHomePay interface, and this is the reason we can decorate WageAdjustment using a decorator subclass (such as CityTax).

❑   If we wanted to extend this application by decorating CityTax with a decorator "subsubclass", that would be allowed within the rules of the Decorator pattern – because CityTax *also* implements the TakeHomePay interface.

❑   And so on, and so on!

The Proxy Design Pattern

> **GoF Intent:** Provide a surrogate or placeholder for another object to control access to it.

The **Proxy** pattern, like the Adapter pattern, adds an extra layer between an object (the **subject**) and its consumer (the **client**). But the purposes of the two patterns are different. While Adapter *changes* the subject's interface, Proxy *preserves* it. Thus:

❑ We use an Adapter when we want to convert the subject's interface into an interface that the client application can use. It works just like a power adapter that takes a 110-volt AC source and converts it to 12-volt DC, so that an electrical appliance can use it.

❑ We use a Proxy to present an interface that is identical to the subject's interface, so the client application cannot tell whether it's dealing with the subject itself or with the subject's proxy. A trivial example would be a device that takes a 110-volt AC source and outputs the same, for a different electrical appliance.

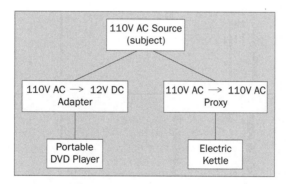

Let's use the power source metaphor for our demonstration of the Proxy pattern. We'll assume that we have a power source (a power generator, for example) that can generate power of any voltage for clients to consume. If a client asks for a 100-volt supply, the power source will fulfill that request. If a client asks for a 2000-volt supply, the source will attempt to fulfill that too.

Now, let's also suppose that there is a design fault deep in the power source, so that if a client requests a power supply of over 1400 volts, the generator hits meltdown. In other words, any request over 1400 volts causes irreparable damage to the source. Unfortunately, when the power source was built, its designers overlooked this issue and didn't build any protection mechanism into the system.

Let's see how we can use the Proxy pattern to solve the problem. We'll propose a design that uses the original source to provide power, but with one constraint: if the requested voltage is *over* 1400 volts, then the voltage supplied will be *exactly* 1400 volts. Further, instead of allowing clients to connect *directly* to the power source, they will only be allowed to connect *indirectly* to the power source via the proxy.

Here's the UML diagram for all that. Notice that the proxy object, `PowerProxy`, keeps a reference (`powerSrc`) of the subject (`PowerSource`) it represents:

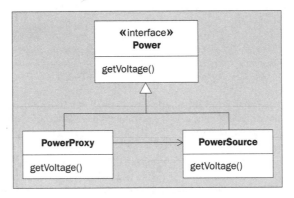

The `Power` interface has only one method, `getVoltage()`, which returns the requested voltage to the caller. Callers specify the voltages they want by setting the `volts` parameter:

```
Interface Power
    Function getVoltage(ByVal volts As Integer) As Integer
End Interface
```

Both `PowerProxy` and `PowerSource` implement the `Power` interface. Here's the `PowerSource` class first:

```
Class PowerSource : Implements Power
    Function getVoltage(ByVal volts As Integer) As Integer
                                         Implements Power.getVoltage

      getVoltage = volts
    End Function
End Class
```

The implementation of the `PowerSource.getVoltage` method will return whatever voltage is specified by the `volts` parameter. It doesn't check the upper limit of its voltage output.

The voltage limit is imposed by a conditional statement within the `PowerProxy` class's implementation of the `getVoltage` method. If the requested voltage is at most 1400 volts, `PowerProxy`'s `getVoltage` method will invoke the `getVoltage` method on `powerSrc`. Otherwise, it will return a supply of 1400 volts:

```
Class PowerProxy : Implements Power
    Private powerSrc As PowerSource

    Public Sub New()
      powerSrc = New PowerSource()
    End Sub

    Function getVoltage(ByVal volts As Integer) As Integer
                                         Implements Power.getVoltage

      If volts <= 1400 Then
        getVoltage = powerSrc.getVoltage(volts)
      Else
        getVoltage = powerSrc.getVoltage(1400)
      End If
```

```
      End Function
    End Class
```

Now let's test this pattern. The client code is shown below. A client device should not access the `PowerSource` directly – it should connect itself to outlets on the power supplier. That's what we do in the client code listed below. We create an instance of `PowerProxy`, and call `getVoltage()` on the proxy without the default constructor:

```
Sub Main()
   Dim power As New PowerProxy()
   Dim voltage As Integer

   Console.WriteLine("Let's request a power supply of 450 volts...")
   voltage = power.getVoltage(450)
   Console.WriteLine("The voltage supplied is {0} volts.", voltage)
   Console.WriteLine("")

   Console.WriteLine("Now let's request a power supply of 2000 volts...")
   voltage = power.getVoltage(2000)
   Console.WriteLine("The voltage supplied is {0} volts.", voltage)

   MessageBox.Show("Click OK to end")
End Sub
```

As you can see from the output below, our implementation of the Proxy pattern ensures we're in no danger of blowing up:

```
Let's request a power supply of 450 volts...
The voltage supplied is 450 volts.

Now let's request a power supply of 2000 volts...
The voltage supplied is 1400 volts.
```

Now let's move on to look at our final category, the behavioral patterns.

Behavioral Patterns

While the creational and structural patterns managed classes and objects, the **behavioral patterns** supervise messages sent between objects. The emphasis is on building objects that prevent ever-changing inter-object communications from ruining a good application.

The GoF cataloged 11 behavioral patterns: Chain of Responsibility, Command, Interpreter, Iterator, Mediator, Memento, Observer, State, Strategy, Template Method, and Visitor. Here, we will examine just four of the most common patterns – namely Observer, State, Strategy and Template Method.

The Observer Design Pattern

> **GoF Intent:** Define a one-to-many dependency between objects so that when one object changes state, all its dependants are notified and updated automatically.

If you've ever worked with events, then you already know something about the **Observer** pattern. In most event models, an object sends messages and other interested objects subscribe to or listen for these messages. The Observer pattern provides a rigorous, standard method for exchanging these messages. It does so in a rather indirect fashion, by requiring one interface for the sender object and another for the observer objects.

Our demonstration assumes that there exists an expense-processing application – this application notifies other applications that use its services:

- ❑ An event takes the form of a call to a method that is specific to the **sender object** (in this example, the ExpensesProcessor.Process() method).

- ❑ The event handlers are implemented though **observer objects**. Each observer object is an implementation of the ExpenseObserver interface, and thus contains a Notify() method.

The drill starts when we have an observer object that is interested in getting event messages from the sender object. We register this interest by "signing up" the observer object (in this example, by calling the sender object's Register() method).

With that done, the client can make calls to the sender object-specific methods (the ExpensesProcessor.Process() method in this example). Each time the Process() method is called, it "informs" each registered observer object of the event – by calling the observer object's Notify method.

The ExpenseObserver interface ensures that all the sender and observer objects involved in this exchange are "on the same wavelength". Here's a UML diagram to capture all this:

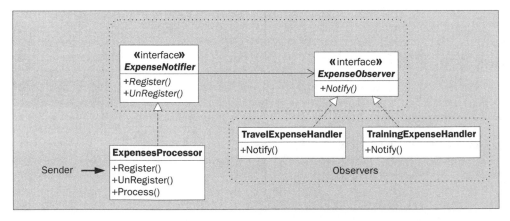

Let's see this in action. First, here are the two interfaces that lie at the heart of our Observer – ExpenseObserver and ExpenseNotifier. These two interfaces enforce the required signatures that allow the pattern to function:

```
Public Interface ExpenseObserver
   Sub Notify(ByRef obj As Object)
End Interface
```

```
Public Interface ExpenseNotifier
   Sub Register(ByRef eo As ExpenseObserver)
   Sub UnRegister(ByRef eo As ExpenseObserver)
End Interface
```

To see how these interfaces enable the pattern to work, let's look at the classes that implement them. First, here is the code for the sender class, ExpensesProcessor. This class implements the ExpenseNotifier interface, by providing implementations for the Register() and UnRegister() methods. It also contains one "event" method, called Process():

```
Public Class ExpensesProcessor : Implements ExpenseNotifier
   Dim m_Observers As New Hashtable()

   Public Sub Register(ByRef eo As ExpenseObserver) _
                                  Implements ExpenseNotifier.Register

     m_Observers.Add(eo, eo)
   End Sub

   Public Sub UnRegister(ByRef ew As ExpenseObserver) _
                                  Implements ExpenseNotifier.UnRegister

     m_Observers.Remove(ew)
   End Sub

   Public Function Process()
     Dim ProcessTime As DateTime = DateTime.UtcNow
     Dim aObserver As ExpenseObserver
     For Each aObserver In m_Observers.Keys
        aObserver.Notify(ProcessTime)
     Next
   End Function
End Class
```

As you can see, an ExpensesProcessor object contains a Hashtable member, which allows it to remember which observer objects are registered. A client can use the Register() method to add observer objects to the list, and the UnRegister() method to remove observer objects from the list.

> *The Hashtable class supports thread-safe instances, allowing us to someday convert our ProcessExpense class into a multithreaded application.*

The key characteristic of the Process() method is that it systematically calls the Notify() method of each of the observer objects in the Hashtable. Thus, each observer object has the opportunity to react to a client calling ExpensesProcessor.Process().

> *Also, you may have noted that the Notify() method of the ExpenseObserver interface expects a single Object parameter. Here, we take advantage of that to pass the call time to each Notify() method.*

Now, let's turn our attention to the two observer objects:

```
Public Class TravelExpenseHandler : Implements ExpenseObserver
  Sub Notify(ByRef obj As Object) Implements ExpenseObserver.Notify
    Console.WriteLine("Travel Expenses processed on " & obj)
  End Sub
End Class
```

```
Public Class TrainingExpenseHandler : Implements ExpenseObserver
  Sub Notify(ByRef obj As Object) Implements ExpenseObserver.Notify
    Console.WriteLine("Training Expenses processed on " & obj)
  End Sub
End Class
```

They're both quite simple. The main characteristic is that each implements a `Notify()` method, which contains the code that needs to be run in response to an `ExpensesProcessor.Process()` method call.

Now let's test all this. Here's a simple client application that does the job:

```
Sub Main()
  Dim objExpensesProcessor As New ExpensesProcessor()
  Dim objTravelExpenseHandler As New TravelExpenseHandler()
  Dim objTrainingExpenseHandler As New TrainingExpenseHandler()

  Console.WriteLine("Register two observer objects...")
  objExpensesProcessor.Register(objTravelExpenseHandler)
  objExpensesProcessor.Register(objTrainingExpenseHandler)
  Console.WriteLine("Now submit first batch of expenses...")
  objExpensesProcessor.Process()

  Console.WriteLine("")
  Console.WriteLine("Now unregister one of the observer objects...")
  objExpensesProcessor.UnRegister(objTrainingExpenseHandler)
  Console.WriteLine("Now submit second batch of expenses...")
  objExpensesProcessor.Process()

  MessageBox.Show("Click OK to end")
End Sub
```

This example gives the following output when run:

```
Register two observer objects...
Now submit first batch of expenses...
Training Expenses processed on 6/14/2002 12:14:21
Travel Expenses processed on 6/14/2002 12:14:21

Now unregister one of the observer objects...
Now submit second batch of expenses...
Travel Expenses processed on 6/14/2002 12:14:21
```

Here's a summary of what's happening here:

❑   The first time we call the `Process()` method, the two observer objects are both registered, so each gets a chance to react to (or handle) the `Process()` method call "event".

❏ The second time we call the `Process()` method, only one observer object is registered (because we just unregistered the other one). Therefore, the one registered observer object gets an opportunity to react to the event.

Given the importance of event programming, it should come as no surprise that .NET introduced an entire family of objects called **delegates** for just such a task. VB.NET uses delegates extensively to implement its event model. The existence of delegates in VB.NET may lead you to wonder whether or not there's a home for the Observer pattern in VB.NET. But don't write it off – in fact, the Microsoft delegate is an Observer in action.

Finally, note that the above interface classes, `ExpenseObserver` and `ExpenseNotifier`, are great examples of when not *to use inheritance. All we wanted was the enforcement of certain method signatures. Interfaces help enforce contracts between objects.*

The State Design Pattern

GoF Intent: Allow an object to alter its behavior when its internal state changes. The object will appear to change its class.

Before we delve into the **State** pattern, a little computer science theory about **state machines** may help to set the stage for our discussion. A state machine stores the status of something at a given time and alters its behavior when the status changes. This not-too-technical definition suggests that a state machine has at least two characteristics:

❏ First, *distinguishable states exist.* In other words, each of the possible states is meaningfully different from the others.

❏ Second, *methods exist that facilitate movement between the states.*

Those of you unfamiliar with state machines may be surprised at their prevalence. For example, they are used aggressively in natural language processing and TCP/IP connections management.

Our demonstration program deals with a group of objects that simulate travel between a number of locations. Like any good state machine, it meets the basic requirements. First, the state objects are noticeably different (for example, the `Hawaii` object does not behave like the `Alberta` object). Second, each state object has methods for getting to other states. Here's the UML:

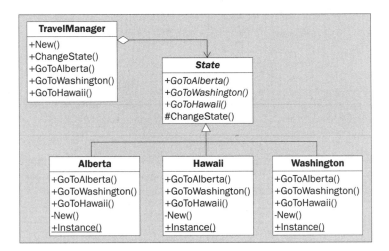

What may not be apparent in the UML is what happens when `TravelManager` decides to travel by calling one of its `GoTo...()` methods. To understand this behavior, we need a brief summary of what the UML tells us:

- ❑ The `TravelManager` object holds a reference to a `State` object (as indicated by the arrow with the hollow diamond).

- ❑ We *cannot* instantiate a `State` object directly (as indicated by the fact that the class name is italicized).

- ❑ Each of the state objects – `Alberta`, `Hawaii`, and `Washington` – is responsible for creating a shared instance of itself.

  (OK, this point may not be obvious without the code. In fact, it is derived from two facts. First, the derived classes' default constructors are hidden; second, the `Instance()` method is a shared method – as denoted by the underline – that might return the object itself. Does all this remind you of a Singleton?)

- ❑ Each of the state objects implements all the `GoTo...()` methods that `TravelManager` calls.

  (Again, this isn't obvious without the code. But, if `TravelManager` implemented the `GoTo...()` methods itself, why would it contain a `State` object?)

Combining these four concepts suggests to us that as `TravelManager` calls a `GoTo...()` method, it first loads an instance of `Alberta`, `Hawaii`, or `Washington`. When the appropriate state object is loaded, it does the work of moving to the next state as requested by executing the `GoTo...()` method.

So, let's have a look at the code. First, the `TravelManager` class. It contains a private `State` member object, which represents the current state of our state machine:

```
Class TravelManager
    Private m_State As State

    Public Sub New()
        Console.WriteLine("Travel Manager starting...")
```

```
      m_State = Washington.Instance
    End Sub

    Public Sub ChangeState(ByVal s As State)
      m_State = s
    End Sub

    Public Sub GoToAlberta()
      m_State.GoToAlberta(Me)
    End Sub

    Public Sub GoToHawaii()
      m_State.GoToHawaii(Me)
    End Sub

    Public Sub GoToWashington()
      m_State.GoToWashington(Me)
    End Sub
  End Class
```

Now let's see the State class itself. Note that it's qualified by the MustInherit keyword. We can't instantiate State objects directly, only through the individual state classes that inherit from it:

```
  MustInherit Class State
    Protected Sub New()
    End Sub

    MustOverride Sub GoToAlberta(ByRef tm As TravelManager)
    MustOverride Sub GoToHawaii(ByRef tm As TravelManager)
    MustOverride Sub GoToWashington(ByRef tm As TravelManager)

    Protected Sub ChangeState(ByRef tm As TravelManager, ByRef s As State)
      tm.ChangeState(s)
    End Sub
  End Class
```

Now here are the individual state classes that inherit from the State class:

```
  Public Class Alberta : Inherits State
    Private Shared m_State = New Alberta()

    Private Sub New()
    End Sub

    Public Shared Function Instance() As State
      Console.WriteLine("Welcome to Alberta!")
      Return m_State
    End Function

    Public Overrides Sub GoToAlberta(ByRef tm As TravelManager)
      Console.WriteLine("You are already in Alberta.")
    End Sub
```

```
      Public Overrides Sub GoToHawaii(ByRef tm As TravelManager)
        Console.WriteLine("Enjoy your flight to Hawaii.")
        ChangeState(tm, Hawaii.Instance)
      End Sub

      Public Overrides Sub GoToWashington(ByRef tm As TravelManager)
        Console.WriteLine("Enjoy the drive to America.")
        ChangeState(tm, Washington.Instance)
      End Sub
    End Class
```

Don't gloss over the GoTo...() methods too quickly. The implementations of these methods are slightly different in each state class, to ensure that each method does the right thing in the context of its current state. For example, the Alberta.GoToAlberta() method above is different to the GotoAlberta() methods in the following two classes:

```
    Public Class Hawaii : Inherits State
      Private Shared m_State = New Hawaii()

      Private Sub New()
      End Sub

      Public Shared Function Instance() As State
        Console.WriteLine("Welcome to Hawaii!")
        Return m_State
      End Function

      Public Overrides Sub GoToAlberta(ByRef tm As TravelManager)
        Console.WriteLine("Enjoy your flight to Canada.")
        ChangeState(tm, Alberta.Instance)
      End Sub

      Public Overrides Sub GoToHawaii(ByRef tm As TravelManager)
        Console.WriteLine("You are already in Hawaii.")
      End Sub

      Public Overrides Sub GoToWashington(ByRef tm As TravelManager)
        Console.WriteLine("Enjoy your flight to Washington.")
        ChangeState(tm, Washington.Instance)
      End Sub
    End Class
```

```
    Public Class Washington : Inherits State
      Private Shared m_State = New Washington()

      Private Sub New()
      End Sub

      Public Shared Function Instance() As State
        Console.WriteLine("Welcome to Washington!")
        Return m_State
      End Function
```

```
      Public Overrides Sub GoToAlberta(ByRef tm As TravelManager)
        Console.WriteLine("Enjoy the drive to Canada.")
        ChangeState(tm, Alberta.Instance)
      End Sub

      Public Overrides Sub GoToHawaii(ByRef tm As TravelManager)
        Console.WriteLine("Enjoy your flight to Hawaii.")
        ChangeState(tm, Hawaii.Instance)
      End Sub

      Public Overrides Sub GoToWashington(ByRef tm As TravelManager)
        Console.WriteLine("You are already in Washington.")
      End Sub
    End Class
```

Here's a little client application to demonstrate these objects:

```
    Sub Main()
      Dim objTravelManager As New TravelManager()

      With objTravelManager
        Console.WriteLine("Requesting a trip to Alberta....")
        .GoToAlberta()
        Console.WriteLine("Now requesting a trip to Hawaii....")
        .GoToHawaii()
        Console.WriteLine("Now requesting a trip to Washington....")
        .GoToWashington()
        Console.WriteLine("Now let's try requesting " & _
                          "the Washington trip again....")
        .GoToWashington()
      End With

      MessageBox.Show("Click OK to end")
    End Sub
```

Here is the output generated by this example:

```
    Travel Manager starting...
    Welcome to Washington!
    Requesting a trip to Alberta....
    Enjoy the drive to Canada.
    Welcome to Alberta!
    Now requesting a trip to Hawaii....
    Enjoy your flight to Hawaii.
    Welcome to Hawaii!
    Now requesting a trip to Washington....
    Enjoy your flight to Washington.
    Welcome to Washington!
    Now let's try requesting the Washington trip again....
    You are already in Washington.
```

The Strategy and Template Method Design Patterns

> **GoF Intent for Strategy:** Define a family of algorithms, encapsulate each one, and make them interchangeable. Strategy lets the algorithm vary independently from clients that use it.
>
> **GoF Intent for Template Method:** Define the skeleton of an algorithm in an operation, deferring some steps to subclasses. Template method lets subclasses redefine certain steps of an algorithm without changing the algorithm's structure.

Providing clients with access to common algorithms is the objective of both the Strategy and Template Method patterns. They accomplish this feat in different ways. **Strategy** employs rich objects that encapsulate the key algorithms. **Template Method** uses lightweight objects and inheritance to serve up their secrets. We'll take a look at two demonstrations in this section, to try to clarify this potentially ambiguous difference.

The Strategy Design Pattern – an Example

Our Strategy application worries about processing credit card transactions. While doing so may only involve a few different calculations, these calculations might include specialized third-party verifications or database queries. Such potential complications clearly suggest separate implementations for each credit card vendor.

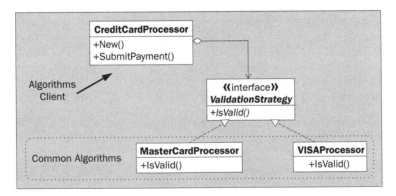

Let's begin by presenting the `ValidationStrategy` interface. This specifies the interface that must be implemented by each of the common algorithm classes:

```
Public Interface ValidationStrategy
    Function IsValid(ByVal Account As String) As Boolean
End Interface
```

Now we'll look at the algorithm classes themselves. In this example we have two, but we could have more if we wanted:

```
Public Class MasterCardProcessor : Implements ValidationStrategy
   Public Function IsValid(ByVal Account As String) As Boolean _
                          Implements ValidationStrategy.IsValid
      If Account.StartsWith("5") Then
        Return True
      Else
        Return False
      End If
   End Function
End Class


Public Class VISAProcessor : Implements ValidationStrategy
   Public Function IsValid(ByVal Account As String) As Boolean _
                          Implements ValidationStrategy.IsValid
      If Account.Length > 5 Then
        Return True
      Else
         Return False
      End If
   End Function
End Class
```

They look quite similar, and they really differ in that they can implement the `ValidationStrategy` interface differently.

In our application, the implementations of `IsValid()` are fairly simple. But a real application would involve either a call to a specialized application or a request to a payment gateway to perform validation services. Both of these processes would most likely entail custom coding specific to the class.

Now let's look at the `CreditCardProcessor` class, which acts as the Strategy pattern's required "switchboard" class (we know from the UML that this class acts like a switchboard – the line with the diamond indicates that a `CreditCardProcessor` object must contain a `ValidationStrategy`-derived object):

```
Public Class CreditCardProcessor
   Private m_ValidationStrategy As ValidationStrategy

   Public Sub New(ByVal vs As ValidationStrategy)
     m_ValidationStrategy = vs
   End Sub

   Public Sub SubmitPayment(ByVal Account As String, _
                           ByVal Amount As Double)
     If m_ValidationStrategy.IsValid(Account) Then
        Console.WriteLine("Request for submitted payment!")
     Else
        Console.WriteLine("Reject this card!")
     End If
   End Sub
End Class
```

Here's a client application to test this out. Based on the validation criteria in the `IsValid()` method implementations, we'd expect the first payment request to be validated while the second one fails:

```
Sub Main()
   Console.WriteLine("Submit payment for $123.45 " & _
                     "on MasterCard #512-125-125")
   Dim objCC As New CreditCardProcessor(New MasterCardProcessor())
   objCC.SubmitPayment("512-125-125", 123.45)

   Console.WriteLine("Submit payment for $10000 on VISA card #123")
   objCC = New CreditCardProcessor(New VISAProcessor())
   objCC.SubmitPayment("123", 10000D)

   MessageBox.Show("Click OK to end")
End Sub
```

And here are the results – just as we expected:

```
Submit payment for $123.45 on MasterCard #512-125-125
Request for submitted payment!
Submit payment for $10000 on VISA card #123
Reject this card!
```

The Template Method Design Pattern – an Example

Our Template Method demonstration has decidedly simpler requirements. It prepares debit and credit transactions in US dollars for an accounting application. The rules are fixed. All amounts must be formatted as integers, with the rightmost two digits equating to cents. Also, debit values are positive, credits negative. Despite these differences both algorithms share the key method, Process().

At first look, it may seem like overkill to create a class hierarchy for a system with so few algorithms. But did you ever write Visual Basic modules housing a collection of common routines? The Template Method pattern serves the same function, except it is less likely to break any applications when altering or adding algorithms:

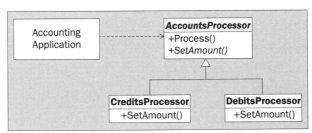

Here's the AccountsProcessor class. It contains a Process() method (with implementation), and a SetAmount() method (whose implementation is left to the classes that inherit from AccountsProcessor):

```
Public MustInherit Class AccountsProcessor
   Protected m_Amount As Integer

   Public Sub Process(ByVal Account As String)
     Console.WriteLine(Account & " adjusted by " & m_Amount)
   End Sub
```

```
        Public MustOverride Sub SetAmount(ByVal Amount As Double)
    End Class
```

Now here are the two classes that inherit from `AccountsProcessor`:

```
    Public Class DebitsProcessor : Inherits AccountsProcessor
        Public Overrides Sub SetAmount(ByVal Amount As Double)
            m_Amount = Math.Round(Amount, 2) * 100
        End Sub
    End Class

    Public Class CreditsProcessor : Inherits AccountsProcessor
        Public Overrides Sub SetAmount(ByVal Amount As Double)
            m_Amount = -1 * Math.Round(Amount, 2) * 100
        End Sub
    End Class
```

Here's an application to test the objects:

```
    Sub Main()
        Dim objDebitsProcessor As New DebitsProcessor()
        Dim objCreditsProcessor As New CreditsProcessor()

        Console.WriteLine("Increment the Training Expense account by $10.50...")
        objDebitsProcessor.SetAmount(10.5D)
        objDebitsProcessor.Process("Training Expense")

        Console.WriteLine("Decrement the Accounts Payable by $10.50...")
        objCreditsProcessor.SetAmount(10.5D)
        objCreditsProcessor.Process("Accounts Payable")

        MessageBox.Show("Click OK to end")
    End Sub
```

And the result is as follows:

```
    Increment the Training Expense account by $10.50...
    Training Expense adjusted by 1050
    Decrement the Accounts Payable by $10.50...
    Accounts Payable adjusted by -1050
```

Choosing between Strategy and Template Method

While these two patterns are implemented quite differently (one with an interface that must be implemented, the other with a `MustInherit`-qualified class and `MustOverride`-qualified methods), it seems at first sight that there's very little to choose between them.

The decision to go with one or the other of these patterns has much to do with the nature of the algorithms under consideration. If the algorithms are relatively simple and unchanging, as in the last demonstration, Template Method is quite effective. If the algorithms are complex, and have very little in common other than an overall goal, then Strategy works best.

An inexperienced software engineer could attempt to use either of these two patterns to achieve the same goal. The effectiveness of the resulting implementation would only become clear with the first round of changes.

For example, suppose our engineer mistakenly used a Template Method when the situation called for a Strategy pattern. Suppose a new requirement demands the creation of another *feature-rich* object. Unfortunately, incorporating it into the Template-based code requires alterations to almost every class since this new object does not conform to the existing classes.

Application of Design Patterns

Each of the examples we've seen in this chapter demonstrates the use of a single GoF design pattern. In your real-life applications, however, you will probably find that design patterns rarely live in isolation. Often, the characteristics of a problem point to a solution composed of two or more design patterns, which takes advantage of the characteristics of each of the patterns.

Some pairs of patterns complement each other particularly well. We will see a number of examples of patterns within patterns, in the remaining chapters of this book. The list below captures just a few of the cohabiting patterns that I have witnessed over the years:

- ❑ Abstract Factory likes to exploit Factory Method for object creation. Some experienced OO programmers even consider this design to be the "real" Abstract Factory.

- ❑ Before an Abstract Factory grabs a specific family of classes, some of the classes within the family are made compatible with the others by application of an Adapter pattern (or even a Façade, which is potentially simpler).

- ❑ The Singleton regularly prevents uncontrolled proliferation of State objects. I suspect many of you were thinking about this as you tried out the examples in this chapter.

- ❑ Strategy patterns may enhance the flexibility of Decorator classes. The Decorator allows us to add responsibilities dynamically; the Strategy allows us to change the way these responsibilities do their job.

The point is that we can think of each individual pattern as a solution template in its own right, but we can also think of it as a *building block* for the creation of more powerful and focused patterns. There is a multitude of information (in technical articles and books) on the subject of composing groups of patterns in order to create more "specialized" patterns that handle specific problems. The Internet is an invaluable resource. For example, there's invaluable information in the pattern literature about how specialized patterns relate to subjects like threading and concurrency. It doesn't matter if this information is presented in an unrelated language like C++ or Java – these resources can often point you in the right direction as you ponder a related problem.

Pattern Selection

The question remains, how do you select the right pattern for a problem? A good start is to examine the characteristics of the problem, and look for a pattern whose intent suggests that it might fit the bill. It helps if you can describe the characteristics of the problem using the same kind of language and terminology the GoF use for the intents of their patterns. Try to match "keywords" to trigger a choice. For example:

- ❑ "This class will need to be *adapted* to handle imperial measurements"
- ❑ "What we need here is a *bridge/ façade/ proxy/ delegate*"
- ❑ "We need to *build* a few variations"

Here are a few other suggestions that the authors find helpful when selecting patterns:

- ❑ **Search for Variability**. Patterns are all about encapsulating variability – they help us to design applications that are extensible, maintainable, and easy to modify. Very often, identifying the most likely elements of variability in the requirements (that is, those business requirements that your client might subsequently want to change) provides crucial clues to the "best" pattern.

- ❑ **Follow the KISS Principle** (Keep It Simple, Stupid!):

  - ❑ Avoid throwing a pattern at a problem that does not need it. For example, if you've got a "family" of classes, but there are actually only two classes in this family, then it's far simpler to use a `select case` structure than an Abstract Factory. Will the family grow in the future? If so, then this is an example of variability, and Abstract Factory could well be justified. If not, it might be better to keep it simple and apply a `select case` structure.

  - ❑ When comparing two or more acceptable pattern-based solutions, favor the *simplest* design. The more complicated design is liable to constrict future architectural options. It is also likely to lengthen the learning curve of the developer who has to maintain the application.

- ❑ **Consider All the Options**. We've already hinted at the notion that there's usually more than one solution to any given problem. It's unlikely that you'll have two complex design solutions to choose between – it's more common that you need to make a choice between different GoF patterns! For example, the situation could arise in which the Abstract Factory and Prototype patterns are both identified as viable solutions. If you have a dilemma like this, you need to look further into how each pattern works, and consider the implications of each pattern within your application.

- ❑ **Know the Scope of the Problem.** It helps to understand whether you're applying a pattern for tactical reasons or for strategic reasons. For example, consider two different applications of the Decorator pattern – if we're using it (say) to embellish a printed report then this is a tactical application, but if it controls the logic of an entire application then this is strategic. An understanding of this difference may help a developer to apply the appropriate type of design. Typically, when selecting a pattern to solve large strategic problems, considerable thought and discussion is required. By constrast, when selecting a pattern to solve a tactical problem, proof-of-concept testing is required.

- ❑ **Patterns *can* Facilitate Bad Designs**. Playing with design patterns is like playing with fire – if you get it right its wonderful, but if you get it wrong it can burn. You can reduce the chances of getting hurt by reading design pattern literature. Most egregious design errors arise when folks simply find something that looks cool and hastily "cut and paste" it into their code. Discussing patterns with team members really helps to avoid selection-related injuries.

Summary

Design patterns constitute a powerful technique for use in the design of systems to be implemented using object-oriented languages like VB.NET. In particular, design patterns can help our applications to be more extensible and maintainable, and better able to react to changes in business requirements.

The most widely-referenced work on design patterns – the GoF's *Design Patterns* book – catalogs some 23 of the most common patterns, describing the characteristics of each problem and of the pattern that is intended to solve it. They categorize their 23 patterns into three groups:

❑ Creational patterns, that attempt to simplify and provide a flexible approach to object creation.

❑ Structural patterns, that attempt to specify how objects and classes should work together.

❑ Behavioral patterns, that attempt to divine an effective structure for inter-object communications.

Aside from those patterns cataloged in the GoF's *Design Patterns* book, the community has identified many other patterns. They cover such diverse topics as asynchronous programming, model-view-controller scenarios, and the use of XML. We'll cover a few non-GoF patterns during the course of this book, and there are plenty of other resources across the Internet.

You don't need to know about hundreds of different design patterns before you can start using them in your application design. In this chapter, we've looked at about a dozen of them, and that is enough to get you started. You may be surprised at how some of the concepts will stay with you. For example, the next time you're presented with a problem that involves a recursive directory structure, I bet the Composite pattern will be somewhere in your thoughts.

In general, it is a pattern's intent that gives us the first indication of whether a given pattern can play a part in the solution to a given problem. Thus, a list of patterns and their intents is probably a useful thing to keep nearby. If a pattern's intent suggests that it might fit the bill, then you can look up the implementation mechanics and begin to consider the implications of using it in your design.

Of course, the more you use design patterns, the more familiar they will become. But there is good reason to start thinking about using design patterns within your very next project – even if you're only armed with the information you've learned in this chapter.

In the next chapter, we'll look at some patterns which we can use to strengthen the development of a data tier for an application.

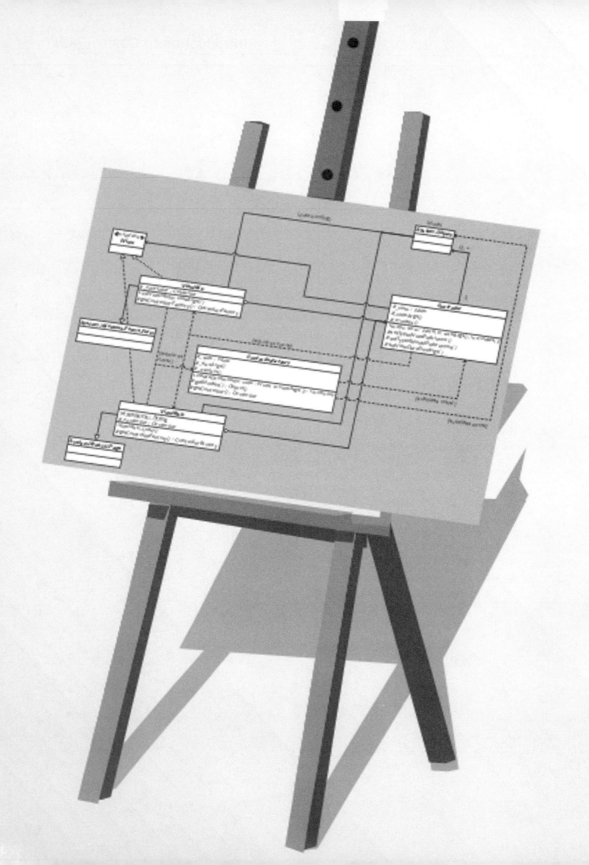

2

Design Patterns in the Data Tier

A typical data tier has a fairly simple *implementation* but is complex in its *operation*. In other words, it is composed of a relatively flat class hierarchy (perhaps only one or two classes deep), is oriented towards one particular type of data store, and presents a relatively simple set of commands to the client applications that use it. However, the underlying operations within those few classes and methods are complex – because the data tier is required to manage issues like security, database connections, reporting errors back to client tiers, database performance optimization, and the execution of complex sequences of transactional queries.

It's also common that a single data-tier application will need to serve numerous data consumers (or client applications), and that each client has its own particular needs in terms of how it expects data to be delivered.

So, in spite of its relatively simple appearance, there are some fairly hefty requirements made of a data tier. We can certainly use the design patterns paradigm in our data tier design – to help create a more flexible data tier and to help shield client application developers from some of the complexity inherent in working with large application databases.

While the design patterns literature probably offers more focus on design patterns in the business rules tier and the presentation tier, they are clearly just as relevant to the data tier. Therefore, in this chapter we will concentrate on the implementation of design patterns in the construction of a data-access tier.

In this chapter we'll focus on several broad objectives:

❑   We'll illustrate the application of design patterns to the task of building a data layer for any *n*-tier .NET application.

❑   We'll showcase several common design patterns, and the benefits and potential pitfalls of implementing those patterns in the data tier.

❑   We'll compare a design patterns approach to software development with other commonly accepted approaches to building a data access tier.

❑   We'll consider design patterns in practice – in particular, by discussing the thought processes involved in the design and coding stages of this case study.

By the end of the chapter, we'll have a functional data-access framework that supports a number of database types, and outputs the data in a number of different formats. Moreover, it is designed in such a way that it can easily be adapted and extended by the reader for real-world applications. Over the course of the chapter, we'll be giving some consideration to the Abstract Factory, Factory Method, and Singleton design patterns.

In this chapter, we will use a design patterns approach to build a more extensible data access layer – it will be sufficiently flexible (in design and implementation) that it will be able to handle a variety of business and technical requirements that could cause problems for some existing data access layers. Here's how this case study will unfold:

❑   We'll start by outlining the problem we've been asked to solve, and listing the requirements of our data access tier. You will probably recognize some of these requirements from your own development experiences.

❑   Then we'll take a look at a "conventional" approach to building a data access layer, and see how well (or how badly) it meets our requirements.

❑   After that, we'll see how we can get a better solution by using a design patterns approach. We'll put some consideration into the design itself; we'll introduce a number of patterns and explain some of the thought behind choosing the right patterns and building them into our design.

❑   Finally, we'll build and test our chosen design, and hence justify our choice.

Requirements of a Data Tier

In the fictitious case study that will form part of this chapter, Northwind Traders is revising its systems infrastructure and overhauling its applications. The company's Technology Manager, Sally Server, has indicated in meetings that as part of this exercise, it would be advantageous to reconsider the way that client applications access the company's databases, and put together a single extensible data tier.

Northwind has a number of local branches, and each branch runs its own implementation of the Northwind database. Most are implemented using Microsoft systems, but for reasons of available technology, one or two distant outposts have versions of the database implemented in Oracle 8i. Therefore, we've been asked to build our data access framework to support many different database platforms, including SQL Server and Oracle.

Northwind has a number of client applications that make use of the data in the Northwind database, and so our data tier will also need to be able to interface with any number of applications.

A Requirements List

Sally and her team have collaborated with some of Northwind's business managers, and come up with a set of business and technical requirements that our data tier will need to satisfy. These points were among the business and technical requirements they came up with:

❑ Each of Northwind's branches has implemented an instance of the Northwind database, but they are not all on the same database platform. Platforms include SQL Server 7.0, SQL Server 2000, and Oracle 8i.

Some branches are planning to implement their Northwind-based applications entirely as a series of web services on SQL Server 2000. They wish to take advantage of some of the new features of SQLXML.

❑ The data access framework must be easy to use. It should also be easily adaptable, so that they can accommodate new releases of database technology. The first operational client will be using SQL Server 2000, so support for that database version is our first priority.

❑ The data access framework must support rich-UI type clients (such as Windows applications), and applications with lighter UI requirements (such as Web, handheld, and wireless applications).

Presentation and middle-tier developers know their particular application requirements in terms of what they will do with data returned from the data tier. Therefore, the data tier must be able to return a variety of data structures to other tiers. Our priority is for a data tier that can return both .NET `DataSets` and `DataReaders` (at the client application's request). This will allow application developers to make the decisions about how best to work with data tier results. The data tier should be adaptable in this respect too. In future, we want (for example) to be able to extend it so it is capable of returning `XmlDocuments`, `XmlReaders`, or scalars (integers, strings, etc.) from a `SELECT`-type command, and of executing non-`SELECT`-type commands (`INSERT`, `UPDATE`, `DELETE`).

❑ The data access framework should support stored procedures and other types of queries (such as requesting a table by specifying the table name).

❑ Northwind is totally committed to new application development using .NET. Therefore the data tier must be written using the .NET Framework.

Our developers are familiar with Visual Basic 6.0, and are being trained in VB.NET. Therefore the learning curve for writing the framework in VB.NET can be assumed to be minimal.

Analysing the Requirements

This requirements list makes for daunting reading! In essence, it looks like we need to create a data tier that can:

❑ Talk to databases implemented on different platforms. This is a fairly common requirement. It provides a certain amount of future-proofing, and also gives the data access tier a certain ubiquity – if it works well, it can be used to access any form of data store. We will find that the .NET Framework classes do a lot of work for us in the end; but the success of the data access tier rests entirely on our data framework design.

❑ Support different types of client applications and output types, or "products". We wish to create a framework that is as flexible as possible when it comes to returning data to the middle or client tiers. A business-tier developer will understand the data requirements of their application better than we do, and we need to accommodate that as flexibly as we can.

Of course, we also have the "make it easy to use" clause – which seems to be omnipresent in requirements documents. In this case we're being asked to create a data tier that is easy for other developers to use. The usability requirement might make us smile, but we will also take note of it.

We'll build a data tier that works nearly the same for all of the different databases we support. It should help to ensure that the data access code used by an application is independent of the database platform being used. If it's successful, then this will have two consequences: first, it means that the client application developer familiar with one database implementation doesn't need to relearn when asked to write an application that must use a database on a different platform; second, it makes it easier to port a client application from one database platform to another, because the data access code used in the application should barely need to change.

We'll meet our other requirements as the chapter progresses, so let's postpone discussion of those requirements and tackle them as the design and code unfold over the next few pages.

To give us something with which to compare a patterns-based approach to building the data tier, let's take a few pages to discuss a common approach we might find in existing data tiers.

Data-Tier Architecture

The purpose of any data tier, however complex, is to wrap data store-specific code (such as the connection code, query and stored procedure execution, error-handling, and manipulation of data into the right format), and hence shield client applications from that code.

Data tiers take many forms – one could be as simple as a class in an application or a set of managed components running on a dedicated server. Regardless of how the data tier is implemented, the result is a single data access API (or other interface) that looks the same to client application developers regardless of the underlying database platform in use. This simplifies the task of the client application developer. Many of us have written our own data tier at some time or other, and many others have at least interacted with such a data tier.

Some data tiers work by exposing commonly used methods that perform functions expressed in an application-oriented context. For instance, one way to provide data services to a Northwind-type application would be to create a flat hierarchy of one or more classes with a variety of methods that might be named `GetCustomer()` or `GetOrders()` or `SaveOrder()`. To use these methods, a middle-tier application developer would pass several input parameters and expect a specific type of return parameter. In previous versions of ADO, that return parameter was usually a `Recordset`. If we employ ADO.NET for our database access, a method like `GetOrders()` would probably return a `DataSet` or `DataReader` object of some sort.

A Simple but Inflexible Data-Tier Example

Here's a very simplified example of such a class – a VB.NET class that exposes a single method called `GetCustomer()`:

```
Imports System.Data.SqlClient
Public Class NWDatabase
  Public Function GetCustomer(ByVal sCustomerID As String, _
                              ByVal sConnectString As String) As DataSet
    Dim sCommand As String
    Dim conSQL As SqlConnection
    Dim cmdSQL As SqlCommand
    Dim daSQL As SqlDataAdapter
    Dim dsReturn As DataSet

    Try
      conSQL = New SqlConnection(sConnectString)
      cmdSQL = New SqlCommand()
      daSQL = New SqlDataAdapter()
      sCommand = "SELECT CustomerID, CompanyName, " & _
            "ContactName, Address, City, PostalCode FROM Customers " & _
            "WHERE CustomerID='" & sCustomerID & "'"

      cmdSQL.CommandText = sCommand
      cmdSQL.CommandType = CommandType.Text
      cmdSQL.Connection = conSQL

      conSQL.Open()
      dsReturn = New DataSet()
      daSQL.SelectCommand = cmdSQL
      daSQL.Fill(dsReturn)
      Return dsReturn

    Catch ex As SqlException
      Debug.WriteLine(ex.Message)
    Finally
      If conSQL.State = ConnectionState.Open Then
        conSQL.Close()
      End If
    End Try
  End Function
End Class
```

As you can see, the method's implementation manages the connection to the database, as well as setting up the command text; it also manipulates the resulting data into a DataSet object (for return to the client) and deals with all its own error-handling.

The exact details of the database connection code aren't important here. What is important is that we note how restrictive this approach is. In particular:

❑   Note that we're using an Imports statement at the top of the class to import classes from the System.Data.SqlClient namespace, which means that we're using the SQL Server .NET data provider. That means that this class will only allow us access to SQL Server (7.0 or 2000) databases. If we wanted to use this class to access a different database platform, we'd need to recode it.

❑   The method returns a DataSet. It can't return a DataReader or an XmlDocument object. So the client application has little control over the format of the data that this data tier method returns, and clearly doesn't satisfy our technical requirements.

Note that method itself contains all the code for connecting to the database and for putting the resulting data into the correct format for output. If we extended this class to contain other methods (such as `GetCustomer()`, `GetOrder()`, etc.) we'd need to rewrite the database connection code and data formatting code into *every* function. If we subsequently decided to support a new format for data output, or if we were asked to extend this data tier to support another data store platform (such as Oracle), the workload would be huge.

This approach is probably common in relatively simple applications and it may be acceptable in many applications whose business requirements never change. However, we've been asked to build a generic data tier, which needs to be adaptable to this kind of change; and the approach outlined above is clearly not sufficiently extensible or adaptable.

A Slightly More Maintainable Example

It seems that we could improve this approach by building a separate database class that executes specific database operations. Our database class could be shared between projects or compiled into a shared binary. It would allow us to remove the database-specific code from each of our `Get...()` methods, which would make the whole thing more maintainable. It also makes things slightly easier when we want to add a new method – because the new method can use our dedicated database-access class to access the database, instead of implementing the data access code itself.

Without getting into the database code too deeply (we'll be doing enough of that later), such a database class would look something like the following:

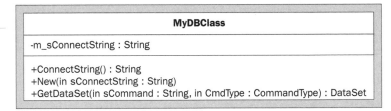

The benefits of such a class are immediately obvious. Any method that needs to generate a `DataSet` can simply instantiate `MyDBClass` and call its `GetDataSet()` method, like this:

```
Public Class NWDatabase
  Public Function GetCustomer(ByVal sCustomerID As String, _
                              ByVal sConnectString As String) As DataSet
    Dim sCommand As String
    Dim oMyDB As New MyDBClass(sConnectString)
    Dim dsReturn As DataSet

    Try
      sCommand = "SELECT CustomerID, CompanyName, " & _
            "ContactName, Address, City, PostalCode FROM Customers " & _
            "WHERE CustomerID='" & sCustomerID & "'"

        dsReturn = oMyDB.GetDataSet(sCommand, CommandType.Text)
    Catch ex As Exception
      Debug.WriteLine(ex.Message)
    End Try

  End Function
End Class
```

As you can see, the client `GetCustomer()` method is now rather simpler than it was – because we've abstracted out most of the database-access code. It's a little less work to create new `Get...()` methods, and a little less effort to maintain the data access code.

However, this approach is no more flexible or adaptable than the previous one. All we've done is move the database-access code from the `NWDatabase` class to the `MyDBClass` class. The code itself would still use the `System.Data.SqlClient` namespace and so it's still only capable of talking to SQL Server database platforms.

Moreover, we haven't done anything about the product type at all: our `GetCustomers()` method is still only capable of returning a `DataSet` object.

There's no obvious way to adapt this code to accommodate access to different database platforms and output types. To make these changes to the existing code, we would probably have to rewrite so much of the code that we'd introduce change control issues – and then the QA people would need to retest most of the application.

Flexibility is a key requirement of our data tier application, and these approaches clearly don't cut the mustard. We need to go back to the drawing board; we'll think about the areas of the application in which we need flexibility, and we'll reconsider our approach with some fresh thoughts in mind.

Creating a Flexible Data Access Framework

The success of our data tier is largely dependent on its ability to support different database platforms, and its ability to return data in different types (`DataSet`, `DataAdapter`, etc.). So let us focus on these two requirements in particular.

In order to access a database and return data, our data tier will make use of the **.NET data providers** and the **objects** that make up those providers. We'll take a look at those now; we'll think about how our data tier needs to use them, and hopefully they will lead us in the direction of a design patterns-based solution to our problem.

The .NET Data Providers

The .NET Framework itself supports different databases using the **.NET data providers**. Each .NET data provider consists of a set of classes that provide access to a particular type of data source. At the time of writing, there are three data providers available from Microsoft:

❑ The **SQL Server .NET data provider** is used for accessing SQL Server 7.0 and SQL Server 2000 databases, and you can also use it for accessing databases hosted in MSDE. This data provider is optimized for SQL Server, and provides excellent performance because it accesses the database server directly (instead of going through an intermediary like OLE DB or ODBC).

The SQL Server .NET data provider classes are contained in the `System.Data.SqlClient` namespace.

❑ The **OLE DB .NET data provider** is used for accessing databases through an **OLE DB data provider** layer. In principle, this means that you can use this .NET data provider to access any database platform that you can access though OLE DB. In practice, in order for the OLE DB .NET data provider to access a database platform, the OLE DB data provider that lies between them most support certain interfaces. At the time of writing, Microsoft says that its OLE DB providers for SQL Server, Oracle, and MS Access have been tested.

The OLE DB .NET data provider classes are contained in the `System.Data.OleDb` namespace.

❑ The **ODBC .NET data provider** works in much the same way as the OLE DB .NET data provider – but this time the layer between the .NET data provider and the database platform is an **ODBC driver**. Again, while in principle you can use any ODBC driver, in practice it must support certain functionality that is required by the .NET data provider. Microsoft has tested its ODBC drivers for SQL Server, Oracle, and Jet (MS Access).

The OLE DB .NET data provider classes are contained in the `Microsoft.Data.Odbc` namespace.

At the time of writing, development is continuing on .NET data providers for other database platforms – for Oracle and Postgresql in particular.

In addition to these data providers, we could also extend our data tier to support SQLXML – a new feature of SQL Server 2000 for retrieving XML. SQLXML services are located in the namespace `Microsoft.Data.SqlXml`, which is available for download at http://msdn.microsoft.com/library (at the time of writing, it is in version 3.0). It's not a data provider in the same way as the others (it doesn't have its own `Connection` object, for a start) – but our data tier should be extensible enough to be able to support it in a future iteration.

The .NET Data Provider Objects

There are four objects that make up a data provider: the **Connection**, the **Command**, the **DataReader**, and the **DataAdapter**. Let's take a very brief look at these objects, because they are important objects to understand – whatever design patterns we decide to employ, these objects are likely to do much of the work for us.

Here's a quick overview to keep in mind as we discuss our data layer design:

Data Provider Class	Description and Usage
Connection	Represents a unique session or connection to a data store
Command	Represents a SQL command or stored procedure that can be executed against a data store
DataReader	Used for returning a forward-only read-only stream of data from a database
DataAdapter	Represents a set of commands and a data connection, and is used to fill a `DataSet` object

Each .NET data provider supplies its own implementation of each of the four classes listed above. The class definitions are contained within the .NET data provider's namespace.

Each data provider names its classes by using a simple prefix – the SQL Server .NET data provider uses the prefix `Sql` and the OLD DB .NET data provider uses the prefix `OleDb`. Moreover, all of the .NET data provider objects are built up on the same four interfaces – `IDbConnection`, `IDbCommand`, `IDataReader`, and `IDbDataAdapter` respectively. Thus, the summary of all the namespaces, object names and parent classes is as follows:

	SQL Server .NET Data Provider	OLE DB .NET Data Provider	ODBC .NET Data Provider
Namespace name	`System.Data.SqlClient`	`System.Data.OleDb`	`System.Data.ODBC`
These classes all implement `IDbConnection`	`SqlConnection`	`OleDbConnection`	`ODBCConnection`
These classes all implement `IDbCommand`	`SqlCommand`	`OleDbCommand`	`ODBCCommand`
These classes all implement `IDataReader`	`SqlDataReader`	`OleDbDataReader`	`ODBCDataReader`
These classes all implement `IDbDataAdapter`	`SqlDataAdapter`	`OleDbDataAdapter`	`ODBCDataAdapter`

The fact that similar classes all implement the same interface (for example, all the `Connection` classes implement `IDbConnection`) is good news for us – because it means that we can program to an interface (such as `IDbConnection`) instead of programming to an implementation of it (such as `SqlConnection` or `OleDbConnection`). That means that we can change data providers with minimal impact in application code.

Our requirements tell us that our data tier must support many different database platforms. The way we'll do that is by supporting the .NET data providers. We'll allow the data providers do all of the work – we just have to know when to use the right provider.

> *There is one object that we have mentioned here, but haven't explained – the `DataSet`. The `DataSet` object is an in-memory set of data – but it is more powerful than the old ADO `Recordset` object. It can hold the result of a query that consists of several tables (and the relationships between the tables), and it can hold the results of several distinct queries (perhaps from distinct data sources) at the same time. The `DataSet` is provider-independent, and consequently is contained in the `System.Data` namespace.*
>
> *We'll make use of the `DataSet` object, along with some of the .NET data provider objects, later in the chapter.*

The Design Patterns Analysis

So, our immediate target is to create a mechanism that is capable of:

❑ Supporting a number of data providers now, and is also sufficiently adaptable that we can add any new data providers that are released by Microsoft or anyone else in the future.

❑ Allowing the client application to select the format of the data that is returned (that is, whether the returned object is a `DataSet`, or a `DataAdapter`, etc.).

Is there a design patterns solution? Well, to look for clues we perhaps need to think about what the data tier does each time we use it:

- ❑ First, it creates the necessary data access objects – `Connection`, `Command`, etc.

- ❑ Then, it uses them to access the data store and perform the required command

- ❑ Finally, it returns any data or other information to the client application

There's clearly a clue in the first of these steps, which is about *creating* the necessary objects. We can hazard a guess we'll need a creational pattern to play a part in our overall design. Back in Chapter 1, we said that the purpose of the creational patterns is to:

"...make applications less dependent on the vagaries of simplistic object construction and class referencing"

The two approaches we've seen so far are certainly guilty of simplistic object construction and class referencing! It sounds like a creational pattern is what we're after. Let's look even closer and consider whether one of the GoF creational patterns will fit our needs.

Considering Creational Patterns

Next, consider *how* our data tier might support each of the .NET data providers. It may be best to build one class for each .NET data provider – and hence a *one-to-one abstraction* of data providers by data tier classes. In a design like that, we could have one class that represents the SQL Server .NET data provider, another for the OLE DB .NET data provider, and so on. We could create one class for each data provider that we intend to support on release; and each time we extend our data tier application to support a new data provider, we'd simply add a new custom class to represent it.

If we structure the data tier correctly, we could easily separate the different data providers (and their requisite `Imports` statements) this way. The classes for a data provider are contained in a dedicated namespace for that data provider – that would make it very convenient to create a separate file for each data provider class. For now, let's deal with a logical arrangement of classes – and we'll work on how we implement our design a little later.

It would be good if our data tier exposes a **standard interface** to our client applications, but gives them the flexibility to choose what type of data provider support the client requires. The client should indicate a choice of data provider to our data tier, and the data tier should respond with an object whose methods can perform database functions using the requested data provider. This object will need to have the same methods and properties, regardless of the data provider the client application requested. This should be enough to satisfy our ease-of-use requirement (because client application developers only need to learn one interface in order to work with many types of data store). It will also mean that if a database is ported from one platform to another, the affected client applications will require very few changes.

So, when a client application requests an interaction with a SQL Server database, then the sequence of events should look something like this:

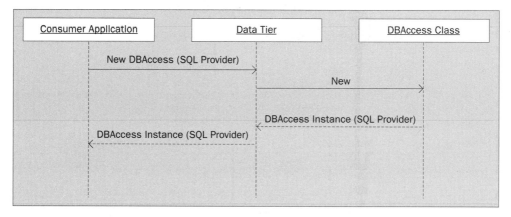

Here, the application communicates to the main interface of our data tier that it needs a database access object, so that it may use it to interact with a SQL Server database (the NewDBAccess() method call). The data tier takes the request and returns an instance of a class that can do the job using the SQL .NET data provider.

There's one more important observation we get from this diagram: namely, that we need a way to parameterize the process of creating the object that will perform the data access.

So, in summary, we need a pattern that will:

❑ Allow us to rely on the various .NET data providers (provided as part of the .NET Framework) for the data access itself

❑ Wrap each of the data providers into its own "wrapper" class (note that each of these wrapper classes should show the same methods and properties)

❑ Have a single point of access, which exposes a parameterized object creation mechanism that can be used by the client application at run time to specify which data provider it needs

Have any of the GoF's creational design patterns sprung to mind during the course of this discussion? Factory Method and Abstract Factory are perhaps the two most obvious candidates. In fact, these two patterns are often confused with one another, so let's remind ourselves of each pattern and consider whether they could be applied to our database-access class scenario.

Factory Method and Multiple Data Providers

Here's a reminder of the GoF intent for the Factory Method pattern:

> **GoF Intent for Factory Method:** Define an interface for creating an object, but let subclasses decide which class to instantiate. Factory Method lets a class defer instantiation to subclasses.

Factory Method is useful in a variety of object-creation scenarios, and we could easily implement a Factory Method pattern for our database-access classes. The client application would create an instance of the Factory class, and ask it to return a concrete instance of the data access class that wrapped the required data provider. Methods of our Factory class might look something like this:

DBAccessFactory
+CreateSQLDBAccess() : IDBAccess +CreateOleDBDBAccess() : IDBAccess +CreateODBCDBAccess() : IDBAccess +CreateSQLXMLDBAccess() : IDBAccess

If a client application required access to (say) a SQL Server database, it would create a `DBAccessFactory` object and then use its `CreateSQLDBAccess()` method to acquire an instance of a concrete class (an implementation of `IDBAccess`) that wraps the SQL Server .NET data provider.

This solution would require one class for each data provider (as expected) – each of these classes would implement the `IDBAccess` interface (and hence they would all expose a common set of methods and properties).

Can this design accommodate the introduction of new data providers? To extend the data tier to support a new data provider, we would need to add a new wrapper class (that implemented `IDBAccess`) and add a `CreateXXXDBAccess()` method to the `DBAccessFactory` class. In other words, we could accommodate extra data providers without changing the overall design of the data tier, and without too much effort.

In short, the Factory Method looks promising so far – it appears to go a long way towards fulfilling the requirements of our data tier.

Factory Method and Multiple Output Types

With the above in mind, we should also consider our other major requirement – that the client should be able to select the type of object (`DataSet`, `DataAdapter`, etc.) in which any resulting data is returned. Things begin to get a little tricky now, and this could turn out to be the downfall of Factory Method as far as our application is concerned. Let's see.

With the "multiple output type" requirement, each of our "wrapper" classes (the classes that implement `IDBAccess` and wrap one of the data providers) must *also* support that functionality for *every one* of the return types we support. Each class must be able to cope with the quirks and implementation details of each return type (as you can imagine, there aren't too many similarities between `DataSet` objects and `XMLDocument` objects). Moreover, each possible return object type has specialized helper objects and methods in the .NET Framework classes.

Because we have to satisfy support for multiple data providers *and* support for multiple return types, the problem as a whole has a 2-parameter feel about it – with data providers represented by one parameter and return types by the second parameter. This 2-dimensionality suggests that Factory Method might not be such a suitable solution after all.

In fact, while it offers a good degree of flexibility, it is also easy to see that a Factory Method-based class model will grow quadratically as we add more data providers and output types. (That is, if we support p data providers and q output types, then we'll need $p \times q$ classes to reflect all the different combinations.) There may be no way around the quadratic growth; but our Factory Method pattern seems more comfortable with a 1-parameter problem. It doesn't really acknowledge the 2-parameter nature of this problem.

This fact, combined with the complexity of dealing with different return types should be enough to make us wonder whether a different pattern would be more scalable and maintainable as we introduce more data providers and output types.

Abstract Factory

So let's consider our other chief candidate – Abstract Factory. Abstract Factory is a little more complicated than Factory Method, but it gives us something subtly different. Let's remind ourselves of the GoF intent for Abstract Factory:

> **GoF Intent for Abstract Factory:** Provide an interface for creating families of related or dependent objects without specifying their concrete classes.

So, with an Abstract Factory pattern, we can deal with families of similar objects when the client application wants to decide at run time which family of objects it wants to use. Each family of objects has its own associated Factory object, and all the Factory objects inherit from a common parent class. At run time, the client application gets the appropriate family of objects by choosing the appropriate *Factory* object, and then using that Factory object to create instances of the family members.

> *In Chapter 1, we used Abstract Factory to create families of* Bear *objects. Our example had two similar families of* Bear *classes – a* GoldenBear *family and a* BrownBear *family. Each family had an associated Factory object. The* GoldenBearFactory *object created members of the* GoldenBear *family and the* BrownBearFactory *object created members of the* BrownBear *family. Both Factory objects inherited from the same parent class.*

How does Abstract Factory relate to our data tier problem? To begin, we need to identify "families" of similar classes – this is the crux of the Abstract Factory pattern.

In fact, the 2-parameter nature of our problem appears to be a strength of Abstract Factory. Recall that our two parameters represented the "data providers" and the "output types". Well, regardless of the data provider that the client application chooses, we will need to support a set of objects capable of returning any of the supported output types. So it seems that:

❑ Each of our supported data providers can be represented by one "family" of objects and an associated Factory object for that family. The Factory object will be able to create instances of any of the classes that belong to that family.

❑ Each family will consist of a number of different members, each of which is capable of returning a different output type.

In other words: each family member is a concrete class that will be able do to return a certain output type using a certain data provider. The other members of the family will return *different* output types using the *same* data provider. Moreover, each member has a "cousin" in each of the other families, which is able to return the *same* output type but does so using a *different* data provider.

This is clearly a more favorable situation than Factory Method was able to provide for us. But there are a number of other considerations, and we should quickly check them to convince ourselves that Abstract Factory really is the right way to proceed:

❑ *The client application's implementation should be independent of how the data access classes are created.* Abstract Factory does satisfy this requirement, because each of the Factory objects inherits the same interface, and the family members all inherit from common interfaces too. In fact, a number of creational patterns give us this capability (including Factory Method), and if this had been the only requirement then we may have chosen a different pattern.

❑ *The client application needs to be shielded from the implementation details of a set of classes, and should only be exposed to its interfaces.* Again, the "common interface" nature of Abstract Factory ensures that the client application works with the interface that represents the concrete class, but never really knows which concrete class it's working with. This should become more apparent when we begin to build the data tier and a sample client application, shortly.

The Abstract Factory pattern is a much closer match for our requirements. We have found some compelling reasons to believe that it is the right pattern, and we haven't found any evidence to persuade us otherwise. So, let's use it to build an implementation of our data access tier.

Building the Data Tier

We have decided that an Abstract Factory pattern will provide the structure of our data access tier. To reach this conclusion we used a decision process that combined analysis and elimination. We first identified the characteristics of our problem. This allowed us to eliminate irrelevant patterns systematically until only a few (in fact, two) candidates remained. Finally, we performed a closer analysis of those patterns to convince ourselves of the suitability (or otherwise) of each candidate.

In this section of the chapter we will draw a UML class diagram of our data tier, so that we can see what classes we need to build and how they relate to the other classes. Then we'll build our implementation of the data tier. In a subsequent section, we will build a client application so that we can test our data tier.

The number of concrete classes in our UML class diagram will still be proportional to the number of data providers we support, and it will also be proportional to the number of output types we support. (This is because, if we support p data providers and q output types, then we'll need $p \times q$ concrete classes.) We don't want to have too many classes in our first iteration – we want to prove that the design works without reproducing reams of code in the chapter. Therefore, for the purposes of the chapter, we will keep things simple. Our first iteration will support only:

❑ Three data providers (the .NET data providers for SQL Server, for OLE DB, and for ODBC)

❑ Two output types (`DataReader` and `DataSet`)

Therefore, the iteration presented in this chapter will do enough to satisfy Northwind Traders' original requirements. Of course, the design of our data tier is extensible, thanks to Abstract Factory, so we'll be able to adapt it to support more data providers and output types quite easily, *after* we've released this first iteration.

In fact, the source code for this chapter includes a second iteration, which supports four data providers and six output types.

A UML Class Diagram

Here is the class diagram for our first iteration of the data tier application:

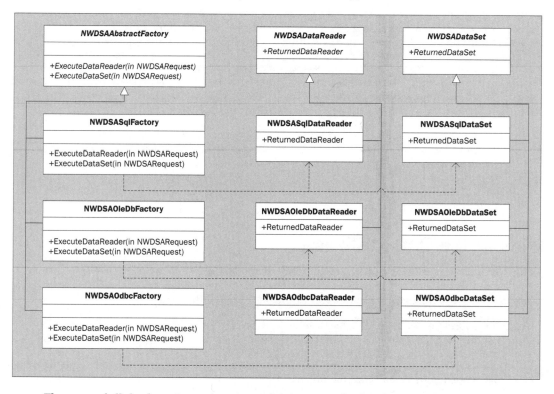

The names of all the classes in our data tier application are prefixed with NWDSA. This acronym stands for Northwind Data Store Access, and we're using the prefix simply to indicate that these classes are part of our data tier solution.

On the right, we can see the families of related concrete classes that we identified. These concrete classes contain the implementation code required to access data though a particular data provider, and return it in the form of a particular output type.

There is one family of concrete classes for each data provider – we've aligned the families of classes into rows so that you can see them more clearly. There are three families here:

SQL Server NWDSA Family	OLE DB NWDSA Family	ODBC NWDSA Family
NWDSASqlDataReader	NWDSAOleDbDataReader	NWDSAODBCDataReader
NWDSASqlDataSet	NWDSAOleDbDataSet	NWDSAODBCDataSet

We can also see the abstract base classes from which these concrete classes inherit. There are just two of those – one for each of the output types we'll support in this iteration. Note that each family contains one family member for each of the supported output types.

On the left of our UML diagram we have the concrete factory objects and the abstract base factory object. In this iteration, there are three concrete factories – one for each family. Each concrete factory class contains the implementation code required to create members of its associated family.

On the left, we can also see the abstract base factory class (this is the class that gives the pattern its name!). Each of the concrete factories inherits from this abstract base class. The client application can create an instance of any of these concrete factory classes, and consider it as an object of type NWDSAFactory.

Remember that with Abstract Factory, the client application can work with instances of the abstract base classes, and avoid over-commiting itself to instances of the concrete classes. In this example, the client application code will declare object references of type NWDSAFactory, NWDSADataReader, and NWDSADataSet – the three abstract base classes in this diagram. They will never create object references of the types of the concrete classes, because that would defeat the purpose of Abstract Factory!

Building the Output Classes

OK, we've talked enough about Abstract Factory that we should be ready to begin our implementation. We'll start by creating the output classes (the classes on the right of our UML class diagram); then in the next section we'll create the factory classes (those on the left of the diagram).

Using Visual Studio .NET, create a blank solution called **NWDSA**. This will contain a project to represent our data tier application; later, we'll also add a test harness project to test the data tier.

So, add a VB.NET Class Library project (also called **NWDSA**) to the solution. Remove the Class1.vb class that is created by default with the project.

The Abstract Base Output Classes

Add a new class file, called NWDSAAbstractProducts.vb, to the project. This file will contain the class definitions for the two abstract base classes from which all our concrete family members will inherit. There is one abstract base class for each output type that we plan to support.

Remove the default code that appears in this file. We'll add two class definitions to the file. Here is the first:

```
Public MustInherit Class NWDSADataReader
  Public MustOverride Property ReturnedDataReader() As IDataReader
End Class
```

Our NWDSADataReader class will be inherited by any class whose job is to return a DataReader object. The NWDSADataReader class is an abstract class, which means that client applications cannot create an instance of this class directly – they can only create an instance of a class that inherits from it. For simplicity, this abstract base class has just one property: the property is ReturnedDataReader, and it returns an object of type IDataReader to the caller. The ReturnedDataReader property is defined as Public MustOverride, which means that any class that inherits from it must provide its own implementation of the property.

Here is the second abstract base class:

```
Public MustInherit Class NWDSADataSet
  Public MustOverride Property ReturnedDataSet() As DataSet
End Class
```

Our NWDSADataSet class will be inherited by any class whose job is to return a DataSet object. It is also abstract, and also has one MustOverride property: the ReturnedDataSet property, which returns an object of type DataSet.

Each of our families of concrete classes will contain a class that inherits from each of these classes, and which implements their MustOverride properties.

We could add more methods and properties to these classes; for example, it might be reasonable for the NWDSADataSet class to contain an UpdateDataSet() method (which would also need to be declared as Public MustOverride). But for simplicity, we limit the functionality in this application.

The Concrete Product Classes

Now we can add the concrete family members. Add three new class files: NWDSASql.vb, NWDSAOleDb.vb, and NWDSAOdbc.vb. These three class files will contain all the code for our three families of concrete product classes. There's rather more work to do here, because we must write one family member for each supported output type (of which there are two), and there are three families to support (one for each supported data provider). So we will write six classes in the following pages.

Fortunately, the classes that inherit from the same abstract base class turn out to be quite similar, so there's not so much work to do. Let's do this one family at a time, beginning with the family of classes for the SQL Server .NET data provider.

The NWDSASql Family

Here's the first family member for this family, which will be used when the client application wants to get a DataReader object from a SQL Server data source. This class inherits from the abstract NWDSADataReader class, and overrides the ReturnedDataReader property:

```
Public Class NWDSASqlDataReader : Inherits NWDSADataReader
  Dim m_oReturnedDataReader As IDataReader

  Public Overrides Property ReturnedDataReader() As IDataReader
    Get
      ReturnedDataReader = m_oReturnedDataReader
    End Get
    Set(ByVal Value As IDataReader)
      m_oReturnedDataReader = Value
    End Set
  End Property
End Class
```

Here is the second member of the NWDSASql object family. It is slightly more complicated, because not only can it return a DataSet from a SQL Server data source, but it can also be used to create a new empty DataSet object. For this reason, the class code also includes a public constructor:

```
Public Class NWDSASqlDataSet : Inherits NWDSADataSet
  Dim m_oReturnedDataSet As DataSet

  Public Sub New()
    If m_oReturnedDataSet Is Nothing Then
      m_oReturnedDataSet = New DataSet()
    End If
  End Sub

  Public Overrides Property ReturnedDataSet() As DataSet
    Get
      ReturnedDataSet = m_oReturnedDataSet
    End Get
    Set(ByVal Value As DataSet)
      m_oReturnedDataSet = Value
    End Set
  End Property
End Class
```

You've probably noticed that there is no reference to the SQL Server .NET data provider in these class definitions, except for the existence of the letters Sql in the class names. In fact, we're going to keep the family member classes quite light, and implement most of the data provider-specific code in the concrete factory classes that we'll meet later.

The NWDSAOleDb Family

Now let's put in the class definitions for the NWDSAOleDb family. Again, there are two classes – one for each supported output type. In fact, these classes are identical to the NWDSAOleDb classes except in name. Here is the class that returns a DataReader object from an OLE DB source:

```
Public Class NWDSAOleDbDataReader : Inherits NWDSADataReader
    Dim m_oReturnedDataReader As IDataReader

    Public Overrides Property ReturnedDataReader() As IDataReader
        Get
            ReturnedDataReader = m_oReturnedDataReader
        End Get
        Set(ByVal Value As IDataReader)
            m_oReturnedDataReader = Value
        End Set
    End Property
End Class
```

Here is the class that returns a DataSet object from an OLE DB source:

```
Public Class NWDSAOleDbDataSet : Inherits NWDSADataSet
    Dim m_oReturnedDataSet As DataSet

    Public Sub New()
        If m_oReturnedDataSet Is Nothing Then
            m_oReturnedDataSet = New DataSet()
        End If
    End Sub
```

```
    Public Overrides Property ReturnedDataSet() As DataSet
        Get
            ReturnedDataSet = m_oReturnedDataSet
        End Get
        Set(ByVal Value As DataSet)
            m_oReturnedDataSet = Value
        End Set
    End Property
End Class
```

At this stage, it's a little difficult to see the benefit of having numerous families of classes whose implementations are all identical. However, the benefits will come when we build subsequent parts of our data tier – and we will see further benefits once this code is in production and a support developer is charged with making modifications and tweaks to support particular data provider implementations.

Specifically, it is my opinion that the existence of concrete classes for each output type will ultimately be useful as we learn more about the way that Microsoft and other vendors implement their data providers. This way, we can be prepared for small variations in behavior in each of the data providers, and these concrete classes will contain the work-around code and implementation of common practices that are specific to a data provider and output-type combination. We'll see.

The NWDSAOdbc Family

Finally, for completeness, here are the class definitions for the NWDSAOdbc family members. Unsurprisingly, they are again similar to the above classes in all but name, so the same comments apply. The NWDSAOdbcDataReader class is responsible for getting a DataReader object from an ODBC data source:

```
Public Class NWDSAOdbcDataReader : Inherits NWDSADataReader
    Dim m_oReturnedDataReader As IDataReader

    Public Overrides Property ReturnedDataReader() As IDataReader
        Get
            ReturnedDataReader = m_oReturnedDataReader
        End Get
        Set(ByVal Value As IDataReader)
            m_oReturnedDataReader = Value
        End Set
    End Property
End Class
```

The NWDSAOdbcDataSet class is responsible for getting a DataSet object from an ODBC data source:

```
Public Class NWDSAOdbcDataSet : Inherits NWDSADataSet
    Dim m_oReturnedDataSet As DataSet

    Public Sub New()
        If m_oReturnedDataSet Is Nothing Then
            m_oReturnedDataSet = New DataSet()
        End If
    End Sub
```

```
    Public Overrides Property ReturnedDataSet() As DataSet
        Get
            ReturnedDataSet = m_oReturnedDataSet
        End Get
        Set(ByVal Value As DataSet)
            m_oReturnedDataSet = Value
        End Set
    End Property
End Class
```

Building the Factory Classes

Per our UML class diagram, we now need to put together a set of concrete factory objects. Each one will have an associated family of concrete classes, and will contain the implementation code that enables data queries using a particular data provider. We'll also need an abstract factory class – this will be the base class from which all our concrete factory classes will inherit. All this structure comes direct from our Abstract Factory pattern.

The task of coding the factory classes is much easier since we already know about the "product" classes that the factories will create and use. But before we start, it's worth reminding ourselves how we expect a client application to make use of these factory objects, so that we get the implementation right.

A client application should be able to ask for (say) an instance of the NWDSADataReader class with little regard to exactly how it's created. In fact, the client application may even be unaware of exactly what type of concrete class the factory returns from such a request (it may be a NWDSASqlDataReader, a NWDSAOleDbDataReader, or a NWDSAOdbcDataReader instance), because the client is actually asking for an instance of an abstract base class (NWDSADataReader) – so all it knows is that it will get an object that inherits from that base class.

Moreover, the client is actually passing the request via a concrete factory object (NWDSASqlFactory, NWDSAOleDbFactory, or NWDSAOdbcFactory). But in terms of the way the client application is coded, it doesn't matter which of these objects is being used – because they all inherit from the abstract factory class called NWDSAAbstractFactory, and therefore expose the same methods and properties.

The Abstract Factory Class

Let's write our abstract factory class first – then we'll write the concrete factory classes that inherit from it. Add a new class file (called **NWDSAAbstractFactory.vb**) to the **NWDSA** project – we'll put this class code in there.

The class itself is quite simple. Like the other abstract base classes we've used, it is declared as MustInherit, which means that it can't be instantiated directly – our client applications can only create instances of the classes that inherit from it.

It also contains definitions for two methods. We have a simple naming convention for these methods. Each name is prefixed with the word Execute, because each one represents the execution of a SQL command. Then, each name is suffixed with the name of an output type – we can do this because each method returns a different output type (one of the two output types we're supporting in this iteration of our data tier). So, we have:

❑ A method whose purpose is to execute a SQL command and return an `NWDSADataReader` object

❑ A method whose purpose is to execute a SQL command and return an `NWDSADataSet` object

Notice how the purpose of each of these methods is very simple – that is what makes it easy for us to abstract them.

So, here is the code for our abstract factory class:

```
Public MustInherit Class NWDSAAbstractFactory
  Public MustOverride Function ExecuteDataReader() As NWDSADataReader
  Public MustOverride Function ExecuteDataSet() As NWDSADataSet
End Class
```

We're starting to bring things together. Our abstract factory class sets the stage for the implementation of a series of concrete factory objects and the products they generate; and it also defines its methods in terms of classes that we've already built.

Notice that the products returned by these methods are all instances of the *abstract* product classes. Each concrete factory will have its own implementation of each of these methods, and it is there that the concrete product type will be determined. That's the key to the Abstract Factory pattern, at least at a high level.

We now have the infrastructure that allows our data tier to support many concrete factories that can return as many concrete products as we'd like to take the time to write. Since our concrete factories correspond to .NET data providers and our abstract products correspond to output types, we've met the two most important requirements of the data tier.

The next thing to do in terms of our Abstract Factory implementation is to write the concrete factory classes. Every concrete factory class will inherit from the abstract factory class above, and will therefore provide its own implementation of the abstract factory's methods. In those method implementations, we will need to write the code that fills and returns the output objects using the appropriate data providers.

But to make these classes easier, it's a good idea to consider how we are going to get the *particulars* of a request from the client application to the appropriate data tier object. We also need to consider how we will manage our connection strings. So let us briefly consider those two issues – once we've solved them, it will be much easier to write the code for the concrete factory classes.

The NWDSARequest Helper Class

We need a way to package the particulars of a request from the client application, so that it can be easily passed from the client app to the data tier. There are a number of approaches to this problem; we'll use a very simple one here.

We'll write a simple class called `NWDSARequest`. An instance of our `NWDSARequest` class represents a single query, and contains all the necessary information about what kind of operation to execute.

Here's the source for our `NWDSARequest` class – you can place it into a new class file called NWDSARequest.vb. First, our `NWDSARequest` contains an enumeration that allows a client application to distinguish between different user roles:

```
Public Class NWDSARequest

   Public Enum UserRole
     External = 1
     Internal = 2
     SuperUser = 3
     Admin = 4
   End Enum
```

This is just an extra little feature – it's a mechanism that allows a client application to indicate the type of end-user who's making a request and use that level of authority to determine the permissions they have on the database. In the case of our Northwind Traders case study:

❑ External users are generally users who are not Northwind employees – such as customers and web users

❑ Internal users are regular Northwind employees

❑ SuperUser users belong to a small group of business users with extra permissions to modify sensitive data

❑ Admin users are application administrators who aren't restricted by any database security

We won't make much of this feature in this chapter, because it's fairly simple and not the main issue of the chapter; but it is as well for you to know that it's there and what it's for.

It also contains a subclass called Parameter, which can represent a parameter to be passed as part of a command. A parameter will be described by two properties – ParamName and ParamValue:

```
Public Class Parameter
   Private m_sParamName As String
   Private m_sParamValue As String

   Public Property ParamName() As String
     Get
       ParamName = m_sParamName
     End Get
     Set(ByVal Value As String)
       m_sParamName = Value
     End Set
   End Property

   Public Property ParamValue() As String
     Get
       ParamValue = m_sParamValue
     End Get
     Set(ByVal Value As String)
       m_sParamValue = Value
     End Set
   End Property

End Class
```

The remainder of the class consists of private member declarations, and public properties to describe the type of user making the request, the type of SQL command being requested, the SQL command itself, any parameters needed for the operation, and a flag for switching transactional processing on and off, and a property for returning exceptions:

```
Private m_lUserRole As UserRole
Private m_lCommandType As CommandType
Private m_sCommand As String
Private m_bTransactional As Boolean
Private m_colParameters As New Collection()
Private m_DataSet As DataSet
Private m_oException As Exception

Public Property Role() As UserRole
  Get
     Role = m_lUserRole
  End Get
  Set(ByVal Value As UserRole)
    m_lUserRole = Value
  End Set
End Property

Public Property CommandType() As CommandType
  Get
     CommandType = m_lCommandType
  End Get
  Set(ByVal Value As CommandType)
    m_lCommandType = Value
  End Set
End Property

Public Property Command() As String
  Get
     Command = m_sCommand
  End Get
  Set(ByVal Value As String)
    m_sCommand = Value
  End Set
End Property

Public Property Parameters() As Collection
  Get
     Parameters = m_colParameters
  End Get
  Set(ByVal Value As Collection)
    m_colParameters = Value
  End Set
End Property

Public Property Transactional() As Boolean
  Get
     Transactional = m_bTransactional
  End Get
  Set(ByVal Value As Boolean)
```

```
        m_bTransactional = Value
      End Set
   End Property

   Public Property Exception() As Exception
     Get
        Exception = m_oException
     End Get
     Set(ByVal Value As Exception)
        m_oException = Value
     End Set
   End Property
End Class
```

We'll make use of this class shortly, when we come to the concrete factory classes. Let's move on to our second side issue – connection string management.

Managing Connection Strings

We've put some considered effort into creating such an adaptable data tier application, and we don't want to spoil all that by hard-coding the connection strings into the data tier, or into the client application that uses it. A much more flexible solution is to store them in an application configuration (.config) file.

Each client application can have its own configuration file – we can use it to hold any configuration information that the application needs. Every application that uses our data tier will need its own app configuration file. (For a Windows application, this file will be called *appname*.exe.config, where *appname*.exe is the name of the executable client application; for an ASP.NET application, it will be called web.config.) This .config file will contain configuration information (such as connection string information) in XML format, and will need to be stored in the same folder as the application.

We'll write a class called NWDSAConnStrings, whose purpose is simply to reach into the client application's .config and grab the necessary connection string. Because we only need one NWDSAConnStrings object per execution, this seems a good place to make use of a Singleton pattern.

Writing the Singleton NWDSAConnStrings Class

Add a new class file called NWDSAConnStrings.vb, and replace the default code with the following:

```
Imports System.Configuration
Imports System.Collections.Specialized

Public Class NWDSAConnStrings
   'based on GoF Singleton defintion
   'and the Chapter 1 example of a Singleton
   Private Shared m_Instance As NWDSAConnStrings
   Private Shared m_Mutex As New System.Threading.Mutex()
   Private Shared m_colConnectStrings As NameValueCollection

   Private Sub New()
     m_colConnectStrings = ConfigurationSettings.GetConfig("appSettings")
   End Sub
```

```
      Public Shared Function GetInstance() As NWDSAConnStrings
        'To be thread safe, we use the Mutex to synchronize threads
        m_Mutex.WaitOne() ' WaitOne() requests a thread
        If m_Instance Is Nothing Then
          m_Instance = New NWDSAConnStrings()
        End If
        m_Mutex.ReleaseMutex()
        Return m_Instance
      End Function

      Public Function GetConnectStringByRole( _
                        ByVal Role As NWDSARequest.UserRole) As String
        'Retrieves configuration file by role name
        Return m_colConnectStrings.Get(Role - 1).ToString
      End Function
    End Class
```

Without going into too much detail, this Singleton pattern works very much like the one we saw in Chapter 1. Among the NWDSAConnStrings class's members is a private shared member of the same type (NWDSAConnStrings) – it's called m_Instance. Client methods cannot access it directly, and they cannot create their own instance of NWDSAConnStrings (because the constructor is declared as Private).

Rather, if a calling method needs an instance of NWDSAConnStrings, it uses an object reference that was declared like this:

```
    Dim g_ConnStrings As NWDSAConnStrings
```

Specifically, it calls its GetInstance() method like this:

```
    m_CS = g_ConnStrings.GetInstance()
```

The GetInstance() method checks to see whether m_Instance has been instantiated; and if not, it instantiates it. Then it returns the instance to the calling method.

So, m_Instance is instantiated exactly once. On the single occasion that it is instantiated, the constructor called the ConfigurationSettings.GetConfig() method to get the appSettings information from the configuration file and store it in the collection object, m_colConnectStrings. Our GetConfig("appSettings") method call looks in the <appSettings> node of our .config file for this information. We'll build a sample .config file in a minute.

Finally, note the GetConnectStringByRole() method, which can be used by the calling method to get at the configuration information, which is now stored in the m_colConnectStrings:

```
    m_ConnString = _
            g_ConnStrings.GetInstance.GetConnectStringByRole(Request.Role)
```

You'll see this code in action in each of the concrete factory objects, shortly.

The Global g_ConnStrings Declaration

So there are two more things we need – a global reference of type NWDSAConnStrings, and a configuration file. Let's deal with the global reference first. Create a new *module* file called **Main.vb**, and make sure it contains the following code:

```
Module Main
    Public g_ConnStrings As NWDSAConnStrings
End Module
```

That's it. When a calling method needs an instance of the NWDSAConnStrings class, it uses the expression g_ConnStrings.GetInstance.

The Application's Configuration File

Finally, let's look at a sample .config file. We don't need to build one just yet, but we will need one later on when we write a test application to test our data tier.

Our connection strings are contained in child nodes of a node called appSettings:

```
<?xml version="1.0" encoding="utf-8" ?>
<configuration>
  <runtime>
  </runtime>
  <appSettings>
    <add
      key="External"
      value="Data Source=lh;Initial Catalog=Northwind;User ID=ext;Password=earth"
    />
    <add
      key="Internal"
      value="Data Source=lh;Initial Catalog=Northwind;User ID=int;Password=wind"
    />
    <add
      key="SuperUser"
      value="Data Source=lh;Initial Catalog=Northwind;User ID=su;Password=and"
    />
    <add
      key="Admin"
      value="Data Source=lh;Initial Catalog=Northwind;User ID=admin;Password=fire"
    />
  </appSettings>
</configuration>
```

There are four keys here – one for each of the entries in the UserRole enumeration contained in the NWDSARequest class, above.

Remember that the name and location of this file is important. For a Windows application, the file should be named *appname*.exe.config (after the client application's executable file, *appname*.exe), and it should live in the same folder as the *appname*.exe file. For an ASP.NET application, the file should be called web.config and live in the root web folder. We'll return to this when we code the test application that will make use of our data tier.

Now we have a way to manage the connection strings and a way to manage the particulars of a request, we can get back to coding the concrete factories.

The Concrete Factory Classes

Now, we can turn to our three concrete factories: NWDSASqlFactory, NWDSAOleDbFactory, and NWDSAOdbcFactory. Each of these three classes will inherit from the abstract base class, NWDSAAbstractFactory, and will implement the ExecuteDataReader() and ExecuteDataSet() methods specified by the base class.

Every implementation of these methods will take an NWDSARequest object as an input parameter. To accommodate this, we'll need to change the definition of our NWDSAAbstractFactory class a little, so return to **NWDSAAbstractFactory.vb** and change the class definition as follows:

```
Public MustInherit Class NWDSAAbstractFactory
   Public MustOverride Function ExecuteDataReader( _
                    ByRef Request As NWDSARequest) As NWDSADataReader
   Public MustOverride Function ExecuteDataSet( _
                    ByRef Request As NWDSARequest) As NWDSADataSet
End Class
```

Our concrete implementations will peel apart the NWDSARequest object, looking for information about how it should perform the database operation that is being requested of it. In the following pages, we'll look at the implementation code for the NWDSASqlFactory class, which make use of the SQL Server .NET data provider.

We'll also see to what extent the implementation code for the NWDSAOleDbFactory and NWDSAOdbcFactory classes differ from that of the NWDSASqlFactory class (recall that they do the same job as NWDSASqlFactory, but they use the OLE DB or ODBC .NET data provider instead).

The NWDSASqlFactory Concrete Factory Class

Let's begin by looking at the implementation of our concrete factory class NWDSASqlFactory, which is the factory that supports the SQL Server .NET data provider. Add a new class file called **NWDSASqlFactory.vb**. We'll start by adding the outline code for this class (without the method implementations):

```
Imports System.Data
Imports System.Data.SqlClient

Public Class NWDSASqlFactory : Inherits NWDSAAbstractFactory
   Private m_conSQL As New SqlConnection()

   Public Overrides Function ExecuteDataReader( _
                    ByRef Request As NWDSARequest) As NWDSADataReader
     implementation_code...
   End Function

   Public Overrides Function ExecuteDataSet( _
                    ByRef Request As NWDSARequest) As NWDSADataSet
     implementation_code...
   End Function
End Class
```

Before we get into the implementation details of these two functions, note the Imports statements at the top of our class definition. In particular, we've included an Imports statement for the System.Data.SqlClient namespace because this is the namespace that contains the SQL Server .NET data provider classes – which we'll be using in this factory class. We've also included an Imports statement for System.Data to give us easy access to the DataSet class.

Note also that the concrete class has a global variable called m_conSQL, which is a SqlConnection object. The reason for this will become clear in the following sections.

> *As we'll see later, our other two concrete factory classes are quite similar to the NWDSASqlFactory class. In fact, they are identical except in their implementation code – which is exactly the purpose of having different factories.*

The NWDSASqlFactory.ExecuteDataReader() Method

Now let's insert the implementation code for the NWDSASqlFactory.ExecuteDataReader() method. I'll add some notes on what the function is doing, as we step through it.

As far as the Abstract Factory design is concerned, we've done most of the hard thinking work – we know that this class will use the SQL Server .NET data provider and will return a SqlDataReader object wrapped in a concrete NWDSASqlDataReader object. So, we can create instances of the Connection and Command objects and other data access objects using the classes contained in the SQL Server .NET data provider:

```
Public Overrides Function ExecuteDataReader( _
                    ByRef Request As NWDSARequest) As NWDSADataReader

    Dim sConnectStr As String
    Dim cmdSQL As New SqlCommand()
    Dim prmSQL As SqlParameter
    Dim oParam As NWDSARequest.Parameter
    Dim colSQLParams As SqlParameterCollection
    Dim drSQL As SqlDataReader
    Dim oDataReaderSQL As New NWDSASqlDataReader()
```

We've used the SQL prefix to reflect the fact that these objects come from the SQL Server .NET data provider.

Next, we need to get a connection string. Recall that the connection string we use is dependent on the user type (Request.Role), and we use our global NWDSAConnectString object, g_ConnStrings, to get it. Remember that g_ConnStrings uses the Singleton pattern, so we don't instantiate it directly – we call its GetInstance() method (which ensures that only one instance exists, and that we have a reference to it). Then we use its GetConnectStringByRole() method to acquire the appropriate connection string from the .config file:

```
Try
    m_conSQL.ConnectionString = _
        g_ConnStrings.GetInstance.GetConnectStringByRole(Request.Role)
```

Now we can open the connection to the data store (using the connection string we've just acquired). We can also set up the SqlCommand object using particulars of the request that have been passed into the method in our NWDSARequest-type argument. Here, were dealing with the command, the command type, and any parameters that were specified in the client request:

```
     ' open connection, and begin to set properties of command
     m_conSQL.Open()
     cmdSQL.Connection = m_conSQL
     cmdSQL.CommandText = Request.Command
     cmdSQL.CommandType = Request.CommandType

     ' add parameters if they exist
     If Request.Parameters.Count > 0 Then
       For Each oParam In Request.Parameters
         prmSQL = cmdSQL.Parameters.Add(oParam.ParamName, _
                                        oParam.ParamValue)

       Next
     End If
```

> Note that `CommandText` can be a SQL statement, a stored procedure name or a table name. The `NWDSARequest` object supports all three.

Now we can execute the command and get the `SqlDataReader` object that contains the data returned from the datastore. We assign our filled `SqlDataReader` object to the `NWDSASqlDataReader.ReturnedDataReader` property, and return the object to the client application:

```
     drSQL = cmdSQL.ExecuteReader()

     oDataReaderSQL.ReturnedDataReader = drSQL
     Return oDataReaderSQL
```

Notice that we *don't* call `drSQL.Close()` here – if we did that then the client application would not be able to access the data in the returned `DataReader` object!

Next, we have some code to handle a couple of exceptions (note that we attempt to catch `SqlExceptions` first, because – as a rule of thumb – we should try to catch specific exceptions first and more general exceptions after):

```
   Catch exSQL As SqlException
     Debug.WriteLine(exSQL.Message)
     Request.Exception = exSQL

   Catch ex As Exception
     Debug.WriteLine(ex.Message)
     Request.Exception = ex
```

Finally, we have the `Finally` clause. It might be tempting to close the open database connection here; but that would create a problem. The problem is that the database connection needs to remain *open* after the `ExecuteDataReader()` method has finished, so that the client app can use the returned `DataReader`. (In fact, this is the reason that `g_conSQL` has global scope, not method scope – it must remain open after the method has finished.)

There are a number of ways to solve this. However we solve it, we *can't* close the connection during the `ExecuteDataReader()` method, so the `Finally` clause is empty:

```
         Finally
            ' do nothing
         End Try
   End Function
```

The NWDSASqlFactory.Finalize() Method

However, we really should make sure we close that connection sometime. We could make it the responsibility of the client application to close the connection – we'd do that by writing another public method called `CloseConnection()` or similar. However, the data tier would be easier to use if we could manage the closure of the connection internally.

Therefore, we'll add the code for that to a `Finalize()` method, that we'll add to the `NWDSASqlFactory` class like this:

```
Public Class NWDSASqlFactory : Inherits NWDSAAbstractFactory
   Private m_conSQL As New SqlConnection()

   Protected Overrides Sub Finalize()
      If Not (m_conSQL.State = ConnectionState.Closed) Or _
         Not (m_conSQL.State = ConnectionState.Broken) Then
         m_conSQL.Close()
      End If
      MyBase.Finalize()
   End Sub

   ' other definitions...
End Class
```

The NWDSASqlFactory.ExecuteDataSet() Method

Now here's the implementation code for the `NWDSASqlFactory.ExecuteDataSet()` method. It's similar to the `ExecuteDataReader()` method, but not identical. Thankfully, the `DataSet` object doesn't give us the same connection problems! We'll highlight the bits that are different.

Again, we use data access objects from the SQL Server .NET data provider, and we name the object references accordingly:

```
Public Overrides Function ExecuteDataSet( _
                          ByRef Request As NWDSARequest) As NWDSADataSet

   Dim sConnectStr As String
   Dim conSQL As New SqlConnection()
   Dim cmdSQL As New SqlCommand()
   Dim prmSQL As SqlParameter
   Dim oParam As NWDSARequest.Parameter
   Dim colSQLParams As SqlParameterCollection
   Dim daSQL As SqlDataAdapter
   Dim oDataSetSQL As New NWDSASqlDataSet()
   Dim tranSQL As SqlTransaction
```

We've got a `SqlDataAdapter` and a `NWDSASqlDataSet` instead of a `DataReader` and a `NWDSASqlDataReader`, and we've also got a `SqlTransaction` object in this example method because a `DataSet` is capable of supporting database updates, and a local connection object.

We grab the connection string, open the connection, and set the command properties (from the client request object) as before:

```
Try
    conSQL.ConnectionString = _
        g_ConnStrings.GetInstance.GetConnectStringByRole(Request.Role)

    ' open connection, and begin to set properties of command
    conSQL.Open()
    cmdSQL.Connection = conSQL
    cmdSQL.CommandText = Request.Command
    cmdSQL.CommandType = Request.CommandType

    ' add parameters if they exist
    If Request.Parameters.Count > 0 Then
        For Each oParam In Request.Parameters
            prmSQL = cmdSQL.Parameters.Add(oParam.ParamName, _
                                          oParam.ParamValue)
        Next
    End If
```

We'll also capture the value of the flag that indicates whether the command should be transactional or not. This value is set by the client application within its request (so we get it from the `NWDSARequest.Transactional` property):

```
    If Request.Transactional Then
        tranSQL = conSQL.BeginTransaction()
    End If
```

If a transaction is required, the code creates a new `SqlTransaction` instance by calling the `SqlConnection`'s `BeginTransaction()` method. Note that the transaction *isn't* managed at the `SqlCommand` level. Rather, transactions are managed above any particular command – so the only logical place to begin, commit, or roll back a transaction is in the `SqlConnection` itself.

Now we create a `SqlDataAdapter` object (using our `Command` object), and use its `Fill()` method to populate the `DataSet` object. Then we return the `DataSet` wrapper, `oDataSetSQL`, to the client application:

```
    daSQL = New SqlDataAdapter(cmdSQL)

    daSQL.Fill(oDataSetSQL.ReturnedDataSet)
    Return oDataSetSQL
```

Note again here, that the returned object is a NWDSASqlDataSet object – because it wraps a DataSet object that was populated using the SQL Server .NET data provider. But all that matters to the client is that this return object is derived from the NWDSADataSet abstract base class.

Finally, we attempt to catch some exceptions (rolling back the transaction if a `Transactional` command was requested – the `tranSql` instance will exist if we called the `conSQL.BeginTransaction` method earlier):

```
Catch exSQL As SqlException
    Debug.WriteLine(exSQL.Message)
    Request.Exception = exSQL
    If Request.Transactional Then
        tranSQL.Rollback()
    End If

Catch ex As Exception
    Debug.WriteLine(ex.Message)
    Request.Exception = ex
    If Request.Transactional Then
        tranSQL.Rollback()
    End If
```

If all goes well, we can commit the transaction. We can also close the connection, because (unlike the DataReader) the DataSet does not depend on it:

```
Finally
    If Request.Transactional Then
        tranSQL.Commit()
    End If
    If conSQL.State = ConnectionState.Open Then
        conSQL.Close()
    End If
End Try
End Function
```

That's it for the NWDSASqlFactory concrete factory class. Now we've built one concrete factory class, the other two are actually quite easy. We'll briefly look at them now.

The NWDSAOleDbFactory Concrete Factory Class

Now let's consider the code for the NWDSAOleDbFactory concrete factory class. How different is it from the code we've just seen? Well, there are two requirements forced on this class by our Abstract Factory design:

❑ Like NWDSASqlFactory, NWDSAOleDbFactory, must inherit from NWDSAAbstractFactory, so it must provide implementations of the same two methods (ExecuteDataReader() and ExecuteDataSet()).

❑ Unlike NWDSASqlFactory, NWDSAOleDbFactory must support a different data provider – the OLE DB .NET data provider – and so it will need use the classes in the System.Data.OleDb namespace (not the System.Data.SqlClient namespace).

Thus, the class (without the method implementations) looks like this. It belongs in a class file called NWDSAOleDbFactory.vb:

```
Imports System.Data
Imports System.Data.OleDb

Public Class NWDSAOleDbFactory : Inherits NWDSAAbstractFactory
    Private m_conOLEDB As New OleDbConnection()
```

```
     Public Overrides Function ExecuteDataReader( _
                         ByRef Request As NWDSARequest) As NWDSADataReader
        implementation_code...
     End Function

     Public Overrides Function ExecuteDataSet( _
                         ByRef Request As NWDSARequest) As NWDSADataSet
        implementation_code...
     End Function

     Protected Overrides Sub Finalize()
        implementation_code...
     End Function
  End Class
```

It's almost exactly the same as the NWDSAOleDbFactory we saw earlier. The class name is different, the Imports statement is different, and the private connection member is different – but otherwise it's identical.

For simplicity, the code for the two Execute...() methods is identical in structure and process. The only difference is that we instantiate OleDb-specific objects (instead of Sql-specific objects), and for clarity, the names of our object references will contain the prefix OLEDB. To illustrate, here's a portion of the code for the NWDSAOleDbFactory.ExecuteDataReader() method, which highlights the lines that are different from the NWDSASqlFactory.ExecuteDataReader() method:

```
     Public Overrides Function ExecuteDataReader( _
                         ByRef Request As NWDSARequest) As NWDSADataReader

       Dim sConnectStr As String
       Dim cmdOLEDB As New OleDbCommand()
       Dim prmOLEDB As OleDbParameter
       Dim oParam As NWDSARequest.Parameter
       Dim colOLEDBParams As OleDbParameterCollection
       Dim drOLEDB As OleDbDataReader
       Dim oDataReaderOLEDB As New NWDSAOleDbDataReader()

       Try
         m_conOLEDB.ConnectionString = _
             g_ConnStrings.GetInstance.GetConnectStringByRole(Request.Role)

         ' open connection, and begin to set properties of command
         m_conOLEDB.Open()
         cmdOLEDB.Connection = m_conOLEDB
         cmdOLEDB.CommandText = Request.Command
         cmdOLEDB.CommandType = Request.CommandType

           etc...
       End Try
     End Function
```

Here's a portion of the code for the NWDSAOleDbFactory.ExecuteDataSet() method, which highlights the lines that are different from the NWDSASqlFactory.ExecuteDataSet() method:

```
Public Overrides Function ExecuteDataSet( _
                    ByRef Request As NWDSARequest) As NWDSADataSet
    Dim sConnectStr As String
    Dim conOLEDB As New OleDbConnection()
    Dim cmdOLEDB As New OleDbCommand()
    Dim prmOLEDB As OleDbParameter
    Dim oParam As NWDSARequest.Parameter
    Dim colOLEDBParams As OleDbParameterCollection
    Dim daOLEDB As OleDbDataAdapter
    Dim oDataSetOLEDB As New NWDSAOleDbDataSet()
    Dim tranOLEDB As OleDbTransaction

    Try
      conOLEDB.ConnectionString = _
          g_ConnStrings.GetInstance.GetConnectStringByRole(Request.Role)

      ' open connection, and begin to set properties of command
      conOLEDB.Open()
      cmdOLEDB.Connection = conOLEDB
      cmdOLEDB.CommandText = Request.Command
      cmdOLEDB.CommandType = Request.CommandType

      etc...
    End Try
  End Function
```

Finally, we should update the `Finalize()` method too:

```
Protected Overrides Sub Finalize()
    If Not (m_conOLEDB.State = ConnectionState.Closed) Or _
       Not (m_conOLEDB.State = ConnectionState.Broken) Then
      m_conOLEDB.Close()
    End If
    MyBase.Finalize()
  End Sub
```

Note that our method implementation code in NWDSAOleDbFactory and NWDSASqlFactory is similar mainly for the sake of simplicity. If it were necessary, we could have coded our concrete factory classes so that their implementations were less similar – provided they stayed within the bounds of the interface.

For example, suppose Microsoft discovered some strange bug that only affected its OLE DB data provider, and recommended a work-around solution to the bug. We would implement this work-around code in NWDSAOleDbFactory, where it was required (and we would not implement it in NWDSASqlFactory, because it was not required there).

The NWDSAOdbcFactory Concrete Factory Class

Again, the code for the NWDSAOdbcFactory concrete factory class is very similar to the code for the other two concrete factory classes:

❏ Like NWDSASqlFactory, NWDSAOdbcFactory, must inherit from NWDSAAbstractFactory, so it must provide implementations of the same two methods (ExecuteDataReader() and ExecuteDataSet()).

❑ Unlike `NWDSASqlFactory`, `NWDSAOdbcFactory` must support a different data provider – the ODBC .NET data provider – and so it will need use the classes in the `Microsoft.Data.Odbc` namespace (not the `System.Data.SqlClient` namespace).

So, the class (without the method implementations) looks like this. It belongs in a class file called NWDSAOdbcFactory.vb:

```
Imports System.Data
Imports Microsoft.Data.Odbc

Public Class NWDSAOdbcFactory : Inherits NWDSAAbstractFactory
  Private m_conODBC As New OdbcConnection()

  Public Overrides Function ExecuteDataReader( _
                    ByRef Request As NWDSARequest) As NWDSADataReader
     implementation_code...
  End Function

  Public Overrides Function ExecuteDataSet( _
                    ByRef Request As NWDSARequest) As NWDSADataSet
     implementation_code...
  End Function

  Protected Overrides Sub Finalize()
     implementation_code...
  End Function
End Class
```

Again, for simplicity, the code for these methods is identical in structure and process, and differs only in that we instantiate `Odbc`-specific objects (instead of `Sql`-specific objects), and we use the prefix `ODBC` in the names of our object references. We'll omit the code here, because you've probably got the idea by now; if you want, you can check it using the source that accompanies the book (downloadable from http://www.apress.com).

Getting the ODBC .NET Data Provider

Note that the ODBC .NET data provider does not ship as part of the .NET Framework. It comes as a separate download, which you can get from Microsoft's web site. Perhaps the easiest way to find it is to go to http://www.microsoft.com/downloads/search.asp and perform a keyword search for the string ODBC .NET data provider. When you've downloaded the file (`odbc_net.msi` – about 850Kb), run it to install the `Microsoft.Data.Odbc.dll` file. Finally, your NWDSA project will need a reference to this DLL.

Compiling the Data Tier Application

We've built everything we need for our first iteration of the NWDSA data tier application. You should be able to compile the solution, and generate a class library called NWDSA.dll.

Now, any client application can perform its data access tasks using the classes on the NWDSA data tier library. All they need to do is reference the DLL, and provide a `.config` file (like the one we described earlier) with the necessary `<appSettings>` node.

Moreover, because of our data tier's Abstract Factory design, we can easily update the class library so that it can support as many data providers and output types as we like – it's just a case of adding more concrete factories, abstract product classes, and concrete product classes. The data tier's design is infinitely extensible in this respect:

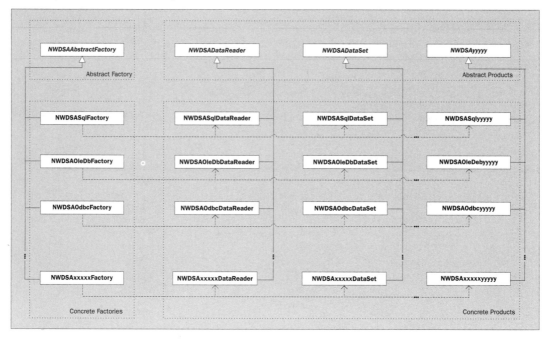

Testing the Data Tier Application

Now it's time to test out our data tier. We'll test it with two different client applications: a Windows application and a web application. We could just as easily test it with a web service application.

A Simple Windows Test Application

Let's build a simple Windows application that uses our data tier to make a query on our Northwind database.

Building the Application

Create a VB.NET Windows Application project, and call it NWDSAWindowsTestApp. You will need to add a reference to the NWDSA data tier application:

- ❑ If the NWDSAWindowsTestApp and NWDSA projects are in different VS.NET solutions, then NWDSAWindowsTestApp will need a reference to NWDSA.dll.

- ❑ If the NWDSAWindowsTestApp and NWDSA projects are in the same VS.NET solution, then NWDSAWindowsTestApp will need a reference to the NWDSA project. (In this case, you should also go into the solution's Properties and set the Startup Project to be NWDSAWindowsTestApp.)

We want our application to be quite simple, but we also want to be able to test all the combinations of data providers and output types in a fairly realistic way. To achieve this, our application will only be able to submit one query (which we'll hard-code into the application), but it will have one button for each output type (DataReader and DataSet). Once we've built and tested this application using a single data provider, we'll prove to ourselves how easy it is to change the application's code to use a different data provider instead.

Delete the Form1.vb file that is created by default, and add a new Windows Form file called NWDSAWindowsTestApp.vb. Add the following controls to the form:

- ❑ Add a Label control. Set its Text property to Customer ID:

- ❑ Add a TextBox control. Set its Name property to txtCustomerID, and clear its Text property

- ❑ Add a Button control. Set its Name property to btnDataReaderTest, and set its Text property to DataReader Test

- ❑ Add a second Button control. Set its Name property to btnDataSetTest, and set its Text property to DataSet Test

- ❑ Add a ListView control. Set its Name property to lstOrders, and set its View property to Details

- ❑ Add a DataGrid control. Set its Name property to dgOrders

If you rearrange all these controls, you should have something that looks like this:

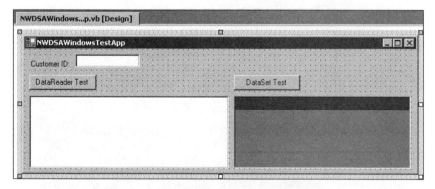

We need to explicitly add some columns to ListView control. To do this, find the Columns property in the Properties pane and click on it to bring up the ColumnHeader Collection Editor:

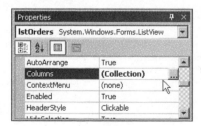

Use the **Add** button to add four columns to the **Members** pane. Then change the **Name** and **Text** properties of the four columns (in the **Properties** pane on the right of this dialog) to reflect the four fields returned from the stored procedure:

Name	Text
OrderID	Order ID
OrderDate	Order Date
RequiredDate	Required Date
ShippedDate	Shipped Date

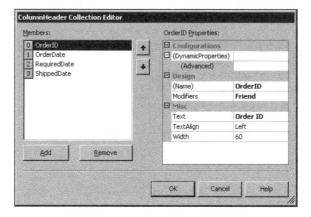

Now, the form should look like this:

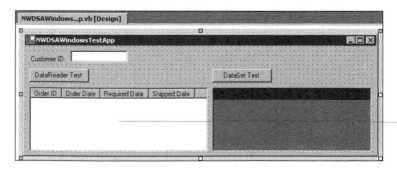

That's all we need to do with the development tools. Now we can turn to the code. At the top of the file, we'll need an `Imports` statement, for our data tier library:

```
Imports NWDSA
```

Now we just have to add `Click` event handlers for the two buttons.

The DataReader Test Event Handler

Let's do the **DataReader Test** button first. We're going to code it so that it uses the SQL Server .NET data provider, via our data tier:

```
Private Sub btnDataReaderTest_Click(ByVal sender As System.Object, _
                                ByVal e As System.EventArgs) _
                                Handles btnDataReaderTest.Click
    Dim oRequest As New NWDSARequest()
    Dim oParam As New NWDSARequest.Parameter()
    Dim oFactory As NWDSAAbstractFactory
    Dim oDataReader As NWDSADataReader
    Dim drOrders As IDataReader
    Dim oItem As ListViewItem

    oFactory = New NWDSASqlFactory()

    With oRequest
      .Command = "CustOrdersOrders"
      .CommandType = CommandType.StoredProcedure

      oParam.ParamName = "@CustomerID"
      oParam.ParamValue = txtCustomerID.Text.Trim()

      .Parameters.Add(oParam)
      .Role = NWDSARequest.UserRole.Internal
      .Transactional = False
    End With

    oDataReader = oFactory.ExecuteDataReader(oRequest)
    drOrders = oDataReader.ReturnedDataReader

    Do While drOrders.Read()
      oItem = New ListViewItem(drOrders.GetInt32(0))
      oItem.SubItems.Add(drOrders.GetDateTime(1))
      oItem.SubItems.Add(drOrders.GetDateTime(2))
      oItem.SubItems.Add(drOrders.GetDateTime(3))

      lstOrders.Items.Add(oItem)
    Loop
    drOrders.Close()
End Sub
```

Before we compose the other `Click` event, let's just look at what is happening in this one. First, our client application specifies which data provider it wants to use. It does so by creating an instance of one of the data tier concrete factory classes. Above, the client is creating a new `NWDSASqlFactory` object – so the client app is saying that it wants to access the data via the SQL Server .NET data provider.

Next, we have `oRequest`, which is an object of type `NWDSARequest` – we use it to represent the particulars of the request. Within the `With` block, we collect all the details of the command and add it to the properties of `oRequest`, so they can be passed to the data tier.

As it happens, we've chosen to test the data tier by requesting the command to run against the Northwind sample database that ships with SQL Server. The command we've chosen here is an existing stored procedure called `CustOrdersOrders`. *When we set up our configuration file in a moment, we'll make sure it points to a Northwind database! (Of course, we could choose a different database, and a different command with different parameters...)*

Then, the client app specifies what output type it wants. It does this by calling the appropriate `Execute...()` method of the concrete factory object. In this case, it calls `oFactory.ExecuteDataReader()` – which specifies that the client app wants a `DataReader`.

Finally, the `ExecuteDataReader()` method returns a `DataReader` object, which we pass to the `ListView` object, `lstOrders`, which then shows it on the screen. When it has finished, it closes the `DataReader` object.

One of the requirements of the data tier application was that it should be easy for client app developers to use. In practice, they only have to make two choices: which concrete factory to use, and which `Execute...()` *method to call. Moreover, they don't have to write many lines of code into our client application. Judging from this simple example, the extra work we put into designing our data tier seems to pave paid off in terms of satisfying the "ease-of-use" requirement.*

Of course, "ease-of-use" is a subjective criterion, but it seems we've made our data tier library very easy to use...

The DataSet Test Event Handler

Now we'll do the **DataSet Test** button's `Click` event handler. Again, we'll code it so that it uses the SQL Server .NET data provider, via our data tier. We'll use shading to highlight the places where it's different from the first event handler:

```
Private Sub btnDataSetTest_Click(ByVal sender As System.Object, _
                                ByVal e As System.EventArgs) _
                                    Handles btnDataSetTest.Click
    Dim oRequest As New NWDSARequest()
    Dim oParam As New NWDSARequest.Parameter()
    Dim oFactory As NWDSAAbstractFactory
    Dim oDataSet As NWDSADataSet
    Dim dsOrders As DataSet

    oFactory = New NWDSASqlFactory()

    With oRequest
      .Command = "CustOrdersOrders"
      .CommandType = CommandType.StoredProcedure

      oParam.ParamName = "@CustomerID"
      oParam.ParamValue = txtCustomerID.Text.Trim()

      .Parameters.Add(oParam)
      .Role = NWDSARequest.UserRole.Internal
      .Transactional = False
    End With
```

```
            oDataSet = oFactory.ExecuteDataSet(oRequest)
            dsOrders = oDataSet.ReturnedDataSet

            dgOrders.SetDataBinding(dsOrders, "Table")
            dgOrders.Refresh()
      End Sub
```

Apart from the event handler name, the only difference is that we're working with a `DataSet` instead of a `DataReader`.

Testing the SQL Server .NET Data Provider

Compile the application; then we just need to sort out the right configuration file. Just use the one that we presented earlier, in the Section entitled *The Client Application's Configuration File*. Don't forget to check the details in the connection strings – make sure they point to the `Northwind` database, and reflect your SQL Server instance and user permissions.

The configuration file must be located in the same folder as the client application's executable file, and it must have the right name. You'll probably find the executable file in the **\NWDSAWindowsTestApp\bin** folder. It will probably be called `NWDSAWindowsTestApp.exe`, in which case you should call the configuration file `NWDSAWindowsTestApp.exe.config`.

Here's what it looks like. On the left, is shown the display if you test for the `DataReader` output type. On the right, is shown the display if you test for the `DataSet` output type:

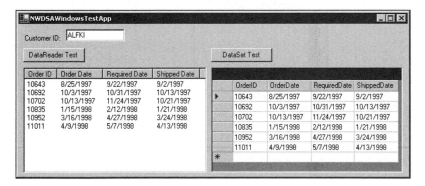

Testing the OLE DB .NET Data Provider

What if the client application developer doesn't have the option of the SQL Server .NET data provider? What if they can only connect to the data store through an OLE DB connection? In that case, they need to do just two things:

- ❑ Recode the event handlers in the client application, so that they use the `NSDWAOledbFactory` concrete factory instead of the `NSDWASqlFactory` concrete factory

- ❑ Ensure that the `.config` file contains connection strings that are suitable for an OLE DB connection.

Let's perform those two steps now, to show how easy it is.

Recoding the Test Event Handlers

Recoding the event handlers for a different data provider couldn't be easier.There are just two lines to change: one in each of the event handlers. In each case, it's the line with which the client application selects which concrete factory to use:

```
Private Sub btnDataReaderTest_Click(ByVal sender As System.Object, _
                                    ByVal e As System.EventArgs) _
                                       Handles btnDataReaderTest.Click
' declaration code as before...
  oFactory = New NWDSAOleDbFactory()
' implementation code as before...
End Sub


Private Sub btnDataSetTest_Click(ByVal sender As System.Object, _
                                 ByVal e As System.EventArgs) _
                                    Handles btnDataSetTest.Click
' declaration code as before...
  oFactory = New NWDSAOleDbFactory()
' implementation code as before...
End Sub
```

Changing the Configuration File

If the application is going to use the OLE DB data provider, it needs a suitable connection string. So you'll need to change all the connection strings in your application's configuration file, NWDSAWindowsTestApp.exe.config, to something of the same form as this:

```
Provider=SQLOLEDB;Data Source=1h;Initial Catalog=Northwind;User ID=ext;Password=earth
```

That's it. Just recompile the solution and run – you should get the same results.

Testing the ODBC .NET Data Provider

To test the ODBC data provider, you'll need to make some similar changes. In the code for the form:

```
Private Sub btnDataReaderTest_Click(ByVal sender As System.Object, _
                                    ByVal e As System.EventArgs) _
                                       Handles btnDataReaderTest.Click
' declaration code as before...
  oFactory = New NWDSAOdbcFactory()
' implementation code as before...
End Sub


Private Sub btnDataSetTest_Click(ByVal sender As System.Object, _
                                 ByVal e As System.EventArgs) _
                                    Handles btnDataSetTest.Click
' declaration code as before...
  oFactory = New NWDSAOdbcFactory()
' implementation code as before...
End Sub
```

Finally, the ODBC .NET data provider expects connection strings of the same form as this:

```
DSN=MYBASE;WSID=local;DATABASE=Northwind;UID=ext;PWD=earth
```

A Simple Web Test Application

Finally, let's quickly put together an. ASP.NET application to test the data tier – to show that it's not only usable in Windows applications! For brevity, we'll just test for the DataSet output type this time. Create a new ASP.NET project called **NWDSAWebTestApp** (set its location to be, say, http://localhost/NWDSAWebTestApp).

Add a reference to the NWDSA class library project (if **NWDSAWebTestApp** is in the same VS.NET solution) or to NWDSA.dll (if **NWDSAWebTestApp** is in a different VS.NET solution).

Delete the form **WebForm1.aspx**, which is provided by default. Then create a new web form called **NWDSAWebTestApp.aspx**. In it, we need to add a few controls:

- ❑ Add a **Label** control. Set its **Text** property to **Orders**. (I've also changed it's **Font** property's **Size** to **X-Large** here.)
- ❑ Add another **Label** control. Set its **Text** property to **Customer ID:**
- ❑ Add a **TextBox** control. Set its **ID** property to **txtCustomerID**, and clear its **Text** property
- ❑ Add a **Button** control. Set its **ID** property to **btnGetOrders**, and set its **Text** property to **Get Orders**
- ❑ Add a **DataGrid** control. Set its **ID** property to **dgOrders**

We need to do a little extra work to the **DataGrid** control. Right-click on it and select the **Property Builder...** option. Select the **Columns** tab on the left – this allows us to add columns to the grid. Select the **Bound Column** option (in the **Available columns** list) and click the > button four times to create four bound columns. Now change the **Header text** and **Data Field** properties of the four new columns to these values:

Header Text	Data Field
Order ID	OrderID
Order Date	OrderDate
Required Date	RequiredDate
Shipped Date	ShippedDate

Uncheck the **Create columns automatically at run time** checkbox, and **Apply** the changes. The dialog should look something like this:

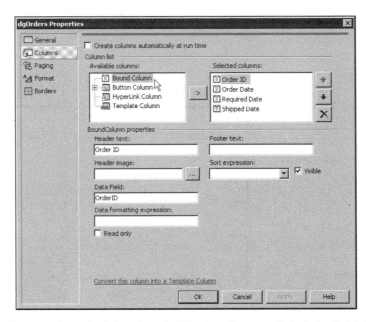

Now select the **Format** tab on the left, select the **Header** object, and click the **Bold** checkbox (to make the DataGrid's header row bold):

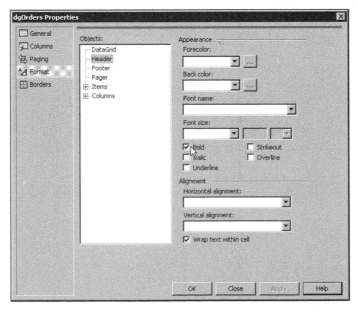

With a little arrangement of these controls, your .aspx page should look something like this:

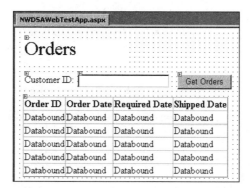

Now we just need to add some code to support the button-click event handler. First, add an `Imports` statement for the NWDSA data tier application that we'll be using, at the top of the `.aspx` file:

```
Imports NWDSA
```

Now add the content of the `Click` event handler:

```
Private Sub btnGetOrders_Click(ByVal sender As System.Object, _
                               ByVal e As System.EventArgs) _
                                            Handles btnGetOrders.Click
    Dim oRequest As New NWDSARequest()
    Dim oParam As New NWDSARequest.Parameter()
    Dim oFactory As NWDSAAbstractFactory
    Dim oDataSet As NWDSADataSet
    Dim dsOrders As DataSet

    oFactory = New NWDSASqlFactory()

    With oRequest
      .Command = "CustOrdersOrders"
      .CommandType = CommandType.StoredProcedure

      oParam.ParamName = "@CustomerID"
      oParam.ParamValue = txtCustomerID.Text.Trim

      .Parameters.Add(oParam)
      .Role = NWDSARequest.UserRole.External
      .Transactional = False
    End With

    oDataSet = oFactory.ExecuteDataSet(oRequest)
    dsOrders = oDataSet.ReturnedDataSet

    Try
      dgOrders.DataSource = dsOrders
      dgOrders.DataBind()
    Catch ex As Exception
      Console.WriteLine(ex.Message)
    End Try
End Sub
```

This code should all look quite familiar – it's practically identical to the code we saw in the Click event handlers of our Windows test application earlier. In this example, we've set oFactory to be a new NWDSASqlFactory object – which means that we're opting to use the *SQL Server* .NET data provider (via the NWDSA data tier application).

Next, we must make sure the web application has the correct configuration information (in this case, the necessary connection strings). Copy the <appSettings> node from the NWDSAWinTestApp.exe.config file we used earlier, and paste it into the web.config file that you'll find in the \NWDSAWebTestApp folder (add it as a child of the <configuration> node).

Finally, set NWDSAWebTestApp.aspx as the startup page (right-click on it and select Set as Startup Page). Now browse to http://localhost/NWDSAWebTestApp/NWDSAWebTestApp.aspx, and submit a customer ID, and you should see something like this:

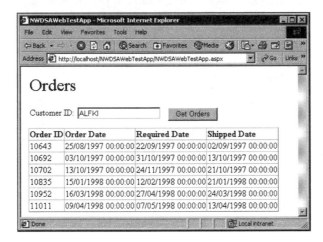

If we wanted to have this client application use one of the other data providers, we do so simply by changing the line that instantiates oFactory. There are two other data providers supported by this iteration of the NWDSA data tier, so we could change the line to either of the following:

```
oFactory = New NWDSAOleDbFactory()
```

```
oFactory = New NWDSAOdbcFactory()
```

Summary

At the beginning of this chapter, we were challenged with the task of designing and building a data tier application. As part of a revision of systems infrastructure, Northwind Traders' managers wanted an application that could act as a layer between their databases and their middle- and presentation-tier applications. To begin, they wanted something that could communicate with SQL Server databases and return DataSets and DataReaders – but they also specified that they wanted an extensible data tier that could (in the future) be easily adapted to provide access to other types of data store, and to return the data in other formats (such as XmlDocuments and scalars).

In order to meet these requirements, our solution design was all-important. After asserting that a design patterns solution may be appropriate, we took a sensible route to deciding which patterns were most relevant:

❑   Examine the characteristics of the problem

❑   Shortlist a number of candidate design patterns that might help solve the problem

❑   Use a process of elimination to establish a suitable choice.

The success of this approach is dependent on selecting the right design pattern, and working out the best way to apply it. In our design phase, we short-listed Factory Method and Abstract Factory. We examined the intents of both patterns. We decided that we *could* have built a solution based on Factory Method, but that the intent of Abstract Factory was better suited to this particular problem, and would probably provide a less complicated and more extensible solution.

In particular, we noticed that the problem involved two "choices" on the part of the client application developer – the data store type and the output type – and that Abstract Factory could reflect these in its concrete factories and its abstract products. Clearly, in this case study it was worth putting in the effort to analyze all the candidate patterns, and work out *how* each pattern would be used. In the end, it was this process that led us to choosing Abstract Factory – it was much better-suited to this particular project.

We built an iteration of our data tier that supports data access via three data providers – the SQL Server .NET data provider, the OLE DB .NET data provider, and the ODBC .NET data provider. It also supports two output types – `DataSets` and `DataReaders`. Consequently, it more than meets the base requirements of the solution.

Moreover, our data tier solution needed to satisfy the extensibility requirement, and so it does. There isn't room in this chapter to prove it, but there is room on our web site. The source code for this book contains a second iteration of this application, which takes advantage of its Abstract Factory design to support no fewer than four data providers and six output types! To build it, we simply needed to add one more concrete factory, three abstract product classes, and 15 concrete product classes. You can get the code at http://www.apress.com.

In the next chapter, we're going to take a look at the application of design patterns in the middle tier of a distributed application, and we're going to meet our first non-GoF pattern.

3

Design Patterns in the Middle Tier

Design patterns and the middle tier were made for each other. Why? Think of it this way. The very nature of the middle tier is to execute business rules. Business rules change as often and quickly as businesses changes. Design patterns exist to encapsulate variability and change. When we put these three assertions together, the conclusion is hard to ignore – design patterns can help developers to manage those never-ending changes to a middle tier application.

In this chapter we will build an application that processes orders. To help us get the job done we will use two types of patterns:

❑ The first type is the now-familiar design pattern that has been best illustrated using UML class diagrams. In fact, our application will utilize some of the basic GoF patterns that we discussed earlier in the book. But, unlike most instances of design patterns that we have talked about so far, here we will use them *in combination* to enhance our solution. We will use the Decorator pattern to manage the overall processing of orders; but hiding underneath it will be the Façade and Strategy patterns.

❑ The second type of pattern we will see is one that constitutes a common architectural approach to a common problem. Our application supports a business-to-business web-based presentation tier – a requirement that demands performance and reliability. Fortunately, developers have already solved this problem with a pattern that we will call Store and Forward (SaF).

Interestingly, such high-level patterns are not necessarily best illustrated using UML class diagrams (like the GoF design patterns). In fact, in this case, the essence of the SaF pattern is much better captured by an activity sequence diagram.

Before we ramp up, there is an interesting side note about the Store and Forward pattern worth mentioning. Even though the SaF pattern lives on a higher conceptual plane than the GoF design patterns, we will need a lowly "bread and butter" design pattern to give it life. Specifically, the Singleton pattern will play a big part in making SaF work.

So, in summary, we'll see the following patterns in application in this chapter:

- ❑ Decorator
- ❑ Façade
- ❑ Strategy
- ❑ Store and Forward (SaF)
- ❑ Singleton

First, we'll look at our business requirements. Then we'll do our analysis, and at that point we'll try to identify the patterns that will best suit our needs. In doing so, we'll examine a few options before finally settling on the approach we've outlined above.

Handling Orders

Before we delve into the detailed analysis and design phase, let's set up our business requirements and "set the scene" for the application and its related technologies. That should help us get a feel for where our application needs to go and how we will get it there.

Business Requirements

Our client is the company called Northwind Traders (that perennial favorite of all Microsoft developers). Currently, Northwind's sales representatives take customer orders over the phone. Sam Spade, Northwind's controller, just finished an order handling benchmarking study and fears that the company's cost per transaction is too high. He has also read about how other companies have lowered their business-to-business (B2B) transaction costs via Internet-based technologies. He thinks that maybe Northwind could, too. With this idea (lowering order transaction costs via the Internet) in mind, Sam starts meeting with the company's Technology Manager, Sally Server, and the Inside Sales Coordinator, Laura Callahan.

During the course of these meetings, it quickly became obvious why order transaction costs were high. Laura informed everyone that while revenues were increasing, customers were placing a higher volume of smaller orders. She said that as a consequence of this change in customers' behavior, Northwind would probably by forced to hire two more sales representatives. And to make matters worse, sales representative costs were increasing since they were now receiving continuous specialized product training.

Since it seemed unlikely that customers would change their ordering behavior, everyone agreed that Northwind needed a way to reduce the labor costs associated with placing orders. At this point, Sam asked Sally whether or not some Internet-based B2B solution might automate the process. She thought this was a good idea, but needed a little more information about how the sales representatives processed orders.

Laura explained that the ordering process was simple; but setting up new customers and answering product questions was complicated! Most existing customers already knew the product line and simply called in their orders to a representative, who then reviewed the order and entered it into Northwind's Order system. This review involved verifying product identification numbers and prices, checking product stock levels, and stopping orders with past delivery dates.

Based on all this information, Sally believed that Sam's initial hunch was a good one. Order processing costs *could* be lowered if the current manual order processing system was replaced with an Internet-based application. The new application could receive customer orders over the Internet, review them, and enter them into the order system. Laura was also enthusiastic; such a system would enable her staff to focus on activities that improve sales, rather than wasting time pushing paper into a computer!

As a result of these meetings, Jack Spratt was hired by Northwind to design and build an order processing application.

Technology Requirements

In this chapter, we'll consider Northwind as a "Microsoft shop". All computer hardware runs on either Windows 2000 Server or Windows 2000 Professional/Windows XP. All business applications are written in Visual Basic. The corporate database is SQL Server 2000.

Sally stated that the new system must utilize these existing technologies. The only exception to the rule would be the development language. She specified VB.NET as the target language for the new application (citing Northwind's recent decision to move onto the .NET platform).

While Jack had not yet started the analysis and design phase for the application, he was nonetheless forming a few ideas about what technologies he might employ for the application. For example, some combination of **MSMQ queuing services** and **multithreading** promised a reliable and responsible order processing application capable of meeting the needs of web-based clients. Also, .NET's **COM Interop** capability might ease communication with the legacy Microsoft-based order system.

Analysis and Design

After several days of discussion with the sales representative, the time came for Jack to document his observations and ideas. He decided to use the Unified Modeling Language (UML) for the job, because of its effectiveness at expressing so many different concepts with its tools. The exercise would also help verify his ideas with the domain expert, Laura, and wrap up any outstanding security and deployment issues with Sally.

If you're unfamiliar with the UML and its notation, you may find the UML Primer (located in Appendix A) to be a helpful resource. The primer is also a great refresher for anyone who has not worked with the UML for a while.

Use Case Diagrams

Jack started by writing the use cases to describe the movement of orders from an ASP.NET page to Northwind's Order system. The resulting use case diagrams provided documentation of many of the application requirements. During the interviews, a name for the new application crystallized – Northwind Order Processing (NOP). The first artifact produced for Laura's review was a preliminary draft of the Primary Use Case. This preliminary draft is shown below.

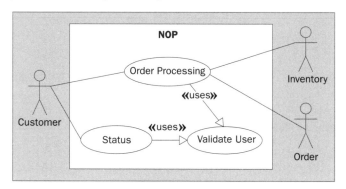

In the simplest terms, NOP identifies a *Customer* actor and allows that actor to perform one of two actions:

❏ Submit an order. The *Order Processing* use case handles this action.

❏ Retrieve order status. The *Status* use case handles this action.

The third use case in this diagram, *Validate User*, does exactly what the name implies: it checks a user's right to perform a particular activity. The remaining actors, *Inventory* and *Order*, represent other Northwind systems external to NOP.

> *If you're new to UML, you might be surprised to see a computer application referred to as an "actor" in a use case diagram. Nonetheless, those cute little stick figures can represent almost anything that interacts with the main use case – human or non-human.*

Laura believed that this preliminary version of the primary use case captured the spirit of the application. She subsequently provided the details needed to construct the business rules for the *Order Processing* use case. (Later, we'll see some activity diagrams that relate much of this information.)

Discussion with Sally cleared up a few key issues suggested by the preliminary Primary Use Case draft:

❏ The web page responsible for accepting customer orders would handle user authentication and authorization. Her team was already building an ASP.NET application utilizing its latest security widgets. Therefore, NOP did not need to validate users.

❏ The *Inventory* actor amounted to a legacy application built with Visual Basic 6. (Jack laughed to himself at hearing a VB6 application described as a "legacy" system.) This system managed Northwind's product price and quantity data.

❏ The *Order* actor provided the big surprise. This actor equaled Northwind's recently-built Order system that incorporated XML and MSMQ. In this system, orders are initiated by dropping an XML-based order document into a specific message queue.

Jack added this newly-acquired information to the diagram, and thus finalized the Primary Use Case:

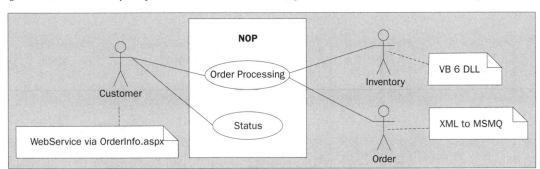

Activity Diagrams

Laura reviewed the activity diagrams that describe the processing that each order is submitted to before it is passed to Northwind's Order system. The preliminary and final diagrams did not vary too much – Jack had captured the business rules quite well! But, once again, the analysis produced a surprise. It turned out that the Order system handles two different types of order documents – and they use different XML document validation specifications! One type (the "Special Order") worked with an older XML validation standard – **DTD** documents. The other ("Order") adhered to the latest standard from the W3C – **XSD**.

There was some similarity in the processes required for the two different types of order: both required a check against the inventory and both resulted in the placement of an order into Northwind's Order system. However, differing business rules complicated things. "Special Order" did not check order credit limits or deal with required ship dates. "Order" *did* check credit limits and ship dates. These different business rules, combined with the different XML document validation specifications, made for a confusing order process!

Jack summarized these differences with a simple table. The first column contains a brief description of the processing action. The second and third columns contain how that action might be effected in NOP. He saw three choices: Not Required, XML Validation, or Code:

Order Processing Action	Effect of Action on Order Processing	
	Special Order	**Order**
Inspect Product ID	Code	XML Validation
Inspect Price	Code	Code
Inspect Quantity	Code	XML Validation
Inspect Date	Not Required	Code
Check Inventory	Code	Code
Check Credit	Not Required	Code
Order Product	Code	Code

Based on this table, Jack produced the following *Order Processing* and *Validate* activity diagrams:

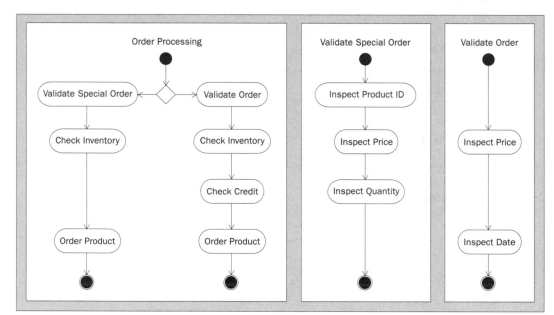

*In the **Validate Order** activity diagram, note that Order does not explicitly need to inspect the ProductID and Quantity, because this is done in the XSD schema.*

It was at this point that Jack started thinking in terms of design patterns. Two ideas came to mind. First, the *Validate Special Order* and *Validate Order* activities hinted that the Strategy pattern might be appropriate when coding the validation process. Second, the similarities of the two order types (outlined above in the *Order Processing* activity diagram) far outweighed their differences. One only needed to drop a few behaviors from one to realize the other. This characteristic suggested a Decorator pattern to Jack.

Homing in on Patterns

Of course, it would be naive to assume that Jack selected these two patterns without some serious thought. In fact, he worked though several possibilities before making these selections. Let's examine Jack's decision-making process in greater detail.

Application of a Decorator pattern wasn't immediately obvious. But Jack looked at the different action states of the *Order Processing* activity diagram, and realized that he could think of them as **responsibilities** that could dynamically be added to (or dropped from) any order. Then he looked again at the Decorator pattern's intent:

> Intent of GoF Decorator: *Attach additional responsibilities to an object dynamically. Decorators provide a flexible alternative to subclassing for extending functionality.*

This was enough to convince him that a Decorator pattern could do the job.

If the activity states had been richer, more complex objects, then the Decorator would have looked less appealing (because the Decorator assumes a certain "likeness" between the supporting objects, which simply "decorate" the common object). In that case another structural pattern, the Composite, would have been more promising. The Composite pattern's intent shows the difference:

> Intent of GoF Composite: *Compose objects into tree structures to represent part-whole hierarchies. Composite lets clients treat individual objects and compositions of objects uniformly.*

(Chapter 1 contains descriptions and demonstrations of both of these patterns. If the Decorator pattern seems a little hazy, you could turn back to Chapter 1 and reacquaint yourself with it. The Decorator plays a central role in our application!)

Finding the most suitable pattern for *Validate Special Order* and *Validate Order* activity states proved a more daunting task. The reason was simple: at first it was unclear to Jack what type of pattern best suited the problem! He took a few minutes to examine the three different GoF design pattern types in turn, remind himself of the high-level purpose of each, and eliminate some pattern types from the hunt:

- ❑ **Creational** patterns **abstract object instantiation**. While this functionality might be required to implement validation, flexible object creation was not really an issue here. (Scratch creational patterns.)

- ❑ **Structural** patterns help **build large, complex objects**. Validation objects did not look like they would end up as multifaceted behemoths. (Scratch structural patterns.)

- ❑ **Behavioral** patterns play with **algorithms and relationships between objects**. Judging from the *Validate Special Order* and *Validate Order* activity diagrams, managing algorithms seemed to hit the mark best.

By deciding upon a behavioral pattern, Jack reduced the problem to picking the best pattern from a smaller pot. Judging from its intent, the Command had some initial appeal:

> Intent of GoF Command: *Encapsulate a request as an object, thereby letting you parameterize clients with different requests, queue or log requests, and support undoable operations.*

But this looked like overkill. Well, what about the Strategy and Template Method patterns? Both intents looked promising:

> Intent of GoF Template Method: *Define the skeleton of an algorithm in an operation, deferring some steps to subclasses. Template Method lets subclasses redefine certain steps of an algorithm without changing the algorithm's structure.*

> Intent of GoF Strategy: *Define a family of algorithms, encapsulate each one, and make them interchangeable. Strategy lets the algorithm vary independently from clients that use it.*

Jack pondered this one for a while, and even looked at some code samples to help get a better take. It was looking at the code that helped him differentiate between these seemingly similar patterns. The Template Method pattern enforced the *same* algorithms. The validation algorithms suggested in the *Order* and *Validate Order* activity diagrams were not so common as to merit a straitjacket approach. Jack felt that the Strategy pattern captured the requirements of the validation activity states much more successfully – they looked like a "family" that needed to be "interchangeable" when it called for it.

Sequence Diagrams

Early on, Jack decided that he would deal with business rules and performance requirements as two different issues. To avoid mixing "plumbing code" with "business code", he decided to split NOP into two applications, `ReceiveDocument` and `ProcessDocument`. `ReceiveDocument` would focus on responding reliably and quickly to web clients; `ProcessDocument` could process order documents. But the decision to split up NOP begs the obvious question – how will all these parts work together?

The UML's sequence diagrams love to answer questions like this. But they do more than just map out the dynamic exchange of messages between objects. Sequence diagrams also give the architect a sense of the chronological ordering of messages. In our case, that's more than a trivial concern, since NOP must support a B2B web-based client. Order processing will most likely be a time-consuming exercise, and clients will not want to wait around for it to finish computing before they get a response! Our sequence diagram will need to demonstrate how the `ReceiveDocument` application will get its job done while keeping client responses timely. Oh, and don't forget, we'd better not lose any orders either. Fortunately, Jack already knew how to handle this problem.

The solution amounts to a two-step process:

❑   First, safely store the end user's request and as quickly as possible return an informative response.

❑   Next, forward the request for processing, and when finished allow the end user to retrieve the result.

Strangely, the pattern is so familiar to developers that build B2B Internet solutions that it doesn't even have a name! So for the sake of simplicity we will refer to it as the **Store and Forward** (**SaF**) pattern.

> *No doubt some readers are probably wondering why the Store and Forward pattern is considered a "true" pattern. After all, there aren't a bunch of classes around to demonstrate it. But a pattern is more than just class diagram; it is a time-tested solution intended to solve a recurring problem. The Store and Forward pattern meet this criterion; it just turns out that a sequence diagram communicates SaF's intent better than a class diagram.*

As we can see in the following sequence diagram, the `ReceiveDocument` application embodies the SaF pattern. It is responsible for storing the order (**Send Message**) and forwarding it to `ProcessDocument` (**Load**). The last function it performs (**Document ID**) will allow the end user to get a Document ID, so they can trace the order in the system.

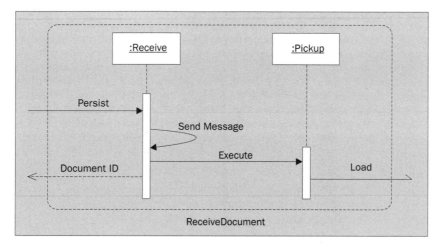

The second sequence diagram shows the whole process, and how `ReceiveDocument` fits into the bigger picture:

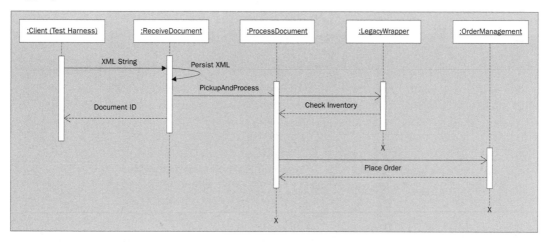

Note that in the first sequence diagram, the **Load** message was drawn as a solid line with a one-sided arrowhead. This notation represents a subtlety of the SaF pattern that is crucial if the pattern is to work properly – namely, that the **Load** method will be an **asynchronous method call** without a return value.

Class Diagrams

With some solid use case, activity, and sequence analysis in hand, Jack was ready to design the class structure. It also helped that he had envisioned the appropriate design patterns! Based on all this analysis he knew that `ProcessDocument` was the only application involving a complex web of classes. So, that was where Jack focused his class design energies.

Some readers may consider this miserly approach to class diagrams to be rather cavalier. We could certainly diagram every class in NOP. But, would all these additional artifacts make us any smarter? Probably not. So why bother generating a lot of near-worthless diagrams?

The Decorator Pattern Classes

To implement the Decorator pattern, Jack needed to identify the concrete class and all of the associated decorator classes. In our case, Jack already knew that the concrete class equated to an order document. So, he aptly entitled this class `Document`. The decorators equated to the different activity states from the *Order Processing* activity diagram. He named each of these classes with a simplistic verb-noun combination indicative of their function. For example, the `CheckInventory` class decorates a document by checking (the verb) inventory (the noun).

Next, Jack decided what methods the concrete `Document` class should contain. This constituted a critical design task since these methods would be available to *every* class in the pattern! He knew to avoid the error of including any optional or specialized methods, since they rightly belonged to decorators. He rightly kept the list focused on those methods most likely required by any and all order documents:

Method/Property	Description
Load()	Loads the order document into a private XML document variable via the private function LoadXMLDoc
DocID	Returns the document's assigned processing referenced ID (not to be confused with an Order ID!)
DocXML	Returns a reference to the private XML document
DocType	Returns the document type (Special Order or Order)
DocStatus	Returns the current status of the document ("processing", "errors", or "complete")
DocErrors	Returns a listing of any errors encountered while processing a document

With the above list of methods, the task of writing the Decorator's interface class (the `ProcessDocument` class) was an academic exercise. Likewise, writing the Decorator pattern's decorator class (the `Processes` class) proved an equally easy task since it just implemented all of the `Document`'s public methods.

The Strategy Pattern Classes

Compared to creating the Decorator, designing the validation processes via the Strategy pattern was straightforward. Jack jumped straight to writing the interface class, `OrderValidationStrategy`. He knew exactly the methods and properties he wanted any order validation class to offer:

Method/Property	Description
IsValid()	Returns a Boolean value indicating whether or not the document is valid
ValidationErrors()	Returns a listing of any errors encountered while validating an order

The Strategy pattern had effectively transferred the "hard work" to the coding of the validation algorithms. And that did not surprise Jack, given the Strategy pattern's intent – *Define a family of algorithms, encapsulate each one, and make them interchangeable...*

The Final Class Diagram

Here's how the Decorator and Strategy patterns combine to produce the final class diagram for the `ProcessDocument` application:

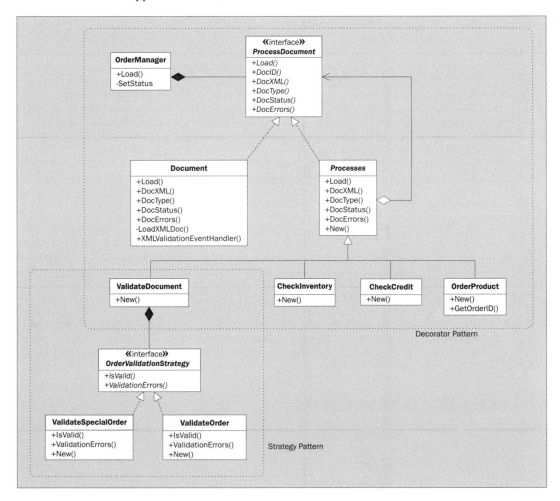

Jack has done enough plotting and planning. Let's move on to the code!

The Coding Part

Our demonstration will be built as a collection of projects sitting within the Visual Studio .NET solution entitled Wrox.ProDPA6985.Ch03. To create the application, there are four major tasks:

❏ Setup the infrastructure (for example, create the database storing document status messages).

❏ Build the debugging and test harness (`TestHarness`) application.

❑   Build the projects for the supporting applications (`LegacyWrapper` and `OrderManagement`).

❑   Build the two NOP applications (`ReceiveDocument` and `ProcessDocument`).

As a side note, you may have noticed that the test harness application is listed *before* the NOP application. This is deliberate. Writing the test harness first helps ensure that we don't "lose sight" of our goal when we actually get coding.

> *This methodology may sound familiar to you. It constitutes a significant part of the "Extreme Programming" practice. One of its tenets holds that developers always build their application test harness first. This forces the developer to be sure of exactly what features the application needs to support, and also facilitates unit testing during the coding phase. There's a lot more to Extreme Programming than this particular tenet. If you wish to learn more about Extreme Programming, Kent Beck's book* Extreme Programming Explained: Embrace Change *(Addison-Wesley, ISBN: 0-201616-41-6) is a good place to start.*

There are a few miscellaneous points worth noting before we start coding.

❑   While NOP will someday support a web service, we're building a fat client for debugging and testing. Bringing web services into the picture during the construction phase only adds an unnecessary layer of complication.

❑   Just because we test with a fat client does not mean we can ignore the requirements of a web service. For example, one of those requirements concerns acceptable parameter data types. The current specification does not allow for passing an XML document as a parameter. Therefore, we used a string value representation of an XML document.

❑   We're not worrying about where our XML validation files are physically located since all of our applications run under one solution. Once loaded into memory by the test client, they remain loaded. In reality NOP would need to look in its own cache for the necessary DTD and XSD validation documents.

Setting up the Infrastructure

Before coding, we need to do a little infrastructure-related work:

1. Register the "legacy" component `Inventory.dll`.

2. Verify (and, if required, install) the Windows MSMQ service.

3. Ensure that our two SQL Server 2000 databases are available.

4. Create a Visual Studio .NET solution.

In this section, we'll cover these four tasks.

Registering Inventory.dll

In spite of all of the new toys and widgets contained in Visual Studio .NET, you still need to make sure that your computer's registry knows about any COM components it might utilize. In this demonstration, the NOP application will make use of the `Inventory.dll` component library.

Save the file `Inventory.dll` to a folder on your hard disk; then navigate a command prompt to that folder and execute the following command:

```
regsrv32 Inventory.dll
```

This will register the component library, and allow us to access it via COM Interop technologies.

We will examine the source code of `Inventory.dll` later in this chapter. The source code and DLL are supplied along with the rest of the code for this book, at http://www.apress.com.

Setting up MSMQ

Microsoft Message Queue (**MSMQ**) provides the private message queue services that NOP relies on to persist order documents. It is a Windows 2000 component that may need to be installed locally. You can check to see whether MSMQ services are installed on your machine, by activating the Computer Management MMC via the Administrative Tools menu. The figure below indicates that MSMQ is installed:

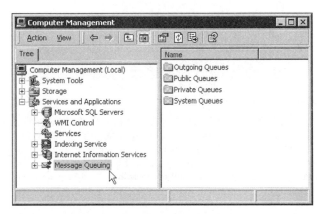

If your computer does not have Message Queuing listed under the Services and Applications node, then install MSMQ via the Control Panel's Add/Remove Windows Components feature.

Setting up the SQL Server Databases

SQL Server 2000 humors two masters in our solution. First, it provides a single table data store for NOP's document processing status messages. Second, it contains product data for the Northwind Inventory system.

The Northwind Database

The legacy component library `Inventory.dll` (which was coded using VB6) retrieves product information from the demonstration Northwind database that comes with SQL Server. You will need to check that this database exists. After that, you will need to modify the connection information located in the data link file. This file is called `Nwind.udl` – you can place it in the same folder as the `Inventory.dll` file. You will probably need to update the password. The following shows what you can expect to find on the Connection tab of the Data Link Properties dialog:

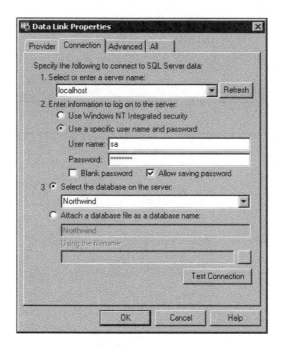

The NWindOrderStatus Database

The other SQL Server database, `NWindOrderStatus`, supports status processing message persistence. You can create it by using the `Create-NWindOrderStatus-Database.sql` script, which is located in this chapter's \SQLScript folder. Before executing this script, you may need to edit the database and log file locations. In particular, if your computer does not have the C:\Program Files\Microsoft SQL Server\MSSQL\data folder (which is assumed in the following lines of the `.sql` script), you'll need to edit the script and set another folder:

```
IF EXISTS (SELECT name FROM master.dbo.sysdatabases
           WHERE name = N'NWindOrderStatus')
  DROP DATABASE [NWindOrderStatus]
GO

CREATE DATABASE [NWindOrderStatus]
ON (
  NAME = N'NWindOrderStatus_Data',
  FILENAME = N'C:\Program Files\Microsoft SQL Server\MSSQL\data\NWindOrderStatus_Data.MDF',
  SIZE = 1, FILEGROWTH = 10%)
LOG
ON (
  NAME = N'NWindOrderStatus_Log',
  FILENAME = N'C:\Program Files\Microsoft SQL Server\MSSQL\data\NWindOrderStatus_Log.LDF',
  SIZE = 1, FILEGROWTH = 10%)
...
```

Note that the `T-SQL CREATE DATABASE` *command will fail if the* `FILENAME` *folders do not exist!*

`Create-NWindOrderStatus-Database.sql` also creates a few other SQL Server objects that our document processing application relies upon. The most important of these, of course, is the `DocumentStatus` table – this is the home of the status records. The other object is a SQL Server-based user identity called `DocWrox`, which has the necessary permissions to access the `NWindOrderStatus` database.

*If your instance of SQL Server 2000 only supports Windows authentication, then you will need to change this option to support SQL Server authentication too. This may be accomplished through the SQL Server Enterprise Manager MMC – select the SQL Server instance's **Properties** page and from there select the **Security** tab. After changing the **Authentication** property, SQL Server will need to be restarted.*

Creating a Visual Studio .NET Solution

In the following section we will start building the first of several VB.NET projects. In order to keep the development effort more manageable, you may at this time want to create a blank solution entitled Wrox_ProDPA6985_Ch03 that will house all of our handiwork. (It's also the way I wrote the source code for this project.) When we are finished coding, our Solution Explorer window should contain five projects as shown below:

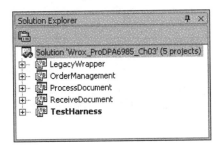

The Inventory

Before delving into Northwind Order Processing (NOP), it's worth taking a moment to inspect the applications that provide product data via Northwind's Inventory application. Accessing this "legacy" application is accomplished via a simple .NET application entitled `LegacyWrapper`.

For once we have a really meaningful (albeit boring) application name – LegacyWrapper! OK, maybe this name is only meaningful to hardcore object-oriented developers. These guys regularly apply the term "wrapper" when they use either the Adapter or Façade patterns to protect the innocent from a legacy application. In our case, our application is using a Façade to "wrap" a dangerous and scary VB6 component! To highlight an extra source of ambiguity, we should note here that the GoF also listed the term "wrapper" as an alternative name for a Decorator design pattern.

The Façade pattern provides us with more than just an exciting lesson in nomenclature. First, it (almost) spares us from having to read the next few paragraphs since it shields us from the inner workings of `Inventory.dll`. Second, it helps keep our architecture simpler. We can get a visual idea of this notion by augmenting a fragment of the `ProcessDocument` class diagram with the `LegacyWrapper` application's `ProductInventory` class diagram, as shown overleaf:

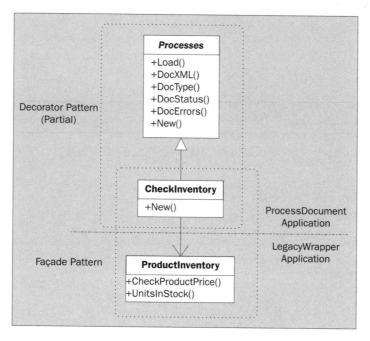

The Legacy Application

We now need to find a few things out about our legacy VB6 application, `Inventory.dll` – and in particular, its single class file, `Product.cls`. If you have Microsoft Visual Basic 6 installed, then it will help to make the code review more palatable; if not, you can also use Notepad to view the code. When looking at the code, pay special attention to any issues that might arise when writing a .NET-based wrapper around `Inventory.dll`. For example:

❑   Are there any data type conversion issues? Remember that the .NET Common Language Runtime (CLR) does not work easily with all Visual Basic 6 data types.

❑   Is the Visual Basic class public? In other words, is the class instancing property set to `MultiUse` rather than `Private`?

Let's step through the code in `Product.cls`, and pick out the key elements. The first thing we notice is that the class instancing property is set to `MultiUse`:

```
VERSION 1.0 CLASS
BEGIN
   MultiUse = -1            'True
   Persistable = 0         'NotPersistable
   DataBindingBehavior = 0  'vbNone
   DataSourceBehavior  = 0  'vbNone
   MTSTransactionMode  = 0  'NotAnMTSObject
END
Attribute VB_Name = "Product"
Attribute VB_GlobalNameSpace = False
Attribute VB_Creatable = True
```

```
Attribute VB_PredeclaredId = False
Attribute VB_Exposed = True
Option Explicit
```

Great! This makes the VB6 `Product` class appear as a normal .NET public class.

There's more good news in the next fragment! Our first function, `InstockCount()`, has a plain old integer data type that .NET happily works with. Also, `ProductID` is passed by value and that minimizes the number of calls between COM and .NET:

```
Public Function InstockCount(ByVal ProductID As Integer) As Integer
    On Error GoTo LocalError
    Dim intResult As Integer
    Dim strQuery As String
    Dim cn As ADODB.Connection
    Dim rs As ADODB.Recordset

    strQuery = "SELECT UnitsInStock FROM Products WHERE ProductID = " & _
                                                        ProductID

    Set cn = New ADODB.Connection
    cn.Open GetConnectionString

    Set rs = cn.Execute(strQuery)
    If Not (rs.BOF Or rs.EOF) Then
      intResult = rs(0)
    Else
      intResult = -1
    End If

    rs.Close
    cn.Close
    GoTo ExitFunction

LocalError:
  Err.Raise Err.Number, "InstockCount", Err.Description
ExitFunction:
    InstockCount = intResult
CleanUp:
  If Not rs Is Nothing Then
    Set rs = Nothing
  End If
  If Not cn Is Nothing Then
    Set cn = Nothing
  End If
End Function
```

The data type of the return value is as important as the function's parameter type, and it is looking good.

The next function, `PriceCheck()`, appears as clean as `InstockCount`, because `Doubles` are as digestible as `Integers`:

```
Public Function PriceCheck(ByVal ProductID As Long, _
                    ByVal Price As Double) As Integer
```

```
    On Error GoTo LocalError
    Dim intResult As Integer
    Dim cn As ADODB.Connection
    Dim rs As ADODB.Recordset
    Dim strQuery As String

    strQuery = "SELECT * FROM Products WHERE "
    strQuery = strQuery & "ProductID = " & ProductID
    strQuery = strQuery & " AND "
    strQuery = strQuery & "UnitPrice = " & Price

    Set cn = New ADODB.Connection
    cn.Open GetConnectionString

    Set cn = New ADODB.Connection
    cn.Open GetConnectionString

    Set rs = cn.Execute(strQuery)
    If Not (rs.BOF Or rs.EOF) Then
      intResult = 1
    Else
      intResult = -1
    End If

    rs.Close
    cn.Close

    GoTo ExitFunction

LocalError:
    Err.Raise Err.Number, "PriceCheck", Err.Description
ExitFunction:
    PriceCheck = intResult
CleanUp:
    If Not rs Is Nothing Then
      Set rs = Nothing
    End If
    If Not cn Is Nothing Then
      Set cn = Nothing
    End If
End Function
```

The VB6 code does not suggest any potentially vexing COM Interop issues. In particular, all method parameters are passed ByVal and the parameters' and return values' data types are all "blittable". (In other words, there are no special data conversion requirements between COM and .NET here. In some cases these requirements do exist. The cost can range from a slight performance degradation to having to tweak the code in places.) Also, there are no complex data types – like VB6 user-defined types (UDTs) or variant arrays (ugh!) – to deal with.

The code does contain one potential problem. Namely, the Inventory application requires the non-.NET version of the ADO libraries. (This problem is so obvious that an experienced developer could easily miss it.) Fortunately, that probably will not be an issue since the .NET runtime installs the latest non-.NET version of ADO. Moreover, Product.cls does not appear to be making any "discontinued" or deprecated ADO method calls.

Many readers of this book will be developers with several ADO libraries installed on their machine, and to those readers this issue may seem academic. But, be warned! You never know what can happen when deploying applications to "normal" desktops!

For those curious souls, `GetConnectionString()` refers to a function in a BAS module (`Main.bas`) that loads the required connection information contained in `NWind.udl`:

```
Public Function GetConnectionString() As String
  GetConnectionString = "file name=" & App.Path & "\NWind.udl"
End Function
```

Finally, if you have Microsoft's Visual Basic 6 installed on your computer, you can test the `Inventory` application using the project contained in the \Legacy\Test folder.

The LegacyWrapper

Building a .NET application that communicates with `Inventory.dll` is a straightforward exercise. After creating a new VB class library project, called `LegacyWrapper`, within our VS.NET solution, we just reference the COM component and write a class that accesses it.

> **Pattern alert! We're creating a reference to another class with the sole intention of merely calling its methods. This is the first step towards implementation of a Façade pattern, as we'll see in this section.**

Here's the Add Reference dialog that is presented by Visual Studio .NET when you add a COM reference to the project:

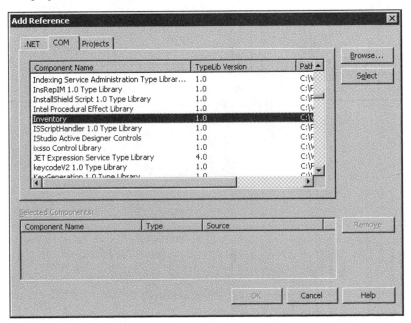

If you do not see `Inventory.dll` *in the list of available components (as shown above), then try registering the component using* `regsvr32` *(as discussed earlier).*

Now change the name of the class file created by VS.NET from `Class1.vb` to `ProductInventory.vb`. We're ready to code our class called `ProductInventory`.

The `ProductInventory` class will be responsible for accessing the Inventory's `Product` class, and is given below. Recall from our object diagrams that this class has two methods, `CheckProductPrice()` and `UnitsInStock()`:

```
Public Class ProductInventory
  Private m_Inventory As New Inventory.ProductClass()

  Public Function CheckProductPrice(ByVal productID As Long, _
                                    ByVal price As Double) As Boolean
    Dim result As Integer

    Try
      result = m_Inventory.PriceCheck(productID, price)
      If result > 0 Then
        Return True
      Else
        Return False
      End If
    Catch e As Exception
      Throw New Exception( _
              "Unable to check price for Product ID = " & productID, e)
    End Try
  End Function
```

In the code above, our reinterpretation of `m_Inventory.PriceCheck()` *now begins to look a little bit like an Adapter pattern! We are definitely entering the territory of a Façade pattern; but whenever code makes incompatible classes hospitable to another class the object-oriented purists might yell, "Adapter!" (Whether or not the* `Product.cls` *code is inhospitable is for the reader to decide...)*

```
  Public Function UnitsInStock(ByVal productID As Long) As Long
    Dim result As Integer

    Try
      result = m_Inventory.InstockCount(productID)
      Return CLng(result)
    Catch e As Exception
      Throw New Exception( _
              "Unable to retrieve units in stock for Product ID = " & _
              productID, e)
    End Try

  End Function
End Class
```

Our interpretation of the information returned from the VB6 application makes it much easier to use `Inventory.dll`. For example, look at the `CheckProductPrice()` method. It ultimately calls `Inventory.Product`'s `PriceCheck()` method, which returns an `Integer`. But the `CheckProductPrice()` method returns a `Boolean`. That's because clients of the `CheckProductPrice()` method just need to know whether or not the submitted product price was correct. They don't care to know about a bunch of integers.

How the Façade Pattern is Helping Us

This situation is a good example of when a Façade comes to the fore. If the Façade pattern is well-implemented here, the `LegacyWrapper` developer will be the only person who ever needs to interpret `PriceCheck()`'s return value. Other developers needing the functionality of the legacy `PriceCheck()` method can bypass learning the intricacies of the `Inventory` application by just calling `CheckProductPrice()`. In this simple example, the overall benefit is rather small. But it's clear that in a similar situation that involved dozens of complex methods, the benefit of the Façade pattern would be multiplied manyfold.

Moreover, there is another way in which the Façade patterns may have simplified working with `Inventory.dll`. Imagine that `Product.cls` contained 40 methods, instead of only two, and that the other 38 of those methods were of no interest to us. We would probably prefer to hide these nonessential routines from `ProcessDocument`. Thus, once again, the Façade helps us by *being selective* – in other words, by excluding `Inventory.dll`'s superfluous methods.

The Test Harness

The NOP test client is a Visual Studio .NET Windows Application named `TestHarness`. We use it to load and submit test versions of the two Northwind order types. More specifically, it places the contents of either an Order or Special Order sample XML document into a textbox control. It also retrieves processing status information after submitting an order. The user interface supports these simple requirements. This is what it should look like:

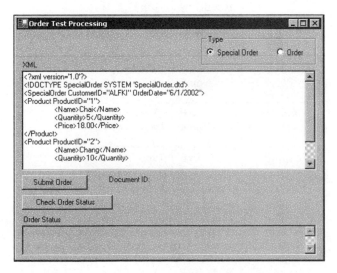

Once you've added the `TestHarness` project to the VS.NET solution, change the name of the file `Form1.vb` to `frmMain.vb`. Next, bring up the **Properties** pane (by hitting *F4* and clicking on the form) and change the **Text** property of the form frmMain from **Form1** to **Order Text Processing**.

Now we can set about building the workings of the test application. First, we'll use the IDE features to add some controls, and then we'll visit the code and add some further implementation.

Adding the Controls

Then we need to use the toolbox to add the necessary controls to the form. The controls are listed below. The table also shows the properties whose values should be changed from the default (use the control's **Properties** pane to set the values of these properties):

Control	Property Name and Value	
Label	Text	XML
Label	Text	Document ID:
Label	Text	Order Status
Label	Text Name	Submit Order `lblSubmitResult`
TextBox	Name Multiline ScrollBars	`txtXML` True Vertical
TextBox	Name Multiline ReadOnly ScrollBars	`txtCheckResult` True True Vertical
Button	Text Name	Submit Order `cmdSubmit`
Button	Text Name	Check Order Status `cmdStatus`
GroupBox	Text	Type
RadioButton	Text Name	Order `rbOrder`
RadioButton	Text Name	Special Order `rbSpecialOrder`

Just in case you're wondering why `txtCheckResult` is a read-only textbox, our intention is that it should resemble a label. The explanation is simple. After submitting an order document, any error message we receive will be displayed here. These error messages are read-only. They may also be quite lengthy – a characteristic that suggests a multi-line feature. Unfortunately a label control lacks a multi-line feature, so we use a textbox control instead.

Adding the Code

Now open the View Code pane, so that we can start adding the necessary implementation code to the application. Start by changing the name of the form class from `Form1` to `frmMain`, and adding the following `Imports` instructions and variable declaration:

```
Imports System.Xml
'Imports ReceiveDocument.Receive

Public Class frmMain
    Inherits System.Windows.Forms.Form
    'Dim m_DocReceive As ReceiveDocument.Receive

    Windows Form Designer generated code
```

Note that the lines referring to the `ReceiveDocument.Receive` class have been commented out. This is because we have not yet built the `ReceiveDocument` application, so we can't reference it yet! By commenting these lines out, we'll be able to test our `TestHarness`'s ability to load and read XML order documents; and later, when we've built the `ReceiveDocument` application, we'll return to the `TestHarness` code and complete its implementation by adding the `ReceiveDocument.Receive` class references.

The Radio Button Change Handlers

After the Windows Form Designer generated code, place the following methods, which handle a change in the radio buttons on the form:

```
    Private Sub rbSpecialOrder_CheckedChanged( _
        ByVal sender As System.Object, ByVal e As System.EventArgs) _
                                Handles rbSpecialOrder.CheckedChanged
    LoadXML()
End Sub

    Private Sub rbOrder_CheckedChanged( _
        ByVal sender As System.Object, ByVal e As System.EventArgs) _
                                Handles rbOrder.CheckedChanged
    LoadXML()
End Sub
```

The radio buttons are used to determine which of the two order documents will be loaded into the big textbox, `txtCheckResult`. In a moment we will add code to make sure that `rbSpecialOrder` is selected by default, thereby loading `SpecialOrder.xml` when the application starts up.

The LoadXML() Method

The workhorse of our test harness, the `LoadXML()` method, picks up one of the two test versions of the order XML documents and then places its string representation into `txtXML`:

```
Private Sub LoadXML()
  Dim objXML As XmlTextReader
  With txtXML
    .Text = "<?xml version='1.0'?>" & vbCrLf
    If rbSpecialOrder.Checked Then
      .Text &= "<!DOCTYPE SpecialOrder SYSTEM 'SpecialOrder.dtd'>" & _
                                         vbCrLf
      objXML = New XmlTextReader( _
                     Environment.CurrentDirectory & "\SpecialOrder.xml")
    Else
      objXML = New XmlTextReader( _
                       Environment.CurrentDirectory & "\Order.xml")
    End If
    While objXML.Read
      .Text &= objXML.ReadOuterXml
    End While
    .Focus()
    .Select(0, 0)
  End With
  txtCheckResult.Text = ""
  lblSubmitResult.Text = ""
End Sub
```

The Button Click Handlers

The command buttons' click events initiate communications with NOP. The cmdSubmit_Click routine pushes an order's string-formatted XML data to ReceiveDocument. The cmdStatus_Click routine retrieves information about how the submitted order fares in ReceiveDocument:

```
Private Sub cmdSubmit_Click( _
      ByVal sender As System.Object, ByVal e As System.EventArgs) _
                                         Handles cmdSubmit.Click
  txtCheckResult.Text = ""
  lblSubmitResult.Text = ""
  'lblSubmitResult.Text = m_DocReceive.Persist(txtXML.Text)
End Sub
```

```
Private Sub cmdStatus_Click( _
      ByVal sender As System.Object, ByVal e As System.EventArgs) _
                                         Handles cmdStatus.Click
  txtCheckResult.Text = ""
  'txtCheckResult.Text = m_DocReceive.GetStatus(lblSubmitResult.Text)
End Sub
```

```
End Class
```

Again, we'll comment out the m_DocReceive.Persist() method calls for now, since we still don't have a reference to the underlying ReceiveDocument.Receive class. We'll return to the application to reinstate these lines of code later.

The Initialization Routine (and an Implementation of Singleton)

Finally, inside the `New()` method that hides inside the designer-generated code region, add the following code before `End Sub`. This code sets the `rbSpecialOrder` radio button to be checked when the application loads. It also loads `txtXML` with data for a "special order" and gets a reference to `ReceiveDocument`:

```
'Add any initialization after the InitializeComponent() call
rbSpecialOrder.Checked = True
cmdSubmit.Focus()
'm_DocReceive = ReceiveDocument.Receive.GetInstance
```

Did this last line of code appear a little unusual? It should have, because we instantiated the `ReceiveDocument.Receive` class in an unusual fashion. We avoided the more typical call to the `New()` constructor method with a custom method entitled `GetInstance()`. The explanation is quite simple – `ReceiveDocument.Receive` implements the Singleton design pattern.

As we described in Chapter 1, the Singleton pattern allows only one instance of the subject class to be created. It accomplishes this by modifying its default constructor from `Public` to `Private`. And with that one alteration only another public method within the class can deliver an instance of the same class. In our case, the static method `GetInstance()` holds the keys to the kingdom.

*Note that only a class's **static** methods can be called when the class is not instantiated.*

The XML Documents

The last step for making `TestHarness` operational is to place the two XML documents referenced in the `LoadXML()` method (`SpecialOrder.xml` and `Order.xml`) and their associated validation documents in the **\TestHarness\Bin** folder. (We can retrieve the folder name using the method `Environment.CurrentDirectory()`.) If the validation documents, `SpecialOrder.dtd` or `Order.xsd`, are not dropped into the **\TestHarness\Bin** folder too, any attempt to read their associated XML documents will result in an ugly error.

*If you are unfamiliar with XML programming, it may prove to be a bit frustrating at first. For example, in our code above, despite including the required validation documents, the XML documents were not **fully** validated on loading. As we will see later, that requires an entirely different step!*

Building and Running the TestHarness Application

There's just one last thing to do: in the **TestHarness** project's properties, ensure that the **Startup** object is set to **frmMain**. Now, if you've followed all the steps, you should be almost ready to build the `TestHarness` application.

Once you've built it, you should be able to use it to load either the "Order" or "SpecialOrder" XML documents (as a string) into the `txtXML` textbox control by clicking one of the radio buttons. While you're testing the application, you may notice that `txtXML` accepts user edits and changes. This feature will eventually allow us to "break" the order for NOP testing and debugging purposes. (That's what this application is for, right?)

*The two sample test XML documents (`Order.xml` and `SpecialOrder.xml`) can be found in the **\TestHarness\bin** folder. If you move them elsewhere, don't forget to grab their soulmates (`Order.xsd` and `SpecialOrder.dtd`), too!*

A Note about the ReceiveDocument.Receive Class Method Calls

There's one last "gotcha" that you might want to keep in mind for when we've created `ReceiveDocument` and we are ready to test. At that time, we not only need to reinstate the commented-out code; we also need to add a reference to the `ReceiveDocument` application. You will know if you forgot this last detail if your uncommented code looks similar to that below:

This is the kind of situation in which it's useful to use the VS.NET IDE's **Task List** feature. Bring up the **Task List** pane (*Ctrl+Alt+K*) and right-click on it to change the filter to **All**. Now right-click on each of the four commented-out lines that refer to the `ReceiveDocument.Receive` class, and select **Add Task List Shortcut**. This will add four tasks to your task list, like this:

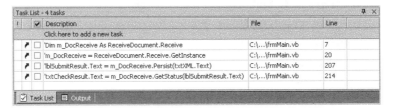

You now have a nice reminder of what to fix patiently awaiting your attention!

The Middle Tier

We are now ready to build Northwind Order Processing (NOP). As soon as its first component, `ReceiveDocument`, begins to take shape, we will be able to start putting our `TestHarness` to work! And when `ReceiveDocument` looks viable, we can then build the "business brains" of our application – the `ProcessDocument` component.

The ReceiveDocument Application

NOP must thrive reliably in a fast-paced Internet environment, and as we've discussed, this suggests a need for the Store and Forward (SaF) pattern. `ReceiveDocument` constitutes the solution to this problem. In effect it is the "plumbing" code for NOP. While `ReceiveDocument` will ultimately send all order documents to `ProcessDocument`, it accomplishes two goals before that handover:

❑ First, order documents are temporarily placed into a local queue. As soon as that is accomplished, it returns document identification to the client. Since this process occurs promptly, the end user experiences a minimal response time to their HTTP-based request.

❑ Second, almost as quickly as the client gets their response, document processing is initiated. During the processing the client can request status messages for this recently submitted order. And when document processing is completed, the client can receive the "official" order identification via the same status messaging feature.

The application contains three significant classes: `QueueManager`, `Receive`, and `Pickup`. I suspect most readers will guess what `QueueManager` does – it creates and provides a reference to a queue. The functions of the other two classes may not be so obvious. Between them they manage the two parts of the Store and Forward pattern: `Receive` manages the "store" part, and `Pickup` manages the "forward" part.

For those who like to read the end of the story first, here is a snapshot of how the `ReceiveDocument` application's **Solution Explorer** should end up:

The QueueManager Class

The `QueueManager` class provides us with one more bit of infrastructure (well, sort of), by performing a role that is vital to the implementation of our Store and Forward pattern. Not only does it return a reference to the queue in which inbound messages are temporarily persisted; if necessary, it also creates the queue.

After creating the **ReceiveDocument** project (a VB.NET Class Library project) to the VS.NET solution, remove the default class file (**Class1.vb**) and add a new class file called **QueueManager.vb**. To the **ReceiveDocument** project you will need to add a reference to the Microsoft messaging component (**System.Messaging.dll**) as shown below:

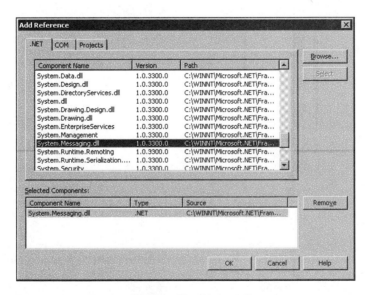

Finally before we start coding the class itself, we'll add the following `Imports` statements (which will help us to keep the object references short):

```
Imports System.Messaging
Imports System.Threading
```

OK, let's get started. The first thing to notice is that we change the class modifier from `Public` to `Friend`, to keep the riff-raff from using the `QueueManager`. Of course, if we had left `QueueManager` public our application would not crash if misused (hopefully). But experienced object-oriented developers might get confused. They expect `Public` classes to be available for public consumption:

```
Friend Class QueueManager
    Private Const QUEUE_NAME As String = "InboundDocuments"
```

The beauty of a centralized queue manager shows up immediately. While we called our queue `InboundDocuments`, you could use any other name here without breaking anything.

The .NET Common Language Runtime (CLR) exposes a wide variety of thread-locking mechanisms. We're not *obliged* to use a `Mutex` object here, but I find it more flexible than VB.NET's `SyncLock` method and easier to work with than `Monitor` objects:

```
Private Shared m_Mutex As New Mutex()
```

It is interesting to note, though, that as we discuss patterns, details such as a language's thread locking and synchronization methods are not too important.

The class has a single method, `GetQueue()`. Note the `m_Mutex.WaitOne()` call here – we'll discuss what the `Mutex` is doing in a moment:

```
Public Shared Function GetQueue() As MessageQueue
    Dim msgQueue As MessageQueue
    Dim msgQueueName As String = ".\private$\" & QUEUE_NAME
    m_Mutex.WaitOne()
```

If we do not have a queue, we'd better create one. We'll use an `If` clause for this:

```
If Not MessageQueue.Exists(msgQueueName) Then
  Try
    msgQueue = MessageQueue.Create(msgQueueName, True)
  Catch e As Exception
    Throw New Exception("Unable to create the " & _
                              QUEUE_NAME & " queue", e)
  Finally
    m_Mutex.ReleaseMutex()
  End Try
```

Setting the second parameter of `MessageQueue.Create()` to `True` creates a transactional queue, rather than the default non-transactional one. When the time comes to process order documents, this queue property will help improve the application's reliability. The feature supports some cool transactional things, such as committing or rolling back retrieved messages. For example, let's say we picked up a message for processing and the process failed. We can automatically put the message back in the queue with a simple abort command.

If the queue already exists, then we use it as follows:

```
      Else
        Try
          msgQueue = New MessageQueue(msgQueueName)
        Catch e As Exception
          Throw New Exception("Unable to access the " & _
                               QUEUE_NAME & " queue", e)
        Finally
          m_Mutex.ReleaseMutex()
        End Try
      End If
      Return msgQueue
    End Function
  End Class
```

The use of the `Mutex` object precludes a significant problem that would otherwise come into play in a multithreaded application such as `ReceiveDocument`. To understand this problem, consider what would happen if two threads both reach the following line of code before the queue `msgQueueName` is available or created:

```
      If Not MessageQueue.Exists(msgQueueName) Then
```

Not surprisingly, in this scenario there would be two efforts to create the same message queue – and this is a behavior that we want to avoid! By locking things up temporarily (via the m_Mutex.WaitOne() method call), we prevent that problem. If you're worried about the performance hit associated with such an approach, note that we avoid that issue by maintaining a reference to this queue in our `ReceiveDocument.Receive` object. This avoids the need to make locking calls to check whether or not the queue exists.

The Receive Class

The `Receive` class gets the ball rolling as far as the presentation tier is concerned. However, it operates in a slightly unusual fashion. Clients cannot instantiate it directly, because `Receive` is designed as a Singleton class. If you're new to design patterns then this paradigm may strike you as strange; however, it provides the application with some significant advantages:

❑   First, clients will not most likely have to wait for an instantiation process with every call. Once a singleton is instantiated, it becomes available to any and all callers. As we saw in Chapter 1, it accomplishes this feat by disallowing arbitrary clients from instantiating it via the default constructor. If a client requests a singleton object, they must acquire it by calling some cleverly-named public method like `GetInstance()`. That method will return a reference to the instantiated singleton object.

This arrangement also absolves the caller from worries relating to instantiation issues. The singleton itself figures out the complexities of instantiation, before returning a reference to itself. In other words, the Singleton pattern even abstracts away any creation woes from the caller. And it does so with minimal cost – the caller only needs to know that magic method that we called `GetInstance()` instead of the default `New()` constructor method.

❑   Second, access to and usage of the application's underlying resources can be optimized. In a moment we will see an excellent example of this feature as we work with a message queue object.

Let's build the `Receive` class. We'll create a new class file, `Receive.vb`, and start to add the following code:

```
Imports System.Messaging
Imports System.Threading
Imports System.Data.SqlClient

Public Class Receive
  Private Const CONNECT_STRING As String _
          = "server=LocalHost;uid=DocWrox;database=NWindOrderStatus"
```

If your SQL Server instance is not hosted on your LocalHost *machine, then you may need to change the* server *attribute here to reflect that. The* uid *and* database *(DocWrox and NWindOrderStatus) were created by the* Create-NWindOrderStatus-Database.sql *script that we ran earlier (in the SQL Server setup section) – you shouldn't need to change those attributes unless you also changed* Create-NWindOrderStatus-Database.sql.

There are three more private member objects that we'll need:

```
Private Shared m_Instance As Receive
Private Shared m_MsgQueue As MessageQueue
'Private m_Pickup As New Pickup()
```

There are a couple of points here. First, in creating m_MsgQueue, we begin the demonstration of how a Singleton pattern helps resource management. We will ultimately set it to a queue once and only once – when we instantiate the Receive object. This minimizes the negative performance impact that we incur by using a Mutex in QueueManager.

Second, note that later on we will need the reference to the Pickup class, but we haven't built that class yet – so for testing purposes we will comment out this line for now. (Again, you could add a task to your **Task List** to remind yourself that we need to return to this!)

The GetInstance() method works in combination with the m_Instance shared variable to provide instances of Receive:

```
Public Shared Function GetInstance() As Receive
  If m_Instance Is Nothing Then
    m_Instance = New Receive()
    m_MsgQueue = QueueManager.GetQueue
  End If
  Return m_Instance
End Function
```

The class needs a New() constructor, but we will set it to Private. If we failed to restrict access to the default constructor, we could bet our lunch money someone will call it! That would nullify our efforts to create a more efficient Receive class:

```
Private Sub New()
End Sub
```

The Persist() method delegates most of its work to two other key methods. The first method, SendMessage(), we will look at shortly. The other temporarily commented one, the Execute() method of the Pickup class, will ultimately contribute significantly to the client's perception of NOP's performance:

```
Public Function Persist(ByVal xmlText As String) As String
  Dim docID As String
  Try
    docID = SendMessage(xmlText)
  Catch e As Exception
    Throw New Exception("Unable to receive document", e)
  End Try
  'm_Pickup.Execute(docID)
  Return docID
End Function
```

Note that in this method, docID is not just another pretty return string. It provides a reference to the client for checking the status of their submitted order documents. Since NOP *doesn't* complete processing before it sends a response, there needs to be a mechanism that allows clients to get information about their submitted orders. In our application, we use "status" messages to provide this service. The following information flow diagram summarizes this process:

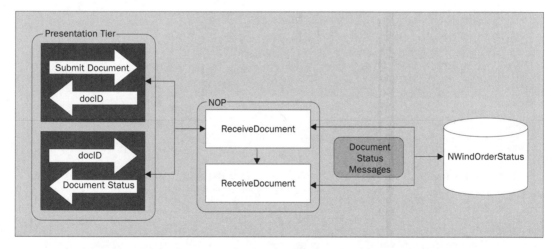

We use a fairly simple but effective method to generate the docID.

The message queue assigns a unique value to each successfully received message (or, in our case, successfully received document). We'll use this identification number for our docID. This identification number possesses another nice feature, aside from uniqueness: embedded within it is a GUID reference to the machine that houses the queue.

> *The value of a reference to a specific machine is really enhanced once NOP is placed on several web servers. Then, if one of these servers breaks down, it's easy for an administrator to check the document status log and see which items were left in limbo. (We could write another application to help manage "lost" messages, but that's another book...)*

We'll take a look at the private SendMessage() method in a moment, but first let's complete the list of public methods by putting down the code for GetStatus(). The GetStatus() method responds to end user requests for information about a specific, recently submitted order. It utilizes basic ADO.NET tools and we will not spend too much time discussing them:

```
Public Function GetStatus(ByVal docID As String) As String
  Dim result As String
  Dim sql As String
  Dim cn As SqlConnection
  Dim cmd As SqlCommand
  Dim param As SqlParameter

  sql = "SELECT TOP 1 Status FROM DocumentStatus"
  sql &= " WHERE DocumentID='" & docID & "'"
  sql &= " ORDER BY StatusID DESC"

  Try
    cn = New SqlConnection(CONNECT_STRING)
    cmd = New SqlCommand()
    With cmd
      .CommandType = CommandType.Text
      .CommandText = sql
      .Connection = cn
    End With
    cn.Open()
    result = CStr(cmd.ExecuteScalar())
    If result Is Nothing Then
      result = "Pending"
    End If
    Return result
  Catch e As Exception
    Throw New Exception("Unable to retrieve status for DocID = " & _
                                              docID, e)
  Finally
    cn.Close()
  End Try
End Function
```

With the public methods out of the way, it's time to look at the heart of the Receive class – the SendMessage() method. It is all about one thing – getting our recently received XML order data into the InboundDocuments queue:

```
Private Function SendMessage(ByVal xmlText As String) As String
  Dim docID As String
  Dim msgDoc As New Message()
  Dim msqTrx As New MessageQueueTransaction()
```

Since we created the InboundDocuments queue as transactional, we need the supporting MSMQ transaction object to send messages. Later on we will harvest the benefits of this additional work.

> *Transactional MSMQ queues are not all the same. In our case, the transaction attribute implies an internal MSMQ-specific transaction. It is not the same type of transaction associated with COM+ Services.*

The first thing to do here is set the properties of the message:

```
With msgDoc
  .Label = Now.ToUniversalTime.ToString
  .Formatter = New BinaryMessageFormatter()
  .Recoverable = True
  .Body = xmlText
End With
```

Setting the message's recoverable property to `True` adds another layer of reliability to our application. It forces MSMQ to persist the message to disk immediately, rather than keeping it temporarily cached in memory until a good moment comes along to flush it to disk. While this feature potentially slows MSMQ a little, it also prevents a crashed web server from losing any messages!

Now we can attempt to send the message:

```
    Try
       msqTrx.Begin()
       m_MsgQueue.Send(msgDoc, msqTrx)
       docID = msgDoc.Id
       msqTrx.Commit()
    Catch e As Exception
       msqTrx.Abort()
       Throw New Exception( _
                 "Unable to send message to the " & m_MsgQueue.QueueName & _
                 " queue", e)
    Finally
       m_MsgQueue.Close()
    End Try
    Return docID
  End Function

  End Class
```

Testing the Receive Class

We can perform some serious testing via the `TestHarness` application. In order to do that, we must first make a few simple modifications to it:

❏   First, remove the comment quotes on the four lines that alluded to `ReceiveDocument` and `Receive`.

❏   Next, add a reference to the `ReceiveDocument` application:

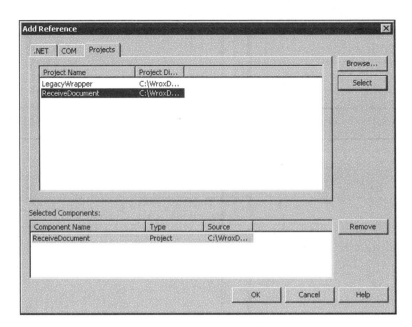

❑　Finally, if you added those four tasks to your Task List, you can remove them now – they have fulfilled their purpose!

After completing these tasks we are ready to rebuild the TestHarness application and use it to submit a few test orders. After submitting some orders, check your Computer Management MMC. If ReceiveDocument executed without any errors, your MMC should resemble the following screenshot. In the sample below, two order messages sit patiently in the inbounddocuments queue:

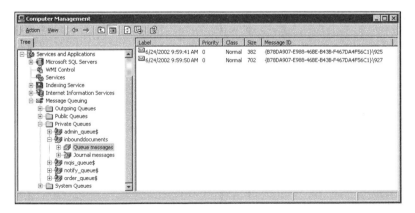

The Pickup Class

The application's last remaining class, Pickup, undertakes another simple responsibility – kicking off a thread that ultimately processes the order currently ensconced in the InboundDocuments queue. Nonetheless, it does so with a degree of panache that fulfills the "Forward" requirement of the Store and Forward design pattern. The magic of threading and transactional queues makes it happen.

We can see where the `Pickup` class comes to the fore, by walking through `ReceiveDocument`'s sequence diagram:

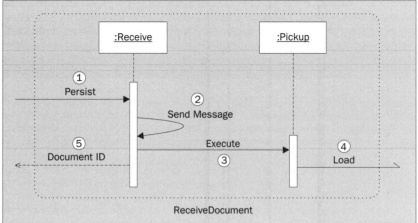

1. **Persist**. Order document is received from the presentation tier (`TestHarness`).

2. **Send Message**. Order document is placed in the `InboundDocuments` queue.

At this stage, the "store" portion of SaF is completed. `Pickup` initiates the "forward" part:

3. **Execute**. Order document is prepared for handoff to the `ProcessDocument` application. This involves wrapping it in a utility class (`PickupAndProcess`) that can be passed inside of a thread.

4. **Load**. `PickAndProcess` object is sent to `ProcessDocument` (via a thread).

With `Pickup`'s processing completed, we go back to `Receive` so it can send the client a response:

5. **Document ID**. After Step 4 has kicked off, the client is sent a reference to their submitted Order document for future status queries.

OK, let's build the `Pickup` class now. Add a new class file, `Pickup.vb`, to the `ReceiveDocument` project. Then, add the following `Import` statements to the file:

```
Imports System.Threading
Imports System.Messaging
'Imports ProcessDocument.OrderManager
```

Once again, we're commenting out the last of these `Import` statements because we haven't built the `ProcessDocument` application yet. We'll return to this code to instate this line once the `ProcessDocument` application is complete; meantime, you might want to add a task to your Task List as a reminder of this.

Now let's move onto the class itself. We'll modify the class to `Friend`. As we discussed earlier, this modification helps ensure that other developers using this application do not accidentally call the `Receive` class:

```
Friend Class Pickup
```

Now here's the `Execute()` method:

```
Public Sub Execute(ByVal docID As String)
  Dim thread As Thread

  thread = New Thread(AddressOf New PickupAndProcess(docID).Execute)
  With thread
    .IsBackground = False
    .Start()
  End With
End Sub
```

By setting the thread's `IsBackground` property to `False`, we prevent it from dying prematurely in the event of the untimely death of a parent thread. Thus, if `ReceiveDocument` encounters severe difficulties, `ProcessDocument` may still complete its task. With a simple line of code we further enhanced NOP's reliability!

The `Execute()` method ultimately initiates the all-important `ProcessDocument`, our yet-to-be-built order processing application, via a .NET thread object.

We're paying particular attention to how we created this thread object, ensuring each thread "keeps to itself" throughout its lifetime. (The last thing we need is for an instance of one `ProcessDocument` to get mixed up with another instance!) We accomplish this feat by including an inner class within `Pickup` that is instantiated with each new thread.

Inner classes are another one of those cool object-oriented features .NET provided for Visual Basic developers. By placing an entire class inside of another class and modifying its accessor to `Private`, only that outer class can instantiate it. This feature comes in handy when developers need a specialized class that only the outer knows about – like in our case!

The heart of the `Pickup` class lies buried deep within its inner class, `PickupAndProcess`. Aside from housing the necessary state data (`docID`), it contains the real `Execute` method:

```
Private Class PickupAndProcess

  Dim m_DocID As String

  Sub New(ByVal docID As String)
    m_DocID = docID
  End Sub

  Sub Execute()
    Dim xmlText As String
    Dim msgQueue As MessageQueue
    Dim msgDoc As New Message()
```

```
      Dim msqTrx As New MessageQueueTransaction()
      'Dim manageOrder As New ProcessDocument.OrderManager()

      msgQueue = QueueManager.GetQueue
      msgQueue.Formatter = New BinaryMessageFormatter()
      Try
        msqTrx.Begin()
        msgDoc = msgQueue.ReceiveById(m_DocID, msqTrx)
        xmlText = CStr(msgDoc.Body)
        'manageOrder.Load(m_DocID, xmlText)
        msqTrx.Commit()
      Catch
        msqTrx.Abort()
      Finally
        msgQueue.Close()
      End Try
    End Sub

  End Class
```

The above `Try...Catch` makes the dream of reliability come true in NOP. With the assistance of our transactional queue we are able to ensure the safety of our original order in the event of a mishap within the `ProcessDocument` application. For example, if `ProcessDocument` fails for some reason, the source order returns to the queue via the `msgTrx.Abort` method. Otherwise, if all goes well, the queue happily gives up the message via `msgTrx.Commit`.

One last noteworthy point about the `Execute()` method – it does not return any values and the thread calling it does not wait for any news to come back. This behavior allows NOP to quickly return the required synchronous HTTP response to end users without waiting for the potentially time-consuming `manageOrder.Load` to finish.

If you're building the application for yourself as you step through this chapter, and you're feeling adventurous, you could take a break now and test your work. Note that in this test scenario, if everything works OK the inbounddocuments queue will be empty. Don't forget to either delete the queue or purge the messages – otherwise, the earlier message will still be sitting there in the queue.

The ProcessDocument Application

The client test utility, `TestHarness`, and the "Store and Forward" application, `ReceiveDocument`, are done. It is now finally time to build NOP's brains – the `ProcessDocument` class library. And while there are quite a few classes inside this application, they are easily categorized by function. At the highest level they either process documents or manage processing.

While we have already seen much of the class diagrams for this application, a quick peek at the application's eventual references and files may be instructive:

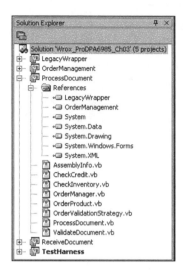

To begin the process of building this application, add a new VB class library project called ProcessDocument to the solution. Don't forget to add the necessary application references, as shown under the References node in the above screenshot. (Unfortunately, one of them, the OrderManagement application, remains a twinkle in our eye; we'll omit that one for now and return to add it later.)

Document Processing with the Decorator Pattern

There are several classes that take part in processing a document, as the class view right amply demonstrates. Nonetheless, processing is coordinated via a single Decorator pattern! In our application, create a class file called ProcessDocument.vb – this will contain most of those interfaces and classes that make up the skeleton of the Decorator. The remaining classes implement the different business rules as discussed in the *Business Rules* section, later in this chapter.

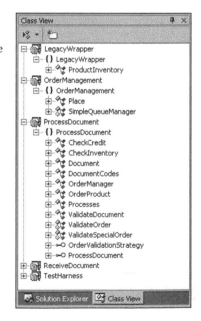

Before diving into the class definitions in `ProcessDocument.vb`, let's add some useful `Import` statements. There are few new ones this time around – `System.IO` and `System.Xml.Schema`. The `IO` class helps when we are manipulating the XML string-formatted data via the `StringReader` class, while `XML.Schema` assists with XML document validation:

```
Imports System.IO
Imports System.Xml
Imports System.Xml.Schema
```

Now let's get onto the class definitions. There will be three classes and an interface in `ProcessDocument.vb` – `ProcessDocument`, `Document`, `Processes`, and `DocumentRoles`.

Some readers may find it disconcerting to put all these classes into a single file. It is certainly hard to argue with the logic of simplicity – one class, one file. Nonetheless, I feel that putting all of the Decorator pattern's "fixed" code in one file is extremely logical. If you disagree, feel free to put 'em anywhere you like!

The ProcessDocument Interface

Since the `ProcessDocument` interface sets the Decorator's rules for all constituent classes, that's a great place to start. These methods and properties were discussed in greater depth in our earlier discussion about NOP's class diagrams:

```
Public Interface ProcessDocument
    Sub Load(ByVal docType As DocumentCodes.Type, _
             ByVal docID As String, ByVal xmlText As String)
    ReadOnly Property DocID() As String
    ReadOnly Property DocXML() As XmlDocument
    Property DocType() As DocumentCodes.Type
    Property DocStatus() As DocumentCodes.Status
    Property DocErrors() As String
End Interface
```

The Document Class (the Decorator Pattern's Concrete Class)

The `Document` class implements these rules. It is the "concrete" class of the decorator for good reason – it manufactures the object that the other class decorates. Let's step through its implementation:

```
Public Class Document : Implements ProcessDocument

    Private m_DocType As DocumentCodes.Type = DocumentCodes.Type.Unknown
    Private m_DocStatus As DocumentCodes.Status = _
                                    DocumentCodes.Status.Processing
    Private m_DocErrors As String
    Private m_DocID As String
    Private m_Xml As New XmlDocument()
```

The `DocumentCode.Type` and `DocumentCodes.Status` enumerations reside in a helper class entitled `DocumentCodes`, which we will visit shortly.

While most of the following routines work as simply as they appear, the `Load()` method kicks off the critical task of sucking up the string formatted XML order document into the application as a certified .NET `XMLDocument` object:

```
Public Sub Load(ByVal docType As DocumentCodes.Type, _
                ByVal docID As String, ByVal xmlText As String) _
                                    Implements ProcessDocument.Load
   m_DocType = docType
   m_DocID = docID
   LoadXMLDoc(xmlText)
End Sub

Public ReadOnly Property DocID() As String _
                                    Implements ProcessDocument.DocID
   Get
      Return m_DocID
   End Get
End Property

Public ReadOnly Property DocXML() As XmlDocument _
                                    Implements ProcessDocument.DocXML
   Get
      Return m_Xml
   End Get
End Property

Public Property DocType() As DocumentCodes.Type _
                                    Implements ProcessDocument.DocType
   Get
      Return m_DocType
   End Get
   Set(ByVal Value As DocumentCodes.Type)
      If m_DocType = DocumentCodes.Type.Unknown Then
         m_DocType = Value
      End If
   End Set
End Property
```

The `DocStatus` and `DocErrors` properties (which follow in a moment) work in combination to ensure that a "broken" document does not subsequently get "fixed". This type of error is particularly endemic of Decorator patterns. This becomes apparent when we consider how a "basic" Decorator pattern manipulates the concrete class:

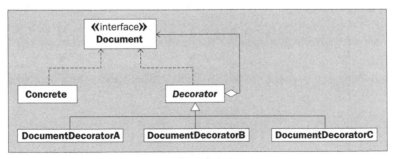

In the diagram above, suppose the *Concrete* class creates a docX object. *DocumentDecoratorA* then works on docX, followed by *DocumentDecoratorB*, and *DocumentDecoratorC*. Suppose you wrote an application based on this pattern – despite the obvious possibility that any of these classes could break docX, this wouldn't worry you. (You just wrote them!) But suppose that, after a few months, another developer comes along and adds a new *DocumentDecoratorD* class.

Suppose further that the *DocumentDecoratorD* developer did not really understand your brilliant application, and that his new class can validate a docX property that *DocumentDecoratorB* occasionally invalidates. The application would then sometimes validate a docX object when it is actually invalid. As a result, the application would be broken.

If the *Concrete* class had included an irreversible flag in docX, then this sad tragedy could have been avoided. For once *DocumentDecoratorB* invalidated docX, *DocumentDecoratorD* could not undo this fact. So, there is a moral to this story. Namely, an irreversible flag (or similar safeguard) is highly recommended with a Decorator, since too many classes have access to the underlying concrete object.

Here's the implementation of the `DocStatus` property:

```
Public Property DocStatus() As DocumentCodes.Status _
                              Implements ProcessDocument.DocStatus
  Get
    Return m_DocStatus
  End Get
  Set(ByVal Value As DocumentCodes.Status)
    If m_DocStatus <> DocumentCodes.Status.Errors Then
      m_DocStatus = Value
    End If
  End Set
End Property
```

And here's the `DocErrors` property:

```
Public Property DocErrors() As String _
                              Implements ProcessDocument.DocErrors
  Get
    Return m_DocErrors
  End Get
  Set(ByVal Value As String)
    m_DocErrors &= Value & vbCrLf
    If m_DocStatus <> DocumentCodes.Status.Errors Then
      m_DocStatus = DocumentCodes.Status.Errors
    End If
  End Set
End Property
```

Note that, aside from providing a way to place errors inside a `Document` object, `DocErrors` also sets the "document broken" flag. Why make a developer write two lines of code to register an error?

The private `LoadXMLDoc()` method implements `ProcessDocument`'s most important function, loading an `XMLDocument` object into the class variable `m_Xml`. Along the way it provides some helpful XML validation services:

```
Private Sub LoadXMLDoc(ByVal xmlText As String)
  Try
```

The next few lines, in conjunction with the `XMLValidationEventHandler` routine, validate the entire XML document line by line. Setting the `XMLValidator.ValidationType` as we do here keeps things simpler by making schema validation automatic – otherwise, the `ValidationType` property must be set manually (and correctly) for each document. This cool feature works well in our application given that our XML documents are not too complex and only use `XMLValidator`'s built-in validation types:

```
        Dim stringReader As _
            New StringReader(xmlText.Replace(ControlChars.Quote, "'"))

        Dim xmlReader As New XmlTextReader(stringReader)
        Dim xmlValidator As New XmlValidatingReader(xmlReader)

        xmlValidator.ValidationType = ValidationType.Auto
        AddHandler xmlValidator.ValidationEventHandler, _
                                AddressOf XMLValidationEventHandler

        While xmlValidator.Read
        End While
```

The `While...End While` loop seems worthless, but in fact it quietly reads each line of XML, firing the `XMLValidationEventHandler` whenever it discovers a validation error. (It could fire for every line in the document!) If we don't run the XML document through this loop, it will not get fully validated. Neither the .NET `XmlTextReader` nor `XmlValidatingReader` classes automatically validate documents. (In fact, `XmlTextReader` cannot validate at all!) And we sure want to take advantage of our DTDs and XSDs.

> The `While...End While` control loop works so well because of the design of the `xmlValidator.Read` method. It returns `False` when there aren't any nodes left to read.

Now, why bother loading our class's `XMLDocument` object if the validation failed? `ProcessDocument` will not be able to do its job without a valid document. So we check for errors before loading the document:

```
        If m_DocStatus <> DocumentCodes.Status.Errors Then
          m_Xml.LoadXml(xmlText)
        End If
```

Recording the errors for the client's information is the only reasonable thing left to do:

```
        Catch e As Exception
          DocErrors = e.Message
        End Try
      End Sub
```

The final method serves as `XMLValidator`'s callback, and is referenced via the `AddHandler` statement we saw a moment ago in the `DocErrors()` method. It does the actual job of placing any validation errors discovered while loading the `XMLDocument` object into a `Document` object:

```
      Public Sub XMLValidationEventHandler(ByVal sender As Object, _
                                        ByVal args As ValidationEventArgs)
        DocErrors = args.Message
      End Sub

    End Class
```

The Processes Class (the Decorator Pattern's Decorator Class)

The next class sitting on `ProcessDocument.vb` is the Decorator pattern's decorator class, `Processes`. While this class cannot be instantiated directly, it contains references to routines that its subclasses may require. All of these references are provided courtesy of a `Document` member object called m_Document:

```
Public MustInherit Class Processes : Implements ProcessDocument
   Protected m_Document As ProcessDocument
```

The class modifier, `Protected`, offers just the right amount of visibility for the decorator. It allows m_Document to be accessible only from within the `Processes` class or from its decorator subclasses.

Here's the decorator class's default constructor:

```
Public Sub New(ByRef doc As ProcessDocument)
   m_Document = doc
End Sub
```

The following methods constitute an excellent example of the powers of an object-oriented language. They exploit containment and inheritance simultaneously! For example, look at the `Load()` method. All the decorator subclasses can load an XML document and process it since they can instantiate a `Document` object via the `Processes` class. And the reason `Processes.Load()` can execute the `Document.Load()` method is because it contains a `Document` object.

```
Sub Load(ByVal docType As DocumentCodes.Type, _
         ByVal docID As String, ByVal xmlText As String) _
                                    Implements ProcessDocument.Load
   m_Document.Load(docType, docID, xmlText)
End Sub

Public ReadOnly Property DocID() As String _
                                 Implements ProcessDocument.DocID
   Get
      Return m_Document.DocID
   End Get
End Property

Public ReadOnly Property DocXML() As XmlDocument _
                                 Implements ProcessDocument.DocXML
   Get
      Return m_Document.DocXML
   End Get
End Property

Public Property DocType() As DocumentCodes.Type _
                                 Implements ProcessDocument.DocType
   Get
      Return m_Document.DocType
   End Get
   Set(ByVal Value As DocumentCodes.Type)
      m_Document.DocType = Value
   End Set
End Property
```

```
   Public Property DocStatus() As DocumentCodes.Status _
                              Implements ProcessDocument.DocStatus
      Get
         Return m_Document.DocStatus
      End Get
      Set(ByVal Value As DocumentCodes.Status)
         m_Document.DocStatus = Value
      End Set
   End Property

   Public Property DocErrors() As String _
                              Implements ProcessDocument.DocErrors
      Get
         Return m_Document.DocErrors
      End Get
      Set(ByVal Value As String)
         m_Document.DocErrors = Value
      End Set
   End Property

End Class
```

The DocumentCodes Class

The next and final class sitting in `ProcessDocument.vb` is the `DocumentCodes` class. Technically speaking, this class is not part of the Decorator pattern. Rather, it simply contains the enumerations for the `Status` and `Type` properties of a document. By putting these enumerations into a class of their own, we succeed in keeping the code more robust and well-organized.

```
Public Class DocumentCodes
   Public Enum Status
      Processing
      Errors
      Complete
   End Enum

   Public Enum Type
      Unknown
      SpecialOrder
      Order
   End Enum
End Class
```

The Business Rules

We are now ready to code with the four decorator classes (`ValidateDocument`, `CheckInventory`, `CheckCredit`, and `OrderProduct`) that mirror the key activities detailed within the Primary Activity Diagram. Together they encompass the business rules for which the Northwind Order Processing was built. Some of them will call upon the services of other applications or classes to get their "business" done. All of them are subclasses of the "decorator" class, `Processes`.

Before we get going, all of the decorator subclasses rely on .NET XML services, so do not forget the following statement on the top of each vb file!

```
Imports System.Xml
```

Implementing the Strategy Pattern: the ValidateDocument Class

By far the most complicated of our business rule classes, ValidateDocument must intelligently deal with at least two different types of order validation. This requirement was not a surprise given the two different Validation Activity diagrams. It must be flexible for two reasons:

❏ Order validation business rules are subject to a great deal of ongoing change

❏ The underlying XML documents may use different XML validation rules (DTD, XDR, XSD, etc.)

The solution to this potentially ugly design problem comes via the Strategy design pattern. It inherently provides the necessary flexibility to call (and change!) the validation code without a lot of hassle. A quick review of a portion of the ProcessDocument class diagram will help clarify this point:

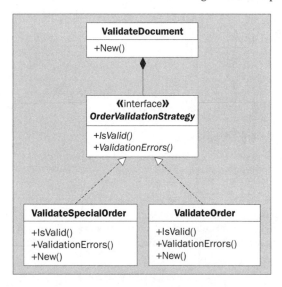

The interface, OrderValidationStrategy, provides the muscle of the Strategy pattern. It guarantees that the decorator class, ValidateDocument, does *not* need to worry about the services ValidateSpecialOrder and ValidateOrder offer. These two validation subclasses will always offer the required methods. And how they implement them is of little concern to ValidateOrder.

That ValidateOrder may remain oblivious of validation details provides a tremendous failsafe mechanism as Northwind's order processing business requirements change. Future developers may successfully break ValidateOrder or ValidateSpecialOrder, but the ProcessDocument application rests safely! (True, letting bogus orders through the system will not make some folks too happy.)

We'll start with the simplest of the depicted classes – ValidateDocument. Create a new class file, ValidateDocument.vb, and insert the following code into it:

```
Public Class ValidateDocument : Inherits Processes

  Public Sub New(ByRef doc As ProcessDocument)
    MyBase.New(doc)

    If doc.DocStatus <> DocumentCodes.Status.Errors Then
      Dim valid As OrderValidationStrategy
      Select Case doc.DocType
        Case DocumentCodes.Type.SpecialOrder
          valid = New ValidateSpecialOrder(doc.DocID, doc.DocXML)
        Case DocumentCodes.Type.Order
          valid = New ValidateOrder(doc.DocID, doc.DocXML)
      End Select

      If valid.IsValid = False Then
        doc.DocErrors = valid.ValidationErrors
      End If
    End If
  End Sub

End Class
```

The simple `Select Case` statement contains the key logic deciding which `OrderValidationStrategy` concrete order validation class is called upon. It is worth noting that if we had not implemented the Strategy pattern, this piece of decision logic code would have been huge! All of the validation code we are about to write would have been sitting in it (or in nearby methods).

The OrderValidationStrategy Interface

Any Strategy pattern's success hinges on its interface. That way, its classes stay "honest" and work without dire consequences when any of them are called upon. Our `OrderValidationStrategy` is no exception to this.

We'll create a class file called `OrderValidationStrategy.vb` file, and add the `OrderValidationStrategy` interface and the concrete strategy classes to it. The first thing to add is an `Imports` statement for the `System.Xml` namespace:

```
Imports System.Xml
```

Now, here's the `OrderValidationStrategy` interface:

```
Public Interface OrderValidationStrategy
  Function IsValid() As Boolean
  Function ValidationErrors() As String
End Interface
```

The ValidateSpecialOrder Concrete Class

With the Strategy pattern interface defined, let's write the class that validates a "Special Order" document. If you remember the Validation Activity Diagram, then what we are inspecting should be quite straightforward!

```
Friend Class ValidateSpecialOrder : Implements OrderValidationStrategy
  Dim m_IsValid As Boolean = True
  Dim m_ValidationErrors As String = ""

  Sub New(ByVal docID As String, ByVal doc As XmlDocument)
    Dim productID As Integer
    Dim price As Double
    Dim quantity As Integer
    Dim productNodes As XmlNodeList
    Try
      productNodes = doc.GetElementsByTagName("Product")
```

My first crack at writing this algorithm taught me an interesting lesson. I discovered the importance of making sure that there were some `Product` nodes to inspect! Under dubious circumstances `GetElementsByTagName("Product")` may not return anything. For this reason, we include the following check on the number of nodes:

```
If productNodes.Count = 0 Then
  m_IsValid = False
  m_ValidationErrors = "Order validation failed; " & _
                       "No product lines identified"

End If
```

With the preliminaries out of the way, it's time to start moving through the order line by line:

```
Dim i As Integer
For i = 0 To productNodes.Count - 1
```

The next test is an example of a business rule-required validation check that a DTD could not provide and an XSD could. DTDs are not very adept at checking numeric values, so we need to do the job.

```
If IsNumeric(productNodes(i).Attributes(0).Value()) Then
  productID = CInt(productNodes(i).Attributes(0).Value())
Else
  Throw New InvalidCastException("Invalid ProductID data: " & _
                    productNodes(i).Attributes(0).Value())
End If

Dim j As Integer
For j = 0 To productNodes(i).ChildNodes.Count - 1
  If productNodes(i).ChildNodes(j).Name = "Price" Then
    price = CDbl(productNodes(i).ChildNodes(j).InnerXml)
  ElseIf productNodes(i).ChildNodes(j).Name = "Quantity" Then
    quantity = CInt(productNodes(i).ChildNodes(j).InnerXml)
  End If
Next j

If productID < 0 Then
  m_IsValid = False
  m_ValidationErrors &= _
        "Unrecoginized ProductID: " & productID & vbCrLf
End If
```

```
        If price < 0 Or quantity < 0 Then
          m_IsValid = False
          m_ValidationErrors &= _
                "Negative price/quantity information submitted " & _
                "for ProductID = " & productID & vbCrLf
        End If
      Next i
    Catch e As InvalidCastException
      m_IsValid = False
      m_ValidationErrors = "Invalid product data submitted: " & e.Message
    Catch e As Exception
      Throw New Exception("Unable to validate order data for DocID = " _
                                                    & docID, e)
    End Try
  End Sub
```

Comparison between this one method and its counterpart in the ValidateOrder class (which follows) reinforces the decision to implement a Strategy pattern. The method above is really just a big algorithm for reading and testing a Special Order. The Order's version (as you'll see) does not look much different. Nonetheless, the algorithms turn out to be *sufficiently* different to justify their own class, as opposed to some gigantic and fragile Select Case statement.

Here's the rest of the ValidateSpecialOrder class:

```
    Function IsValid() As Boolean _
                        Implements OrderValidationStrategy.IsValid
      Return m_IsValid
    End Function

    Function ValidationErrors() As String _
              Implements OrderValidationStrategy.ValidationErrors
      Return m_ValidationErrors
    End Function

End Class
```

The ValidateOrder Concrete Class

The run-of-the-mill "Order" looks a lot like the "Special Order" validation class. Of course, it worries about a slightly different set of business rules. We'll highlight the differences as we go:

```
Friend Class ValidateOrder : Implements OrderValidationStrategy
  Dim m_IsValid As Boolean = True
  Dim m_ValidationErrors As String = ""

  Sub New(ByVal docID As String, ByVal doc As XmlDocument)
    Dim productID As Integer
    Dim price As Double
    Dim requiredDate As Date
    Dim productNodes As XmlNodeList
    Try
      productNodes = doc.GetElementsByTagName("Product")
      If productNodes.Count = 0 Then
        m_IsValid = False
```

```
        m_ValidationErrors = "Order validation failed; " & _
                           "No product lines identified"
    End If

    Dim i As Integer
    For i = 0 To productNodes.Count - 1
        productID = CInt(productNodes(i).Attributes(0).Value())
```

Unlike a Special Order, we did not have to verify that the productID was an Integer – the .NET XmlValidatingReader did that already!

```
        Dim j As Integer
        For j = 0 To productNodes(i).ChildNodes.Count - 1
            If productNodes(i).ChildNodes(j).Name = "Price" Then
                price = CDbl(productNodes(i).ChildNodes(j).InnerXml)
            ElseIf productNodes(i).ChildNodes(j).Name = "RequiredDate" Then
                requiredDate = CDate(productNodes(i).ChildNodes(j).InnerXml)
            End If
        Next j

        If price < 0 Then
            m_IsValid = False
            m_ValidationErrors &= _
                    "Negative price information submitted " & _
                    "for ProductID = " & productID & vbCrLf
        End If
```

Here's a validation check unique to an Order document. Special Orders do not have a RequiredDate property to contend with:

```
        If requiredDate < Now Then
            m_IsValid = False
            m_ValidationErrors &= "Invalid required due date " & _
                            "for ProductID = " & productID & vbCrLf
        End If
    Next i
    Catch e As Exception
        Throw New Exception("Unable to validate order data for DocID = " _
                                            & docID, e)

    End Try
End Sub

Function IsValid() As Boolean _
                    Implements OrderValidationStrategy.IsValid
    Return m_IsValid
End Function

Function ValidationErrors() As String _
            Implements OrderValidationStrategy.ValidationErrors
    Return m_ValidationErrors
End Function

End Class
```

The CheckInventory Class

Through .NET COM Interop services, CheckInventory makes calling upon the legacy Inventory system via the LegacyWrapper application a snap. But despite this "code saver" we still need to write code that loops through the XMLDocument. Let's create a file called CheckInventory.vb and start adding the following code:

```
Imports System.Xml
Imports System.Threading
Imports LegacyWrapper
```

Read on if you are wondering why we imported System.Threading. All will become clear. Here's the CheckInventory class:

```
Public Class CheckInventory : Inherits Processes

  Public Sub New(ByRef doc As ProcessDocument)
    MyBase.New(doc)
    If doc.DocStatus <> DocumentCodes.Status.Errors Then
      Dim productID As Integer
      Dim price As Double
      Dim quantity As Integer
      Dim productNodes As XmlNodeList

      Threading.Thread.CurrentThread.ApartmentState = ApartmentState.STA
```

Here's why we needed System.Threading. Setting the currently running thread's apartment state to STA (single-threaded apartment) may help improve performance. Since we know that the underlying COM application, the VB6-based Inventory.dll, runs as a single threaded apartment, we prevent .NET from first trying to run it within a multithreaded threaded apartment (MTA).

> *Don't bother trying to figure out why VB.NET always tries to execute a COM application in an MTA thread. I have been told by smarter folks that it just does. I suspect that the really smart folks who designed VB.NET had their reasons.*

```
      Dim m_Inventory As New LegacyWrapper.ProductInventory()
```

After creating the reference to Inventory.dll, accessing it is as simple as declaring the variable m_Inventory!

```
      Try
        productNodes = doc.DocXML.GetElementsByTagName("Product")
        If productNodes.Count = 0 Then
          doc.DocErrors = "Can not check inventory; " & _
          "no product lines identified."
        End If

        Dim i As Integer
        For i = 0 To productNodes.Count - 1
          productID = CInt(productNodes(i).Attributes(0).Value())
          Dim j As Integer
          For j = 0 To productNodes(i).ChildNodes.Count - 1
            If productNodes(i).ChildNodes(j).Name = "Price" Then
```

```
            price = CDbl(productNodes(i).ChildNodes(j).InnerXml)
        ElseIf productNodes(i).ChildNodes(j).Name = "Quantity" Then
            quantity = CInt(productNodes(i).ChildNodes(j).InnerXml)
        End If
    Next j
```

We make our first of two calls to the legacy `Inventory` application – checking whether or not the product price submitted by the customer is correct:

```
If Not m_Inventory.CheckProductPrice(productID, price) Then
    doc.DocErrors = "Product ID #" & _
                    productID.ToString & " is improperly priced."
End If
```

Now we make sure that the product is in stock!

```
        If m_Inventory.UnitsInStock(productID) < quantity Then
            doc.DocErrors = "Product ID #" & productID.ToString _
                        & " out of stock"
        End If
    Next i
    Catch e As Exception
        Throw New Exception("Unable to check inventory for DocID = " _
                                                    & DocID, e)
    End Try
  End If
End Sub
End Class
```

The CheckCredit Class

The `CheckCredit` class really is too simple. But them's the business rules…

Seriously, while I kept the business rules quite simple for this demonstration application, credit checking is an entire industry. Here we will just make sure that the order's total sales amount doesn't exceed a constant value (MAXIMUM_ORDER_TOTAL). This code goes into a new class file called `CheckCredit.vb`:

```
Imports System.Xml

Public Class CheckCredit : Inherits Processes
    'A cleverer developer would grab this value from a config file...
    Private Const MAXIMUM_ORDER_TOTAL As Double = 500D

    Public Sub New(ByRef doc As ProcessDocument)
        MyBase.New(doc)
        If doc.DocStatus <> DocumentCodes.Status.Errors Then
            Dim productID As Integer
            Dim price As Double
            Dim quantity As Integer
            Dim totalOrder As Double
            Dim productNodes As XmlNodeList
```

167

```
      Try
        productNodes = doc.DocXML.GetElementsByTagName("Product")
        If productNodes.Count = 0 Then
          doc.DocErrors = "Can not check credit; " & _
                            "no product lines identified."
        End If

        Dim i As Integer
        For i = 0 To productNodes.Count - 1
          Dim j As Integer
          For j = 0 To productNodes(i).ChildNodes.Count - 1
            If productNodes(i).ChildNodes(j).Name = "Price" Then
              price = CDbl(productNodes(i).ChildNodes(j).InnerXml)
            ElseIf productNodes(i).ChildNodes(j).Name = "Quantity" Then
              quantity = CInt(productNodes(i).ChildNodes(j).InnerXml)
            End If
          Next j
          totalOrder += price * quantity
        Next i

        If totalOrder > MAXIMUM_ORDER_TOTAL Then
          doc.DocErrors = "Total Amount of order exceeds " & _
                                    MAXIMUM_ORDER_TOTAL.ToString
        End If
      Catch e As Exception
        Throw New Exception("Unable to check credit for DocID = " _
                                          & DocID, e)
      End Try
    End If
  End Sub

End Class
```

The OrderProduct Class

If everything goes well, the OrderProduct class places an order into Northwind's order system. We'll put this code into another new class file, OrderProduct.vb.

Since the OrderManagement application to do that does not exist yet, we need to comment out its references for the moment. The OrderManagement application is responsible for actually placing orders. When we are finished with ProcessDocument, we will finally build the OrderManagement application, which is is responsible for actually placing orders. Then, we'll come back to this application and reinstate the commented-out lines:

```
'Imports OrderManagement.Place
```

Now for the class itself:

```
Public Class OrderProduct : Inherits Processes
  Dim m_OrderID As String = ""
```

As long as the other business classes did not generate any errors, the order gets placed via the Place() method call in the constructor:

```
Public Sub New(ByRef doc As ProcessDocument)
    MyBase.New(doc)
    If doc.DocStatus <> DocumentCodes.Status.Errors Then
      'Dim place As New OrderManagement.Place()
      'm_OrderID = place.NewOrder(doc.DocXML)
      If m_OrderID.Length > 0 Then
        doc.DocStatus = DocumentCodes.Status.Complete
      End If
    End If
End Sub
```

Unlike the other business rule classes, we included a method other than New(). Adding methods and properties to a Decorator pattern's derived class is not unusual. One of the reasons that it is so common is the very same reason we added a property here – we needed to obtain information from the class. In our case we wanted to make the newfound m_OrderID available outside of OrderProduct:

```
Public Function GetOrderID() As String
    Return m_OrderID
End Function

End Class
```

There are a lot of other reasons for adding additional routines to a decorator beyond public access to a variable. Remember what the Decorator aims to accomplish – attaching additional responsibilities. And if you add additional responsibilities to a class, you will most likely need to give clients access to them.

The Processing Manager – the OrderManager Class

The "processing manager" classes worry about one thing – managing how documents are processed. That essentially translates into how the different decorators' derived classes are applied, if at all! This function becomes critical when utilizing the Decorator design pattern since the pattern by its very nature offers a wide variety of processing options. For example, a regular "Order" passes through the CheckCredit class, while "Special Order" documents do not.

The official GoF Decorator pattern does not mandate a "managing class". Nonetheless, I have learned through experience that using one prevents misuse of a decorator's derived classes.

Since our application worries about orders, we only need one of these specialized classes – OrderManager. Some readers may question why we bother with an OrderManager class. Couldn't we just bury the code that builds the appropriate decorators somewhere else? Of course we could. But doing so limits the ease of updating NOP. For example, suppose Northwind decides to allow customers to place order inquiries and cancellations. Where would the developer responsible for implementing these features begin? Maybe check the client code? How about the decorator? If the decorator, where? Will I break any other applications when I add the new derived classes supporting the additional responsibilities?

Like a good manager, our "processing manager" class keeps everyone informed. It accomplishes this with the same status message system we discussed earlier. Placing the code responsible for inserting status messages in the NWindOrderStatus database in OrderManager offers another advantage – it does not "pollute" the business rules classes with unrelated activity.

Create another new class file, called **OrderManager.vb**, to the **ProcessDocument** application. Now we can start to add code to it. First, here is the single `Imports` statement we'll need:

```
Imports System.Data.SqlClient
```

Now here's the `OrderManager` class. Again, if your SQL Server instance is not hosted on your `LocalHost` machine, then you may need to change the `server` attribute here to reflect that:

```
Public Class OrderManager
    Private Const CONNECT_STRING As String _
            = "server=LocalHost;uid=DocWrox;database=NWindOrderStatus"
```

Here's the class's `Load()` method. Its first call to `SetStatus()` allows the curious customer to find out that their submitted order is being processed:

```
Public Sub Load(ByVal docID As String, ByVal xmlText As String)
    Dim tagOpen As Long
    Dim tagClose As Long
    Dim statusField As String
    Dim docType As String
    Dim order As OrderProduct

    SetStatus(docID, Now.ToString & " Processing")
```

Instantiating `doc`, the decorator's concrete object, starts the ball rolling! Then we use the `If...ElseIf...Else...End If` clause to decide how to decorate `doc`. Remember that NOP possesses two different order types, which require slightly different processing by the same components:

```
Dim doc As New Document()
If InStr(xmlText, "SpecialOrder.dtd") > 0 Then
  doc.Load(DocumentCodes.Type.SpecialOrder, docID, xmlText)
  order = New OrderProduct(New CheckInventory( _
                                 New ValidateDocument(doc)))

ElseIf InStr(xmlText, "Order.xsd") > 0 Then
  doc.Load(DocumentCodes.Type.Order, docID, xmlText)
  order = New OrderProduct(New CheckCredit( _
            New CheckInventory(New ValidateDocument(doc))))

Else
  Throw New Exception("Unknown document type of " & _
  docType & " for DocID = " & docID)
End If
```

There are a lot of ways to decide what XML document is being sent to NOP. Using the document's referenced validation schema though does have an advantage. It *almost* guarantees that inbound XML documents are routed appropriately. We could improve these odds for XSD documents by searching for a fully qualified URI, such as http://NorthwindTraders.com/Order.xsd:

```
    Select Case order.DocStatus
      Case DocumentCodes.Status.Errors
        statusField = Now.ToString & " Errors: " & vbCrLf & _
                                              order.DocErrors()
      Case DocumentCodes.Status.Complete
        statusField = "Order ID: " & order.GetOrderID
      Case Else
        statusField = Now.ToString & " Processing Incomplete"
    End Select
    statusField = statusField.Replace("'", "")
```

Our last call to SetStatus() hopefully contains good news – a submitted order's OrderID, for the curious customer:

```
    SetStatus(docID, statusField)
  End Sub
```

And here is the SetStatus() method:

```
  Private Sub SetStatus(ByVal docID As String, ByVal Status As String)
    Dim sql As String
    Dim cn As SqlConnection
    Dim cmd As SqlCommand
    Dim param As SqlParameter

    sql = "INSERT DocumentStatus (DocumentID, Status) VALUES("
    sql &= "'" & docID & "'"
    sql &= ", "
    sql &= "'" & Status & "'"
    sql &= ")"

    Try
      cn = New SqlConnection(CONNECT_STRING)
      cmd = New SqlCommand()
      With cmd
        .CommandType = CommandType.Text
        .CommandText = sql
        .Connection = cn
      End With

      cn.Open()
      cmd.ExecuteNonQuery()

    Catch e As Exception
      Throw New Exception("Unable to save status(" & _
                          Status & ") for DocID = " & docID, e)
    Finally
      cn.Close()
    End Try
  End Sub

End Class
```

Testing the ProcessDocument Application

Now is a good time to test what's been written so far. If you haven't done so already, you'll need to go back and complete all those outstanding tasks:

❑ In the `TestHarness` project, ensure you've reinstated the four lines in `frmMain.vb` that refer to `ReceiveDocument.Receive`. Also make sure `TestHarness` has a reference to the `ReceiveDocument` project

❑ In the `ReceiveDocument` project, reinstate the two lines in `Receive.vb` that refer to `ReceiveDocument.Pickup`

❑ Also in the `ReceiveDocument` project, reinstate the three lines in `Pickup.vb` that refer to `ProcessDocument.OrderManager`. Also make sure `ReceiveDocument` has a reference to the `ProcessDocument` project.

Compile the solution, run **TestHarness.exe**, and submit a few orders. You probably won't see the messages in the **inbounddocuments** queue in the MMC, because they pass through too quickly. However, you should begin to see the order status entries appear in the **DocumentStatus** table of the **NWindOrderStatus** database:

StatusID	DocumentID	Status	
1	b78da907-e988-46be-b43b-f467da4f56c1\2061	6/24/2002 09:17:21 AM	Processing
2	b78da907-e988-46be-b43b-f467da4f56c1\2061	6/24/2002 09:17:33 AM	Processing Incomplete
3	b78da907-e988-46be-b43b-f467da4f56c1\2063	6/24/2002 09:47:09 AM	Processing
4	b78da907-e988-46be-b43b-f467da4f56c1\2063	6/24/2002 09:47:10 AM	Processing Incomplete

OrderManagement

This little application provides the last service NOP requires before we can finish up. It will just place orders into the Northwind Order system. This task only requires placing the order in a specific MSMQ `NewOrder` queue. We'll add one more application with two classes: `SimpleQueueManager` and `Place`.

After adding a VB class library project entitled **OrderManagement** to the solution, add a reference to `System.Messaging.dll`. Also, remove the default class file **Class1.vb**. Now we're ready to add our two new classes.

The SimpleQueueManager Class

Add a new class file called **SimpleQueueManager.vb**, and add the following code to it:

```
Imports System.Messaging

Friend Class SimpleQueueManager

  Private Const QUEUE_NAME As String = "NewOrders"

  Public Shared Function GetQueue() As MessageQueue
    Dim msgQueue As MessageQueue
    Dim msgQueueName As String = ".\private$\" & QUEUE_NAME
    If Not MessageQueue.Exists(msgQueueName) Then
      Try
```

```
                msgQueue = MessageQueue.Create(msgQueueName)
            Catch e As Exception
                Throw New Exception("Unable to create the " & QUEUE_NAME & _
                                                      " queue", e)

            End Try
        Else
            Try
                msgQueue = New MessageQueue(msgQueueName)
            Catch e As Exception
                Throw New Exception("Unable to access the " & QUEUE_NAME & _
                                                      " queue", e)

            End Try
        End If
        Return msgQueue
    End Function

End Class
```

The Place Class

Next, add a class file called **Place.vb,** and then add the Place class detailed below. It provides the only public method, NewOrder(), in the OrderManagement application:

```
Imports System.Messaging

Public Class Place

    Public Function NewOrder(ByVal xmlDoc As Xml.XmlDocument) As String
        Dim orderID As String
        Dim msgQueue As MessageQueue
        Dim msgDoc As New Message()
        msgQueue = SimpleQueueManager.GetQueue

        With msgDoc
            .Label = "Order " & Now.ToUniversalTime.ToString
            .Body = xmlDoc.InnerXml
        End With

        Try
            msgQueue.Send(msgDoc)
            orderID = msgDoc.Id
        Catch e As Exception
            Throw New Exception("Unable to send order to the " & _
                                    msgQueue.QueueName & " queue", e)
        Finally
            msgQueue.Close()
        End Try

        orderID = "NW000" & _
                    Right(orderID, orderID.Length - InStr(orderID, "\"))
        Return orderID
    End Function

End Class
```

There is one small point worth observing before we move on to system testing. Until now, the returned identification numbers existed to keep tabs on a document's passage through the Northwind Order Processing application. It is only here, at the very end of the drill, that the customer obtains a "real" order identification number!

System Testing

Speaking of testing, now we can test the entire system we've created. There are a couple of outstanding tasks to complete:

- ❏   In the `ProcessDocument` project, ensure you've reinstated the three lines in `OrderProduct.vb` that refer to `OrderManagement.Place`

- ❏   Make sure `ProcessDocument` has a reference to the `OrderManagement` project

Now compile the solution and run the **TestHarness.exe** application one last time. If everything ran as hoped your Computer Management MMC should contain something resembling the sample below:

This sample shows that two orders were submitted via the `TestHarness` application sitting in the **neworders** queue. (If we inspect the **inbounddocuments** queue, it should be empty.)

Of course, you do not have to keep checking your queues to know whether or not orders arrived safely. After submitting an order, we can use the `DocumentID` to obtain its status, which is now being recorded in the **DocumentStatus** table of the **NWindOrderStatus** database:

StatusID	DocumentID	Status
11	b78da907-e988-46be-b43b-f467da4f56c1\2071	6/24/2002 11:22:31 AM Processing
12	b78da907-e988-46be-b43b-f467da4f56c1\2071	Order ID: NW0002073
13	b78da907-e988-46be-b43b-f467da4f56c1\2074	6/24/2002 11:41:53 AM Processing
14	b78da907-e988-46be-b43b-f467da4f56c1\2074	Order ID: NW0002076

By clicking the `TestHarness`'s **Check Order Status** button, the `txtCheckResult` **Order Status** control should display the order number:

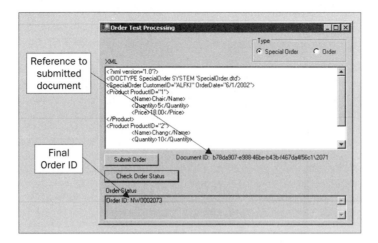

Summary

We built a middle-tier application capable of supporting a web service in this chapter. Northwind customers will soon be submitting their orders via the web. Northwind sales representatives won't waste any more time keying in orders.

Along the way we incorporated several basic GoF patterns that contributed significantly to our application's success. And while it is usually difficult to "pin the feature on the pattern", we can list a few patterns and their contributions:

❏ The Singleton pattern enhanced performance in the `ReceiveDocument` application

❏ The Decorator facilitated the application of business rules within the `ProcessDocument` application

❏ The Strategy pattern kept order validation flexible within the `ValidateOrder` class

❏ The Façade pattern simplified access to a legacy `Inventory` system

These design patterns will also facilitate implementing Northwind's inevitable business rule changes. This is obvious with the `ValidateOrder` class, where the Strategy pattern eases any validation algorithm changes. But even the entire order processing procedures realizes greater flexibility with a design pattern! The Decorator that it was built with inherently supports additional order responsibilities.

Finally, our application also demonstrated an implementation of the more complex Store and Forward pattern, a perennial favorite of Internet-based business-to-business applications concerned with reliability and performance. It also provided a nice demonstration of transactional MSMQ queues and the .NET threading class.

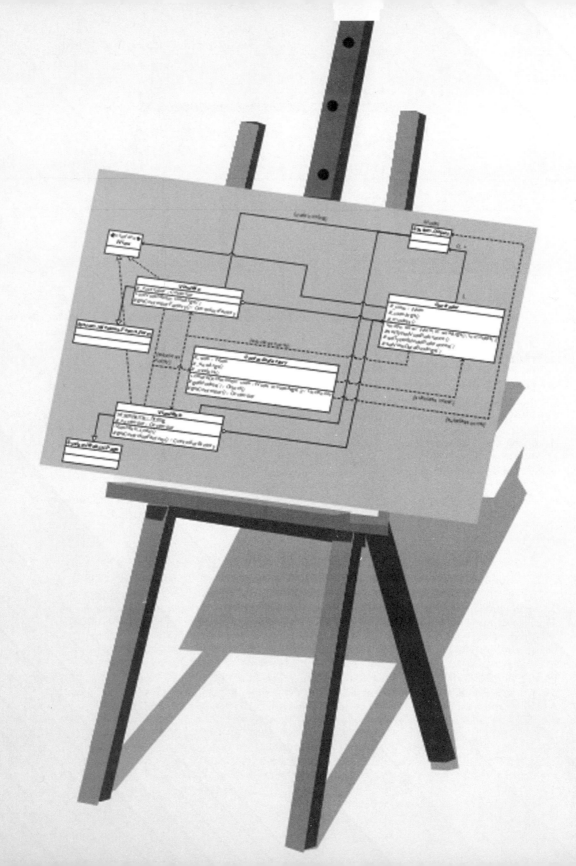

Design Patterns in the Presentation Tier

Congratulations! You've made it through the design of the data and middle tiers and now it's time to figure out how to present your wonderful application to the end user. Unfortunately, this task is not quite as simple as you'd hoped. Are you going to use a web user interface or go with a rich user interface like Windows Forms? What about a thin client on a PDA? What if your business requires you to do all of the above?

Regardless of what types of user interfaces (UIs) you end up implementing in your presentation tier, design patterns can be very useful in making your presentation tier work right, especially when you're faced with a complex presentation tier that may contain a number of different UIs for the same enterprise application.

In this chapter we will be looking at various design patterns and architectures that will hopefully clear the muddy water of designing the presentation tier. We will be using several of the GoF design patterns we first met back in Chapter 1 – including Observer, Composite, Strategy, and Factory Method.

The Problem with the Presentation Tier

I don't know if you've noticed over the years, but the presentation tier has become a very complicated part of the enterprise application. In the good old days of the mainframe, one could get away with a dummy terminal, which presented a very simple (and often difficult-to-use) UI to the unfortunate user. Then graphical operating systems and the client–server innovation produced a richer and more usable UI for the user, with windows and buttons and that friendly little hourglass.

Eventually, technological innovations and higher performance requirements pushed our enterprise apps to span to three or more logical tiers. This fact, coupled with the advent of such things as the Internet, PDAs, and really cool cell phones, has forced the presentation tier to grow into a host of diverse UI technologies. The architect whose task it is to design this complex presentation tier needed much grace.

As a result of the demands placed on application designers to deliver these types of presentation tiers, many applications today are plagued with over-complexity, non-reusable code, and poor usability. Moreover, the heavy cost of such inefficient design becomes apparent when the time comes to upgrade the application. If you're in this position now, you could be facing the task of rewriting each UI, or switching architectures and starting from scratch.

Well, we technical design purists know that this situation just won't do. We are now in the application packaging business, in which applications are marketed with different UIs. As designers and developers, we need to follow a methodology of working that minimizes this complexity of development and maintenance. In this environment, there is a very important role for design patterns!

Introducing Model/View/Controller

Unfortunately, given the complex nature of the ever-evolving presentation tier, it became apparent to many designers that throwing a handful of design patterns at the problem wouldn't be enough. There needed to be a more concise architecture or high-level pattern that could accurately model the interactions of the presentation tier. There needed to be something that could provide the abstraction and decoupling needed in order to promote proper flexibility and code reuse and still maintain performance and scalability.

Several years ago, the Smalltalk programming language innovated such an architecture – it is called **Model/View/Controller**, or **MVC**. MVC dissects an application into three distinct types of objects: models, views, and controllers. We'll take a closer look at each of these object types, and how they interact, in the next section. But for now, understand that MVC can be thought of as a high-level design pattern or architecture since it really encompasses several of the low-level (GoF) design patterns. MVC separates the problem of the presentation tier into manageable pieces that designers can feel comfortable working with, and it uses design patterns to make these pieces work together.

> *To see what the Smalltalk community is up to today, visit http://www.smalltalk.org.*

The majority of us have experienced the effects of MVC in the technologies we've been using over the years. For example, Sun embraced MVC and made it one of the fundamental drivers for J2EE Servlets. Microsoft saw the power in using MVC to decouple visual presentation from presentation logic, and produced the event-driven Windows forms we've all come to know and love.

Over the years, MVC has become established as a valid architecture for addressing the problem of the presentation tier. Therefore, MVC will be at the core of our discussion throughout the rest of this chapter.

It's important that we first get a solid understanding and lay out some common MVC terminology. Let's take a few minutes to go over MVC and provide a foundation for continuing our discussion.

MVC in a Nutshell

As I've already mentioned, MVC is made up of **model**, **view**, and **controller** elements. These elements are actually different types of classes in the implementation of the architecture:

❑   A **model** represents the data of the application and the business rules that govern the manipulation of that data. In *n*-tier terminology, the model is the middle tier.

❑   A **view** is a visual representation of the model. It could be a Windows Form, or a web page, or a UI form on a PDA. A key to the MVC architecture is that multiple views can exist simultaneously for a given model, with all of those views displaying the same underlying data (but in different formats or with different technologies). The beauty of this concept is that it addresses the multi-UI problem discussed above. Each view is responsible for making sure it is displaying the most current data. It does this by either subscribing to state change events broadcast by the model or by making periodic queries to the model.

❑   Finally, for every view there is at least one **controller**. The controller decouples the visual presentation from the underlying presentation logic by handling user interactions and controlling access to the model. Depending on what these user gestures are, the controller can modify the existing view, request state changes to the model, or select a new view to be displayed to the user. Therefore, the brains of the presentation tier lie within the controllers; hence their name.

Here's a high-level graphical representation of MVC and how each element interacts. Also shown in this diagram are the design patterns used by MVC (we'll describe these patterns shortly):

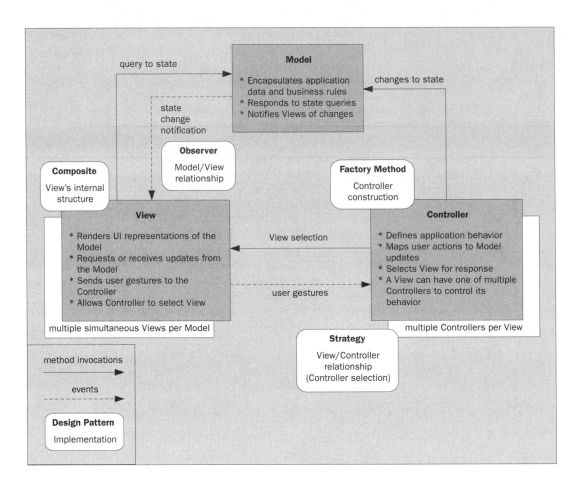

The Power of MVC

MVC is not the architecture for all presentation tiers. It is specifically tailored for medium to large presentation tiers that contain several views and are potentially hosted in a variety of **UI types** (rich UIs, websites, PDAs, etc). MVC solves the problem of unmanageable code that typically occurs in large applications, by breaking it down into manageable building blocks (models, views, and controllers) that, through the power of OO techniques, design patterns, and now .NET, can be easily designed, implemented, and maintained.

Like many design pattern situations, the power of MVC is in **decoupling**. We all know that if an application is coupled too tightly, then it tends initially to be easy to code and subsequently to be very difficult to maintain and update. By contrast, too much decoupling can overcomplicate an application to the extent that we lose track of the application's original purpose. MVC strikes a perfect decoupling balance, and polishes things off by specifying the proper interactions between each decoupled element.

Decoupling the Model and the View

The first decoupling scenario of interest occurs between the model and the view. You may have already recognized this decoupling concept from the classic *n*-tier architecture. The basic premise is that you separate the business logic (the middle tier) from the presentation. In MVC terms, the middle tier is the model. In very simple cases, the model may represent the database itself. However, in most applications it should represent a middle-tier API, which sits *on top* of the data tier. Then the business logic can be easily shared between all UI types. I don't think there is too much need to preach about the value of this separation, since *n*-tier architecture is generally assumed throughout this book.

However, to re-emphasize the practical value of model/view decoupling, remember that most large applications have several separate developers and often separate teams that work on each UI type. One group may work on the web site and one on the internal rich-UI app. Having a model that is decoupled and common to all UI types prevents the all-too-common scenario in which one team incorporates some piece of custom business logic (such as a direct ADO call against the database) that breaks existing business logic in another UI type. In a simple application, this might be easy to fix. In a large and complex application, this can be very costly and difficult to debug.

Decoupling the View and the Controller

If we decouple business logic from the presentation, we're on the right track. However, the front ends of larger apps still tend to be unmanageable *even* when there is a nice set of friendly business objects to talk to. There's one more step we can take within the presentation tier: to decouple the visual presentation from the presentation logic. This one concept is really the core of MVC and this chapter. There are two main benefits to decoupling visual presentation (views) and presentation logic (controllers) into separate classes.

The first benefit is that decoupling allows a single view to have multiple controllers. Controllers define the behavior of a view. Therefore, if a view requires multiple behaviors, controllers can do the trick. There are several cases in which a single view may require variable behavior. Here are a few examples:

❑ A view may work with multiple user types that need to see different things and experience different behaviors from the visual elements within a view, depending on their access rights.

❑ A view may be hosted on multiple platforms, each of which may require slight modifications to the way the view is rendered for compatibility. On the rich-UI side, there may be slight but important differences in the way Windows 98 and Windows XP render the same view. On the web side, you may have a view (that is, a web page) that needs to run against different browser types.

❑ A view may also need to be altered depending on the state of the model. Instead of creating multiple views for each variation of the model state, a single generic view with multiple controllers can provide a more elegant solution. We'll see an example of this in our sample application later in the chapter.

Since each controller is a separate class from the view, a controller can be swapped out at either design time or run time to suit the needs of the application. Swapping out a *view* in this fashion (especially at run time) can be much more difficult to pull off. Having multiple controller classes also means we can add future controllers very easily. If a new user type is conceived, or if we decide to push our application to a new platform, adding a new controller for each affected view is much easier than modifying each view or (worse yet) adding completely new views to the application.

The second benefit is that it actually helps the decoupling of the view from the model. .NET data binding (which we will discuss in more detail later) allows the view to receive updates automatically when the model changes. Instead of configuring the data binding within the view itself, it can instead be done in the controller. This means that UI designers can create views without any concern for the *exact* model that their view is representing. Sure, they'll probably still have to have a general idea of the data elements of the model (that is, the fields) that their view is representing, but they won't have to do the work of (for example) actually connecting their First Name textbox with the CUST_FName field in the database or the FirstName property of a business object, since that is now taken care of by the controller.

MVC can be a very powerful architecture for the presentation tier. Without much surprise, the mechanics behind the magic are done using design patterns.

The Design Patterns Used in MVC

Let's take a look at the design patterns that make up MVC. The following table includes a reminder of the GoF intent of each pattern, and notes its role within MVC:

Design Pattern	GoF Intent	How it's used in MVC
Observer (behavioral)	Define a one-to-many dependency between objects so that when one object changes state, all its dependents are notified and updated automatically.	MVC uses the Observer pattern to keep each view in sync with the model. Therefore, whenever data within the model changes, each subscribing view (whether it's a web page, a Windows form, or a form on a PDA) gets notified.
Composite (structural)	Compose objects into tree structures to represent part-whole hierarchies. Composite lets clients treat individual objects and compositions of objects uniformly.	Each view potentially uses the Composite pattern to make up its internal structure of visual elements (buttons, textboxes, scrollbars, etc.). Composite allows us to organize all of the components of the view as a hierarchy and treat the entire view as a whole.
Strategy (behavioral)	Define a family of algorithms, encapsulate each one, and make them interchangeable. Strategy lets the algorithm vary independently from clients that use it.	The Strategy design pattern defines the relationship between view and controller. The idea is that multiple controllers (algorithms) could be used with a single view, depending on the current state of the application. Strategy treats a controller as a swappable algorithm; it allows you to interchange the controller of a view when needed at design time and at run time.
Factory Method (creational)	Define an interface for creating an object, but let subclasses decide which class to instantiate. Factory Method lets a class defer instantiation to subclasses.	There are a few ways you can choose the default controller for a view when it's first rendered; we're going to do it using a variation of the Factory Method, which delegates controller class construction to a related hierarchy of factory objects.

MVC in VB6

Believe it or not, a simplified (and very limited) form of MVC can be implemented in VB6! You may have already recognized a number of MVC concepts that transfer over to VB6. Over the next four or five pages, let's take a very brief look at some VB6 code and see how it works. Then we'll build on this code when we transition into our examination of VB.NET. This example will be limited to a Windows forms application; we'll postpone the discussion of other view types (such as a web page) until the VB.NET section that follows.

> **Wait a minute! Why are we talking about VB6? The answer is simple. Like me, many readers of this book will have entered into the VB.NET world from VB6. When learning VB.NET concepts, I'm sure many of these readers have attempted to draw comparisons to things they know in VB6. The presentation functionality in VB6 has some of its roots in MVC – therefore, it makes sense to show a little of that to get the ball rolling.**
>
> **However, I'm *not* trying to say that you can do MVC just as easily in VB6 as in VB.NET. I'm merely using VB6 as a starting point in our example code. When we get into the VB.NET code in the next section, you will begin to see the limitations of VB6 when it comes to implementing MVC – and how VB.NET is far superior.**

VB6 MVC Class Diagram

We don't want to dwell on VB6 for any longer than necessary. Therefore our VB6 sample app will be simple enough that we can bypass most of the design discussion that we *will* work through in the upcoming VB.NET section. For now, let's look at a simple class diagram that shows the pieces to our MVC application in VB6:

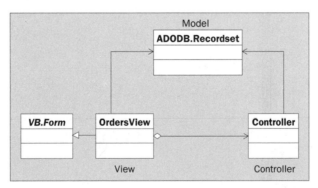

We'll discuss this in more detail, and lay out the code for each part of this diagram, in a moment; but first allow me to summarize what we're about to create. Our model, as you will see, will be nothing more than a disconnected ADO `Recordset` class. Our view will be a VB6 Form called `OrdersView`, which, by nature of all VB6 Forms, inherits from the VB `Form` class.

> *It's important to note that this is one of the few times implementation inheritance actually happens in VB6. As you may already know, you cannot create custom classes in VB6 and inherit both interface and implementation from them; you can only inherit the interface. Nor can you inherit in this way from other COM classes. However, as a very special case, custom Form classes do inherit (both interface and implementation) from the VB. `Form` class by virtue of the VB6 runtime.*

`OrdersView` will hold a reference to the `Controller` class, which contains all of the logic to control the behavior of the view and updates to the model.

The Model Class

Let's start with the model. The VB6 application and our upcoming .NET application will use a "disconnected" model. This means that instead of talking to a separate physical or logical middle tier, we're going to keep it simple and talk to a local representation of the middle tier. In our case we're going to end up working with a disconnected data object as a substitute for the middle tier, so our presentation tier can have a model to work against. For our VB6 example, we'll use a disconnected ADO `Recordset`.

To get things going, create a Standard EXE project in VB6 called MVCVB6. In the project, add a reference to the **Microsoft ActiveX Data Objects 2.7 Library**.

> *If you don't have MDAC 2.7 installed, version 2.0 or later will do.*

Add a Basic Module (you can leave it with the default name, **Module1**). In it, insert the following code:

```
Option Explicit

Public Function getModel() As ADODB.Recordset
  Dim rs As ADODB.Recordset
  Set rs = New ADODB.Recordset

  With rs
    .CursorLocation = adUseClient
    .LockType = adLockBatchOptimistic

    'create schema
    .Fields.Append "OrderID", adInteger
    .Fields.Append "CustomerID", adBSTR
    .Fields.Append "OrderDate", adDate
    .Fields.Append "OrderType", adSmallInt

    'add sample data
    .Open
    .AddNew
    .Fields("OrderID") = 100
    .Fields("CustomerID") = "pete"
    .Fields("OrderDate") = #1/1/2002#
    .Fields("OrderType") = 0
    .AddNew
    .Fields("OrderID") = 101
    .Fields("CustomerID") = "jon"
    .Fields("OrderDate") = #2/1/2002#
    .Fields("OrderType") = 1
  End With

  Set getModel = rs
End Function
```

This code is pretty simple; we have a `Public` function that returns a disconnected `Recordset` full of data, which could represent a subset of data returned by an actual call to the middle tier. We have a model.

Obviously, our `getModel()` method over-simplifies the access to the model. In most situations, we would have a much more complicated API in the middle tier to retrieve and modify the model (and much less hard-coding). Almost certainly, we'd also connect to a real database instead of generating a makeshift `Recordset` full of data, as we've done here. But for the purposes of this demonstration, `getModel()` will do.

The View Class

The view will be a VB6 form. Go back to the form that was auto-generated by VB6 when you created the project – change its name from `Form1` to `OrdersView`. Next, slap a `DataGrid` control (Microsoft DataGrid Control 6.0 (SP5) (OLEDB)) on the form and rename the control to `ordersGrid`. You may need to add this control to your IDE toolbox before you can add it to your form, since it's not there by default (to do that, right-click on the toolbox and select **Components...**). Finally, add a button to the form. Label it **Click Me** and name it `clickMeButton`. The final product should look something like this:

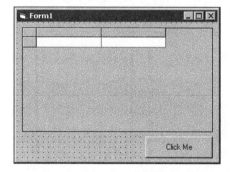

The Controller Class

Finally, we come to the fun part. Create a new class module called **Controller**. In it, place the following code:

```
Option Explicit

Private m_model As ADODB.Recordset
Private WithEvents m_ordersView As Form
Private WithEvents m_ordersGrid As DataGrid
Private WithEvents m_clickMeButton As CommandButton

Public Sub init(ByRef ordersView As Form, _
                ByRef ordersGrid As DataGrid, _
                ByRef clickMeButton As CommandButton)
  Set m_ordersView = ordersView
  Set m_ordersGrid = ordersGrid
  Set m_clickMeButton = clickMeButton
End Sub

Private Sub m_OrdersView_Load()
  Set m_model = getModel()
  With m_ordersGrid
```

```
      Set .DataSource = m_model
   End With
End Sub

Private Sub m_clickMeButton_Click()
  With m_model
    .MoveFirst
    .Fields("OrderDate") = Now
  End With
End Sub
```

Our `Controller` class basically acts as a stand-in for the code one would normally place in the Form itself. (Normally, we would take all the logic behind all of the events of the controls on our form, and place them in the Form instead. In this case, we're porting all of that code over to a *separate* controller class that can handle all the same events that the Form can handle.) At the top of the `Controller`'s code, you can see variable declarations that reference the underlying Form and all of the controls we need to work with. Then, we use the values of those variables, which are passed into the `Controller`'s init method, in the `Controller` class's implementation of the `Load` and `Click` event handlers. Thus, this class is able to handle the `Load` event of our `OrdersView` form and the `Click` event of our `clickMeButton`, just as the underlying Form could have done.

The last step is to code the link between the view and controller. To do this, add the following code to the `OrdersView` form:

```
Option Explicit

Private m_controller As Controller

Private Sub Form_Initialize()
  Set m_controller = New Controller
  m_controller.init Me, ordersGrid, clickMeButton
End Sub
```

Our view then creates an instance of the `Controller` and initializes it by passing all of the references to the controls that the controller needs via the `init()` method.

Running and Analysing the Application

That's it! If you run the application you'll see the `orderGrid` populate with the data from the disconnected `Recordset`. If you click the `clickMeButton`, the controller will intercept that event and make a change to the state of the underlying `Recordset` (the model). You'll see the `ordersGrid` automatically update itself when this happens; it is using the Observer design pattern to do this. The nice thing about it is that here, we didn't need to implement the Observer pattern – it's already provided via the data binding.

The `OrdersView` form also uses the Composite pattern, since it is a composition of multiple child controls, all of which act as a whole.

What about Strategy? We could have easily created several controller classes, each of which could handle the same form and controls. Then we could have instantiated the proper one at run time and given it control of the `OrdersView`, thereby dynamically selecting the actual behavior of the view.

A clean way to implement multiple controller classes in VB6 would be to create a controller interface, so the view could have a reference to this interface instead of an actual controller class. Then, when the controller class was instantiated at run time, the view would still have an early-bound reference to the controller.

Is It Worth It?

All this extra work to implement a controller might seem a bit extravagant. It's much easier to just place all the controller code within in the Form itself. But then the view and the controller would no longer be decoupled. The decision to go with an MVC approach and decouple view and controller is like many of the decisions we face when thinking about design pattern application. You have to weigh the value of the flexibility you gain with the design pattern against the cost it takes to implement it.

We've just seen a very simple and stripped down implementation of MVC. There are many things that are very difficult (or impossible) to achieve in VB6, that are now readily available in VB.NET due to its true OO capabilities. Let's take a look.

MVC in VB.NET

A true design pattern enthusiast would probably say that our VB6-based MVC is full of holes, and they would probably be right. Sure, we kind of got the basic structure and behavior down, but it really didn't gain us much (except some decoupling):

❑ You may have noticed that our Strategy implementation wasn't really complete since we had no way of sub-classing controller classes. (Recall from Chapter 1 that the Strategy pattern involves a client object holding an *abstract* reference to an algorithm object, which can be swapped out with whatever concrete algorithm class is necessary. Here, the client object equates to the view and the algorithm object equates to the controller.)

❑ We also couldn't make hierarchical families of interrelated view/controller combinations. At best, we could have generated a flat set of controller classes that all implemented a common interface, but there would have been no code reuse.

❑ VB6's data binding is also quite inferior to that of VB.NET (which is really just .NET data binding). We'll see shortly how this new data-binding technology really makes our Observer pattern work well.

To really cash in on the power of MVC and its underlying design patterns, we need a real OO language. Enter VB.NET.

VB.NET has removed the gap between VB and MVC, in that all of the design patterns discussed above can be fully implemented in VB.NET. Also, with some additional tools at our disposal in Visual Studio .NET, you'll find that the task of slapping MVC together is much easier and more powerful than it was in VB6. First, let's briefly take a look at some of the more MVC-ish aspects of .NET that we get out of the box. This, along with the sample VB6 app we put together above, will provide a good context for what's coming up next.

Inherited Forms

As mentioned before, having true implementation inheritance is an absolute requirement for making most design patterns work. Because of this, we're sure to be able to code up a fully functional representation of the Strategy pattern that describes the relationship between view and controller.

Another nifty tool that comes with Visual Studio.NET is the capability to easily create **inherited Windows Forms** in the Visual Studio.NET IDE, in which we can create a child form that inherits all of its code and visual elements from a parent form.

> *Unfortunately, ASP.NET Web Forms cannot inherit in the same way. Inherited Windows Forms classes inherit everything in a Windows Form superclass (the visual elements and the code behind) since everything is contained within a single class. By contrast, ASP.NET Web Forms separate their visual elements and their code-behind into separate classes that end up in separate assemblies. All code-behind classes get compiled into an assembly at design-time (that typically has the same name as the web application), which lives in the web application's /bin directory. The .aspx page itself is different – it becomes a separate class that inherits from its code-behind class and is compiled into a separate assembly at run-time that ends up in a temporary .NET directory. Each time an .aspx page is served up by IIS, the ASP.NET infrastructure checks to see if the page's .aspx code (though not the code-behind) has changed. If it has, this .aspx assembly gets recompiled on the fly. This class and assembly separation makes for easy script-like updates to the .aspx page that still become compiled code when the page is accessed by the user. However, this architecture doesn't allow for the same visual inheritance that we get with Windows Forms since we can't inherit from the .aspx page class itself, which contains all of the visual elements of the Web Form; we can only inherit from the code-behind class. Perhaps in future editions of .NET, a mechanism will exist that will allow complete Web Form inheritance.*

To make inherited Windows Forms work, all we need is a base form – either in our current project or in an assembly in our project's references – and we're in business. The following figure shows an example of a simple VB.NET Windows Form (called Form1) that we can use to inherit:

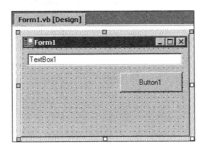

There's nothing special about this form. It has two controls: a TextBox and a Button. To create an inherited form, the project containing the base form needs to be built first. Then it's as simple as adding an Inherited Form item from the Add New Item dialog:

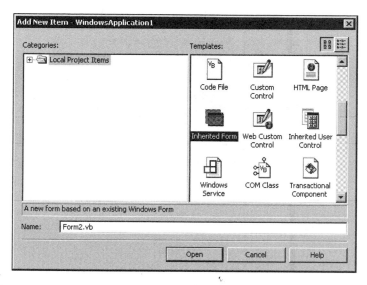

When you do this, Visual Studio .NET prompts you to choose one of the available forms in the scope of your project, which can come either from the current project, or from a referenced project, or from any referenced assembly. Here we see the Form1 form that we just created as an available form to inherit from:

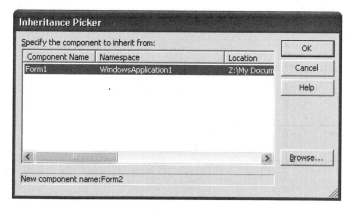

When the new inherited form is displayed in the Windows Form designer, it looks just like the base form, with of all of its controls in place. The only difference is the inherited controls are locked from being edited during design time, but they can be modified at run time. Also, you are free to add new controls to the inherited form and modify those during design time. Of course, from here you can keep creating new forms and sub-forms to build your desired UI hierarchy:

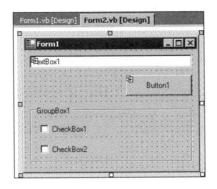

This trick can also be used to create inherited controls for Windows Forms. However, like ASP.NET Web Forms, custom ASP.NET server controls cannot inherit both visual elements and code-behind as custom Windows Forms controls can.

ASP.NET Web Forms

.NET Windows Forms are a successor to VB6 Forms in many ways, and as we mentioned at the beginning of the chapter, both provide an MVC-ish separation of visual elements from the code-behind using event-driven code. ASP never had this built-in separation until ASP.NET Web Forms came along. With classic ASP, processing user input was very tedious as it either required a separate ASP page or a very complex postback mechanism within a single page; all of which had to hand-coded. ASP.NET Web Forms provide an event-driven code model that will make our MVC implementation in ASP.NET almost identical to the one we use with .NET Windows Forms.

ASP.NET Server Controls

Like, Windows Forms, ASP.NET Web Forms wouldn't be complete without controls. ASP.NET Server Controls provide the visual elements that the code-behind responds to. Server Controls also allow ASP.NET Web Forms to fully implement the Composite design pattern since a Web Form is really a hierarchical collection of Server Controls.

Event Handling and Delegates

As in the days of VB6, we can still take advantage of event handling with our VB.NET objects. As you will see, events are the key tool that allows a controller to respond to user gestures from a view. Also, events are the underlying mechanism for making data binding work, which is a great way to implement the Observer pattern between model and view.

Events are actually a subset of a more powerful mechanism in .NET called **delegates**. A delegate is basically an object that references (and can invoke) a procedure, which is called an **invocation**. That procedure can be any member type (subroutine, function, or property) of any visibility (public, private, protected, or friend) in any object. This procedure can also be either a shared or instance member of its class. Once a delegate is created and mapped to a particular procedure, it can be passed around to external objects, giving these objects the ability to invoke the associated procedure at any time.

A single delegate object can also map to and invoke several target procedures. This is how events work in .NET. An event is nothing more than a delegate object that clients can use to map to their corresponding event-handling procedures. When the event is raised, it's actually executing the delegate, which in turn invokes each of the event-handling procedures in the listening objects in turn. Of course, VB.NET hides the complexity of implementing event-like behavior with delegates by providing Events instead. However, we can achieve the same results by using delegates explicitly, if we want.

Multithreading and Asynchronous Programming

It's probably worth mentioning in a presentation tier discussion that VB.NET now has full **multithreading** capabilities. In VB6, multithreading could only be partially achieved by doing fancy tricks with events and working with out-of-the-box controls that had multi-threading capabilities themselves (like the Timer control). Now, with true multithreading we can develop UIs that can be more efficient in servicing user requests. Of course, multithreading can also be very dangerous if its not implemented properly. Most experienced programmers who've done a lot with multithreading will tell you that there are more cases than not where a single thread of execution is sufficient to get the job done.

A subject related to multithreading is what .NET has termed **Asynchronous Programming**. It's actually referred to as a design pattern in the .NET documentation (we won't be using this pattern in this chapter, but look for it in Chapter 5, which discusses inter-tier design patterns). The pattern implements asynchronous behavior using delegates and is designed in such a way that a client object can call any member of a server object asynchronously, regardless of whether the server object's member was actually implemented to be asynchronous.

This can be a handy design pattern to use in all tiers of an application, but particularly in the presentation tier. How many times has a user tried clicking a button, only for the whole UI to suddenly freeze while the underlying form waits for the executing process to complete? A better approach would be to fire off the underlying process *asynchronously*, and give the user some real-time feedback as to the status of the operation (or even allow them to do something else with the UI in the meantime).

There are many situations in which the presentation tier is executing a middle-tier operation that might take an undesirably long time to complete. A great example is a middle tier that has a web service as its interface for the presentation tier. Of course, web service method calls can be lengthy (due to the parsing overhead of SOAP or simply because the network is slow). Having a more responsive middle tier is ideal and is one of the reasons we implemented MSMQ in Chapter 3.

VB.NET has a lot to offer out of the box that makes MVC more possible than ever before. However, it would nice to be able to harness these capabilities into a framework of classes that could be used to generate new presentation tiers that specifically subscribe to the MVC architecture. Next, we will do just that, and when we're finished we'll have a solid MVC class framework that can be used for any presentation tier that wishes to implement MVC. Then we'll put it to the test by employing it within a presentation tier for the sample application we learned about in the previous chapter.

Building an MVC Framework for .NET

A **framework** is really nothing more than a collection of classes that can be used as a foundation for the design (or parts of the design) of a real application. The .NET Class Library is itself a framework of classes used by .NET applications either to access system resources or to implement and extend certain object types and designs. In this section we're going to build an MVC framework of classes that can be extended in any application to generate new models, views, and controllers.

The MVC Framework Class Diagram

Before we dive into the code, let's put this framework together using class diagrams. Perhaps the easiest way to do this is to start with a simple MVC class diagram and slowly evolve it into something practical that we can code up and use in .NET.

A Simple MVC Class Diagram

So, let's start with this very simple class diagram:

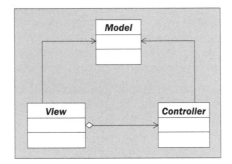

Here we see the basic relationships between the model, view, and controller classes. All three classes are shown as abstract, so that real applications have to extend them in order to use them.

We've already discussed the general roles that each class plays, but it still might be difficult to see how this diagram is represented in a real application. Perhaps it would be helpful to compare this to a class diagram for a more typical presentation tier:

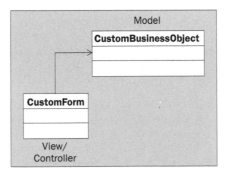

This presentation tier has a Windows Forms UI with a single custom form communicating to a custom business object. It's simplistic; in fact, to help keep the class diagram simple, it doesn't show the `CustomForm` class inheriting from the `System.Windows.Forms.Form` class. However, it does describe the typical relationship between the presentation tier and the middle tier: you have a main UI class of some kind (such as a Windows form or a web page) that communicates directly to the middle tier via a business object.

Comparing the Two Class Diagrams

There is one main difference between our class diagram for a typical presentation tier, and the MVC class diagram presented just before it. This difference is very important and it's worth remembering, because it's one of the main reasons why MVC has been so successful over the years:

> **Normally, visual elements and presentation logic are contained within a single UI class. In MVC, they are decoupled into view and controller classes.**

You might argue that Windows Forms and ASP.NET web pages are *made* to contain! This is true; but if we place all of your presentation logic (the code-behind) within the event-handling procedures of those classes then we bind the underlying logic to the views. As we've already pointed out, there are several advantages to separating visual presentation (views) from presentation logic (controllers).

Associations in the MVC Class Diagram

Now that we understand the importance of the different roles of our three MVC classes, let's examine each association in the MVC class diagram:

Association	Comment
View/Controller	The relationship between a view and its controller is probably the most important relationship. As we've already hinted, this relationship is described by the Strategy design pattern. This means that one of several concrete controller classes can be chosen to service the view.
View/Model	The relationship between view and model is defined by the Observer design pattern. This means whenever there is a change in the important data within the model, the view receives an update. We've displayed this association as a reference from the view to the model. However, we'll see shortly how we might loosen this association a bit, given the use of .NET data binding.
Controller/Model	The relationship between controller and model isn't described by any particular design pattern, since it is nothing more than a simple reference from the controller to the model. The controller has the sole responsibility of updating the state of the model, so a simple reference does the trick.

It's important to note that the model itself really has no awareness of any existing views or controllers. Therefore, it contains no direct references back to views or controllers. As we will see, this is primarily because the model can be just about any type of object, so we can't assume it knows how to interact with views and controllers. Allowing this condition makes our MVC framework very flexible since it can then incorporate any object type as the model.

Incorporating the MVC Class Diagram into .NET

Our simple MVC class diagram works great on paper, but there are a few issues when we try to make it fit practically in .NET. In this section we will re-examine our basic MVC diagram, address any issues that may arise when implementing it in .NET, and modify it accordingly.

Upgrading the View/Model Association for Data Binding

One way for our view to observe state changes in the model is to listen for events of the model, since the .NET Event architecture closely matches the Observer design pattern. In its current form, our MVC class diagram displays this scenario with a reference from the view to the model. In VB.NET, the view would probably declare its reference to the model using the `WithEvents` keyword, which would allow for easy placement of view update code in the associated event handling procedures.

The following is a snippet of code from a hypothetical view class with a `WithEvents` reference to a model class called `MyModel`. It then shows code that updates the view when the `MyModel` object's `ModelChanged` event fires:

```
Public Class MyView
  ...

  Private WithEvents _model As MyModel
  ...

  'MyModel class has a ModelChanged event
  Public Sub _model_ModelChanged() Handles _model.ModelChanged
    'code to examine the model and update the view...
  End Sub
  ...

End Class
```

This approach works, but it has one major problem: the view is only able to update itself when events are fired from the model. Therefore, when the model does fire an event, it's up to the *view* to determine what parts of the model's state have changed, so it can properly update itself. Even worse, what if the model doesn't have any events? Then the view is left to manually check the model for updates, which can lead to periods of time when the view is outdated.

> *There is a good rebuttal to the problem of the model having no events. It is that we would implement standard events in our model abstract base class. However, coming up we will see why we might not have this much control over concrete model classes.*

A better scenario would be to somehow bind visual elements of the view to data elements within the model, so that when state changes do occur within the model (especially those parts of the state that the view is showing) the view would be updated automatically. This is known as **data binding** and it is a very powerful technology in .NET – even more so than it was in VB6. For now you can data bind almost any kind of control to just about any kind of data source, even custom classes! Therefore, in our scenario we are going to employ data binding instead of event handling in order to facilitate the Observer design pattern relationship between the view and the model.

> *It should be noted that .NET data binding isn't completely magical. For example, setting the data source of a textbox to a property of a custom class only makes data binding work in one direction. If the user modifies a value in the textbox, the underlying class property is modified. On the other hand, if some other application procedure or the underlying object itself modifies the class property, the textbox value will not be automatically updated. This is because in order for this kind of data binding to work, the custom class needs to implement certain system interfaces (namely `IEditableObject` for single objects and `IBindingList` for lists of objects), so the textbox can automatically register event handlers with events within those system interfaces when data binding is specified.*

The DataSet object already implements the required interfaces to make this two-way data binding work (this is why we'll be using it as our underlying model in our sample application, later in the chapter). However, it is very feasible to assume that, in a full-blown application, other data sources (like custom classes that implement the necessary data binding interfaces) may be used instead.

As you will see in the code, data binding will allow us to place the data binding implementation code within the controller instead of the view. The advantage of this is that the view then becomes totally decoupled from the model; it's the controller that determines the data relationship between view and model. Therefore, the view will no longer need a direct reference to the model. However, an implied association still exists via data binding. So, let's update the class diagram to show this:

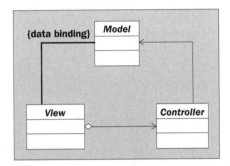

Here we see the association line between view and model *without navigation* occurring from the view to the model, since the view will not need to hold a reference to the model.

As we continue to develop the MVC framework class diagram over the following pages, we will highlight association and association text changes using bold lines and text (as above). We will also highlight class changes by gray-shading the affected classes.

A Free Model

One of the more vague issues up to this point in the chapter has been: what exactly is the **model** in MVC? We've made the assertion that the model represents the middle tier of our application; but what does that look like in a class diagram?

Our current MVC class diagram shows an abstract model class that the controller has a direct reference to. Unfortunately, by having the model class as abstract, we will force all concrete model classes to inherit from it. This may prove too constrictive. Why? Because we want to let the model be whatever it needs to be. Maybe it's a full-fledged business object. Maybe it's simply an ADO.NET DataSet object. Or maybe it's a legacy COM object on the middle tier.

If we avoid forcing the model to inherit from a specific type, we will be able to plug any object into our MVC presentation tier and call it the model. It's the job of the controller to determine what the model is, how to get a reference to it, and how to specify the data-binding between it and the view. Therefore, we need to specify our model as generically as possible, and there's nothing more generic than the System.Object class.

Finally, we don't want to limit our controller to a single model object either. In reality, a controller may need to work with several models at once in order to service its view. Therefore our controller/model association has an explicit multiplicity of one-to-many.

There are several cases in which multiple models may need to be accessed by a controller within the presentation tier. Perhaps there is more than one middle-tier or back-end entity with which the presentation tier needs to communicate (such a web service) or that adds value to the application (like a mapping engine that generates driving directions). Perhaps there is an additional temporary model that needs to stay alive during a user session like search results or the contents of a shopping cart.

Let's update our class diagram to show a generic multi-object model:

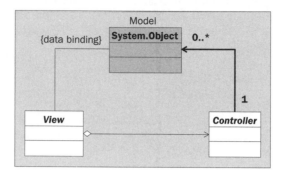

Notice that we actually notate the model end of the controller/model association as *zero*-to-many. This allows for the rare situation in which there are zero models required.

So far, we've tweaked the model and the relationship between the model and the view. Now, let's examine the view.

Multiple Abstract Views

Like the model, the view has a similar problem. If we really wanted to, we could build an abstract view class from the ground up that could manifest itself as multiple UI types (Windows form, Web page, smart device UI, etc.). However, it would make much more sense to leverage classes already in the .NET Framework to produce views. By "leverage existing classes", I mean that the abstract view class would inherit from the `System.Windows.Forms.Form` class to represent a Windows form, or from the `System.Web.UI.Page` class to represent an ASP.NET web form, or from whatever .NET class it needed to represent whichever type of UI was required. The problem is that the classes in .NET can't inherit from multiple superclasses (in fact, this is also true in most other object-oriented platforms). This means we can't have a single abstract view class.

So what can we do? We fudge a little by creating a view interface (we'll call it `IView`) and separate abstract view classes for each type of UI we wish to service. In our framework we're going to create a separate abstract class for Windows forms called `ViewWin`, and a separate abstract class for ASP.NET web forms called `ViewWeb`. Unfortunately, we do have to repeat standard view code in each of these abstract view classes (don't worry, there isn't much). However, our `IView` interface serves as a generic type that other classes can use to reference and pass around view classes, regardless of their inheritance origins.

So, let's replace our single abstract view class with two separate view abstract classes that implement the `IView` interface – one for Windows forms and one for ASP.NET web forms:

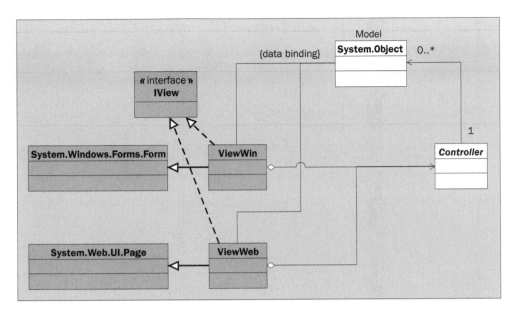

You may notice that the `ViewWin` and `ViewWeb` classes in the above diagram are not being shown as abstract. In theory they should be. Unfortunately, the Visual Studio.NET IDE has problems with Windows Forms and ASP.NET Web Forms that inherit from abstract classes. For example, if you create an inherited form from the `ViewWin` class in Visual Studio.NET (using the inherited Windows forms technique discussed earlier in the chapter), the Windows Forms designer displays an error message similar to the following:

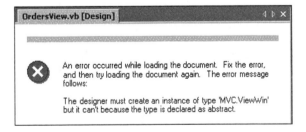

Similarly, if you create a new ASP.NET Web Form, open its underlying `.aspx.vb` file, and set the class to inherit from `ViewWeb`, you get the following error when you go back to the ASP.NET Web Forms designer:

These errors occur within the respective Visual Studio.NET designers for the simple reason that the designers need to create their own instances of the super class. If the super class is abstract, you can't create an instance of it; hence, the error.

In fact, we could leave `ViewWin` and `ViewWeb` abstract if we decided we weren't going to use Visual Studio .NET to develop our concrete views (for example, if we were planning to develop everything in Notepad). However, in this chapter we want to take advantage of the tremendous power of VS.NET as a tool for developing .NET applications (especially, given its visual nature, the presentation tier). Therefore, we will make `ViewWin` and `ViewWeb` non-abstract, predominantly because we will be developing our concrete views in Visual Studio .NET.

A Reference from the Controller to the View

The only abstract class we haven't messed with yet is the **controller**. The good news is that we don't have to. As you may have noticed already, the controller is really the brains of an MVC application; it's where all of the presentation logic lives. The controller doesn't need to represent or extend any other type of object; therefore it can remain abstract and all concrete controller classes can extend it. This is good because the controller defines many of the behaviors and relationships with the other MVC classes. Encapsulating this into a single abstract base class makes good object-oriented sense.

In order for the controller to know when to execute its presentation logic, it needs to be able to respond to user-generated events (user gestures) within the view. Our current diagram shows an aggregate association from the view to the controller, since a controller is technically part of a view. But the controller will also need a reference back to the view, so that concrete controllers can set event-handling references to the view or to visual elements within the view. For example, if a concrete view contains a button control that the user is to click, then the concrete controller needs to have a `WithEvents` reference to that button, so it can handle the `Click` event. The abstract controller can't contain a reference to the button control since it knows nothing about the concrete view that would actually contain the button. However, the abstract controller should have a general reference to the *view*, so that concrete controllers can cast references to the concrete view and/or visual elements within the view as needed.

This reference from the view back to the controller may seem a bit confusing right now, as it's hard to really see its purpose until we start coding. But it is necessary. Let's take a look at the class diagram now with this modification:

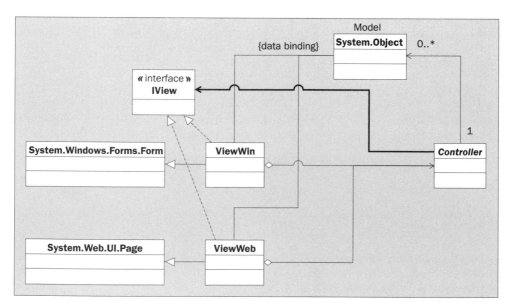

This new reference from the controller to the view is actually to the IView interface. This way, the abstract controller can contain a reference to any type of view (ViewWin, ViewWeb, etc.).

The Controller Factory

We're going to dive deeper into the details of the concrete class construction within our MVC framework of classes in just a bit. But for now, let's consider at a high level the construction of concrete controller classes. Since the Strategy pattern relationship between the view and its controller allows for one of many controllers to be selected for the view, there is some logic involved in determining exactly what concrete controller gets instantiated. Since the view contains the controller, we could place this logic within the view, but once again, that would bind the logic to that view. A better approach is to put the construction logic within a **factory object**, and better yet within a family of factory objects that have a parallel class hierarchy to the controller classes they're creating. The Factory Method design pattern fits this situation perfectly.

This may look like overkill at the moment. However, as we lay out the complete concrete class diagram for our NOP presentation tier, you will see why Factory Method works so well in constructing concrete controller classes. For now, it will be sufficient to add a single abstract ControllerFactory class to the diagram. The view will construct and have a reference to this ControllerFactory class, and it's up to the concrete view class to determine which concrete ControllerFactory is necessary to construct its concrete controller class:

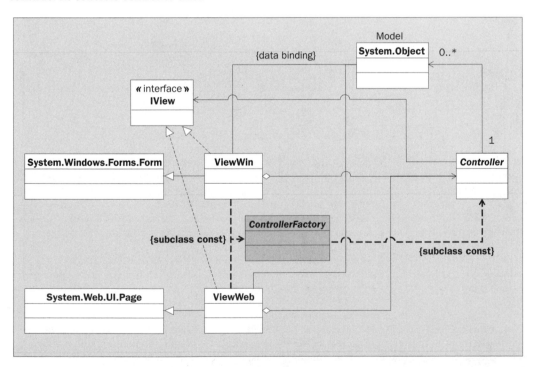

You will notice the {subclass const} constraint (which stands for subclass construction) next to the construction lines. The construction lines by themselves would be invalid since the classes they point to that are being constructed are abstract (and abstract classes can't be constructed). Instead, this notation implies that it's a subclass that does the constructing and it's a subclass that is constructed.

The Final Construction

While we're on the subject of class construction, we might as well finish up our class diagram and show the rest of the construction lines. Like the construction line from `ControllerFactory` to controller, these additional lines represent construction occurring within subclasses. However, it is useful to see this construction relationship between our high-level MVC classes, especially in the next section when we lay in the class schema:

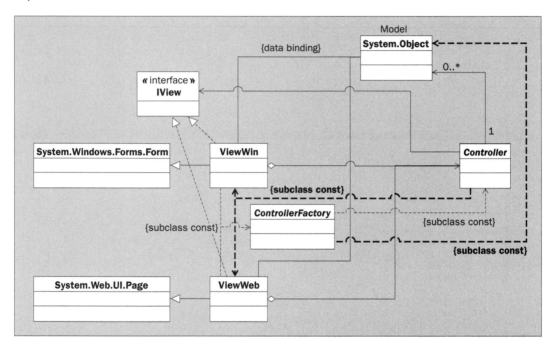

Here you can see that the `ControllerFactory` is not only responsible for creating controller classes, but it also creates references to the model as well (these references get passed into the new controller when it's constructed by the `ControllerFactory`). Intuitively, one would expect the controller to be the class to construct its own references to the model. But as we get further into our design we will discover how the `ControllerFactory` may need to know the state of the model ahead of time, because it can use that state as a criterion for selecting and constructing the proper controller class.

Finally, concrete controller classes are responsible for creating new views. This is consistent with the controller's role of handling view selection. When the user clicks a button that is intended to open up or navigate them to a new view, it's the job of the controller to determine which view that is, and to construct it.

Now, there is one last interesting note regarding our class construction. Notice how all construction occurs from either the `Controller` class or the `ControllerFactory` class. This is good because all of the presentation logic is also contained within these two classes. Having all construction occurring within the same classes that contain all the logic helps produces a sound MVC architecture.

The MVC Framework Class Schema

Well, we finally have a complete set of MVC framework base classes. We also have an understanding of how the classes relate and which objects construct which objects. In this section we will define all the necessary schema members for each class. Let's first update our class diagram with the necessary schema, and then we'll discuss it:

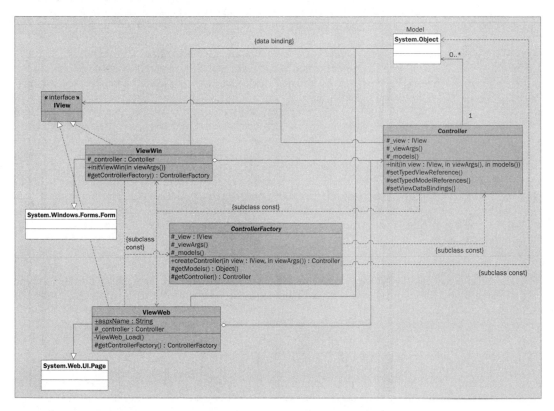

Next, we will discuss the general reasons for each schema member for each class. The mechanics behind these members will probably become clearer in the next section when we talk about passing information between views and finally when we start coding up the framework.

Model Members

Since we completely scrapped any abstract form of the model and left it to be any necessary object (or collection of objects), there's no schema to mention for the model. It is up to the controller to use whatever model is necessary.

View Members

As we've seen already, all view classes implement the `IView` interface. `IView` is simply a type used to generically reference and pass around view classes, without having to use the exact type. The `ControllerFactory` and controller classes make extensive use of the `IView` interface in this way. Interestingly enough, `IView` itself contains no members, as there are no common *public* members that both the `ViewWin` and `ViewWeb` classes can share.

The ViewWin and ViewWeb classes have several other common members, since they were supposed to be a single abstract class (remember, we had to break them up due to the single inheritance rule). Each class contains a protected attribute that is a reference its controller object (_controller). The attribute is protected so that it is accessible by subclasses. Each class also contains a protected abstract method called getControllerFactory(), which is a place for view subclasses to put code that instantiates the proper concrete ControllerFactory class for the view. The getControllerFactory() method is called automatically by both the ViewWin and ViewWeb classes: ViewWin calls it in its initViewWin() method and ViewWeb calls it during its Load event.

As we just mentioned, the ViewWin class has a special public method called initViewWin(). This method takes an Object array argument called viewArgs, which, as you will see, is used to pass information to the current view when it's created. initViewWin() is usually called by whatever client constructed the view; typically this is the controller of a different view. Besides calling getControllerFactory(), initViewWin() also calls the createController() method of the ControllerFactory class that was created by getControllerFactory(). It then sets the view's internal _controller reference to the controller returned by createController().

The ViewWeb class doesn't have the same initViewWin() method. Instead, it executes all of the same logic within its Load event handler. The main reason for this is that ViewWeb classes cannot be created directly by other classes (namely controllers of other views), so no method like initViewWin() can be called. Consequently, there is no viewArgs argument being passed into the ViewWeb class. So how does a ViewWeb class get passed its information from a calling client? We will learn shortly (in the next section entitled *Views Calling Other Views*) just exactly how view classes call each other and pass information.

The ViewWeb class has an additional attribute called aspxName, which is actually a constant. ViewWeb classes can only be created when the ASP.NET infrastructure serves up the associated .aspx page (since they inherit from the System.Web.UI.Page class). The aspxName constant is a convenient place to store the associated .aspx page name of a ViewWeb subclass, since it can be overridden by concrete subclasses (using the VB Shadows keyword). It can then be accessed easily by clients who wish to call the ViewWeb subclass. The necessity of this constant will also become clearer in the upcoming section, *Views Calling Other Views*.

ControllerFactory Members

The primary purpose of a ControllerFactory class is to create a concrete controller class. Therefore, its most important member is the createController() public method. This method cannot be overridden, since it executes the plumbing necessary to build any controller class. It does this by calling the two protected methods, getModels() and getController(), which must be overridden. We'll explain these two methods next.

The ControllerFactory class has a secondary purpose, and that's to get references to all of the models that the controller will need. This is done in the getModels() method, which is the first protected method that createController() calls. The getModels() method returns an array of type Object, so it can contain anything that the controller needs to do its job. As we've mentioned before in our MVC class framework discussion, the model is free; and this provides as much flexibility as the controller would need. Once this model array is created, it's stored and eventually passed into the new controller class created by the next protected procedure called by the createController() public method, getController().

The real logic for choosing the correct concrete controller class is contained within the getController() method, which has to be implemented by a subclass. One nice thing is, by the time getController() is called, the references to the model are already established (via the getModels() method); so the logic within getController() can use the state of the model (if it needs to) as a criterion for its selection of the concrete controller. In our sample application coming up, we will do just that.

After calling getModels() and getController() to get the model and the controller, the createController() public method rounds off by calling the init() method of the new controller returned by getController(). init() takes references to just about everything obtained up to this point in the process: a reference to the view, a reference to the information passed to the view (viewArgs), and (of course) a reference to the model (or models array).

The getModels() and getController() methods may need access to the view and the viewArgs passed into the createController() method. Therefore, createController() also sets class-level references to these objects (the _view and _viewArgs protected attributes). Also, once getModels() has returned its model, a class-level reference (the _models protected attribute) is set to that array so the getController() method can access it as well. These three protected attributes are not necessary, but they provide a convenient way for all ControllerFactory methods to access these objects.

Controller Members

The controller has the largest number of abstract members of the bunch. This is because most of the presentation logic and plumbing occurs here and it's important to impose as much control over the subclasses as possible.

The Controller class has three protected attributes, all of which are passed to the Controller via the public init() method, which is called by a ControllerFactory class:

- ❑ The first attribute, _view, is a reference to the hosting view.

- ❑ The second, _viewArgs, is an Object array that contains the viewArgs passed to the ControllerFactory's createController() method from the view itself.

- ❑ The third attribute, _models, is another Object array containing references to all of the models, which was created in the ControllerFactory's createController() method.

The Controller class also has four protected abstract methods that subclasses must override and implement. Each of these methods is called in proper sequence by the init() method. This enforces the proper configuration of the controller as it relates to all of the other classes in the MVC framework:

- ❑ The setTypedViewReference() and setTypedModelReferences() methods are not as important as the other protected methods. They are simply there as convenient places for subclasses to set strongly typed references to the view and the model.

  By "strongly typed reference" we mean a variable that's declared using the concrete class (such as CustomerView) instead of the abstract class or interface (such as IView).

The view and the model come into the controller as generic types via the `init()` method (`IView` in the case of the view, and an array of `System.Object` type in the case of the model). Both the view and the model are typically used several times within the logic of controller subclasses. Therefore, it's handy for the controller subclasses to have strongly typed references to the view and the model. These strongly typed references should be class-level variables declared as `Protected` so they can be accessed by other subclasses. The strongly typed view reference should also be declared using the `WithEvents` keyword, so subclasses can handle events from the view itself (like the `Load` event).

❑ The `setViewWithEventsReferences()` protected method is a place where controller subclasses should set variable references to all the visual elements (for example, controls) within the view whose events need to be handled within the controller. These references should be declared as class-level variables within the controller subclass using the `WithEvents` keyword, thus allowing the subclass to handle the associated events.

References to the necessary visual elements within the view can be obtained if these elements are made available as properties or fields in the containing view's public interface. If both the view and the controller are within the same assembly, then these properties or fields can be declared as `Friend`; if they're in separate assemblies, then they have to be declared as `Public`. By default in Visual Studio .NET, controls within a Windows form (`ViewWin` class) declare themselves as `Friend` fields. By default, server controls within an ASP.NET web form (`ViewWeb` class) declare themselves as `Protected` fields. Therefore ASP.NET server control fields would have to be modified to at least `Friend` to be accessed by controller classes. We'll see how this is done in more detail once we start coding our sample application.

❑ Finally, the `setViewDataBindings()` method is where controller subclasses should bind all the necessary visual elements (the `WithEvents` references we just mentioned) within the view to the corresponding data elements within the model. Once these data bindings are set, the view/model Observer design pattern relationship is in place.

Views Calling Other Views

Most applications need more than one view to make up the presentation tier. Therefore there are many cases where one view is calling another:

❑ When a new view is required to show more detail of the current view. For example, a CustomerList view might open a Customer view to show (and allow editing of) the details of an individual customer.

❑ When the user is navigating to a totally different area of the application. For example, when the user jumps from the Products view to the ShoppingCart view.

Regardless of the situation, a somewhat complex scenario occurs when there is a **parent view** that needs to create and pass control over to a **child view**. In many cases, there is also a need to pass *information* to the child view so it can properly render itself. To complicate things further, it's really the controllers that need to communicate to each other, not the views. This is because it's the controllers that contain the presentation logic. Therefore, when a parent view calls a child view, what's really happening is the controller hosted in the parent view (which we'll call the **parent controller**) is trying to call the child view and (potentially) send information to the controller hosted in child view (which we'll call the **child controller**). This scenario of views calling other views needs to be addressed when designing the MVC framework classes.

It would be very difficult to have a common API for calling new views for all types of views (ViewWeb, ViewWin, etc.), due to architectural differences between different views. For example, a new ViewWin class can be instantiated and activated directly by a parent controller. However, a ViewWeb class cannot since it can only be instantiated by the ASP.NET infrastructure when its associated .aspx page is served up by IIS. Therefore, to simplify the matter, let's decide that each view type can implement its own approach to constructing child views and passing information to them.

Calling New ViewWin Views

As we just stated, creating and activating a new ViewWin class is actually pretty straightforward. The calling code resides in the parent controller, typically in an event handling procedure of a control on the associated view (like the click event of a button). The parent controller simply instantiates the desired concrete child view class, calls its initViewWin() method, and then calls either the Form.Show() or Form.ShowDialog() method to display the view. Information is passed to the new view via the initViewWin() method's viewArgs argument. The viewArgs argument of initViewWin() is actually declared using the VB ParamArray keyword, so zero to many arbitrary arguments can be passed.

The code within the parent controller might look something like this:

```
Private Sub _myButton_Click(ByVal sender As System.Object, _
                        ByVal e As System.EventArgs) _
                                            Handles _myButton.Click
    Dim myChildViewWin As New MyViewWeb()
    With myChildViewWin
        .initViewWin(arg1, arg2, arg3)
        .ShowDiaglog()
    End With
End Sub
```

There's a lot going on behind these few lines of code (specifically within the initViewWin() method call). Here's a sequence diagram that shows the complete process of a parentController calling and activating a new child ViewWin class:

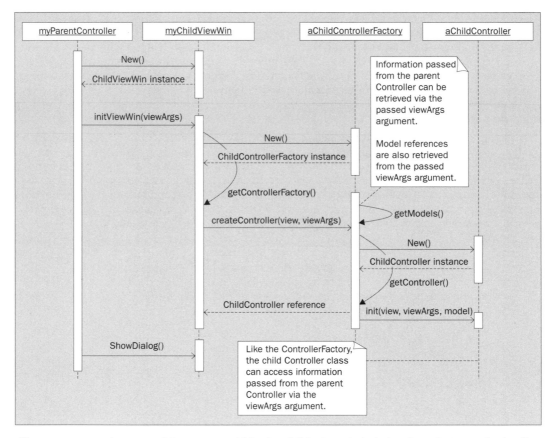

Here we can see that everything occurs within the child ViewWin's initViewWin() method call. initViewWin() automatically calls the protected method getControllerFactory(), which creates an instance to the required ControllerFactory class. initViewWin() then calls the createController() method of the new ControllerFactory to obtain a reference to the required Controller class, which the view holds on to for the duration of its lifetime.

The ControllerFactory class's createController() method does most of the real plumbing work. It gets a references to the model (by calling the protected getModels() method), creates a new concrete Controller class, and then initializes that Controller class by calling its init() method. Finally, it returns the finished product (an initialized Controller class) to the hosting view.

Information is passed from the parent controller all the way to the child controller via the viewArgs argument, which is passed to ViewWin.initViewWin(), then to ControllerFactory.createController(), and then finally to Controller.init().

Calling New ViewWeb Views

Creating and activating a new ViewWeb class is a little more indirect than a ViewWin class. This is because ViewWeb classes are only instantiated when their associated .aspx pages are served up to a browser (which is because ViewWeb classes inherit from the System.Web.UI.Page class). So, how does code in a parent controller call a new ViewWeb class and pass information? There are several approaches and each depends upon how you want the new web page (the ViewWeb object) to behave when it is created.

The easiest approach is for the parent controller to handle a **user gesture event** of a server control contained within the view (like the click event of a button), and perform a `Server.Transfer` method call to the `.aspx` page of the new view.

User gesture events are events that occur due to user interactions with the view, like the `Click` event of a button. Non-user gesture events are events that automatically occur within a view, like a `Load` event.

ASP.NET's `Server.Transfer` (which is really the `System.Web.HttpServerUtility.Transfer` method) is analogous to the old ASP 3.0 `Server.Transfer` method, which was available in IIS 5.0. Like the ASP `Server.Transfer` method, the new method transfers execution from one `.aspx` page to another. However, the new `Server.Transfer` is more flexible: it allows you to pass querystring data along with the page path. Here's a sample showing what the code in the parent controller might look like to call a new `ViewWeb` class called `ChildViewWeb` via the `Server.Transfer` method:

```
Private Sub _myButton_Click(ByVal sender As System.Object, _
                    ByVal e As System.EventArgs) _
                                    Handles _myButton.Click
  _parentViewWeb.Server.Transfer(ChildViewWeb.aspxName & _
                        "?arg1=a&arg2=b&arg3=c")
End Sub
```

In this code, we see the `Click` event handler of a button within a parent view. `ChildViewWeb` is a concrete `ViewWeb` class that is to be the child view. We're using its `aspxName` constant (which can be called without creating an instance of a `ChildViewWeb` class) to get the actual `.aspx` page name associated with the `ChildViewWeb` class. The `Server.Transfer()` method takes that page name plus a few querystring arguments, which allow custom information to be passed to the `ChildViewWeb` view when it is finally created by the ASP.NET infrastructure. As you can see, the actual querystring name-value pairs are completely arbitrary; it all depends on what the child controller hosted by the `ChildViewWeb` view is looking for. When the transfer has executed and the `ChildViewWeb` object and its associated child controller object are finally created, the passed querystring information can be extracted using the ASP.NET `Request` object.

Let's take a look at a sequence diagram of the `ViewWeb` scenario. There are two sequences: a request and a response. Let's first look at the request:

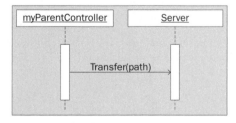

The first sequence takes place within the context of the parent view's `.aspx` page (in this case `ParentView.aspx`). Once the `Server.Transfer` method is completed, control is passed over to the new view's `.aspx` page. Here's the sequence diagram for the `ChildView.aspx` response, which is where all the work is happening:

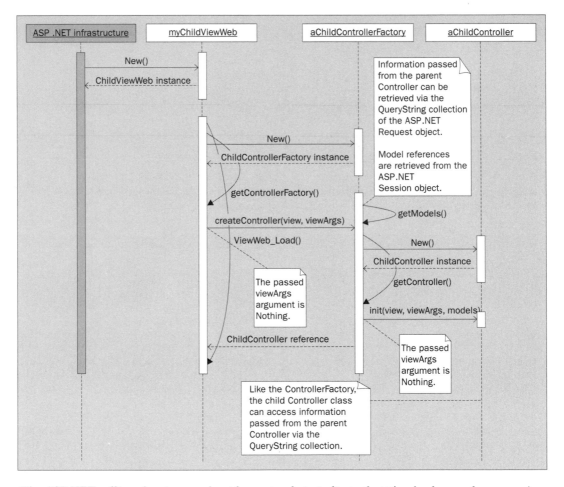

The ASP.NET calling class is grayed out here, simply to indicate that it's a background process. As we've already mentioned, the ViewWeb scenario is a little more complicated in comparison to ViewWin, since the parent controller cannot directly create and reference the child view. In the ViewWin class, most of the work occurs within the initViewWin() method. By contrast, in the ViewWeb class, all of this work occurs within the ViewWeb_Load() procedure, which is the Load event handler of the System.Web.UI.Page superclass. Information can't be passed directly from the parent controller to the child view, so it's passed via querystring, which can be picked up by the child ControllerFactory and controller classes in the new child view.

You may also notice that the child ControllerFactory is getting model references from the ASP.NET Session object. The ASP.NET Session object is a good place to store references to .NET reference types that need to stay alive between page calls (maintaining session state). You can easily pass value type information via the querystring, but there are limits. The Session object can hold references to large amounts of data or to model references that can't be represented and passed between pages via a querystring or form post. When we code up our sample application, we'll see how we can easily store model information within the Session object.

You may be wondering why we're trying to keep a reference to the model when we move from one view to another instead of going and getting an updated model from the middle tier. The need for this is totally dependent upon the situation. In many cases when navigating from one view to another, a fresh model is required. However, if the state of the model hasn't changed and it's not critical that the new view get the absolute latest model, then we have a mechanism here to maintain a local reference to the model until a reconnection to the middle tier is finally required.

This technique may also be important for maintaining a reference to the model between postbacks of a single view. HTTP is a stateless protocol and as you may know, ASP.NET Web Forms use tricks like view state to maintain the state of Server Controls between page postbacks. However, references to complex objects (such as a model) need to be maintained within something that stays on the server, like the ASP.NET Session *object.*

As we've already mentioned, sometimes a view works with several models. One model may have data that needs continuous updating with the middle tier. Another may use data that is only relevant to a user's session (like cached search results or the contents of a shopping cart) and doesn't need to be connected back to the middle tier between views. The Session *object is a good place to store additional models that live and die with a user's session.*

The Server.Transfer approach is simple, but it has the limitation of creating the new view within the same browser window. Most often, this behavior is acceptable, but sometimes it is necessary to create the new view within a new browser window (such as a pop-up). There are many ways you could implement this. A simple way would be to put a Hyperlink server control (System.Web.UI.WebControls.Hyperlink) in the parent view. Then the parent controller could handle the Load event of that control and set its NavigationURL property to specify the .aspx page of the child view along with any querystring arguments. The Target property could also be set here, to specify the exact name of the browser window in which the child view would render. The code might look something like this:

```
    Private Sub _myHyperLink_Load(ByVal sender As Object, _
                            ByVal e As System.EventArgs) _
                                Handles _myHyperLink.Load
    With _myHyperLink
        .NavigateUrl = PopUpView.aspxName & "?title=My Popup"
        .Target = "popup"
    End With
End Sub
```

In this code, the child view (the PopUpView class) and its child controller are expecting the parent controller to pass the title text of the pop-up window. We're seeing that in the appended querystring.

This discussion on views calling views pretty much wraps up the design portion of our MVC class framework. In the next section we'll see how all of this design manifests itself into real code.

MVC Framework Code

We finally get to do some coding! The ironic part is that there really isn't much code within the MVC framework classes themselves. The power of the framework is really in the abstraction and relationship between the classes, not in numerous lines of code.

We're going to place the MVC framework code and all of the sample application code into one Visual Studio .NET solution called MVCPresTier. We'll subdivide everything into separate projects (which become separate assemblies when compiled) as needed. To start, create the new solution and add a new Class Library project called MVC. This will produce the DLL assembly that will contain our MVC framework of classes.

Even though it won't be shown in any of the code to follow, every source file will have Option Explicit *and* Option Strict *switched* On. *With* Option Explicit On *(which is actually the default in VB.NET), we are forced to declare all variables. Turning* Option Strict On *(the default in VB.NET is* Off*) will force our code to do manual data conversions. Both of these* Option *settings are good coding practices for new code written in VB.NET.*

The Model

You may have already guessed it, but there isn't any code to write for the model since the model can be anything the controller wants it to be. However, when we get into the sample application, we'll produce some model classes that simulate the NOP middle tier from Chapter 3.

The View

Per our MVC framework class diagram, we have one interface (IView) and two classes (ViewWin and ViewWeb) associated with the view.

The IView Interface

First, let's add the IView interface. Rename the Class1.vb file (which is automatically generated by Visual Studio.NET) to View.vb. Then replace the Class1 class definition in the file with the following code:

```
Public Interface IView
End Interface
```

IView has no members, so it's pretty simple; it's just an interface definition. However, this interface is used extensively by many other classes within the MVC framework.

The ViewWin Class

Next, we'll add the ViewWin class. Since ViewWin is really a Windows Form class (that is, it inherits from System.Windows.Forms.Form), the easiest way to add its code is to add a new Windows Form to the project, copy the code it generates into View.vb, and modify it to meet the schema of the ViewWin class. When you add the temporary Windows Form class to the project, name the file ViewWin.vb so its class name is already set. Then cut and paste the ViewWin class code from ViewWin.vb to View.vb. Then clean up by deleting the temporary ViewWin.vb file.

Finally, modify ViewWin so it looks like the following class. The gray background indicates the code that you'll need to add to the initial Windows Form code:

```
Public Class ViewWin
    Inherits System.Windows.Forms.Form
    Implements IView
```

```
      Protected _controller As Controller

   Windows Form Designer generated code

      Public Sub initViewWin(ByVal ParamArray viewArgs() As Object)
         'get concrete ControllerFactory class
         Dim controllerFactory As ControllerFactory = getControllerFactory()

         'createController is called and viewArgs are passed
         If Not controllerFactory Is Nothing Then
            _controller = controllerFactory.createController(Me, viewArgs)
         End If
      End Sub

      Protected Overridable Function getControllerFactory() _
                                                    As ControllerFactory
         'subclass must implement and return a concrete ControllerFactory class
      End Function
   End Class
```

The line `Windows Form Designer generated code` *above represents the collapsed region of code generated by Visual Studio .NET when you create a new Windows Form class. We're not placing any new code within this region, so I've shown it in its collapsed form for brevity.*

`ViewWin` implements `IView` and contains the members discussed previously in the schema section. Notice how the `initViewWin()` method (which cannot be overridden) automatically calls the protected `getControllerFactory()` method, which returns an instance of a concrete `ControllerFactory` class. It then uses the `ControllerFactory` object to call the `createController()` method, which returns the concrete controller class for the view; and since this is a `ViewWin` class, `viewArgs` are passed to `createController`.

Interestingly, if the `getControllerFactory()` method returns `Nothing` (that is,. it's not implemented by the view subclass), then the `createController()` method is never called. This produces a view with no controller. There are cases where this scenario may be desirable (for example, a view that is in a disabled state), so this makes for a good default behavior for a view. We will see this same code in the upcoming `ViewWeb` class.

The ViewWeb Class

Codewise, `ViewWeb` is very similar to `ViewWin`. Since `ViewWeb` is really an ASP.NET web form, we could also use the same trick of creating a separate web form to get the skeleton code to add to `View.vb`. However, Visual Studio .NET doesn't allow you to add Web Form items to Class Library projects, so you'd have to add a new ASP.NET Web Application project to the solution first. This is a little more work than it's worth, so we'll just hand-code it all instead.

First, add a reference to the `System.Web.dll` assembly in the `MVC` project. Now we're ready to type the code. Here is the full listing for the class:

```
Public Class ViewWeb
   Inherits System.Web.UI.Page
   Implements IView
```

```
    Public Const aspxName As String = "ViewWeb_baseclass.aspx"
    Protected _controller As Controller

#Region " Web Form Designer Generated Code "

  'This call is required by the Web Form Designer.
  <System.Diagnostics.DebuggerStepThrough()> Private Sub _
                                          InitializeComponent()

  End Sub

  Private Sub Page_Init(ByVal sender As System.Object, _
                    ByVal e As System.EventArgs) Handles MyBase.Init
    'CODEGEN: This method call is required by the Web Form Designer
    'Do not modify it using the code editor.
    InitializeComponent()
  End Sub

#End Region

  'ViewWeb_Load will occur automatically when the .aspx page loads
  Private Sub ViewWeb_Load(ByVal sender As Object, _
                    ByVal e As System.EventArgs) Handles MyBase.Load
    'get concrete ControllerFactory class
    Dim controllerFactory As ControllerFactory = getControllerFactory()
    'createController is called and no viewArgs are passed
    If Not controllerFactory Is Nothing Then
      _controller = controllerFactory.createController(Me, Nothing)
    End If
  End Sub

  Protected Overridable Function getControllerFactory() _
                                          As ControllerFactory
    'subclass must implement and return a concrete ControllerFactory class
  End Function
End Class
```

Once again, we use the gray background to highlight the code we've added to the standard Web Form template code.

The ViewWeb class sets its aspxName constant equal to a generic value. Subclasses will Shadow this constant and specify the name of their associated .aspx page.

The getControllerFactory() method is identical to the one declared in ViewWin and serves the same purpose. The main difference between the ViewWin and ViewWeb classes is how they initialize themselves. As we've seen, the ViewWin depends on the client (parent controller) to call its initViewWin() method directly – the method takes a viewArgs argument so information can be passed to the new view. ViewWeb classes can't be called directly by clients since they can only be instantiated by the ASP.NET infrastructure. Therefore, the code corresponding to the initViewWin() method of ViewWin is the Load event handler in ViewWeb. Since no viewArgs argument is passed to ViewWeb_Load(), the value of Nothing is passed to the ControllerFactory.createController method for its viewArgs argument. As we've already discussed, the ControllerFactory and Controller classes then use other means to obtain information passed to the view (such as the ASP.NET Request object).

The Controller

The classes related to the controller (`ControllerFactory` and `Controller`) are the only abstract classes in our framework. But this is good because the controller classes are the core of MVC; the fact that they are truly abstract means we have more control over the subclass implementation.

Add another class file to the project – call it `Controller.vb`. There are two controller-related classes, `Controller` and `ControllerFactory`.

The Controller Abstract Class

The `Controller` abstract class comprises mostly empty protected abstract methods that are placeholders for subclasses to replace with all the necessary logic to make a controller work. All of these protected methods are called in the right sequence by the `init()` method:

```
Public MustInherit Class Controller
  Protected _view As IView
  Protected _viewArgs() As Object
  Protected _models() As Object

  Public Sub init(ByRef view As IView, ByRef viewArgs() As Object, _
                                  ByRef models() As Object)
    'set reference to View
    _view = view
    'set reference Model(s)
    _models = models
    'set reference to view arguments
    _viewArgs = viewArgs
    'allow subclasses to set strongly typed reference to View
    setTypedViewReference()
    'allow subclasses to set strongly typed Model references
    setTypedModelReferences()
    'allow subclasses to set View event handling references
    setViewWithEventsReferences()
    'allow subclasses to set View data binding
    setViewDataBindings()
  End Sub

  Protected MustOverride Sub setTypedViewReference()
  Protected MustOverride Sub setTypedModelReferences()
  Protected MustOverride Sub setViewWithEventsReferences()
  Protected MustOverride Sub setViewDataBindings()
End Class
```

One interesting thing to note is that we're not making use of any custom constructors in our MVC framework classes. Specifically, instead of the `init()` method shown above, we could have had a constructor for the `Controller` class that took the same arguments as `init()`. However, constructors that take arguments are not inherited into the public interface of a subclass. In other words, a `CustomerController` subclass would have to declare an identical constructor with all of the same arguments as the `Controller` class's constructor. `CustomerController` probably wouldn't need to add any additional code to its constructor, so all it would be doing is passing the same constructor arguments on to the `Controller` base class constructor. However, the public `init()` method is inherited by a subclass's public interface and therefore automatically works without any additional subclass coding.

The ControllerFactory Abstract Class

The ControllerFactory abstract class looks similar to Controller. It too has a group of protected abstract methods that subclasses are forced to override and are all called within a public worker method, in this case createController():

```
Public MustInherit Class ControllerFactory
   Protected _view As IView
   Protected _viewArgs() As Object
   Protected _models() As Object

   Public Function createController(ByRef view As IView, _
                           ByRef viewArgs() As Object) As Controller
     _view = view
     _viewArgs = viewArgs
     _models = getModels()
     Dim controller As Controller = getController()
     controller.init(view, viewArgs, _models)
     Return controller
   End Function

   Protected MustOverride Function getModels() As Object()
   Protected MustOverride Function getController() As Controller
End Class
```

Believe it or not, we now have a fully functional MVC class framework that we can use in a real application. Go ahead and compile this class library project into the MVC.dll assembly. We will reference it up next, when we code up our sample application.

A Front End for Northwind Order Processing

At Northwind Traders, Laura Callahan hired consultant Jack Spratt to develop the middle tier of the Northwind Order Processing (NOP) application. However, she already had some internal developers working on the front end of NOP. Bill Ulrich is the man who has been charged with leading his internal development team to produce the presentation tier. We'll get to learn about his endeavors to implement MVC, which will include the integration of the MVC framework we just developed.

The NOP application needed a front end to provide users access to the middle tier. The primary UI was to be an ASP.NET web site that would allow customers who were currently calling the sales reps, to place orders manually over the Internet, thereby reducing the cost per transaction. However the sales team felt a little threatened by being replaced by a web site, so the head of sales, Gladys Forbes, convinced Laura to build a second UI just for the sales team. It would allow them to handle orders more efficiently – they could use it to place any telephone orders that came through and to support any order problems that initiated from the web site. The internal UI team suggested building a rich UI client with .NET Windows Forms, since it would provide a similar look and feel to the existing client–server app the sales team was currently using. Finally, in their discussions (as we hinted in Chapter 3) it was noted that a web service could be a part of the presentation tier (though we won't implement it in this chapter). If customers had the technology to consume the web service, then they could seamlessly integrate NOP into their own enterprise applications.

For our sample application we're not going to pour over the dozens of use case, activity, and sequence diagrams that represent Bill's future presentation tier and try to come up with the associated classes and then make it all fit on top of our MVC framework. Although this is probably Bill's goal in the end, it would be out of the scope of our chapter to tackle the complete presentation tier design. Instead we're going to take a very small piece of it and call it Bill's pilot application for MVC. Bill will use this pilot app to test the waters a bit and see just how flexible MVC is. Then, when he feels comfortable, he can tackle the rest of the application.

Just because we're taking on a subset of the real presentation tier, doesn't mean we're not going to get a lot of value out of our pilot application. The basic premise of the pilot will be to take a simple presentation tier use case and represent it in both a Windows forms UI and a web UI. Hopefully the pilot application will show us how MVC makes developing each type of UI better and how the development of multiple types of UIs is better.

Use Case Diagrams

Bill Ulrich knew the most important use case to focus on was allowing the end user to submit an order. In the case of a customer, orders were placed one at a time. However, sales reps wanted the capability to place multiple orders at the same time for multiple customers. These requirements produced the following simple use case diagram, which Bill felt was the perfect candidate for his pilot application.

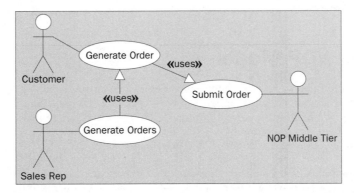

Activity Diagrams

The activity of this use case is also quite simple, and doesn't provide much more information than the use case diagram. The goal is to generate an order or group of orders to be submitted. Each order contains one or more products:

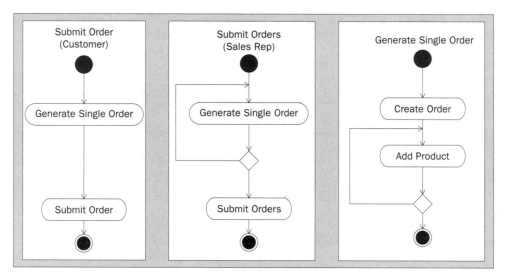

The use case diagram and the associated activity diagram pretty much encapsulate the requirements for Bill's pilot app. Next, we're going to generate a stand-in model that the pilot app can use that represents the NOP middle tier. Then we'll get into the class design of both UI types and finally put it all together in code.

A Common NOP Model

Before we can get to the fun part of creating actual views and controllers in our NOP pilot app, we should put together a common set of model classes that each UI can use to simulate the NOP middle tier. Since this is just a pilot application, our model will not actually be the real NOP middle tier itself, but rather a simplified representation of it. However, given the flexibility of our MVC framework, swapping this model out for the real one should be relatively easy.

To make data binding easy, the core of our model (that is, our "database") will be a .NET DataSet class (System.Data.DataSet). We will then wrap it with a utility class called NOPData and a couple business object classes (Orders and Order) that simply query against this DataSet, retrieving DataView objects that show the part of the model the business object needs to represent. Here's a quick class diagram that shows what we're after:

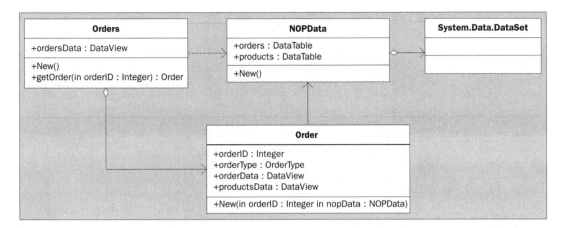

The Orders class represents a business object that provides access to multiple orders at once, while the Order class gives access to a single order and the products within that order. Both classes reference the NOPData utility class which contains the actual DataSet object with all of the data. On NOPData's construction, the DataSet is loaded with hard-coded dummy data (since we're not actually going to develop a real database) that both Orders and Order can utilize.

The only class that will be creatable outside of the NOP model assembly will be Orders. Therefore, it will also be the gateway for accessing individual Order objects, which is done via the Orders.getOrder() method. The NOPData class will be declared as Friend so it can't be created and it can't be referenced outside of the assembly.

The NOPData Class

Add a new Class Library project to our current MVCPresTier solution in Visual Studio.NET – call it NOPModel. We don't need to add a reference to the MVC project we created earlier, since the model doesn't need direct access to views or controllers (remember, the model is oblivious to views and controllers).

We'll start by coding the NOPData class. In the new project, rename the Class1.vb file to Model.vb and replace the Class1 skeleton code with the following:

```vb
Imports System.Data

Friend Class NOPData
  Private _ds As New DataSet()
  Private _orders As New DataTable("Order")
  Private _products As New DataTable("Product")

  Public Sub New()
    'locals
    Dim orderOrderIDColumn As New DataColumn("OrderID", _
                                    Type.GetType("System.Int32"))
    Dim productOrderIDColumn As _
              New DataColumn(orderOrderIDColumn.ColumnName, _
                                    Type.GetType("System.Int32"))
    Dim productIDColumn As New DataColumn("ProductID", _
                                    Type.GetType("System.Int32"))
```

```
Dim orderRowRelation As DataRelation
Dim row As DataRow
Dim rowValues As Object()

'build schema
With _ds
  'Order table
  .Tables.Add(_orders)
  With _orders.Columns
    .Add(orderOrderIDColumn)
    _orders.PrimaryKey = New DataColumn() {orderOrderIDColumn}
    .Add(New DataColumn("CustomerID", Type.GetType("System.String")))
    .Add(New DataColumn("OrderDate", Type.GetType("System.DateTime")))
    .Add(New DataColumn("OrderType", _
                              Type.GetType("NOPModel.OrderType")))
  End With
  'Product table
  .Tables.Add(_products)
  With _products.Columns
    .Add(productIDColumn)
    _products.PrimaryKey = New DataColumn() {productIDColumn}
    .Add(productOrderIDColumn)
    .Add(New DataColumn("Name", Type.GetType("System.String")))
    .Add(New DataColumn("Qty", Type.GetType("System.UInt32")))
    .Add(New DataColumn("Price", Type.GetType("System.Double")))
    .Add(New DataColumn("RequiredDate", _
                              Type.GetType("System.DateTime")))
  End With

  'Order/Product relationship
  orderRowRelation = .Relations.Add("Order_Product", _
                        orderOrderIDColumn, productOrderIDColumn)
  'constraints
  With orderOrderIDColumn
    .Unique = True
    .ReadOnly = True
    .AutoIncrementSeed = 100
    .AutoIncrementStep = 1
    .AutoIncrement = True
  End With
  With productOrderIDColumn
    .ReadOnly = True
  End With
  With productIDColumn
    .Unique = True
    .ReadOnly = True
    .AutoIncrementSeed = 200
    .AutoIncrementStep = 1
    .AutoIncrement = True
  End With
End With
```

```
'sample data
row = _orders.Rows.Add(New Object() {Nothing, "pete", _
                                      #1/1/2002#, OrderType.Normal})
_products.Rows.Add(New Object() {Nothing, _
                                 row(orderOrderIDColumn.ColumnName), _
                                 "beer", 100, 3.5, #1/2/2002#})
_products.Rows.Add(New Object() {Nothing, _
                                 row(orderOrderIDColumn.ColumnName), _
                                 "pizza", 3, 10, #1/2/2002#})
row = _orders.Rows.Add(New Object() {Nothing, "jon", _
                                      #2/1/2002#, OrderType.Special})
_products.Rows.Add(New Object() {Nothing, _
                                 row(orderOrderIDColumn.ColumnName), _
                                 "milk", 50, 1.5, #2/2/2002#})
End Sub

Public ReadOnly Property orders() As DataTable
  Get
     Return _orders
  End Get
End Property

Public ReadOnly Property products() As DataTable
  Get
     Return _products
  End Get
End Property

End Class
```

This class is somewhat lengthy simply because it has so much hard-coded data within it. There's nothing really too fancy going on, except for the fact that (for the purposes of demonstration) we're constructing a `DataSet` object from scratch (instead of getting the data from a database). The class first generates the schema of the `DataSet`, which contains an `Order` and a `Product` table, which look something like this:

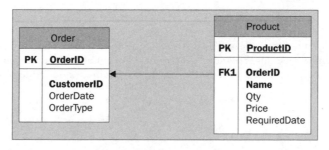

It then adds some sample data that consists of two orders and three products. And since it's a `DataSet` under the hood, we really have a miniature in-memory database, including an enforced parent-child relationship between the Order and Product tables. The other two classes in `NOPModel` (`Orders` and `Order`) can be used by controllers to gain access to our `DataSet`.

The Orders Class

Next, let's code the `Orders` class. It will live in the `Model.vb` file as well:

```
Public Class Orders
  Private _nopData As NOPData
  Private _ordersData As DataView = New DataView()

  Public Sub New()
    _nopData = New NOPData()
    With _ordersData
      .Table = _nopData.orders
    End With
  End Sub

  Public ReadOnly Property ordersData() As DataView
    Get
      Return _ordersData
    End Get
  End Property

  Public Function getOrder(ByVal orderID As Integer) As Order
    Return New Order(orderID, _nopData)
  End Function
End Class
```

The `Orders` class provides access to the underlying data via the `ordersData` property, which exposes a reference to a `DataView` object. `DataViews` (`System.Data.DataView`) are special ADO.NET objects that represent subsets of data within a `DataSet`. `DataViews` are fully data-binding capable, so they will make a good data source when we get to the data-binding stage in our view and controller classes. The `Orders` class also provides the `getOrder()` method, which takes an order ID as an argument. This method can be used by clients to gain access to individual `Order` objects. The `getOrder()` method automatically persists the state of the `NOPData` object (and therefore the underlying `DataSet`) by passing it to the constructor of the new `Order` object.

The Order Class

So, let's take a look at the `Order` class. This class actually contains an enumeration called `OrderType`, which is used to identity whether the underlying order is a normal order or a special order. We'll show the `OrderType` enumeration along with the `Order` class, which are both added to the `Model.vb` file:

```
Public Enum OrderType
  Normal
  Special
End Enum

Public Class Order
  Private _nopData As NOPData
  Private _orderID As Integer
  Private _orderType As orderType
  Private _orderData As DataView = New DataView()
  Private _productsData As DataView = New DataView()
```

```
Friend Sub New(ByVal orderID As Integer, ByRef nopData As NOPData)
   'nopData
   _nopData = nopData
   'orderID
   _orderID = orderID
   'orderData
   With _orderData
      .Table = _nopData.orders
      .RowFilter = "OrderID = " & orderID
   End With
   'orderType
   Dim orderRow As DataRow = _orderData.Item(0).Row
   _orderType = CType(orderRow.Item("OrderType"), OrderType)
   'productsData
   With _productsData
      .Table = _nopData.products
      .RowFilter = "OrderID = " & orderID
   End With
End Sub

Public ReadOnly Property orderID() As Integer
   Get
      Return _orderID
   End Get
End Property

Public ReadOnly Property orderType() As NOPModel.OrderType
   Get
      Return _orderType
   End Get
End Property

Public ReadOnly Property orderData() As DataView
   Get
      Return _orderData
   End Get
End Property

Public ReadOnly Property productsData() As DataView
   Get
      Return _productsData
   End Get
End Property
End Class
```

The Order class also provides properties that return DataView types: orderData and productsData. These properties will also be used for data binding purposes by views in controllers later on in our pilot application.

Well, that pretty much wraps up our simplified NOPModel project. Compile this into a NOPModel.dll class library and it should be ready to use in the upcoming code.

Concrete Views and Controllers

Finally, the fun part! We've worked hard to develop a solid MVC framework and it's now time to start using it to create real views and controllers.

NOPWin for the Sales Reps

The first UI that we're going to tackle is the Rich UI for the sales team. This way we can see the Visual Studio .NET inherited form feature in action and earn some brownie points with the sales reps at the same time. We will then create exactly the same views in a web UI. Both UI types will use the same model and will have a very similar structure.

The NOPWin Class Diagram

Our Rich UI application will be called **NOPWin**. Let's take a look at a class diagram that will show for the first time a set of concrete model, view, and controller classes that extend our MVC class framework:

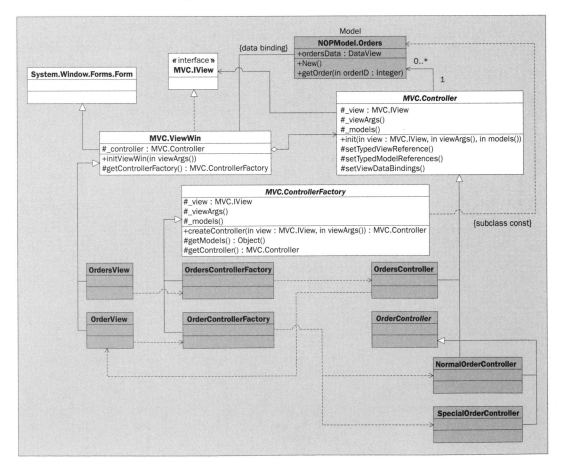

This class diagram is really an extension of the MVC framework class diagram we put together earlier in the chapter. For clarity, all classes from the MVC assembly are prefixed with MVC (which is also their namespace name) and the added concrete classes are highlighted in gray. Since NOPWin is only extending the ViewWin view class, the ViewWeb class is not shown. Also, you can see that we were able to remove most of the construction lines labeled {subclass const} from the original framework diagram and replace them with real construction lines between concrete classes. The only one we left was the construction line from the ControllerFactory to the model, since showing separate construction lines from each concrete ControllerFactory class would add no value to the diagram and only make it more cluttered.

So, what is this class diagram going to produce? Well, it shows two views that the user can work with. The startup view is the OrdersView. As we shall see in our code, it will contain a data grid showing all the orders in the model. Each order can be navigated to by the click of a button, which renders an OrderView class. From within the OrderView view, the user can either edit the products in the order (which are also contained in a data grid) or they can click a button to place the order.

Now, the fun part is that there are two different types of orders: normal orders and special orders. Both types need to be displayed differently in the OrderView view. One approach would be to subclass OrderView into NormalOrderView and SpecialOrderView. However, this is a little extreme since the visual differences between the two views are very small. Instead, our design subclasses the associated OrderController class. Then the OrderControllerFactory class constructs the proper controller by examining the model to establish whether the current order is a normal order or a special order.

This illustrates one of the powerful features of MVC: the decoupling of the view from the controller. In the future, if a new order type were to be added to the NOP application, the presentation tier would only need to add a new OrderController subclass and alter the logic within the ControllerFactory.createController() method to construct the new concrete view when the order was of that order type. The behavior of any view can be altered easily, by adding new controllers to the presentation tier in this way.

Without further delay, let's start coding. Start by adding a new Windows Application project (called NOPWin) into our MVCPresTier solution. You will need to add references to both the MVC and NOPModel projects we created earlier. Delete the Form1.vb file automatically created by the new Windows Application project.

The OrdersView View

The first concrete view we're going to tackle is OrdersView, which is used to manage multiple orders. Add an inherited form (called OrdersView) to the NOPWin project – have the form inherit from the MVC.ViewWin class in our MVC framework.

There are several things that need to be done to this form to make it the Orders view that we want. First, change the **Text** property of the form (which is the caption) from **ViewWin** to **Orders**. Then:

❑ Add a DataGrid control. Set its **Name** property to **ordersGrid**.

❑ Add a Button control. Set its **Name** property to **viewOrderButton**, and set its **Text** property to **View Order**.

❑ Add another Button control. Set its **Name** property to **orderAllButton**, and set its **Text** property to **Order All**.

Arrange these controls so that the form looks something like this:

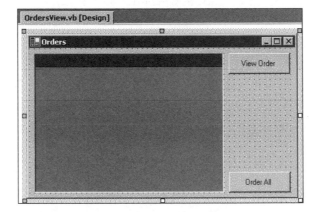

To make the order data display within the DataGrid in a more user-friendly fashion, we will modify the TableStyles collection property of the ordersGrid control:

❑ Select the orderGrid control and click to open up its TableStyles Collection Editor from the orderGrid's properties window:

❑ Add a member to the collection and name it ordersGridTableStyle. Set its MappingName property to Order (so it maps to the Order table in our NOPModel's underlying DataSet):

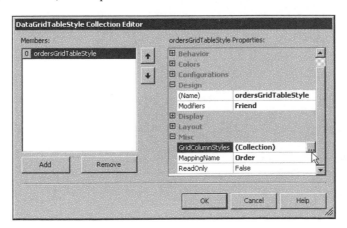

❑   Click the **GridColumnStyles** property button (shown in the dialog above) to open the DataGridColumnStyle Collection Editor:

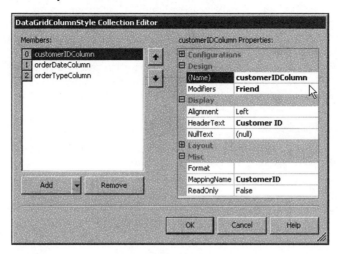

❑   As shown above, we need to add textbox columns for each column of the Orders table in our DataSet. Each column has a **Name**, **HeaderText**, and **MappingName** property that need to be set:

Name	Header Text	Mapping Name
customerIDColumn	Customer ID	CustomerID
orderDateColumn	Order Date	OrderDate
orderTypeColumn	Order Type	OrderType

Finally, we need to modify the code within the OrdersView class (OrdersView.vb) in order to specify the corresponding concrete ControllerFactory:

```
Imports MVC
Public Class OrdersView
   Inherits ViewWin

   Windows Form Designer generated code

   Protected Overrides Function getControllerFactory() As ControllerFactory
     Return New OrdersControllerFactory()
   End Function
End Class
```

Once again, the code we need to add is highlighted with the gray background. This view code is typical of all the view code we will see in our sample application where the only thing we really need to do is override the getControllerFactory() protected method and return an instance of the concrete ControllerFactory required for the given view. In this case, OrdersView returns an instance of the OrdersControllerFactory class. Now, when you add the getControllerFactory() method above to your code, you should see a blue squiggly line show up under the OrdersControllerFactory class name and a build error in your **Task List** that states: **Type OrdersControllerFactory is not defined**. This is because we haven't coded the OrdersControllerFactory class yet. But, before we do that, let's code up OrdersController first.

The OrdersController Class

Add a new **Class** item (called OrdersController.vb) to our **NOPWin** project. In it, place the following code for the OrdersController class:

```
Imports MVC
Imports NOPModel

Public Class OrdersController
  Inherits Controller

  'strongly typed View reference
  Protected WithEvents _ordersView As OrdersView
  'strongly typed Model references
  Protected _orders As Orders
  'View WithEvents references
  Protected WithEvents _ordersGrid As DataGrid
  Protected WithEvents _viewOrderButton As Button
  Protected WithEvents _orderAllButton As Button


  'overriden Controller members

  Protected Overrides Sub setTypedViewReference()
    _ordersView = CType(_view, OrdersView)
  End Sub

  Protected Overrides Sub setTypedModelReferences()
    _orders = CType(_models(0), Orders)
  End Sub

  Protected Overrides Sub setViewWithEventsReferences()
    With _ordersView
      _ordersGrid = .ordersGrid
      _viewOrderButton = .viewOrderButton
      _orderAllButton = .orderAllButton
    End With
  End Sub

  Protected Overrides Sub setViewDataBindings()
    _ordersGrid.DataSource = _orders.ordersData
  End Sub
```

```
'View event handling procedures
Private Sub _viewOrderButton_Click(ByVal sender As Object, _
                                   ByVal e As System.EventArgs) _
                                   Handles _viewOrderButton.Click

    Dim orderRow As DataRow = _
           _orders.ordersData.Item(_ordersGrid.CurrentRowIndex).Row
    Dim orderID As Integer = CInt(orderRow.Item("OrderID"))
    Dim orderView As New OrderView()
    With orderView
        .initViewWin(_orders, orderID)
        .ShowDialog()
    End With
End Sub

Private Sub _orderAllButton_Click(ByVal sender As Object, _
                                  ByVal e As System.EventArgs) _
                                  Handles _orderAllButton.Click

    MsgBox("All orders have been placed!")
End Sub
End Class
```

Controller subclasses contain most of the code within a presentation tier since that's where most of the presentation logic is. The OrdersController class contains several references to controls within the OrdersView view and it overrides all of the required protected abstract methods from the inherited Controller class. It also handles a few user-gesture events from OrdersView. The first event is the Click event of OrdersView's viewOrderButton control.

The viewOrderButton control is referenced by OrderController's _viewOrderButton class-level variable, hence its use in the code of the event handling procedure.

In this event handler, we see code to call and activate the OrderView view, passing the order ID and a reference to the Orders model object as viewArgs to the OrderView's initViewWin() method. This demonstrates in full detail how ViewWin parent views call and pass information to child views, as discussed earlier in the chapter.

> **An important thing to point out here is that the controller doesn't have to set references to all composite objects within the corresponding view, only the ones it's interested in. In this case, OrdersController needs to handle events from the viewOrdersButton and orderAllButton controls and potentially handle events from ordersGrid as well.**

The second event handled by OrdersController is the Click event of the orderAllButton control. There's nothing special going on here except that the application displays a message box. The reason for the existence of this button is that NOPWin is an application for the sales people and needs a way to submit multiple orders at once. While we're not actually implementing the code that sends the orders, this would be the place that action would occur.

An important overridden method to take a quick look at is setViewDataBindings(). All it takes is a single line of code that binds the ordersGrid DataGrid object to the ordersData property of the Orders object (which is a DataView type). OrdersView and OrdersViewController are now bound and the Observer design pattern is in place.

The OrdersControllerFactory Class

OrdersController also needed a factory class (so we can get rid of that build error in OrdersView.vb). In OrdersController.vb, add the following class code:

```
Public Class OrdersControllerFactory
  Inherits ControllerFactory

  'overriden Controller factory members
  Protected Overrides Function getModels() As Object()
    Dim orders As New Orders()
    Dim models() As Object = {orders}
    Return models
  End Function

  Protected Overrides Function getController() As Controller
    Return New OrdersController()
  End Function
End Class
```

Remember, a ControllerFactory subclass has two jobs. The first is to obtain references to models and the second is to create an instance of a concrete controller class. This is done by overriding the protected abstract methods getModels() and getController() respectively. The OrdersControllerFactory class above overrides getModels() to return a brand-new reference to an Orders object from our NOPModel assembly. It actually sticks this in an Object array since this is how the model is then passed to the controller. OrdersControllerFactory then overrides getController(), which simply returns a new instance of the OrdersController class. We'll see a more elaborate selection process in the getController() method of the *Order*ControllerFactory class coming up since it can create multiple concrete controller classes.

We've completed the OrdersView class and related classes (OrdersController and OrdersControllerFactory). Now it's time to code OrderView, which is the child view that OrdersView calls when the user wishes to drill into a particular order.

The OrderView View

We'll take similar steps to add all of the classes related to OrderView. Add another inherited form, called OrderView (OrderView.vb), to the NOPWin project – have it inherit from the MVC.ViewWin class in our MVC framework too.

Again, we need to add a few controls, before it will be the **Order** form that we want. Change the **Text** property of the form from **ViewWin** to **Order**. Then:

❑   Add a Label control named **Label1**. Set its **Text** property to **Customer ID**.

❑   Add another Label control named **Label2**. Set its **Text** property to **Order Date**.

❑   Add one more Label control, named **Label3**. Set its **Text** property to **Products**.

Now add three controls to accompany these three labels, and a Button control, as follows:

❑   Add a TextBox control. Set its **Name** property to **customerIDText**, and clear its **Text** property.

❏ Add another `TextBox` control. Set its **Name** property to **orderDateText**, and clear its **Text** property.

❏ Add a `DataGrid` control. Set its **Name** property to **productsGrid**.

❏ Add a `Button` control. Set its **Name** property to **orderButton**, and set its **Text** property to **Order**.

By arranging these controls accordingly, the form should look something like this:

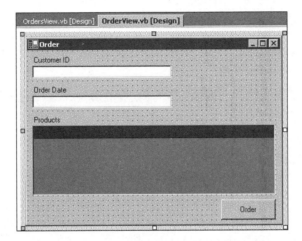

Like the `OrdersView` class, the `OrderView` has a `DataGrid`. We need to add `TableStyles` to this `DataGrid` to make it display the product data better. The process is almost identical to what we did with the `OrdersView` class, except there are different names:

❏ Add a member to `productsGrid`'s **TableStyles** collection – call it **productsGridTableStyle**. Set its **MappingName** property to **Product**:

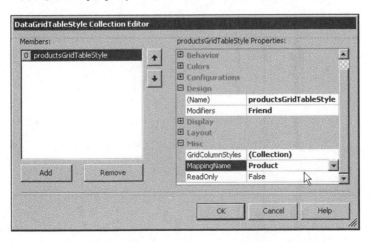

❑ Add four textbox columns to the GridColumnStyles collection, in the same way that we did before:

Name	Header Text	Mapping Name
nameColumn	Name	Name
quantityColumn	Quantity	Qty
priceColumn	Price	Price
requiredDateColumn	Required Date	RequiredDate

When you've done that, the DataGridColumnStyle Collection Editor should look something like this:

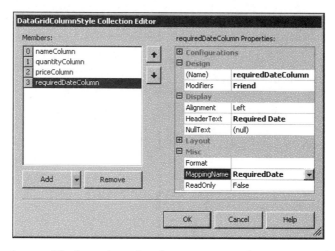

Once again we need to modify the code within the OrderView class so it uses the correct concrete ControllerFactory class:

```
Imports MVC
Public Class OrderView
   Inherits ViewWin

   Windows Form Designer generated code

   Protected Overrides Function getControllerFactory() As ControllerFactory
      Return New OrderControllerFactory()
   End Function
End Class
```

The OrderController Abstract Class

Our OrderView view can use one of two concrete controller classes. Both of these classes share a lot of common logic that we consolidate into an abstract super class called OrderController. Add a new Class item to the NOPWin project – call it OrderController.vb. In it, place the following code for the OrderController abstract class:

```
Imports MVC
Imports NOPModel

Public MustInherit Class OrderController
  Inherits Controller

  'strongly typed View reference
  Protected WithEvents _orderView As OrderView
  'strongly typed Model references
  Protected _order As Order
  'View WithEvents references
  Protected WithEvents _orderButton As Button
  'other class-level variables
  Protected _orderData As DataView
  Protected WithEvents _productsData As DataView

  'overriden Controller members

  Protected Overrides Sub setTypedViewReference()
    _orderView = CType(_view, OrderView)
  End Sub

  Protected Overrides Sub setTypedModelReferences()
    _order = CType(_models(0), Order)
  End Sub

  Protected Overrides Sub setViewWithEventsReferences()
    With _orderView
      _orderButton = .orderButton
    End With
  End Sub

  Protected Overrides Sub setViewDataBindings()
    With _orderView
      'order data
      _orderData = _order.orderData
      .customerIDText.DataBindings.Add(New Binding("Text", _orderData, _
                                                   "CustomerID"))
      .orderDateText.DataBindings.Add(New Binding("Text", _orderData, _
                                                  "OrderDate"))
      'products data
      _productsData = _order.productsData
      .productsGrid.DataSource = _productsData
    End With
  End Sub

  'View event handling procedures

  'other event handling procedures

  Private Sub _productsData_ListChanged(ByVal sender As Object, _
               ByVal e As System.ComponentModel.ListChangedEventArgs) _
               Handles _productsData.ListChanged
    If e.ListChangedType = _
```

```
                        System.ComponentModel.ListChangedType.ItemAdded Then
              'set the OrderID field of a newly added product
              _productsData.Item(_productsData.Count - 1)("OrderID") = _
                                                         _order.orderID
         End If
      End Sub
   End Class
```

Like `OrdersController`, `OrderController` contains `WithEvents` references to important controls within its associated view class, `OrderView`. It also overrides all necessary protected methods. Notice that its `setViewDataBindings()` method is a little more involved since it has to set data bindings for several controls, not just a `DataGrid` control.

A new event handling procedure, `_productsData_ListChanged()`, is also present. This procedure was not in `OrdersController`, and is required here in order for new products to be added to the `productsGrid` control and also successfully to the underlying `DataSet`. Since the `productsGrid` maps to the `Products` table in the `DataSet`, which is a child table to the `Order` table, the order ID has to be properly set in the new product row, otherwise an error occurs.

Next, we'll code the two concrete `OrderViewController` classes that inherit from `OrderController`.

The NormalOrderController Class

Add a new class to the `OrderController.vb` file with the following code:

```
Public Class NormalOrderController
   Inherits OrderController

   'View event handling procedures

   Private Sub _orderView_Load(ByVal sender As Object, _
                  ByVal e As System.EventArgs) Handles _orderView.Load
      _orderView.Text = "Normal Order"
   End Sub

   Private Sub _orderButton_Click(ByVal sender As Object, _
               ByVal e As System.EventArgs) Handles _orderButton.Click
      MsgBox("Order sent from NormalOrderController!")
   End Sub
End Class
```

The `NormalOrderViewController` class handles the load event of the `OrderView` class so it can set the caption of the form to **Normal Order**. It also displays a unique message when the user clicks the `Order` button.

The SpecialOrderController Class

Add another new class to the `OrderController.vb` file, with the following code:

```
Public Class SpecialOrderController
  Inherits OrderController
  'View event handling procedures

  Private Sub _orderView_Load(ByVal sender As Object, _
                   ByVal e As System.EventArgs) Handles _orderView.Load
    With _orderView
      .Text = "Special Order"
      .productsGridTableStyle.GridColumnStyles.Remove(.requiredDateColumn)
    End With
  End Sub

  Private Sub _orderButton_Click(ByVal sender As Object, _
             ByVal e As System.EventArgs) Handles _orderButton.Click
    MsgBox("Order sent from SpecialOrderController!")
  End Sub
End Class
```

The `SpecialOrderController` class does the same things as `NormalOrderViewController`, except it also removes the `requiredDateColumn` `GridColumnStyle` from the `productsGrid` `DataGrid` control. This is because special orders don't display a required date.

This shows an example of how sub-classing controller classes can even change the actual look of the view they're associated with. Creating a new controller class is much easier (and produces more code-reuse) than sub-classing a new view class, especially if the visual differences are small.

The OrderControllerFactoryClass

Finally, our family of `OrderController` classes needs a factory class. Add another new class to the `OrderController.vb` file with the following code:

```
Public Class OrderControllerFactory
  Inherits ControllerFactory

  'overriden Controller factory members

  Protected Overrides Function getModels() As Object()
    'get orders from view args
    Dim orders As Orders = CType(_viewArgs(0), Orders)
    'get order id from view args
    Dim orderID As Integer = CInt(_viewArgs(1))
    'get order
    Dim order As Order = orders.getOrder(orderID)
    'populate and return models array
    Dim models() As Object = {order}
    Return models
  End Function
```

```
      Protected Overrides Function getController() As Controller
        Dim order As Order = CType(_models(0), Order)
        'return proper OrderController depending on type of order in Model
        Select Case order.orderType
          Case OrderType.Normal
            Return New NormalOrderController()
          Case OrderType.Special
            Return New SpecialOrderController()
        End Select
      End Function
    End Class
```

The `OrderControllerFactory` class has a little more to do to get its reference to the model for the concrete `OrderController`. Instead of creating a new instance to the `Orders` object, it's able to get the reference that was passed from the `OrdersController` that called the `OrderView` in the first place. It extracts this from the `viewArgs` argument that was passed into the `ControllerFactory.createController()` method. It also grabs the passed order ID and is able to obtain a reference to an `Order` object within `Orders` by calling the `Orders.getOrder()` method. This `Order` object then becomes the model for the new concrete `OrderController` class.

The overridden protected `getController()` method then uses the order type of the newly acquired model (`Order` object) to select which concrete `OrderController` to construct.

NOPWin Startup

Finally, the `NOPWin` application needs some startup code to create and activate the initial view. Add a **Module** item called `Startup.vb` to the `NOPWin` project, and add the following code:

```
Imports MVC

Module Startup
  Public Sub Main()
    Dim ordersView As New OrdersView()
    With ordersView
      .initViewWin()
      .ShowDialog()
    End With
  End Sub
End Module
```

This code is exactly the same code that a controller would use to call and pass control to a new `ViewWin` view. So, in a sense, the `Startup` module is like a startup controller.

*You may also need to check that the NOPWin project recognizes the `Startup` module as its startup object. To do this, check that the **Startup Object** setting in the project's properties is set to **Startup**.*

If we compile and run the NOPWin application, here's what we see:

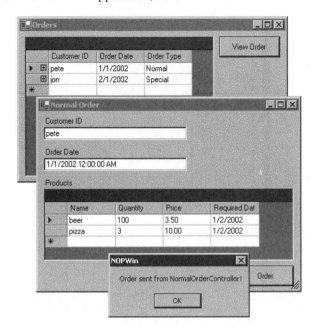

We've successfully implemented our first concrete Model/View/Controller application! Next we'll do same thing except in the web environment. You'll see the many similarities and the subtle differences between implementing MVC in both UI types.

NOPWeb for the Customers

The NOPWin Rich UI application was for the sales staff. Bill was able to do a short presentation of his NOPWin app and they seemed to like it. However, now it was time to think about the real front end of the NOP application, which was for the web site customers. Bill would call this web site pilot application **NOPWeb**. As per the use case, all the customer would really need is an OrderView web page (view) since customers are only allowed to work with a single order at a time. However, Bill wanted NOPWeb really to be a web version of NOPWin with all the same views and logic so he knew how well his MVC framework could handle either UI type. Therefore the NOPWeb pilot app would also have an OrdersView web page for consistency, even though it might not show up in the final version of the web site since customers would never use it.

The NOPWeb Class Diagram

The NOPWeb class diagram is very similar to NOPWin's class diagram:

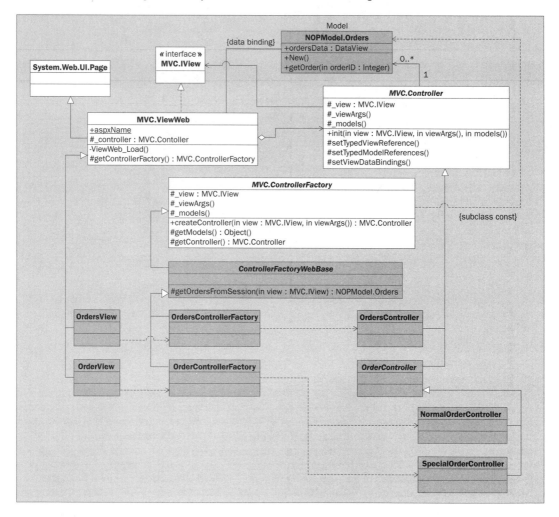

Here are the differences:

❑ NOPWeb views inherit from the `ViewWeb` class instead of the `ViewWin` class. `ViewWeb`, as we've designed it in the MVC framework, has a slightly different schema and a very different way that it's constructed and activated.

❑ There is no construction line from the `OrdersController` concrete class to the `OrderView` concrete class. This is because controllers cannot directly instantiate new view classes. As we've discussed before, the controller has to provide some way for the view's associated `.aspx` page to be rendered.

❏ All the concrete `ControllerFactory` classes inherit from an abstract class called `ControllerFactoryWebBase`. This class contains a single protected method called `getOrdersFromSession()` that retrieves a stored reference of an `Orders` object from the ASP.NET `Session` object. If the reference isn't there, the method instantiates a new one and puts it there. Then `ControllerFactory` subclasses can call this method in order to get a reference to `Orders` object that stays alive between page calls.

Let's get started with NOPWeb's code. Start by adding an **ASP.NET Web Application** project to our `MVCPresTier` solution in Visual Studio .NET. Create the web application as a virtual directory called `NOPWeb` off of your `localhost` web site. The complete web application URL would then be:

http://localhost/NOPWeb

Like `NOPWin`, `NOPWeb` needs a reference to both the `MVC` and `NOPModel` projects. Finally, delete the **WebForm1.aspx** file that Visual Studio.NET automatically generated.

The OrdersView View

Let's add our first view to the web site. Unlike with Windows Forms, we can't add inherited Web Forms to web site applications. Therefore, add a new **Web Form** item to the NOPWeb project and name its file **OrdersView.aspx**.

To make the view inherit from the `ViewWeb` class, change the class it inherits from in the code from `System.Web.UI.Page` to `ViewWeb`. You'll also have to add an `Imports` statement (for the `MVC` namespace) to allow this `Inherits` modification to work without producing a build error. `OrdersView`'s code (`OrdersView.aspx.vb`) will then look like this:

```
Imports MVC

Public Class OrdersView
   Inherits ViewWeb

   Web Form Designer Generated Code

End Class
```

Now we can start adding server controls to the `OrdersView` web page so it looks like the `ViewWin`'s `OrdersView`. Make the following amendments to the web form in its **Design** view:

❏ Add a `Label` control whose **ID** is **Label1**. Set its **Text** property to **Orders**. (I've also changed it's **Font** property's **Size** to **X-Large** here.)

❏ Add a `DataGrid` control whose **ID** is **ordersGrid**

Now you should have something that looks like this:

237

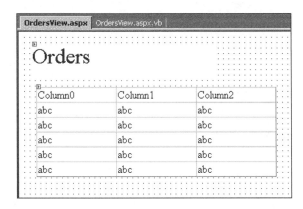

Like the data grid controls in the NOPWin application, we need to configure ordersGrid to display the proper columns, which map to the proper data fields during data-binding. Right-click on the orderGrid DataGrid and select the **Property Builder** option. This opens a more advanced property dialog for the DataGrid. Select the **Columns** tab on the left. Here is where we add columns to the grid:

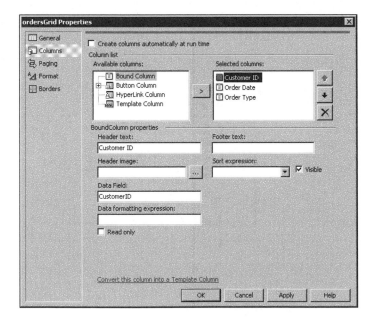

Uncheck the **Create columns automatically at runtime** checkbox. Now add the following **Bound Column** items as shown in the figure above:

Header Text	Data Field
Customer ID	CustomerID
Order Date	OrderDate
Order Type	OrderType

We also need to add a **Button Column** to the `DataGrid`, so users can click it to open the `OrderView` representing the associated order. To do this, drill into the **Button Column** node in the **Available columns** tree and pick the **Select** button. Then click the add arrow button to add the **Select Button Column** to the list on the right. Then set the **Text** property of the new **Select Button Column** to **View** and set the **Command name** property to ViewOrder. This button will actually be a link, so leave the **Button type** as LinkButton:

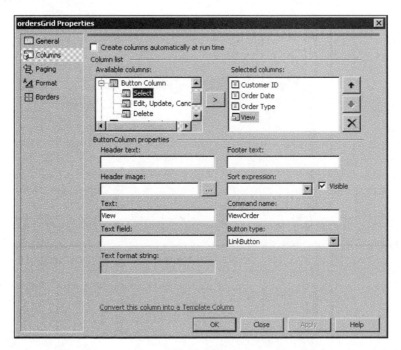

Finally, select the **Format** tab in the **ordersGrid Property Builder** dialog. We're going to set the `DataGrid`'s **Header** to be in bold by checking the **Bold** checkbox as shown overleaf:

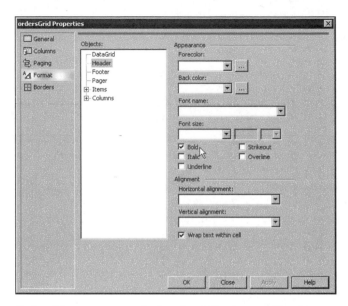

After all that, your **OrdersView.aspx** page design should look more like this:

Now, let's finish up the code work for the `OrdersView` view, in `OrdersView.aspx.vb`:

```vb
Imports MVC

Public Class OrdersView
  Inherits ViewWeb

  Public Shadows Const aspxName As String = "OrdersView.aspx"
  Protected Friend WithEvents Label1 As System.Web.UI.WebControls.Label
  Protected Friend WithEvents ordersGrid _
                        As System.Web.UI.WebControls.DataGrid

  Web Form Designer Generated Code

  Protected Overrides Function getControllerFactory() As ControllerFactory
    Return New OrdersControllerFactory()
  End Function
End Class
```

Once again, the code in the gray background shows changes from the last time we touched this class:

- ❏ We need to override the `aspxName` constant (using the `Shadows` keyword) so the correct `.aspx` page name can be associated with the view (in this case `OrdersView.aspx`).

- ❏ Unlike Windows Forms, ASP.NET Web Forms don't declare their contained controls as `Friend` variables (or fields), but rather as `Protected` variables. However, having them protected means that other classes cannot access these controls unless they inherit from the class itself. Our controller classes will need to have access to the server controls within all of our `ViewWeb` views. Therefore we've added the `Friend` keyword to all the server control variable declarations.

  ASP.NET Web Forms declare their contained controls as `Protected` fields because the `.aspx` page becomes a separate class that inherits the code-behind class at run-time. Therefore, declaring the controls as `Protected`, allows the `.aspx` subclass to inherit the code-behind behavior.

- ❏ Finally, we need the standard `getControllerFactory()` protected method override, which `OrdersView` uses to return an instance to the `OrdersControllerFactory` class.

The OrdersController Class

The `OrdersController` class is practically identical to NOPWin's `OrdersController` except it has to handle ASP.NET server controls instead of Windows form controls. Create a new class item in the NOPWeb project with a file named `OrdersController.vb`. In it, add the following code:

```vb
Imports MVC
Imports NOPModel

Public Class OrdersController
  Inherits Controller

  'strongly typed View reference
  Protected WithEvents _ordersView As OrdersView
  'strongly typed Model references
  Protected _orders As Orders
  'View WithEvents references
  Protected WithEvents _ordersGrid As DataGrid

  'overriden Controller members

  Protected Overrides Sub setTypedViewReference()
    _ordersView = CType(_view, OrdersView)
  End Sub

  Protected Overrides Sub setTypedModelReferences()
    _orders = CType(_models(0), Orders)
  End Sub

  Protected Overrides Sub setViewWithEventsReferences()
    With _ordersView
      _ordersGrid = .ordersGrid
    End With
  End Sub
```

```
Protected Overrides Sub setViewDataBindings()
  With _ordersGrid
    .DataSource = _orders.ordersData
    .DataBind()
  End With
End Sub


'View event handling procedures

Private Sub _ordersGrid_ItemCommand(ByVal source As Object, _
         ByVal e As System.Web.UI.WebControls.DataGridCommandEventArgs) _
         Handles _ordersGrid.ItemCommand
  Select Case e.CommandName
    Case "ViewOrder"
      Dim orderRow As DataRow = _
                        _orders.ordersData.Item(e.Item.ItemIndex).Row
      Dim orderID As Integer = CInt(orderRow.Item("OrderID"))
      'pass data to new View via query string
      Dim viewURL As String = _
                    OrderView.aspxName & "?order_id=" & CStr(orderID)
      _ordersView.Server.Transfer(viewURL)
  End Select
End Sub
End Class
```

The main difference is that we're using a **Select Button Column** in the DataGrid to send the user to the OrderView page instead of the regular button that we used in the NOPWin application. Hence the _ordersGrid_ItemCommand() private procedure, which handles the ItemCommand event of the ordersGrid control. Within this procedure we see how the OrdersController passes control over to the OrderView view by using the Server.Transfer method.

The ControllerFactoryWebBase Class

As we saw in NOPWeb's class diagram, ControllerFactoryWebBase is an abstract class that both of the concrete ControllerFactory classes inherit from. It contains a single protected method called getOrdersFromSession() that retrieves a reference to an Orders object in the ASP.NET Session object if it exists. If it doesn't exist, it is created and added to the Session object. Here's the code for ControllerFactoryWebBase, which also belongs in the file OrdersController.vb:

```
Public MustInherit Class ControllerFactoryWebBase
  Inherits ControllerFactory

  Protected Function getOrdersFromSession(ByRef view As IView) As Orders
    'constants
    Const CorderModelSessionKeyName As String = "orders_model"
    'get orders data from ASP.NET session
    Dim viewWeb As ViewWeb = CType(view, ViewWeb)
    Dim session As System.Web.SessionState.HttpSessionState = _
                                                  viewWeb.Session

    Dim orders As Orders
    If session.Item(CorderModelSessionKeyName) Is Nothing Then
      'generate new Orders object and persist it to session
      orders = New Orders()
```

```
            session.Item(CorderModelSessionKeyName) = orders
      Else
        'get orders from session
        orders = CType(session.Item(CorderModelSessionKeyName), Orders)
      End If
      Return orders
    End Function
End Class
```

The OrdersControllerFactory Class

Finally, the OrdersControllerFactory class inherits from ControllerFactoryWebBase so it can use this getOrdersFromSession() method in its overridden getModels() method. Put this class code into OrdersController.vb, too:

```
Public Class OrdersControllerFactory
  Inherits ControllerFactoryWebBase

  'overriden Controller factory members

  Protected Overrides Function getModels() As Object()
    Dim orders As Orders = getOrdersFromSession(_view)
    Dim models() As Object = {orders}
    Return models
  End Function

  Protected Overrides Function getController() As Controller
    Return New OrdersController()
  End Function
End Class
```

The overload getController() method is identical to the implementation in NOPWin, returning an instance the concrete OrdersController class.

The OrderView View

OrderView is going to be the main page that customers will use. The OrderView class we code up in NOPWeb is very similar to the one we did in NOPWin. Add another **Web Form** item to the NOPWeb project and name its file OrderView.aspx.

Once again we need to modify the inheritance of the new web form by tweaking the underlying code a bit in OrderView.aspx.vb:

```
Imports MVC

Public Class OrderView
  Inherits ViewWeb
    Web Form Designer Generated Code
End Class
```

Once again, we need to add a number of controls to the Web Form, via the Visual Studio .NET Web Forms designer:

- ❏ Add a `Label` control whose ID is orderLabel. Set its Text property to Order. (Again, I've also changed it's Font property's Size to X-Large here.)

- ❏ Add another `Label` control whose ID is Label1. Set its Text property to Customer ID

- ❏ Add another `Label` control whose ID is Label2. Set its Text property to Order Date

- ❏ Add another `Label` control whose ID is Label3. Set its Text property to Products

Now add some controls to accompany those last three labels:

- ❏ Add a `TextBox` control whose ID is customerIDText

- ❏ Add another `TextBox` control whose ID is orderDateText

- ❏ A `DataGrid` control whose ID is productsGrid

Finally:

- ❏ Add a `Button` control whose ID is orderButton. Set its Text property to Order

- ❏ Add a `Label` control whose ID is messageLabel. Set its ForeColor property to Red, and clear its Text property

- ❏ Add a `Button` control whose ID is backToOrdersButton. Set its Text property to < Back to Orders

After all that, with the appropriate arrangement, you should have something that looks like this:

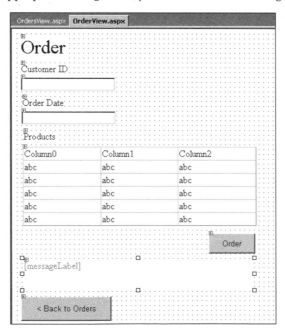

`OrderView` also has a `DataGrid` control that needs some modifications, so right-click on it and select the Property Builder dialog:

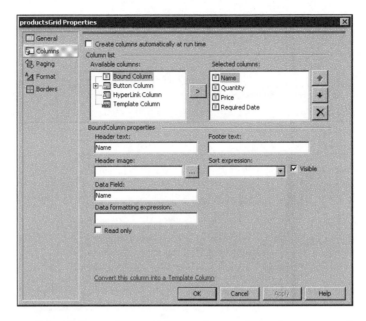

In the same way we did with the `ordersGrid` control on `OrdersView` page, make the following changes to `productsGrid`:

❑ Uncheck the **Create columns automatically at runtime** checkbox.

❑ Add the following **Bound Column** items as shown in the figure above:

Header Text	Data Field
Name	Name
Quantity	Qty
Price	Price
Required Date	RequiredDate

❑ Set the **Header** format of the `DataGrid` to be **Bold**.

Now the page design should look like this:

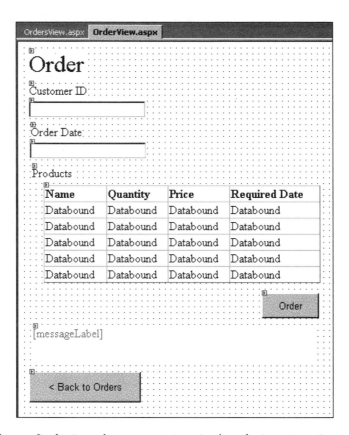

Now we can make our final minor changes to OrderView's code, in OrderView.aspx.vb:

```
Imports MVC

Public Class OrderView
  Inherits ViewWeb

  Public Shadows Const aspxName As String = "OrderView.aspx"

  Protected Friend WithEvents orderLabel As System.Web.UI.WebControls.Label
  Protected Friend WithEvents Label1 As System.Web.UI.WebControls.Label
  Protected Friend WithEvents Label2 As System.Web.UI.WebControls.Label
  Protected Friend WithEvents Label3 As System.Web.UI.WebControls.Label

  Protected Friend WithEvents customerIDText _
                                As System.Web.UI.WebControls.TextBox
  Protected Friend WithEvents orderDateText _
                                As System.Web.UI.WebControls.TextBox
  Protected Friend WithEvents productsGrid _
                                As System.Web.UI.WebControls.DataGrid
```

```
      Protected Friend WithEvents orderButton _
                                     As System.Web.UI.WebControls.Button
      Protected Friend WithEvents messageLabel _
                                     As System.Web.UI.WebControls.Label
      Protected Friend WithEvents backToOrdersButton _
                                     As System.Web.UI.WebControls.Button

   Web Form Designer Generated Code

      Protected Overrides Function getControllerFactory() As ControllerFactory
        Return New OrderControllerFactory()
      End Function
   End Class
```

The changes in gray are the same kinds of changes we did with the `OrdersView` class. `OrderView` just has a few more controls.

The OrderController Class

`OrderView` needs concrete controller classes and a `ControllerFactory` class. Add a new **Class** item to the NOPWeb project and name the file `OrderController.vb`. In it place the following code:

```
Imports MVC
Imports NOPModel

Public MustInherit Class OrderController
   Inherits Controller

   'strongly typed View reference
   Protected WithEvents _orderView As OrderView
   'strongly typed Model references
   Protected _order As Order
   'View WithEvents references
   Protected WithEvents _customerIDText As TextBox
   Protected WithEvents _orderDateText As TextBox
   Protected WithEvents _productsGrid As DataGrid
   Protected WithEvents _orderButton As Button
   Protected WithEvents _backToOrdersButton As Button
   'other class-level variables
   Protected _orderData As DataView

   'overriden Controller members

   Protected Overrides Sub setTypedViewReference()
     _orderView = CType(_view, OrderView)
   End Sub

   Protected Overrides Sub setTypedModelReferences()
     _order = CType(_models(0), Order)
   End Sub
```

```
    Protected Overrides Sub setViewWithEventsReferences()
      With _orderView
        _customerIDText = .customerIDText
        _orderDateText = .orderDateText
        _productsGrid = .productsGrid
        _orderButton = .orderButton
        _backToOrdersButton = .backToOrdersButton
      End With
    End Sub

    Protected Overrides Sub setViewDataBindings()
      'order data
      _orderData = _order.orderData
      _customerIDText.DataBind()
      _orderDateText.DataBind()
      'products data
      With _productsGrid
        .DataSource = _order.productsData
        .DataBind()
      End With
    End Sub

    'View event handling procedures

    Private Sub _customerIDText_DataBinding(ByVal sender As Object, _
                                   ByVal e As System.EventArgs) _
                  Handles _customerIDText.DataBinding
      If _orderView.IsPostBack Then
        _orderData.Item(0).Item("CustomerID") = CStr(_customerIDText.Text)
      Else
        _customerIDText.Text = CStr(_orderData.Item(0).Item("CustomerID"))
      End If
    End Sub

    Private Sub _orderDateText_DataBinding(ByVal sender As Object, _
                                    ByVal e As System.EventArgs) _
                  Handles _orderDateText.DataBinding
      If _orderView.IsPostBack Then
        _orderData.Item(0).Item("OrderDate") = CDate(_orderDateText.Text)
      Else
        _orderDateText.Text = CStr(_orderData.Item(0).Item("OrderDate"))
      End If
    End Sub

    Private Sub _backToOrdersButton_Click(ByVal sender As Object, _
                                   ByVal e As System.EventArgs) _
                  Handles _backToOrdersButton.Click
      'switch View to OrdersView
      _orderView.Server.Transfer(OrdersView.aspxName)
    End Sub
  End Class
```

As with NOPWin, NOPWeb's `OrderController` class is abstract and it gets inherited by subclasses for both the normal order and the special order types. This `OrderController` also has to handle a few extra events in order to get the web form data binding to behave properly. The private methods `_customerIDText_DataBinding()` and `_orderDateText_DataBinding()` do this by making sure the bound data in the underlying `DataSet` object is either being set when the page reposts or retrieved when the page is being rendered for the first time.

The _backToOrdersButton_Click() private method handles the Click event of the backToOrdersButton server control. Here we see the view calling a view scenario happening in reverse. Now it's OrderView that's the parent view calling back to the OrdersView child view. The Server.Transfer method is once again used here to make the view calling work.

The NormalOrderController Class

NOPWeb's NormalOrderController class is virtually identical to NOPWin's. It sets the page title to read **Normal Order** and when the user clicks the **Order** button a message is displayed in the messageLabel control. This class code also belongs in the file OrderController.vb:

```
Public Class NormalOrderController
  Inherits OrderController

  'View event handling procedures

  Private Sub _orderView_Load(ByVal sender As Object, _
                              ByVal e As System.EventArgs) _
                                            Handles _orderView.Load
    _orderView.orderLabel.Text = "Normal Order"
  End Sub

  Private Sub _orderButton_Click(ByVal sender As Object, _
                              ByVal e As System.EventArgs) _
                                            Handles _orderButton.Click
    _orderView.messageLabel.Text = "Order sent from NormalOrderController!"
  End Sub
End Class
```

The SpecialOrderController Class

The same thing goes for SpecialOrderController. Like NOPWin's SpecialOrderController class, this one removes the RequiredDate column from the DataGrid since special orders don't display a required date. This class code also belongs in the file OrderController.vb:

```
Public Class SpecialOrderController
  Inherits OrderController

  'View event handling procedures

  Private Sub _orderView_Load(ByVal sender As Object, _
                              ByVal e As System.EventArgs) _
                                            Handles _orderView.Load
    With _orderView
      .orderLabel.Text = "Special Order"
      'remove RequiredDate field from the DataGrid
      With .productsGrid.Columns
        .Item(.Count - 1).Visible = False
      End With
    End With
  End Sub
```

```
      Private Sub _orderButton_Click(ByVal sender As Object, _
                              ByVal e As System.EventArgs) _
                                      Handles _orderButton.Click
      _orderView.messageLabel.Text = "Order sent from SpecialOrderController!"
    End Sub
End Class
```

The OrderControllerFactory

This is our last class to code! OrderControllerFactory overloads its getModels() and getController() methods much like NOPWin's did. But like OrdersControllerFactory, it gets its reference to the Orders object from the protected getOrdersFromSession() method of its super class, ControllerFactoryWebBase(). This class code also belongs in the file OrderController.vb:

```
Public Class OrderControllerFactory
    Inherits ControllerFactoryWebBase

    'overriden Controller factory members

    Protected Overrides Function getModels() As Object()
        'get orders from Session
        Dim orders As Orders = getOrdersFromSession(_view)
        'get order id from Request
        Dim httpRequest As HttpRequest = CType(_view, ViewWeb).Request
        Dim orderID As Integer = CInt(httpRequest.QueryString.Item("order_id"))
        'get order
        Dim order As Order = Orders.getOrder(orderID)
        'populate and return models array
        Dim models() As Object = {order}
        Return models
    End Function

    Protected Overrides Function getController() As Controller
        Dim order As Order = CType(_models(0), Order)
        'return proper OrderController depending on type of order in Model
        Select Case order.orderType
          Case OrderType.Normal
            Return New NormalOrderController()
          Case OrderType.Special
            Return New SpecialOrderController()
        End Select
    End Function
End Class
```

The Finished NOPWeb Application

Well, we don't need to add any special startup code for the NOPWeb application to work. You can just browse right to their respective .aspx pages and the views render.

You can start with the OrdersView.aspx page, which looks something like this:

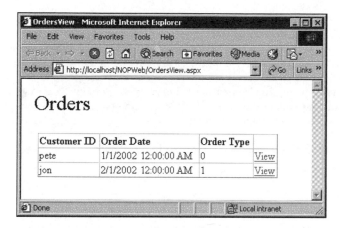

If you click one of the View links, you are taken to the OrderView.aspx page (via the Server.Transfer method):

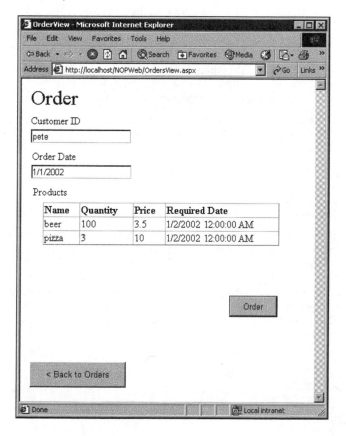

Here you can click the order button to get a notification of the type of order that was sent. You can make changes to the **Customer ID** and **Order Date** fields as well. If you click either button on the form, they are persisted to the underlying `Orders` object stored in the ASP.NET session. You can click back to the `OrdersView.aspx` page and see that any changes you made show up there as well.

The `OrderView.aspx` page can also be browsed to directly (perhaps by a customer). You do have to specify a querystring that contains an order ID otherwise the page will throw an error. Therefore, if you wanted to see Pete's order, you could browse directly to:

> http://localhost/NOPWeb/OrderView.aspx?order_id=100

Summary

In this chapter we tackled the problem of designing against a complicated presentation tier. We chose to use a very popular and effective design pattern architecture called Model/View/Controller (MVC). With an understanding of this architecture, we were able to build a framework of classes that we used to implement a rich UI application and a web application (both talking to the same middle tier).

We found out that MVC uses the following GoF design patterns under the hood:

❑ *Observer* – This pattern describes the relationship between the model and the view in which each view automatically gets updated whenever the state of the model changes. We employed .NET's data binding technology to implement this pattern.

❑ *Composite* – The internal structure of a view is based on the Composite pattern in which all the controls within a view form a hierarchy that can be treaded as a whole. Both Windows Forms and Web Forms use this design pattern to make up their hierarchies of child controls.

❑ *Strategy* – Strategy describes the relationship between a view and its aggregate controller. A view can potentially use one of multiple control classes that each specifies a different behavior for the same view. We saw how we could alter the behavior of our `OrderView` form with specialized controller classes for normal orders and special orders.

❑ *Factory Method* – We found a good way to construct our controller classes was to use the Factory Method design pattern, which abstracted the construction of the actual controller class into factory objects.

Finally we learned that the principle purpose of MVC for the presentation tier was to decouple the visual presentation (views) from the presentation logic (controllers), This produces several benefits that are especially useful to the larger, more complex presentation tiers that are commonly found in today's enterprise applications.

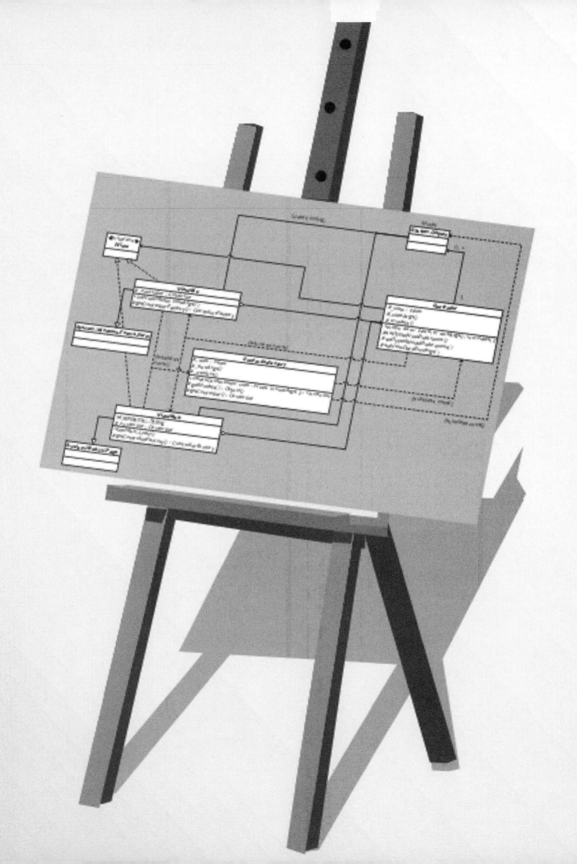

5

Between the Tiers: Design Patterns and .NET Remoting

In each of the Chapters 2, 3, and 4, our study of design patterns was focused onto one of the three tiers of a 3-tier architecture – the data layer, the business rules layer or the presentation layer. In this chapter, we acknowledge the fact that a tiered application may very well be distributed; and so we consider the value of design patterns in a distributed system – specifically, one that uses **.NET Remoting**.

.NET Remoting is a development framework that assists developers in creating applications that are distributed across process boundaries and machine boundaries. In this chapter we will see how design patterns can pay their part in implementing the distributed nature of a distributed application.

Moreover, we will see how .NET Remoting, as a development framework, has recognized the potential of certain design patterns in the field of distributed applications, and also aids developers in the use of design patterns. With the help of the right tools, many of the pattern details are shielded and much boilerplate code is already implemented, and hence we can avoid implementing those patterns from the ground up. Of course, the benefits of that are obvious: we save ourselves work and brain power, reduce the risk of error-prone implementations, and thus create time to focus on other more specific problems.

In this chapter, we will build a simple distributed application whose implementation is aided by use of a number of GoF patterns: Singleton, Proxy, Adapter, Observer, Decorator and Template Method. The application will also make use of a non-GoF pattern known as the Asynchronous Programming pattern. We'll illustrate how the .NET Remoting framework supports the use of these patterns in a developer's design of a distributed system as we walk through the example.

.NET Remoting – A Primer

Let's start with a quick tour of some basics of .NET Remoting. We'll briefly go through some concepts and terms in .NET Remoting in this section and set the background for later discussion. .NET Remoting is a complex subject, and an introductory treatment of the subject is beyond the scope of this book. There are a number of resources on the Web; and for a good introduction to .NET Remoting for VB.NET developers, try a title like *Professional VB.NET, Second Edition* (ISBN 1-86100-716-7).

Like a number of other technologies (DCOM, Java RMI, CORBA's IIOP/GIOP), the objective of **.NET Remoting** is to help in the development of objects (or components) that can be consumed remotely in an object-oriented way. When we say that an object is *consumed remotely*, we mean that it is called by another application that exists in a different process – possibly on another machine. The following diagram shows the relationship between a .NET Remoting server and client, and how they fit into the big picture:

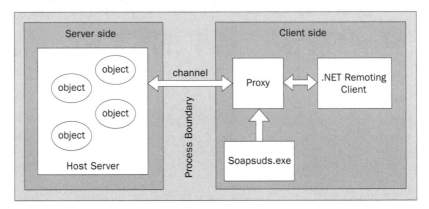

Remoting Objects and the Host Server

In the diagram, the first thing we see is that Remoting objects reside in a **host server**. (In the sample application in this chapter, the host server will be an .exe executable application.) The objects themselves are classified into three types – **Client-activated**, **SingleCall**, and **Singleton**. Each Remoting object falls into one of these three categories, depending on how the object is activated and how its state (the values kept by its member variables) is maintained:

- ❑ A client-activated object is, quite simply, an object that is activated at the client's request. A client-activated object can hold state information between any number of method calls triggered by the same client. However, a client-activated object does not allow you to share state information among several clients – it is associated with one client only.

- ❑ A SingleCall object is a server-activated object. A new SingleCall object is created each time one of its methods is called, and the object is destroyed when the call is completed. Consequently, a SingleCall object holds no state information between method calls.

- ❑ A Singleton object is also a server-activated object – but this type of object is one that services *multiple* clients. There can be only one object instance of a Singleton class. The state of a Singleton object is shared among clients. This type of object is called *Singleton* precisely because it follows the GoF Singleton design pattern.

A Remoting object can reside within a host application (an .exe file) of its own; alternatively, it may be hosted by IIS or by the .NET Component Service.

During the course of the sample application in this chapter, we'll build remote objects of all three types.

Channels and Protocols

Communication channels between client and server can include HTTP, SMTP, TCP, and so on. Note, however, that only TCP and HTTP channels are included as part of the .NET Remoting framework.

When using an HTTP channel, we send request and response messages using the **Simple Object Access Protocol** (**SOAP**). SOAP is the protocol at the core of web services. Like DCOM's ORPC (Object Remote Procedure Call) and IIOP/GIOP, SOAP is a protocol for consuming server objects remotely. But unlike its counterparts, SOAP messages are in XML format.

> *If you'd like to know more, you can find the SOAP specification at http://www.w3c.org. Don Box's article* SOAP Increases Interoperability Across Platforms and Languages *(MSDN Magazine, March 2000) is also an invaluable read.*

The Client, the Proxy, and the soapsuds.exe Utility

The figure above also shows one of a number of ways that a client can generate a proxy for a remote server object.

Also in the diagram above, we can see that the client application uses a **proxy** to communicate with the remote server object. The proxy **represents** the server object on the client side. In order to represent the remote server object, it needs to know about the server object's type information.

The diagram shows just one of several ways that a client can get information about a remote server object. The soapsuds.exe utility is provided by .NET, and can be used by the client to get the service description of a Remoting object. The service description contains the server object's type information. If the client has a local copy of the .NET Remoting server assembly, soapsuds.exe can also use it to generate a proxy. .NET Remoting is all about exposing remote objects for clients to consume.

The Configuration File, Default.cfg

.NET Remoting allows us to extract some attributes of server objects and put them into a separate **configuration file**, called Default.cfg. We can use Default.cfg to specify what port and protocol the server object will use to communicate with clients, whether the server object is a Singleton, SingleCall, or ClientActivated object, and sometimes what formatter should be used to serialize objects into streams.

The advantage of this design is that it allows us to change the behavior of the Remote object simply by changing the settings in the object's Default.cfg file. It means that we don't have to recompile the source code for the Remote object itself or the application that hosts it.

We will make use of this fact during the course of the sample application in this chapter. As you may recall, earlier in this chapter we noted that a Remoting object can be hosted in IIS, in the .NET Component Service, or as an executable application (an .exe file). In this chapter's example, we will write a number of host programs, compile them into executable files and run them simultaneously to host our remote objects. Each executable will run in its own process space, and hence the overall solution is truly distributed.

A Call Event Coordinator Example

In this chapter, we'll illustrate how the .NET Remoting framework itself uses design patterns, and also how the .NET Remoting framework supports the use of design patterns in a developer's design of a distributed system. To do this, we'll be developing a sample application – a (rather simplified) distributed **call routing system** for call centers.

System Requirements

The application will listen for incoming calls, and redirect each incoming call to one of a number of customer service representatives (CSRs). When we look at the nature of the application, and the situations in which it will be deployed, we can quickly draw up a list of requirements for the application:

- ❑ **Requirement 1:** In practice, we expect that our call routing system will be deployed at many different call centers, and we also expect that some of those call centers may have different phone systems. Therefore, our sample application should be able to **interface with any phone system** that is already installed into a call center.

- ❑ **Requirement 2:** Each call center has its own rules and policies for routing phone calls to its CSRs. So it's important that our application is sufficiently flexible that it can **accept whatever call routing policies** a call center has and act accordingly.

- ❑ **Requirement 3:** Sometimes, a scenario might require that a calling customer is put on hold while a CSR is processing the customer's request. Other scenarios might require that the CSR calls the customer back after he has finished processing the customer's request. In other words, **call events might be dispatched to CSRs synchronously or asynchronously**.

- ❑ **Requirement 4:** Our system should have a single point for coordinating all customer calls. Therefore, there should be **only one call event coordinator** in a call center.

Perhaps, as you read these requirements, you are already casting your mind back to patterns that we've met in previous chapters – and thinking about how they might be candidate patterns for some of the requirements in this system! In order to meet these four requirements, we will build the application in phases, and visit a number of patterns along the way.

The Players in the System

The diagram below shows the players in our call routing system. It's a typical view of a call center, and a high-level view of our sample application:

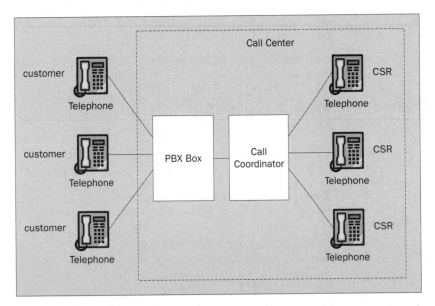

In the system, each call is an event, and there is an event coordinator (the call coordinator) that dispatches phone call events to the call center's CSRs. The job of a CSR is to answer customer phone calls.

The event coordinator accepts phone call events from the **PBX** (private branch exchange) **box**, which is the telephone switching system of the call center. All phone calls to the call center go through the PBX box, before they are picked up by the event coordinator one at a time.

We could augment this basic model by introducing an adapter, which would lie between the PBX box and the event coordinator. Its purpose would be to shield the details of a PBX box from the event coordinator, and thus provide a consistent interface to the event coordinator. Thus, if we were to change the PBX box, we wouldn't need to change the event coordinator; we would just need to change the adapter. Indeed, it makes developing and deploying the sample application easier, because it means that we would need only one implementation of the event coordinator for all situations – in deployment, we'd simply interface with the existing PBX box by choosing the appropriate adapter.

In practice, the adapter would be our solution to Requirement 1. However, in this chapter, our focus is not on the details of individual phone systems; it is on the business logic and design structure of a call routing system. Therefore, we will simplify that part of the system by using a **simulation program** that (a) simulates the PBX box–adapter combination, and (b) simulates customer phone calls by triggering phone call events.

The Tiers of the System

While our application is distributed in the technical sense of the word (that is, it involves a number of different processes working together across process boundaries), we've kept the tiers of the application very simple in order to avoid unnecessary complexity:

❑ You can think of the simulation program as being the application's presentation tier.

❑ The application has no data tier. (In practice, the system might retrieve customer data from some data store upon receiving a phone call from customer; but we really want to focus on .NET Remoting issues, so such data access features are left as an exercise to readers.)

❑ The most significant part of our application is the middle tier, which itself is distributed – in that it is made up of a number of processes that work together.

We'll implement the middle tier classes in three phases. By doing this, we can emphasize how little the code changes when our system requirements change – which is the very objective of patterns.

The Development Phases of our Application

Here's a rundown of what we'll do in the three development phases of our application:

❑ In the first phase, we'll implement the two main classes in the middle tier of our application. One is the EventCoordinator class that represents the (call) event coordinator; the other is the CSR class that represents a customer service representative. We'll make use of the GoF Singleton pattern, which is already implemented in .NET Remoting, to ensure that we have only one instance of the EventCoordinator class running (and thus we will meet Requirement 4).

The EventCoordinator instance will dispatch phone call events to instances of the CSR class, and here we'll take advantage of the Observer pattern. The event coordinator will play the role of the sender (sometimes called the notifier or observable object) in the Observer pattern, and will notify the observer object when an event occurs. Each CSR instance plays the role of observer in the Observer pattern, by observing call events triggered by the EventCoordinator.

The EventCoordinator and CSR instances are remote objects. Even if they are instantiated on the same physical machine, in this example those instances are hosted by different processes and therefore are "remote" from one another. In deployment, it's likely that the host applications would be deployed onto different machines in a network. Either way, we use proxies – each CSR application uses a proxy that represents the remote event coordinator, and the event coordinator uses proxies to represent the remote CSR instances. In implementing this part of the solution, we'll see how .NET Remoting utilizes the Proxy pattern and how we use it.

We'll also get to see how .NET applies the GoF Adapter pattern in its design of Delegates.

❑ In the second phase of the example, we'll meet Requirement 3 by making the call events asynchronous. In order to do this, we will introduce a non-GoF pattern called Asynchronous Programming. The Asynchronous Programming pattern might seem convoluted and mysterious at first; but once we've seen the main operations .NET Framework does behind the scenes for the pattern, you'll see that turning a synchronous method call to an asynchronous one (or vice versa) is actually very simple, and requires very few code changes.

❑ In the third and final phase, we will achieve the goal set in Requirement 2 (the acceptance of whatever call routing policies are implemented locally) by utilizing two GoF patterns – Decorator and Template Method. What's more, we will *embed* the Template Method pattern within the Decorator pattern, and show the benefits of that "complex" design.

Phase 1 – The Basic Application

In this phase, we'll build a first release of the application that satisfies Requirement 1 (by using a simulator program to represent the PBX box and adapter, and to simulate customer phone calls by triggering call events) and Requirement 4 (by implementing exactly one EventCoordinator object).

Collecting and Distributing Calls

As we've already discussed, the basic purpose of the application is to collect customer calls as they come in, pick them up, and distribute them to CSRs as appropriate. If you studied the Observer pattern back in Chapter 1, you may already have spotted similarities between that pattern and our system's characteristics. You may recall the intent of the Observer pattern:

> **Intent of GoF Observer:** Define a one-to-many dependency between objects so that when one object changes state, all its dependants are notified and updated automatically.

In this sample application, the arrival of a customer call will cause a change to the state of the event coordinator object; then we'll use the Observer pattern to ensure that the dependent CSR objects are notified of the call as necessary.

Here is our first draft UML class diagram, in which we begin to depict the participants of the Observer pattern in the context of our example:

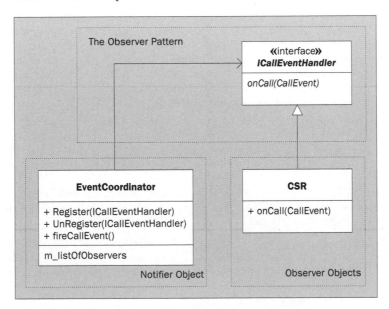

This class diagram has a slightly different structure to the one we saw in Chapter 1 – that's because we're beginning to adapt it for the purposes of this application. I'll explain that further in a moment; but first let's have a quick reminder of how Observer works.

Recalling the Observer Pattern

Let's look more closely at each of the participants in the above figure, and remind ourselves of how the Observer works:

❑ The `EventCoordinator` object is the sender or notifier object. It has an internal private member, `m_listOfObservers`, which represents a list of all the "observer" objects that wish to be notified whenever a call event occurs. It also has two methods, `Register()` and `UnRegister()`, which are used to add observers to the `m_listOfObservers` list and remove observers from the list. When a call event happens, `EventCoordinator`'s `fireCallEvent()` is called – this will invoke the `onCall()` method of each registered `CSR` object, passing a `CallEvent` object (which contains information about the event) as the method's single parameter.

❑ Each `CSR` object is an observer object. When the `EventCoordinator` object notifies the `CSR` object of an event (by calling its `onCall()` method), the method executes and thus handles the call event.

❑ A `CallEvent` object is passed as a parameter to the `CSR` object's `onCall()` method, and allows event-specific information to be passed from the notifier to the observer (so that it can be used by the `CSR` object when handling the event). In our example, the `CallEvent` object will carry a collection of name–value pairs, which contain information such as the caller's phone number and member ID.

❑ The `ICallEventHandler` interface is the abstraction of the `CSR` observer object. In particular, it abstracts the `onCall()` method so that *all* observer classes interested in the call event implement a common interface. (What this means is that an observer object doesn't have to be a `CSR` object – it can be *any* object that implements the `ICallEventHandler` interface. Note that the input parameters of the `Register()` and `UnRegister()` methods are of type `ICallEventHandler`, not type `CSR`. This feature of the Observer pattern captures the spirit and essence of method polymorphism, and makes our object model more extensible in the face of changes in business requirements.)

A Variation on the Observer Pattern

Now, if you're comparing this class diagram with the class diagram we used for the Observer example in Chapter 1, you may notice that it is a little different. Specifically:

❑ In the example in Chapter 1, the sender (or notifier) object, `ExpensesProcessor`, implements an interface called `ExpenseNotifier`, which contains the two methods `Register()` and `UnRegister()`.

❑ In the example above, the notifier object, `EventCoordinator`, does not implement a similar interface containing the two methods `Register()` and `UnRegister()`. Indeed, there is no corresponding interface in the example above, and the class diagram above shows `Register()` and `UnRegister()` as its own methods.

As I mentioned, this is because we're adapting the Observer slightly to reflect the needs of this application. In the Chapter 1 example, the existence of the `ExpenseNotifier` interface means that we can create other notifier classes. Creating another notifier class for that example is simple: we just have the new class implement the `ExpenseNotifier` interface just as the `ExpensesProcessor` class does. Each such class will implement the `Register()` and `UnRegister()` methods, and thus will be able to act as notifier.

In this example, we don't implement the abstraction because, as we'll explain shortly, we don't need to provide the `Register()` and `UnRegister()` methods in the `EventCoordinator` class. Consequently, there's really not much to abstract into an interface.

Taking Advantage of the Event and Delegate

As we've said, .NET recognizes the popularity of the Observer pattern, it provides some constructs that make it easier for developers to implement the pattern. The constructs we are talking about here are the **event** and the **delegate**.

The event construct is no stranger to VB developers. By contrast, the delegate construct is introduced for the first time in VB.NET, and might be new to some of us. As we step through the example, we'll remind ourselves of the event construct and also take a good look at the delegate. We'll see that by employing the delegate, the EventCoordinator object no longer needs to implement the Register() and UnRegister() methods, and it doesn't need to keep an m_listOfObservers member variable full of registered listeners. All this kind of thing is taken care of by the runtime.

With that in mind, let's revise our UML class diagram, adding a .NET delegate to the picture and showing the new relationships among the classes we'll implement in this phase of the example:

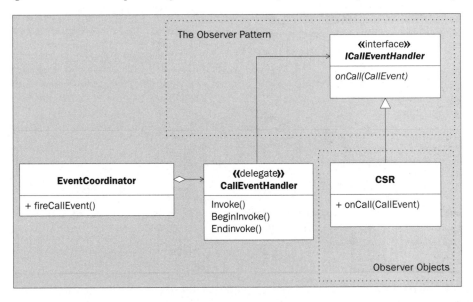

Notice that in the figure, there's no Register() function and no UnRegister() function. We've also removed the m_listOfObservers variable, because the EventCoordinator class no longer needs to maintain a list of registered observers. We'll see how the delegate and event constructs replace these, as we build the example.

Building the Application

It's time to start implementing our application, based on the refined Observer pattern we've outlined above. We'll do it in three steps, as outlined below. In the first two steps we'll build the server-side stuff, and in the final step we'll build a client-side application:

❏ First, we'll build two class libraries, which will house the remote server objects:

❑ We'll call the first one CallCenter.dll, because it will be used in a host application that represents the call center itself. This DLL will contain class definitions for the EventCoordinator class and its delegate.

❑ We'll call the second one Representative.dll, because it will be used in a host application that represents a customer service representative. This DLL will contain the class definitions for the CSR class and the ICallEventHandler interface.

❑ Second, we'll use the class libraries to build the host applications that will host the remote server objects. We'll need one for the call center (CallCenterHost.exe), and one for each of the CSRs (CSRHost.exe).

❑ Third, we'll create one more application – the PBX simulator called ClientSimulator.exe. This will be a client application that makes remote calls to the server-side objects (by simulating customer calls).

The Remote Notifier Object (EventCoordinator) and the Delegate

First, let's build the CallCenter class library. This library contains the "notifier" portion of our Observer pattern – specifically, the EventCoordinator class and the CallEventHandler delegate.

We'll put all the source code for the CallCenter class library into a file called CallCenter.vb. In the following subsections we'll walk through the source code for this class library. We begin with Imports statements for the namespaces we'll need in the library. We'll also place the code for the class library into its own namespace:

```
Imports System
Imports System.Runtime.Remoting
Imports System.Collections

Namespace CallCenter
```

Within the namespace, we will define three things: a delegate (called CallEventHandler), the notifier class (called EventCoordinator), and a public helper class (called InfoItem), that we haven't mentioned before.

The CallEventHandler Delegate

First, we define the delegate to be a subroutine that expects a single parameter, an ArrayList:

```
Public Delegate Sub CallEventHandler(al As ArrayList)
```

The purpose of the delegate is to wrap function pointers that point to the onCall() method of each observing CSR object. Here's how it will work. When a customer call is received, the PBX box calls the EventCoordinator's fireCallEvent() method, which in turn calls an instance of this delegate. The delegate itself then calls each of the observing methods (the event handlers) that are bound to it. (When we look at the client code for our PBX box simulator, we'll see how to use a method called System.Delegate.Combine() to bind a number of event handlers to a delegate.)

The EventCoordinator Notifier Class

Now we have our delegate, we can use it in the definition of the notifier class, EventCoordinator. This class contains two members. One is m_evntCall, which is an instance of the CallEventHandler delegate. The second is a private array, m_CallInfoArray, which (as we'll see shortly) contains a list of name/value pairs representing the properties of a customer call:

```
Public Class EventCoordinator
  Inherits MarshalByRefObject

  Public m_evntCall As CallEventHandler        ' Delegate instance
  Private m_CallInfoArray As ArrayList       ' Call event's properties
```

In a more complex application, involving a number of different types of event and different types of event property set, it would make sense to derive each of the event properties classes from a single base class – the EventArgs base class (provided by the .NET framework class library). This would allow us to treat all of the derived event property classes equally in polymorphic fashion. In our example, with only one type of event (the call event), we'll use ArrayList for this class for simplicity. ArrayList is not derived from EventArgs.

The EventCoordinator class has a method called fireCallEvent():

```
' This method is called to trigger the Call event.
Public Sub fireCallEvent()
  Console.WriteLine("EventCoordinator.fireCallEvent() called.")
  m_evntCall(m_CallInfoArray)
End Sub
```

When a call event occurs, the fireCallEvent() method is called. The fireCallEvent() method passes the call event's properties (contained in the member variable m_CallInfoArray) to the delegate m_evntCall, which will ultimately pass the array to each observing CSR object (via the CSR object's onCall() method). We'll return to the subject of delegates in a moment.

The m_CallInfoArray member is private. Therefore, in order to allow a client application to access the call event's properties collection, the EventCoordinator class has public methods Add() and RemoveAll(), and read-only properties Count and Item:

```
' Methods and properties to allow client to access m_CallInfoArray
Public Sub Add(infoItem As InfoItem)
  m_CallInfoArray.Add(infoItem)
End Sub

Public Sub RemoveAll()
  m_CallInfoArray.Clear()
End Sub

Public ReadOnly Property Count() As Integer
  Get
    Return m_CallInfoArray.Count
  End Get
End Property

Public Default ReadOnly Property Item(ByVal index As Integer) _
                                                As Object
  Get
    return m_CallInfoArray.Item(index)
  End Get
End Property
```

Finally, we include a public constructor method for the `EventCoordinator` class:

```
Public Sub New()
  m_CallInfoArray = New ArrayList()
End Sub
End Class
```

As you can see, our `EventCoordinator` class doesn't provide `Register()` and `UnRegister()` functions, nor does it use a data structure to keep track of registered observer objects. So where is the plumbing code for the Observer pattern? It's all taken care of by the delegate, as we'll explain now.

Events, Delegates, and the Adapter Pattern

Event coding in Visual Basic is probably quite familiar to many readers of this book. An event is fired by a **publisher**, which is like our notifier – it exposes the event by using the `Event` keyword, and triggers events by using the `RaiseEvent` keyword. Events are handled by a **subscriber**, which creates instances of the publisher class by using the `WithEvents` keyword, and binds event handlers to events by using the `Handles` keyword.

On the publisher side, we can register an event-handler by using `AddHandler`, and unregister it using `RemoveHandler`. On the subscriber side, we can use a combination of `AddHandler` and `AddressOf` to bind an event handler to an event, and we can unbind that event handler by using a combination of `RemoveHandler` and `AddressOf`.

In VB.NET, we have all these conveniences plus some more. In particular, VB.NET introduces the concept of a **delegate**, which is a wrapper of one or more function pointers. (This has some desirable features that traditional function pointers lack. For example, delegates are type-safe and object-oriented, whereas function pointers are neither.)

In order to combine function pointers into a delegate, we use the `System.Delegate.Combine()` method. To remove a function pointer from the invocation list of another delegate, we use the `System.Delegate.Remove()` method. As we'll see in the example, this technique is used on the "subscriber" side – that is, by the client application that simulates our PBX box. We don't need a data structure in our observable class to maintain the list of observers, because the delegate does it for us.

Note also that when we declare a delegate like `CallEventHandler`, the compiler actually generates a class. The generated class will have the same name as the delegate, and will be derived from `System.Delegate`. Therefore, our generated class will have three inherited member functions: `Invoke()`, `BeginInvoke()`, and `EndInvoke()`. The signatures of these functions depend on the signature of the observer object's `onCall()` method (that is, the function whose pointer `CallEventHandler` wraps). This is important to know because later in the second phase of our example, we'll use the three compiler-generated functions to send `Call` events asynchronously.

Finally, note that the delegate is an example of the GoF Adapter pattern. You may recall from Chapter 1, that the purpose of an Adapter is to convert a class's interface into one that clients expect. A delegate is an Adapter because it converts the interface of a function pointer to another interface. Instead of working with a function pointer, clients work with the new interface exposed by the delegate. As we mentioned earlier, the new interface provides compiler-generated methods. It also can be passed to `System.Delegate.Remove()` and `System.Delegate.Combine()`, which certainly won't accept function pointers as input parameters.

The InfoItem Helper Class

There's one last part of the CallCenter class library that we haven't covered – that's the InfoItem helper class. This is simply an abstract data type for a name/value pair. Instances of InfoItem are used here in our example to represent the caller's phone number, member ID and area code, so that these values can be passed from the notifier to each observer as properties of the call event. Here is the InfoItem class's definition:

```vb
<Serializable()> Public Class InfoItem
    Private m_strName As String
    Private m_strValue As String

    Public Property Name() As String
      Set(ByVal strName As String)
        m_strName = strName
      End Set
      Get
        Return m_strName
      End Get
    End Property

    Public Property Value() As String
      Set(ByVal strValue As String)
        m_strValue = strValue
      End Set
      Get
        Return m_strValue
      End Get
    End Property

    Public Sub New(strName As String, strValue As String)
      Me.Name = strName
      Me.Value = strValue
    End Sub

  End Class

End Namespace
```

One important thing to note about InfoItem is that it must be marked with the <Serializable()> attribute. This is because we pass an ArrayList of InfoItem instances by value from EventCoordinator to CSRs. To pass an object by value across application domains, that object must be serializable so that the framework can serialize it into byte streams.

The Remote CSR Server Object

Now the source code for CallCenter.dll is complete, let's move onto the source code for the Representative.dll class library. Recall that this class will be used in a host application that represents a customer service representative. It contains class definitions for the CSR class and the ICallEventHandler interface.

We'll put all the code for this class into a source file called Representative.vb. It starts with the Imports statements, and then opens the namespace that we'll use for the Representative code:

```
Imports System
Imports System.Threading
Imports System.Runtime.Remoting
Imports System.Runtime.Remoting.Messaging
Imports System.Collections
Imports Microsoft.VisualBasic
Imports CallCenter

Namespace Representative
```

As you can see, it uses a number of the .NET Framework classes here. It will also use the `CallCenter` class library that we've just coded.

The ICallEventListener Interface

Here is the code for the `ICallEventHandler` interface:

```
Public Interface ICallEventHandler
    Sub onCall(al As ArrayList)
End Interface
```

Note the signature of the `onCall()` method. Later, we'll use the same signature for the function pointer wrapped by a delegate.

The CSR Observer Class

Next and last, here is the observer class, `CSR`, which represents a customer sales representative. The `CSR` class implements the `ICallEventHandler` interface:

```
Public Class CSR
    Inherits MarshalByRefObject
    Implements ICallEventHandler

    'Event handler function
    Public Sub onCall(al As ArrayList) Implements ICallEventHandler.onCall
        Console.WriteLine("Event passed with an array of {0} properties:", _
                        al.Count)
        Dim infoItem As InfoItem
        For Each infoItem In al
          Console.WriteLine("   {0}: {1}", _
                            infoItem.Name, infoItem.Value)
        Next
        Thread.Sleep(10000)
        Console.WriteLine("Slept 10 seconds.")
    End Sub 'onCall
End Class

End Namespace
```

Notice that the `CSR` class inherits `MarshalByRefObject`. This is mandatory for every remoting object, regardless of whether it is a `Singleton`, `SingleCall` or `ClientActivated` remote object. By inheriting `MarshalByRefObject`, the `CSR` class tells the .NET Remoting infrastructure that its instances are remote objects and they should be marshaled by reference (not by value) when accessed by clients.

As we've already mentioned, the CSR class's onCall() method expects a single argument of type ArrayList as input from EventCoordinator. Our implementation of this method assumes that the ArrayList contains an array of InfoItem elements (which contain name/value pairs representing call properties like name, phone number, etc.). For simplicity, our example doesn't do anything fancy – it just outputs these name/value pairs to the console window and then sleeps for 10 seconds before returning.

The Host Applications

Now we've got the source code for the notifier and observer class libraries, we can build them into applications. In principle, we can host these applications at different places across a network, and they will work together using .NET Remoting techniques. In practice, for simplicity, we will host these applications on a single machine. As we've said, this still forms a "distributed" solution, because the individual applications must communicate across process boundaries.

We will organize the notifier application and CSR applications by placing them into different subfolders of the \Phase1 folder:

❏   We'll have a subfolder called \EventCoordinator to represent the call center

❏   We'll have two subfolders called \EventHandler1 and \EventHandler2, to represent two customer service representatives

In the following two sections, we'll briefly describe these applications. We will not describe the compilation in detail here, as it's fairly straightforward. The source code for this chapter includes a batch file called Phase1CompileAll.bat, which compiles the entire application in one go (using VB.NET command-line compilation tools) – you'll be able to compile everything by using that batch file, or you can use it for guidance.

The CallCenter Application and the Singleton Pattern

The call center application takes the form of an executable file called CallCenterHost.exe, which hosts the EventCoordinator remote server object. This application makes use of the CallCenter.dll class library (whose source we have already seen), and a configuration file Default.cfg.

The code for the host program CallCenterHost.exe is listed below. You'll find it in the file Host.vb:

```
Imports System
Imports System.IO
Imports System.Runtime.Remoting

Public Class Host

  Public Shared Sub Main()
    VBMain(System.Environment.GetCommandLineArgs())
  End Sub

  Public Shared Sub VBMain(args() As String)
    RemotingConfiguration.Configure("Default.cfg")

    Console.WriteLine("Host is ready.")
```

```
      Console.WriteLine("Press RETURN to exit at any time.")
      Console.WriteLine("")
      Dim keyState As String
      keyState = Console.ReadLine()
      Console.WriteLine("End")
    End Sub

  End Class
```

Because we want to have a *single* event coordinator to coordinate all call events, we'll configure our EventCoordinator object to be a Singleton remote server object. We do this within the configuration file, Default.cfg, which is used in the Configure() method above. Here's the full listing for Default.cfg for the CallCenter application:

```
<configuration>
  <system.runtime.remoting>
    <application name="CallCenter">
      <service>
        <wellknown mode="Singleton"
                   type="CallCenter.EventCoordinator, CallCenter"
                   objectUri="EventCoordinator.soap"
        />
      </service>

      <channels>
        <channel ref="http" port="999" />
      </channels>
    </application>
  </system.runtime.remoting>
</configuration>
```

As you can see, the configuration file specifies that the mode of our event coordinator is Singleton (and also that the port the event coordinator listens on is 999). In fact, this is how .NET Remoting facilitates the application of the GoF Singleton pattern in object creation. Instead of writing our own implementation of the Singleton pattern, we simply use the mode="Singleton" attribute – this will ensure that the CLR will create only one instance of the EventCoordinator object.

The Default.cfg file makes it very easy to configure the CallCenter application without recompiling it. For example, there is a limit to the traffic that a Singleton EventCoordinator can handle, so at some time in the future we may find it appropriate to make our event coordinator a SingleCall object instead. To do that, all we have to do is edit the Default.cfg file. That's it – there is no need to recompile anything.

Note also that in this simplified scenario, there is only one PBX box in the call center. In a more practical situation, our singleton event coordinator might need to be able to receive call events all from a number of PBX boxes. In that case, access to the singleton coordinator's states would need to be synchronized.

To build the call center application, we simply need to compile the executable CallCenterHost.exe and the class library CallCenter.dll:

```
vbc /debug+ /r:System.Runtime.Remoting.dll -out:CallCenterHost.exe Host.vb
vbc /debug+ /t:library -out:CallCenter.dll CallCenter.vb
```

The CSR Application

Each CSR application also takes the form of an executable file called `CSRHost.exe`. This executable hosts the CSR remote server object; it makes use of the `Representative.dll` class library (whose source we saw earlier), and the `CallCenter.dll` library that we've just built; and it also uses its own configuration file, which is also called `Default.cfg`.

> *You've probably noticed that all the configuration files here carry the name* `Default.cfg`. *We distinguish between them by putting them into different folders. The configuration file for the* `CallCenterHost.exe` *application is stored with* `CallCenterHost.exe` *in the* *EventCoordinator folder. The configuration file for each* `CSRHost.exe` *application is stored with* `CSRHost.exe` *in the* *EventHandlerx folder.*

To build the host program `CSRHost.exe`, we can use the same source code (`Host.vb`) we used to build the `CallCenterHost.exe` application above. (We could write new source code for `CSRHost.exe`, if we wanted to. But we note that the two host applications have very similar characteristics – they're intended to host instances of remote server objects – and that the only essential differences between the host applications are differences that we can capture in the applications' `Default.cfg` files.)

So, let's just look at the `Default.cfg` file used by one of these CSR applications:

```
<configuration>
  <system.runtime.remoting>
    <application name="Representative">
      <service>
        <wellknown mode="SingleCall"
                   type="Representative.CSR, Representative"
                   objectUri="CSR.soap"
        />
      </service>

      <channels>
        <channel ref="http" port="888" />
      </channels>
    </application>
  </system.runtime.remoting>
</configuration>
```

Here, we use the `<wellknown>` element's `mode` attribute to indicate that each CSR object is a `SingleCall` server object. This is because the CSR object does not maintain any state information. It is created when the client invokes the `onCall()` method, and destroyed when `onCall()` finishes processing the event.

> *Later, in the third phase of our example, we'll change the CSR class to be client-activated.*

Also in the `<wellknown>` tag, we use the `type` attribute to specify the full type name of the CSR remote object. The full type name is composed of the object's class type (`Representative.CSR` in this case) and the assembly name (`Representative` in this case), separated by a comma. Last, we use the `objectUri` attribute to specify the URI of the remote object (`CSR.soap` in this case).

Finally, our configuration also specifies that instances of the CSR class hosted by this application will listen on port 888 using the HTTP protocol. In fact, as we've already mentioned, we will have two CSR host applications, and each application will listen on a different port. The application in the \EventHandler1 folder will listen on port 888, and the application in the \EventHandler2 folder will listen on port 889.

To build each CSR application, we simply need to compile the executable `CSRHost.exe` and the class library `Representative.dll` (notice that the compilation requires a copy of `CallCenter.dll`):

```
vbc /debug+ /r:System.Runtime.Remoting.dll -out:CSRHost.exe Host.vb
vbc /debug+ /t:library /r:CallCenter.dll -out:Representative.dll
                                            Representative.vb
```

We need to do this twice – once for each CSR application.

The Client Application

We've covered everything we need for our remote server objects. Now let's build a client application that will make use of them. Our client application is an executable called `ClientSimulator.exe`, and it plays the part of a PBX box and simulates an incoming customer call. The source code for our client application is contained in the file `ClientSimulator.vb`.

First, here are the necessary `Imports` statements. In addition to classes in the listed .NET Framework namespaces, our client application also makes use of the `CallCenter` and `Representative` namespaces that contain the class definitions for our server objects:

```
Imports System
Imports System.Runtime.Remoting
Imports System.Runtime.Remoting.Channels
Imports System.Runtime.Remoting.Channels.Http

Imports CallCenter
Imports Representative
```

Now we can look at the `Client` class itself. First, it uses the `Activator.GetObject()` method to call across the Internet and get references to the necessary server objects – the `EventCoordinator` object and the two `CSR` objects:

```
Public Class Client

    Public Shared Sub Main()
        ChannelServices.RegisterChannel(new HttpChannel(0))

        'Get references to CSR and EventCoordinator Remoting objects.
        Console.WriteLine("Preparing server object references...")
        Dim CSRep1 As CSR = _
                CType(Activator.GetObject(GetType(CSR), _
                                        "http://localhost:888/CSR.soap"), _
                    CSR)
        Dim CSRep2 As CSR = _
                CType(Activator.GetObject(GetType(CSR), _
                                        "http://localhost:889/CSR.soap"), _
                    CSR)

        Dim EventCrd As EventCoordinator = _
                CType(Activator.GetObject(GetType(EventCoordinator), _
                            "http://localhost:999/EventCoordinator.soap"), _
                    EventCoordinator)

        Console.WriteLine("Server object references are ready.")
```

Next, it creates two delegates – one for the `onCall()` event handler of each of the two CSR objects – and uses `System.Delegate.Combine()` to register them with the `EventCoordinator`:

```
'Register the event handlers with the call event
Console.WriteLine("Registering observers...")
Dim callHandlerCSR1 as CallEventHandler
callHandlerCSR1 = New CallEventHandler(AddressOf CSRep1.onCall)
Dim callHandlerCSR2 as CallEventHandler
callHandlerCSR2 = New CallEventHandler(AddressOf CSRep2.onCall)
EventCrd.m_evntCall = _
        System.Delegate.Combine(callHandlerCSR1, callHandlerCSR2)

Console.WriteLine("Observers registered.")
Console.WriteLine("")
```

At this point, the remote server objects are set up and ready to receive calls.

Now our client application can turn call simulator, by generating a call event (just as if a real customer was calling). To do this, it first creates some properties of the call (one for the phone number, one for the member ID, both represented by `InfoItem` instances). We add these properties to the `EventCoordinator` object's internal `m_CallInfoArray` (using the `Add()` method), and then trigger the call event via the `fireCallEvent()` method:

```
'Set properties of the Call.
Console.WriteLine("Setting properties and simulating call event...")
Dim InfoItem1 As New InfoItem("Phone number", "312-398-8000")
EventCrd.Add(InfoItem1)
Dim InfoItem2 As New InfoItem("Member ID", "37662")
EventCrd.Add(InfoItem2)

'Fire Call event
EventCrd.fireCallEvent()
```

Finally it cleans up the `m_CallInfoArray` member and writes a note to the console window:

```
    EventCrd.RemoveAll()

    Console.WriteLine("Call event fired. Simulation ends.")
  End Sub
End Class
```

To build the client application, we simply need to compile the `ClientSimulator.vb` code into an executable, using the following command (notice that the compilation requires a copy of `CallCenter.dll` and `Representative.dll`):

```
vbc /debug+ /r:System.Runtime.Remoting.dll
            /r:CallCenter.dll /r:Representative.dll ClientSimulator.vb
```

Running the Example Application

Running the application is simplicity itself. We simply need to start the server services, and then run the client application:

- ❑ First, start the EventCoordinator service by navigating to the \EventCoordinator folder and double-clicking the CallCenterHost.exe file

- ❑ Second, start the two CSR services by navigating to each \EventHandler*x* folder and double-clicking its CSRHost.exe file

- ❑ Finally, run the client simulator application by navigating to the \ClientSimulator folder and double-clicking its ClientSimulator.exe file

Alternatively, you can run the two batch files (Phase1RunServices.bat then Phase1RunClient.bat) that are provided with the source code for this chapter, or you can use the commands contained within those batch files to run the whole thing from the command line.

As you'll recall, the two CSR instances are configured to listen on two different ports – 888 and 889. A port is the labeled endpoint of a network connection. For example, the default HTTP web service listens on port 80 for client requests; similarly, we have configured our two CSR applications to listen on ports 888 and 889 for requests.

This configuration allows us to run all these "distributed" applications on a single machine (the machine called localhost). If the machine receives a client request at port 888, then one of the CSR services will pick it up; if it receives a client request at port 889, the other CSR service will pick it up. If it receives a client request at port 999, the EventCoordinator service picks it up.

If the ports we've chosen for this example (888 and 889 for CSR instances and 999 for the event coordinator) are already used by other services on your machine, then you can use the configuration files (and the code in ClientSimulator.vb) to specify different ports. You have to go to the configuration files and assign other port numbers to the remote objects to make the example work. If you want to run the example across a number of machines in the network, you can do so by specifying the IP addresses and port numbers of the server machines in the client application, like this:

```
'Get references to CSR and EventCoordinator Remoting objects.
Dim CSRep1 As CSR = _
        CType(Activator.GetObject(GetType(CSR), _
                              "http://10.0.0.2:888/CSR.soap"), _
            CSR)
Dim CSRep2 As CSR = _
        CType(Activator.GetObject(GetType(CSR), _
                              "http://10.0.0.3:888/CSR.soap"), _
            CSR)

Dim EventCrd As EventCoordinator = _
        CType(Activator.GetObject(GetType(EventCoordinator), _
                  "http://10.0.0.1:999/EventCoordinator.soap"), _
            EventCoordinator)
```

As we've seen, the PBX client application creates references to the remote server objects, performs the necessary registering, and then triggers a call event and waits for the event to finish. In total, you'll see four console windows, each of which represents a different process within the example:

The top window here shows the output from the EventCoordinator process. The next two show the output from the CSR processes (these two windows show the same output – a future task is to adjust the EventCoordinator so that it only passes a customer call to *one* of the CSRs, not to all of them!). The bottom window shows the output from the client process.

A Note on the Proxy Pattern

The coordinator dispatches call events to CSRs through .NET Remoting channels. The coordinator and CSRs are remote objects, and are marshaled by reference (not by value); therefore clients cannot create a new instance of a remote object locally. Consequently, instances of the InfoItem class are not remote objects. This is because InfoItem class is serializable – so they must be passed by value. The state information of an InfoItem instance is serialized whenever the instance crosses a context boundary or AppDomain. A client can then deserialize the received byte stream, and create a new local instance of type InfoItem that has the same state.

Since clients of remote objects can only access the objects remotely, they need local representatives of the remote objects to give them the illusion that they are working with local objects. A local representative of such an object is called a **proxy** of the remote object. This is a good example of the GoF Proxy pattern. In our sample code, we use proxies to represent the coordinator to CSRs and the PBX client. They are also used to represent CSRs to the event coordinator.

The proxy represents a remote server object on the client side, and it obviously needs to know about the server object's type information in order to represent it. In the realm of COM, type information can be exchanged using type libraries or interface definition files. The **MIDL** can help you extract type information from type libraries. In .NET, it's the **soapsuds** utility that helps us to extract type information from the compiled assembly.

Now we're going to move onto Phase 2 of our development, in which we will implement the asynchronous call-handling requirement.

Phase 2 – Asynchronous Call Handling

Let's suppose that we shipped and deployed our example program to a number of call centers, and that customers are happy with it for quite a while. Then one day a new business requirement comes in. One call center wants the event coordinator to dispatch call events to CSRs in an **asynchronous** fashion. Customers want this feature because some actions performed by CSRs take a long time to finish, and our customers want the event coordinator to come right back after dispatching call events to CSRs and be notified by the CSRs when they finish their tasks.

Fortunately, our system has a well designed structure; and moreover, .NET supports this kind of change with the **Asynchronous Programming** pattern. Therefore, adding such a business requirement to our system is a breeze. In this phase of our example, we'll see how .NET supports the use of this pattern.

The Asynchronous Programming Pattern

The Asynchronous Programming pattern is not a GoF pattern – it's a Microsoft-devised pattern. Microsoft suggests that developers utilize the pattern when sending asynchronous events.

One advantage that asynchronous call events can bring to our application is that it will give increased call handling capability for the event coordinator. In its current form, call events are processed synchronously, which means that the event coordinator must wait for a CSR to finish processing a call event before it can respond to the customer and then get ready for the next customer call. By introducing asynchronous events, the event coordinator no longer has to wait for a CSR to finish processing the call, so it can come right back after dispatching the event to a CSR and be ready for the next customer call.

This increased call handling capability is especially important in our case because the event coordinator is a Singleton object. As we saw earlier in the chapter, Requirement 4 states that the application must have a single event coordinator – and therefore it must be a Singleton. Unlike SingleCall and ClientActivated objects, which can have multiple instances serving client requests in parallel threads, a Singleton object can (by definition) have only one instance, serving client requests one at a time.

There are a few ways to work around this problem. One is to use multi-threading when passing synchronous call events from event coordinator to CSRs. An alternative method is to turn synchronous events into asynchronous ones. This latter method is the one we'll show in this phase of the example.

If you've read the Asynchronous Programming sections in the .NET documentation (http://msdn.microsoft.com/library/en-us/cpguide/html/ cpconasynchronousprogrammingdesignpattern2.asp), you're probably already fascinated by the benefits that this pattern promises. The .NET documentation says that the caller decides if a call should be asynchronous. That is, we don't need to make any changes to the callee class (the CSR class in our example).

Understanding the Pattern

Before we look at the code, let's take a look at the pattern itself. The participants of the Asynchronous Programming pattern include:

- A client (the PBX client)

- An event source (the `EventCoordinator`)

- An event-handling delegate (the `CallEventHandler` delegate)

- An `AsyncCallback` delegate (the `onCallEventHandlerReturn` delegate we'll see later in the code list)

The following UML sequence diagram shows the interactions among these participants in the context of our example. We've seen all the participants in Phase 1, with the exception of the `AsyncCallback` delegate. The `AsyncCallback` delegate is a special type of delegate provided by the .NET class library. It is like ordinary delegates in that it is a wrapper of function pointers; but it is different in that it has certain methods that get called by the CLR at certain times. We'll get to understand this better as we trace the method calls shown in the diagram, in the following paragraphs:

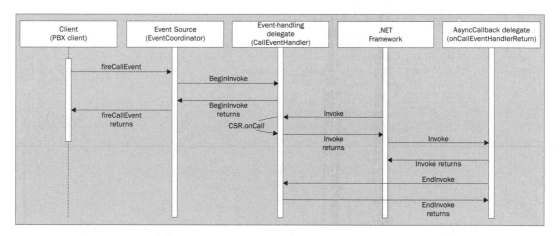

- First, the PBX client calls the event coordinator's `fireCallEvent()` to fire a call event.

- The event coordinator then immediately dispatches the call event by calling `BeginInvoke()` on the event-handling delegate. Because this is an asynchronous event, `BeginInvoke()` returns immediately without waiting for the result of event handling.

- Behind the scenes, as soon as the `BeginInvoke()` is called on the `CallEventHandler` delegate, an item is put in the work queue of the thread pool provided by the CLR.

- When the .NET Framework checks the queue and sees the item, it will call `Invoke()` on the event-handling delegate.

- When the `Invoke()` method is called, the event-handling function itself (CSR's `onCall()` method) is invoked as shown in the above figure. The `onCall()` method call itself works in just the same way as it did in Phase 1. The CSR object doesn't know whether the call event is synchronous or asynchronous.

- After the `onCall()` method finishes processing, the .NET Framework will call `Invoke()` on the `AsyncCallback` delegate to notify the event coordinator of the completion of the `Call` event processing.

❑ In the `AsyncCallback` delegate, we can fetch the event processing results by calling `EndInvoke()` on the event-handling delegate. The `EndInvoke()` method must be called manually in the function wrapped by the `AsyncCallback` delegate.

As we mentioned in the *Events, Delegates, and the Adapter Pattern* section, the signature of the `EndInvoke()` method depends on the signature of `CSR.onCall()`, the function wrapped by the event-handling delegate. This is why we can get the results of `CSR.onCall()` by calling `EndInvoke()`. In our example code, since `CSR.onCall()` has no return value and accepts no out parameters (parameters passed by reference, not by value), we won't need to call `EndInvoke()`.

Readers interested in the details of how to fetch the result of asynchronous calls can find examples in the .NET Framework documentation.

Amending the Application

As we've already noted, the .NET *Asynchronous Programming* documentation says that it should be the *caller* that decides whether a call should be asynchronous. This means that we don't need to make any changes to the callee `CSR` class in our example. It is the `EventCoordinator` object in our example that decides whether its call to the `CSR.onCall()` method should be synchronous or asynchronous.

So, the only change we need to make is to the `EventCoordinator` class definition, in `CallCenter.vb`. We'll highlight the changes from the Phase 1 version of `CallCenter.vb` by using gray highlighting.

First, we'll be making use of the .NET Framework's `AsyncResult` class, which belongs to the `System.Runtime.Remoting.Messaging` namespace. So it's useful to add an extra `Imports` statement for that namespace:

```
Imports System
Imports System.Runtime.Remoting
Imports System.Runtime.Remoting.Messaging
Imports System.Collections
```

The next thing to do is define `onCallEventHandlerReturn()`:

```
Public Class EventCoordinator
  Inherits MarshalByRefObject

  Public m_evntCall As CallEventHandler      ' Delegate instance
  Private m_CallInfoArray As ArrayList       ' Call event's properties


  'Function wrapped by AsyncCallback delegate
  Public Sub onCallEventHandlerReturn(ar As IAsyncResult)
    Console.WriteLine("onCallEventHandlerReturn() call complete.")
  End Sub 'onCallEventHandlerReturn
```

In our example, the event coordinator doesn't have to do anything when a `CSR` object finishes processing a call event, so we simply write a string to the console confirming that the `onCallEventHandlerReturn()` is indeed called back by the framework.

Next we make some changes to the `fireCallEvent()` method. To begin, we declare a local variable cb of type `AsyncCallback`. The variable is an `AsyncCallback` delegate that wraps the `onCallEventHandlerReturn()` method of `EventCoordinator`. That means that when a CSR finishes processing a `Call` event, the .NET Framework will invoke `onCallEventHandlerReturn()`:

```
'This method is called to trigger the Call event.
Public Sub fireCallEvent()
    Console.WriteLine("EventCoordinator.fireCallEvent() called.")
    Dim cb As AsyncCallback = AddressOf Me.onCallEventHandlerReturn
```

Now that we've seen the `AsyncCallback` delegate and the `onCallEventhandlerReturn()` method it wraps, we're ready to see how to call `BeginInvoke()` on `m_evntCall`. Recall that `BeginInvoke()` will put an item in the work queue of the thread pool, so that when the .NET Framework checks the queue and sees the item, it will call `Invoke()` on the event-handling delegate.

The `BeginInvoke()` call is performed within `fireCallEvent()`. In Phase 1, we passed `m_CallInfoArray` to the `m_evntCall` delegate in the `fireCallEvent()` method to dispatch synchronous `Call` events to CSRs. Here, we replace that line with one that invokes the `BeginInvoke()` method on a delegate.

Because `m_evntCall` is a delegate that might wrap more than one function pointer, we use `m_evntCall.GetInvocationList()` to get a list of them all. Each delegate in the list wraps a function pointer to a CSR's `onCall()` method. For each delegate on the list, we call its `BeginInvoke()` method:

```
    Dim state As New Object
    Dim ar As IAsyncResult
    Dim invokeList() As System.Delegate = m_evntCall.GetInvocationList()
    Dim callHandler As CallEventHandler

    For Each callHandler In invokeList
      callHandler.BeginInvoke(m_CallInfoArray, cb, state)
    Next

    Console.WriteLine("EventCoordinator now ready for next call event...")
End Sub

'Other class members...
End Class
```

Notice that we pass a number of parameters to the `BeginInvoke()` method of the compiler-generated `CallEventHandler` class. We mentioned in the *Events, Delegates, and the Adapter Pattern* section that the compiler will generate a class for us based on the `CallEventHandler` delegate we declared. You may recall that the generated class is named `CallEventHandler`, and that it is derived from `System.Delegate`. One of its member functions is `BeginInvoke()` and the signature of `BeginInvoke()` depends on the signature of `CSR.onCall()`, the function whose pointer the `CallEventHandler` delegate wraps.

So what would the signature of `BeginInvoke()` be? Well, `BeginInvoke()` will take whatever parameters `CSR.onCall()` takes, *plus* an `AsyncCallback` delegate and a `state` object. For this reason, we pass `m_CallInfoArray`, the `AsyncCallback` delegate, and a dummy `state` object to `BeginInvoke()`:

- ❑ We pass m_CallInfoArray so that the .NET Framework can propagate it to the onCall() method of each CSR.

- ❑ We pass the AsyncCallback so that the .NET Framework knows which function to call back when a CSR's onCall() method finishes processing the Call event.

- ❑ The state object is there for you to maintain any state information you want across the whole process of the asynchronous event (there is none in this example, so the state object is a dummy one).

That's all we need to do to turn the synchronous Call event into an asynchronous one. There's no change in the event handler class CSR, as promised by the pattern in the .NET documentation.

Building and Running the Example

The steps for building the Phase 2 example are identical to those for the Phase 1 example. If you're using the source code that accompanies the book, then you'll need to compile everything in the \Phase2 folder – you can do that by running the Phase2CompileAll.bat batch file that is contained within the \Phase2 folder. By contrast, if you've built Phase 2 by making changes to your Phase 1 solution, then you only have to recompile CallCenter.dll and distribute it to the appropriate places.

Running the application also requires identical steps to before. Start the server programs first, and then run the client program. You'll see that the PBX client triggers the Call event and finishes execution right after that. However, because the event notifications are sent to CSRs from the event coordinator asynchronously, the event coordinator is not sitting idly and doing nothing. The event coordinator prints out the string **EventCoordinator now ready for next call event...**, to indicate that it has passed on the event asynchronously (using BeginInvoke()) and is now ready for the next call.

In the meantime, the two CSRs are processing the call event in the onCall() method. Here, in the onCall() method, we simulate the processing of the event-handler by making it sleep for 10 seconds (using the Thread.Sleep() method). At the end of the 10 seconds, the CSRs wake up; the processing of the call event finishes, the EventCoordinator is notified and its onCallEventHandlerReturn() is called twice – once by each CSR.

Here's the output you'll see. Once again, the EventCoordinator's output is in the top window. The last two lines of its output appear 10 seconds later than the rest of the text:

Phase 3 – Flexible Policy Management

The product manager calls another urgent meeting. This time the feature request we got from clients is to impose call-handling policies on CSRs:

❑ One client wants to have calls from San Jose, California (area code 408) handled by one group of CSRs, while calls from South Dakota (area code 605) are handled by a different group of CSRs

❑ Another client awards his "gold members" with MemberIDs between 100 and 200, and it wants calls from those members to be handled by a more experienced CSR

The topic of Phase 3 is the question of how to add such a feature into our current example – with minimum impact on the system's structure and maximum flexibility in policy management. We'll see how a combination of two patterns – Decorator and Template Method – provide a neat solution to our problem.

Adjusting the Application Design

At first glance, adding the policy checking feature to our example doesn't seem to be a big issue. It looks like a case of simply adding more classes to represent the introduction of call-handling policies and different types of CSR:

❑ To represent different call-handling policies, we could introduce a base interface and a number of different derived classes. The base interface could be called `Policy`, and it would have a method called `doPolicyCheck()`. Each call-handling policy would be represented by a class that derives from `Policy` – its policy rules would be implemented in the derived class's override of `doPolicyCheck()`. We'd have one `Policy`-derived class for checking the MemberID, one for checking the caller's area code, and (say) one for checking the caller's name.

❑ To represent different types of CSR, we could subclass our existing CSR class and create four new classes: one for experienced CSRs, one for less experienced CSRs, one for CSRs that handle calls from San Jose, CA and one for CSRs that handle calls from South Dakota.

How would these work together? The onCall() method of each CSR subclass would call the doPolicyCheck() method of the relevant Policy subclasses, and decide (based on the results) whether it needs to handle the call. An example is shown in the diagram below. In the diagram, our client divides its service force into four types of CSR (denoted C1, C2, C3, C4), and it has three policies for call handling (denoted P1, P2, P3). In the pseudocode box in the diagram, we see that CSR instances of type C1 are governed by policies P1 and P2:

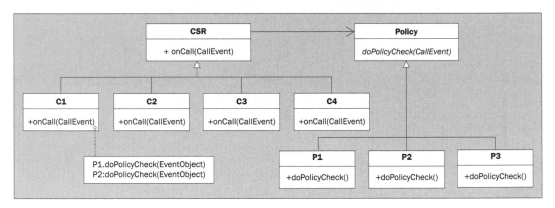

However, it doesn't take much to start picking out the flaws in this design:

❑ It's fairly clear from the diagram how quickly the class hierarchy grows as we add more CSRs and policies.

❑ What if we have another client who wants the CSR subclasses distinguished by (say) product lines, not policies? In that case, the above design doesn't give us an intuitive view of things – we'd prefer to have CSR-derived classes for each product line than CSR-derived classes for each policy combination.

❑ There's also a lack of flexibility in policy management. This design embeds the relationships among CSRs and policies in the classes themselves. If we want to change the relationships, we have to recode all the CSR subclasses. It would make more sense to store details of which policy applies to which CSR in a configuration file; then, changing the relationships would simply be a case of editing the configuration file.

Of course, we want to create a solution that is rather more robust than this. In fact, we can create a much more flexible and extensible solution with a little judicious application of the Decorator and Template Method patterns.

Considering a Design Pattern Solution

Before we look at how the Decorator pattern can help us, let's remind ourselves of the pattern's intent, as phrased by the GoF:

> **GoF Intent for Decorator:** Attach additional responsibilities to an object dynamically. Decorators provide a flexible alternative to subclassing for extending functionality.

The Decorator's intent describes exactly the kind of thing we're looking for here. We want to add extra "policy-handling" functionalities to our CSR objects, but we don't want to achieve it via subclassing.

As you will recall from Chapter 1, the idea of the Decorator pattern is that it uses a decorator object to add extra functionality to "concrete" classes that implement a certain interface. (In the example in Chapter 1, we used the WageAdjustment decorator class to decorate the Employee concrete class; but in fact it could also decorate *any* class that implemented the TakeHomePay interface.)

This requirement fits our situation well. Our concrete class is the CSR class, and it implements the ICallEventHandler interface; so we already have some of the class structure that will make up our Decorator pattern. We'll call our decorator class PolicyDecorator. Now our Decorator pattern is beginning to take shape:

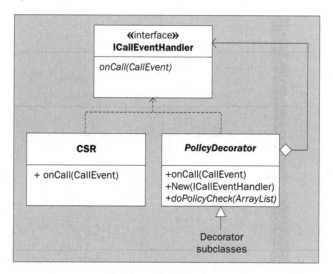

In order to keep within the rules of the Decorator pattern, we'll also need to note the following:

- ❑ The decorator object must keep the top-level interface public. In this case, the PolicyDecorator is the decorator object, and it must reveal the details of the ICallEventHandler interface. It will do this by using the Implements keyword (as we'll see when we get to the code).

- ❑ Once we've implemented the decoration, the outside world should no longer access the concrete object or its parent interface directly – they can only be accessed via a decorator object. In this case, we'll have to make sure that the onCall() method is no longer called directly through a CSR object; we'll have to use PolicyDecorator.onCall() to access the CSR's implementation of onCall() indirectly instead.

❑ As the name of the pattern implies, the job of a decorator is to decorate the concrete class (that is, to add extra functionalities to it), but not to obsolete it. So our `PolicyDecorator` decorator class will still need implementations of the interface it decorates – the `ICallEventHandler` interface – to get the job done. (This is the reason `PolicyDecorator` aggregates `ICallEventHandler`, as indicated by the diamond in the diagram above.)

Deciding on the Decorators

Finally, you may recall that we used "cascading" decorators in Chapter 1, to add further decoration to the main decorator class. (In that example, we used three decorator subclasses – `CityTax`, `RetirementPlan`, and `CountryTax` – to decorate the main `WageAdjustment` decorator class with even more functionality. It's worth turning back to Chapter 1 to remind yourself what we did in that example. In fact, in that example the main `WageAdjustment` decorator acts as a layer of abstraction for the more complex decorator subclasses, in that it abstracts out the functionality that is common to `CityTax`, `RetirementPlan` and `CountryTax`.)

We still need to decide how we're going to arrange the decorator classes for our call center example. Should we use a single decorator class, or should we implement a number of more complex decorator subclasses which further decorate the main decorator? To help us decide, let's consider the following questions:

❑ What additional functionalities will our Decorator pattern add to the `ICallEventHandler` interface?

❑ How will the Decorator pattern add these functionalities?

We know the answer to the first question: the purpose of our Decorator pattern is to decorate our `ICallEventHandler` interface with a `doPolicyCheck()` method, which checks a certain characteristic of the calling customer.

What about the second question? One quick and dirty technique is to put the additional functionalities within a decorator's implementation of `onCall()`. However, this makes the code more difficult to maintain and reuse. It's better to implement each of those extra functionalities within their own methods. Moreover, if we declare these methods as virtual methods within the `PolicyDecorator` main decorator class, each decorator subclass must override them and provide its specific implementations of those methods.

In fact, this part is starting to sound a little more like the Template Method, so let's remind ourselves of the intent for that pattern:

> **GoF Intent for Template Method:** Define the skeleton of an algorithm in an operation, deferring some steps to subclasses. Template Method lets subclasses redefine certain steps of an algorithm without changing the algorithm's structure.

That sounds about right. The main decorator will contain a virtual doPolicyCheck() method declaration, and the decorator subclasses will use that "template" to define their own versions of the doPolicyCheck() algorithm. So, we can complete our class diagram by adding these decorator subclasses:

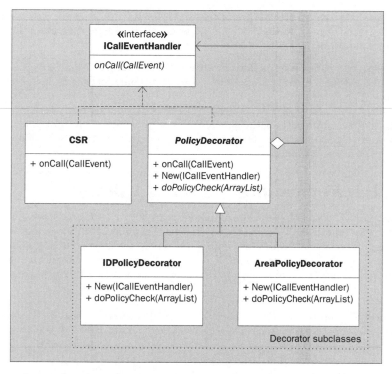

As you can see, the result is a combination of the Decorator pattern and the Template Method pattern:

- ❑ At the top of the diagram, we see the heart of the Decorator pattern. We have the ICallEventHandler interface, which is implemented by the concrete CSR class and decorated by the PolicyDecorator class.

- ❑ Further down the diagram, we see the heart of the Template Method pattern. We have the two PolicyDecorator subclasses, IDPolicyDecorator and AreaPolicyDecorator, each of which implements its parent class's doPolicyCheck() algorithm in a different way.

  Of couse, the IDPolicyDecorator and AreaPolicyDecorator classes could also add their own classes and hence further decorate the PolicyDecorator class (this is the cascading technique that we mentioned in Chapter 1). However, our requirements don't demand that, so we will not use it here.

Now we have seen all the participants of the Decorator pattern and the Template Method pattern in one UML diagram, we are ready to begin coding. Let's summarize those five participants, before we start:

- ❑ The ICallEventHandler interface is the same as it was in the previous two phases. It has only one method, onCall(). No change is made to this interface.

- ❑ The CSR class also requires no changes. When it is decorated with a subclass of PolicyDecorator, the behavior of its onCall() method will be different.

- ❑ The PolicyDecorator decorator class is a new class – the base class for the decorator subclasses listed below. PolicyDecorator keeps a reference to the ICallEventHandler interface that it decorates via aggregation.

❑ The `IDPolicyDecorator` decorator subclass is intended to decorate the `CSR` class with a `doPolicyCheck()` method. When a `CSR` is decorated with this decorator, it will only answer customer calls from members whose IDs are in a certain range.

❑ The `AreaPolicyDecorator` decorator subclass also decorates the `CSR` class. When a `CSR` is decorated with this decorator, it will only answer customer calls from members with certain area codes.

As required by the Decorator pattern, the concrete class and decorator classes (`CSR`, `PolicyDecorator`, `IDPolicyDecorator` and `AreaPolicyDecorator`) will *all* have to implement the `ICallEventHandler` interface.

Amending the Representative Class Library

Remember our goal in this phase is to change the behavior of `CSR.onCall()` dynamically. We want to check the caller's MemberID and area code according to our policy, before passing the call to a `CSR`. We have decided not to accomplish this by putting the policy-checking code in the `onCall()` method of the `CSR` class. Instead, we have decided to leave the `CSR` class intact, and attach decorators to it on the fly. Therefore, we don't need to make any change to the `ICallEventHandler` interface and the `CSR` class.

In this phase, we'll implement three new classes: `PolicyDecorator`, `IDPolicyDecorator` and `AreaPolicyDecorator`. These three classes are all decorators. They are all subclasses of the `ICallEventHandler` interface, and (as we've said) they can be used to decorate `ICallEventHandler` and any class derived from `ICallEventHandler`.

The PolicyDecorator Class

Let's start, then, by writing the code for the `PolicyDecorator` class. We'll add the source code for this class to the file `Representative.vb`. Note first that our class inherits `MarshalByRefObject` (to tell the .NET Remoting infrastructure that its instances are remote objects and should be marshaled by reference, not by value). Note also that the class also implements `ICallEventHandler`, as we said it must do:

```
Public Class PolicyDecorator
  Inherits MarshalByRefObject
  Implements ICallEventHandler
```

Next, we need a member variable to reference the object that the `PolicyDecorator` object will decorate. This could be a `CSR` object, or another object that implements `ICallEventHandler` – our `PolicyDecorator` object will treat it as `ICallEventHandler` in a polymorphic fashion. We'll instantiate it within the class constructor:

```
Private m_CallEventHandler As ICallEventHandler

Public Sub New(callEventHandler As ICallEventHandler)
  Console.WriteLine("Constructing PolicyDecorator " & _
                    "using {0} constructor ", callEventHandler)
  m_CallEventHandler = callEventHandler
End Sub
```

For our information, the constructor also writes the typename of the constructed object to the console.

Next comes the `PolicyDecorator`'s `onCall()` method. It performs the policy check (by calling its own `doPolicyCheck()` method), uses the result of this check to decide whether to call the `onCall()` method of the object it decorates. Finally, we see the `doPolicyCheck()` method itself:

```
    Public Sub onCall(al As ArrayList) Implements ICallEventHandler.onCall
        If doPolicyCheck(al) Then
          m_CallEventHandler.onCall(al)
        End If
    End Sub

    Overridable Protected Function doPolicyCheck(al As ArrayList) _
                                                    As Boolean
        doPolicyCheck = True
    End Function

  End Class
```

There are a few observations we should make about this class. First, note that we've initialized `m_CallEventHandler` in the constructor, and set its value to the constructor's input parameter. This approach has one desirable feature: namely, that it allows us to cascade several decorators at object creation. For example, at the time we create an instance of class `CSR`, we can decorate it with *both* the `IDPolicyDecorator` and `AreaPolicyDecorator`, like this:

```
  Dim CSRep As New AreaPolicyDecorator(New IDPolicyDecorator(New CSR()))
```

Is it always best to initialize `m_CallEventHandler` in the constructor? In reality, it depends on the problem you are solving. In another situation, it might be appropriate to initialize `m_CallEventHandler` in a member function such as the `onCall()` method. For example, you might use this technique to delay initialization until the point at which the object is needed.

Second, note that the `m_CallEventHandler` reference is *private*; this shields the object reference from subclasses of `PolicyDecorator`. Hence, subclasses will only be able to override the virtual (overridable) `doPolicyCheck()` method. They will not have any knowledge about the object that we're decorating. This is possible because we utilize the Template Method pattern to make `PolicyDecorator`'s `onCall()` method a template method. The logic that describes how to pass a call event on to the aggregated object's `onCall()` method is hidden in the template method.

Finally, it's worth noting a difference between this decorator class and the one we saw in the example in Chapter 1. Namely, this one is public creatable, while the `WageAdjustment` decorator class in Chapter 1 is a `MustInherit` class. Why? It's simply that in this example, we would like to use `PolicyDecorator` as a decorator class in its own right; while in Chapter 1, we use `WageAdjustment` simply as an abstraction of the three decorator subclasses in that example.

The IDPolicyDecorator Class

Now let's see the implementation of `IDPolicyDecorator`. The source for this class will also go in the `Representative.vb` file.

The `IDPolicyDecorator` class derives from `PolicyDecorator`. It inherits everything from `PolicyDecorator` and overrides the `doPolicyCheck()` method where it checks if the caller's MemberID is between 100 and 200:

```
Public Class IDPolicyDecorator
  Inherits PolicyDecorator

  Public Sub New(callEventHandler As ICallEventHandler)
    MyBase.New(callEventHandler)
    Console.WriteLine("Constructing IDPolicyDecorator " & _
                      "using {0} constructor ", callEventHandler)
  End Sub

  Overrides Protected Function doPolicyCheck(al As ArrayList) As Boolean
    Dim bResult As Boolean = False
    Dim infoItem As InfoItem
    For Each infoItem In al
      If infoItem.Name = "Member ID" Then
        Dim iMemberID As Integer
        iMemberID = Convert.ToInt32(infoItem.Value)
        If (iMemberID >= 100 And iMemberID <= 200) Then
          Console.WriteLine("Member with MemberID {0} accepted.", _
                            iMemberID)
          bResult = True
        Else
          Console.WriteLine("Member with MemberID {0} rejected.", _
                            iMemberID)
          bResult = False
        End If
      End If
    Next
    doPolicyCheck = bResult
  End Function
End Class
```

As `PolicyDecorator`, the constructor of `IDPolicyDecorator` takes an input parameter of type `ICallEventHandler` so that we can cascade `IDPolicyDecorator` with other decorators. The constructor of `IDPolicyDecorator` does not do anything to the input parameter. It just passes its input parameter to the base class's constructor.

The AreaPolicyDecorator Class

Next is the implementation of `AreaPolicyDecorator`. It's identical to the implementation of `IDPolicyDecorator`, except that in the `doPolicyCheck()` method it checks caller's area code instead of member ID.

Once again, the source code for this class will go in the file `Representative.vb`:

```
Public Class AreaPolicyDecorator
  Inherits PolicyDecorator

  Public Sub New(callEventHandler As ICallEventHandler)
    MyBase.New(callEventHandler)
    Console.WriteLine("Constructing AreaPolicyDecorator " & _
                      "using {0} constructor ", callEventHandler)
  End Sub

  Overrides Protected Function doPolicyCheck(al As ArrayList) As Boolean
    Dim bResult As Boolean = False
    Dim infoItem As InfoItem
    For Each infoItem In al
      If infoItem.Name = "Area Code" Then
        If infoItem.Value = "408" Then
          Console.WriteLine("Call from area code {0} accepted.", _
                            infoItem.Value)
          bResult = True
        Else
          Console.WriteLine("Call from area code {0} rejected.", _
                            infoItem.Value)
          bResult = False
        End If
      End If
    Next
    doPolicyCheck = bResult
  End Function
End Class
```

The Configuration File, Default.cfg

We noted earlier that PolicyDecorator inherits from MarshalByRefObject, and that
IDPolicyDecorator and AreaPolicyDecorator inherit from PolicyDecorator. Consequently,
all three decorator classes are subclasses of MarshalByRefObject. This means that they are remoting
objects in the same way as the CSR and EventCoordinator classes.

However, unlike CSR and EventCoordinator, our decorator classes are not well-known SingleCall
or Singleton types. They are client-activated. In order to allow clients to get a handle of these types,
we have to modify the Default.cfg configuration file for the CSRHost.exe application, by adding an
<activated> tag for each of the three types:

```
<configuration>
  <system.runtime.remoting>
    <application name="Representative">
      <service>
        <wellknown mode="SingleCall"
                   type="Representative.CSR, Representative"
                   objectUri="CSR.soap" />
        <activated type="Representative.PolicyDecorator, Representative" />
        <activated
                   type="Representative.IDPolicyDecorator, Representative" />
        <activated
                   type="Representative.AreaPolicyDecorator, Representative" />
      </service>
```

```
        <channels>
          <channel ref="http" port="888" />
        </channels>
      </application>
    </system.runtime.remoting>
  </configuration>
```

Each `<activated>` tag has a `type` attribute, in which we identify the class by giving its full type name (such as `Repersentative.PolicyDecorator`) and its assembly name (`Representative`).

Building a Client Program

In order to demonstrate decorator objects being attached to instances of the CSR class in a dynamic fashion, we'll need to modify the client side code a little bit. The decoration is dynamic because decorators are attached to instances of the CSR class on the fly. For example, if we want to impose the member ID policy on a CSR, we do so by coding the following statement:

```
Dim CSRep As New IDPolicyDecorator(New CSR())
```

By contrast, if we want to impose the area code policy on a CSR, we do so by coding this statement instead:

```
Dim CSRep As New AreaPolicyDecorator(New CSR())
```

And if we want to impose *both* the member ID *and* area code policies on a CSR – in that order – we do so by cascading the two policy decorators like this:

```
Dim CSRep As New AreaPolicyDecorator(New IDPolicyDecorator(New CSR()))
```

Notice that we don't create a new subclass of CSR each time we have a new combination of policies. The information that dictates which policies to impose on which CSR is not embedded in class hierarchy. Instead, it can be stored in a policy file. Although we don't show this in our example code, a more generic client program might read some policy file at runtime and attach decorators to CSR instances accordingly via reflection.

We also want to try something new at the client side. In this example, we will not call `ChannelServices.RegisterChannel()` to register channels and `Activator.GetObject()` to get proxies of well-known server objects. Instead, we'll compose a `Default.cfg` configuration file (just as we did for the remote server objects); we will pass the configuration file to the `RemotingConfiguration.Configure()` method, and get proxies to client-activated server objects by using the `New` keyword.

Here's the source code for our sample client application. This source code will go into the file called `ClientSimulator.vb`, and will eventually be compiled into `ClientSimulator.exe`.

When the `ClientSimulator.exe` program runs, it first reads the settings in `Default.cfg` (using the `RemotingConfiguration.Configure()` method) and uses the `New` keyword to get proxies to instances of CSR and `EventCoordinator`.

```
Imports System
Imports System.Runtime.Remoting
Imports System.Runtime.Remoting.Channels
Imports System.Runtime.Remoting.Channels.Http

Imports CallCenter
Imports Representative

Public Class Client

Public Shared Sub Main()
  Console.WriteLine("Preparing server object references...")
  RemotingConfiguration.Configure("Default.cfg")
  Dim CSRep5 As New AreaPolicyDecorator(_
                             New IDPolicyDecorator(New CSR()))
  Dim EventCrd As New EventCoordinator()
  Console.WriteLine("Server object references are ready.")

  'Subscribe to the Call event.
  Console.WriteLine("Registering observer...")
  Dim callHandlerCSR5 As New CallEventHandler(AddressOf CSRep5.onCall)
  EventCrd.m_evntCall = callHandlerCSR5
  Console.WriteLine("Observer registered.")
  Console.WriteLine("")
```

After the references (or proxies) to the server objects are ready, our client application changes hats, and plays the part of a customer call simulator:

```
Console.WriteLine("First simulated call: " & _
               "should be rejected because area code is not 408")
Dim InfoItem1 As New InfoItem("Phone number", "000-0000")
Dim InfoItem2 As New InfoItem("Member ID", "7654")
Dim InfoItem3 As New InfoItem("Area Code", "650")
EventCrd.Add(InfoItem1)
EventCrd.Add(InfoItem2)
EventCrd.Add(InfoItem3)
EventCrd.fireCallEvent
EventCrd.RemoveAll()

Console.WriteLine("Second simulated call: " & _
        "should be rejected because MemberID is not between 100 and 200")
InfoItem1 = New InfoItem("Phone number", "222-2222")
InfoItem2 = New InfoItem("Member ID", "7654")
InfoItem3 = New InfoItem("Area Code", "408")
EventCrd.Add(InfoItem1)
EventCrd.Add(InfoItem2)
EventCrd.Add(InfoItem3)
EventCrd.fireCallEvent
EventCrd.RemoveAll()
```

```
    Console.WriteLine("Third simulated call: " & _
                      "CSR should answer the phone call")
    InfoItem1 = New InfoItem("Phone number", "777-7777")
    InfoItem2 = New InfoItem("Member ID", "150")
    InfoItem3 = New InfoItem("Area Code", "408")
    EventCrd.Add(InfoItem1)
    EventCrd.Add(InfoItem2)
    EventCrd.Add(InfoItem3)
    EventCrd.fireCallEvent
    EventCrd.RemoveAll()

    Console.WriteLine("All call events fired. Simulation ends.")
    End Sub

End Class
```

As you can see, the call simulator fires the call event three times:

❑ For the first call event, the area code property is not 408 – and therefore the call should be blocked by the AreaPolicyDecorator.

❑ For the second call event, the MemberID property is not between 100 and 200 – so the call should be blocked by the IDPolicyDecorator.

❑ For the third call event, the area code property is 408 and the MemberID property is 150 (which is between 100 and 200) so the call should be passed on to a CSR.

We'll test this out shortly, but there is a little more work to do first.

The Configuration File, Default.cfg

There's one more piece of code to present, and that is the Default.cfg configuration file that will contain the settings for the remote server objects to be used by the client program (just as we did on the server side for remote server objects). The code list of the configuration file is listed below; it's pretty much the same as the configuration file for server side remote objects. We need to place this Default.cfg file in the same folder as the ClientSimulator.exe application that will use it:

```
<configuration>
  <system.runtime.remoting>
    <application name="CallClient">
      <client url="HTTP://localhost:888">
        <activated type="Representative.PolicyDecorator, Representative" />
        <activated
            type="Representative.IDPolicyDecorator, Representative" />
        <activated
            type="Representative.AreaPolicyDecorator, Representative" />
        <wellknown type="Representative.CSR, Representative"
                url="http://localhost:888/CSR.soap" />
        <wellknown type="CallCenter.EventCoordinator, CallCenter"
                url="http://localhost:999/EventCoordinator.soap" />
      </client>
    </application>
  </system.runtime.remoting>
</configuration>
```

The configuration file is in XML format. In our `ClientSimulator.vb` source code, we referenced five remote server objects:

- ❏ One is the SingleCall `CSR` listening on port 888

- ❏ One is the Singleton `EventCoordinator` listening on port 999

- ❏ The other three are client-activated decorator classes

The settings for those five remote objects are contained within the `<client>` tag in our configuration file.

Building and Running the Example

The steps for building the Phase 3 example are almost identical to those for the earlier phases. The main difference is that in this phase of the example, we provided only one CSR – which is listening on port 888.

If you're using the source code that accompanies the book, then you'll need to compile everything in the **\Phase3** folder – you can do that by running the **Phase3CompileAll.bat** batch file that is contained within the **\Phase3** folder. By contrast, if you've built Phase 3 by making changes to your Phase2 solution, then you have to recompile `Representative.dll` and distribute it to the appropriate places. You also have to recompile `ClientSimulator.exe`.

Running the application also requires similar steps to before. Start the server programs first (using `Phase3RunService.bat`, or by double-clicking on `CallCenterHost.exe` then `CSRHost.exe`). Two console windows will appear. Then run the PBX client program (by using `Phase3RunClient.bat`, or by double-clicking on `ClientSimulator.exe`).

The following screenshot shows what you should see. The console window for the CSR service (the middle window here) shows output that reflects the three call events that are fired by the PBX client. It shows that it rejects calls whose area code or member ID don't conform to the constraints set by the `AreaPolicyDecorator` and `IDPolicyDecorator`. Only the last of the three call events satisfies the constraints and is passed on to a CSR. The last line of the output (**Slept 10 seconds**) is the output that is generated by the CSR, which (as you may recall) simulates the call processing by running the `Thread.Sleep()` method. That line of output appears when the CSR reawakens, 10 seconds after the previous line of output:

The top window here contains the output from the event coordinator service. The first two `onCallEventHandlerReturn()` output lines are caused by the two rejected call events. Because the call events are rejected by policy decorators, you'll see these two lines on the screen almost immediately after you start the PBX client program. The third and final `onCallEventHandlerReturn()` output line is caused by the successful call event, and therefore will show up about 10 seconds later than the rest of the output.

Summary

In this chapter, we focused on the .NET Remoting framework, and what it provides for the development of distributed systems. We built an example in three phases to emphasize how design patterns help us reduce the total amount of code that needs to be changed when a client requests new system requirements.

❑ In the first phase, we saw some good use of a couple of GoF design patterns – specifically the Observer and Adapter patterns. We also showed how .NET Remoting makes it easy to use certain GoF design patterns such as Singleton and Proxy – by providing ready-made constructs that save us from having to do all the hard work.

❑ In the second phase of the example, we applied the Asynchronous Programming pattern to turn synchronous events into asynchronous ones. We achieved that with less than 10 lines of code, because (once again) the .NET Framework does most of the work for us behind the scenes.

❑ In the last phase of our example, we made use of the Decorator and Template Method patterns to extend our design.

One curious thing about design patterns is how some of them look very similar to one another – that is, until you look more closely at them. A consequence of that is that, when you first examine a design problem, you sometimes find that there are a number of candidate patterns that might provide a good solution. For example, in Phase 3, we might have found it appropriate to apply the Proxy pattern, or another GoF pattern, or an aspect-oriented method (such as message sinks in .NET Remoting), instead of the Decorator pattern.

We might also have decided to implement Decorator in a different way. For example, we applied the Decorator pattern at the server side (with the decorator objects residing on the same machine as the objects they decorate), but we might have found a solution in which the Decorator pattern was applied on the client side (with the decorator objects residing on the same machine as the clients that use the decorated objects). In our example, putting decorator objects at the client side reduces network traffic and increases performance. However, malicious attackers having access to the client machine can bypass the policy check by sending requests directly to the CSR objects.

Ultimately, knowing what patterns to use – and how to use them – requires a good deal of thought and experience, and it's always worth investing some time to consider the implications of a pattern-powered design, before you start building it.

Generally, after you've dissected a software system into three tiers (a presentation tier, a business logic tier and a data tier), you'll do an assessment and choose for your project a suitable framework for building the distributed components. The decision made at this stage will have a great impact on subsequent development. The more we know about patterns and frameworks, the more informed our decision will be. It takes time to gain familiarity with a framework like .NET Remoting, because it encompasses a broad territory. Getting really familiar with patterns requires a certain degree of hands-on experience. As VB.NET developers, the good news is that we have intrinsic support from .NET Remoting for using various design patterns in a more intuitive and effortless manner.

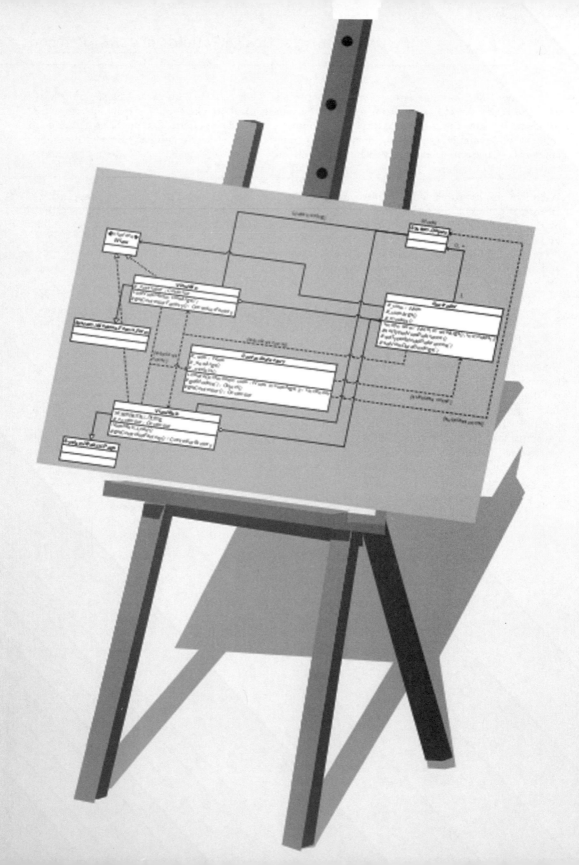

6

What Next?

It is our hope that this book has brought you closer to the world of design patterns. We've covered many ideas and concepts – some of which will be new to even the most experienced VB developers – and we've demonstrated by example how you can enhance your VB.NET solutions by application of OOP, UML and design patterns.

The next thing to do is keep going! Read more about design patterns; introduce them to your development team. Think about the last project you completed – could you have improved its design with a little judicious application of a design pattern or two? And keep design patterns in your mind when you're looking at the requirements of your *next* project.

That's not all you can do. In this chapter we would like to suggest a couple of areas that are closely related to the design patterns paradigm – **refactoring** and **antipatterns**. While our treatment is certainly brief, it should provide you with a few ideas and enough appetite to explore them further as you hone your design pattern skills.

At the end of the chapter, there is a list of resources and suggested further reading.

Refactoring

In this book we've learned about patterns by observing them in demonstration applications and in sample code snippets. We've seen case study situations in which developers carefully consider the requirements of an application, weigh up the options, and choose a design pattern solution that suits the problem well.

But that's not the only way that design patterns find their way into our solutions! It is often the case that a developer only spots the suitability of a design pattern after much of the code has already been written (or even after the application has been released!). Consequently, design patterns are often introduced into an application during the **software refactoring** process.

The term *software refactoring* applies to the practice of improving existing code. There are lots of reasons why we might want to refactor an existing implementation. For example, we might refactor an application in order to:

❑ Simplify and streamline the source code (perhaps to reduce long-term maintenance costs)

❑ Improve the application's performance

❑ Make the application more scalable

❑ Improve the error-handling capabilities of the application

❑ Prepare the source code for the addition of new features

Sometimes we will undertake a refactoring exercise to achieve a specific goal (like one of the goals listed above). But more often, refactoring occurs when we're fixing bugs or adding new features.

The concept of refactoring is so widely appreciated in the object-oriented programming community that several rules of thumb have come into general acceptance regarding the introduction of design patterns. Let's take a look at a couple of refactoring examples that demonstrate a typical refactoring exercise.

Extract Class

Imagine an application that contains a class responsible for widgets. When first coded it looked like any other respectable, everyday, ordinary class. It contained one `CreateWidget()` method and a bunch of `DoWidgetStuff()`-type methods. As time marches on, users begin to demand different types of widgets; and support developers add extra creation methods to the class to reflect the users' demands.

Before long, the class's widget-creation methods almost outnumber all its other methods. All those creation methods have polluted the original `Widget` class – its interface is becoming increasingly clumsy and its implementation is growing bigger and bigger. All those different widget-creation methods require a lot of code that is unrelated to working and managing widgets! Over time, the modifications to the class have seen it evolve into something that is unnecessarily complicated.

Based on a suggestion by Fowler *et al* in their book *Refactoring: Improving the Design of Existing Code* (Addison-Wesley, 1999, ISBN 0-201-48567-2), we decide to write a specialized **extract class** which handles object creation. The UML below captures the essence of this refactoring recommendation:

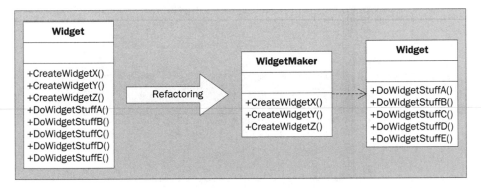

One very useful aspect of formalized refactoring is the inclusion of a roadmap for the conversion. In our case, such a conversion involves just four steps:

1. Create the class responsible for object creation (the WidgetMaker class)

2. Migrate the creation methods from the original class to the class responsible for object creation

3. Remove the creation methods from the originally overburdened class (the Widget class)

4. Update creation method class references where needed (that is, update application code to call WidgetMaker.CreateWidgetX() instead of Widget.CreateWidgetX())

The point of all this is that a potentially tricky problem is made much easier to solve because Fowler *et al* have done all the approach work for us. Let's look at one more refactoring example.

Parameterize Method

Suppose we have an application that contains a class that was originally designed with a simple set of methods and properties. However, over time new services were required of the class, so support developers have extended it by adding new methods. Some of these additional methods are very similar to the class's original methods. It might make sense to apply a refactoring, to consolidate those methods that have very similar behavior.

Suppose the class in question is the Gizmo class, and that this class originally had a method called ChangeColorToRed() that would change the object's color to red. In a subsequent release of the application, the Marketing team realized more colors for our gizmo, so ChangeColorToWhite() and ChangeColorToBlue() were added. Obviously, it's quite bulky to have a completely separate method for each color, especially if more and more colors are to be added in the future. However, it is understandable why this predicament occurred – since in the original application, red was the only color in conception.

The **parameterize method** refactoring technique comes to our aid here. It helps us consolidate all of our ChangeColorToX() methods into one method – by creating a single method that takes a color as a parameter:

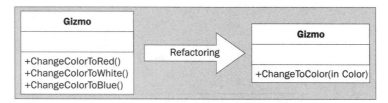

Once again, there is a step-by-step conversion process that allows us to implement the parameterize method as illustrated above (these are just as outlined in the *Refactoring* catalog at http://www.refactoring.com/catalog/):

1. Create a parameterized method (`ChangeToColor()`) that can be substituted for each repetitive method (`ChangeToColorX()`)

2. Compile

3. Replace the body of one method (`ChangeColorToRed()`) with a call to the new method (`ChangeToColor()`)

4. Compile and test

5. Use Inline Method on the old method

6. Repeat for all the methods

The Inline Method is another refactoring. Its idea is that when you have a method with a small body, whose purpose is as clear in the body as it is in the name, it may be appropriate to copy the method body into the body of the method's callers, and remove the method altogether. A method like `ChangeColorToRed()` *is likely to fit this description well, and so we could consider applying the Inline Method here.*

Now we can choose to keep the old methods if we wish (for compatibility reasons) or just remove them altogether if we have control over and can update all of the clients that are using our `Gizmo` class. Our new `ChangeToColor()` method can now provide the same services as `ChangeColorToRed()`, `ChangeColorToWhite()`, and `ChangeColorToBlue()` could. Moreover, it can easily accommodate new colors that may be required in the future.

Once again, Fowler *et al* have done the approach work and made our refactoring task much easier. Given the importance of refactoring techniques in the maintenance and upgrade of applications – particularly in a design patterns-driven environment – it's worth getting to know them a little.

Antipatterns

If you have never read about them before, it is perhaps easiest to think of an **antipattern** as a misapplied design pattern. Imagine that a developer faces a problem (which we'll call Problem A), and decides that a particular design pattern (Pattern X) offers an acceptable design solution. Unfortunately, our errant developer did not take the time to fully understand the context and characteristics of Problem A. He implements Pattern X, but it is not the correct pattern for the job. Consequently, the application's architecture is now crippled rather than enhanced.

If we've ever experienced a disaster like this, or we hear anecdotal evidence of similar disaster stories, then it might be enough to put us off design patterns for life. "Once bitten, twice shy," we'd say. But we can reduce our chances of a similar experience with a little appreciation of antipatterns.

It turns out that our developer is not alone – he is one of many developers who have made the same mistake. In fact, the case of mismatched Problem A and Pattern X is so common (and so predictable) that some clever folks recognized it, named it *Antipattern A–X*, and documented it with a description of the original problem, the erroneous solution, and the negative consequences that derive from this ill-fated pairing.

The Antipatterns Bible

The clever folks in question are Brown, Malveau, McCormick, and Mowbray, whose book *Antipatterns: Refactoring Software, Architectures, and Projects in Crisis* (Wiley, 1998, ISBN 0-471-19713-0) does for antipatterns what the GoF did for patterns.

The *Antipatterns* book is an entertaining exposition of the purpose and usage of antipatterns, and a catalog of more than 40 antipatterns. Each pattern is fully documented with background, general form, symptoms and consequences, typical causes, known exceptions, and a refactored solution for unfortunate developers who have fallen into the trap of bad pattern implementation. It also describes examples and variations of each antipattern.

To give you a flavor, the following are some of the most common antipatterns worth recognizing and avoiding!

The Blob

When one class dominates your application, you have the makings of a **Blob**. This steroid-enhanced class probably contains all of the application's methods and operations. The application may have other lesser classes, which perform trivial chores and helper functions. But the gargantuan Blob class is hard to handle – it makes testing difficult and enhancements practically impossible.

Fortunately, the process of intelligent application of design patterns mitigates the risk of creating blobs.

Here are some common symptoms of the Blob:

- ❑ One huge class with many properties and methods
- ❑ A class whose properties and methods appear to be unrelated to a common purpose
- ❑ Difficult to debug and almost impossible to test

Lava Flow

The **Lava Flow** antipattern is associated with the fragments of code that slowly flow into an application over the years. These code fragments have long since lost their value; nonetheless, they remain like hardened lava rock.

While this problem does not occur too often with new applications, use of the Adapter and Façade patterns could easily result in Lava Flow. For example, consider a Façade wrapped around some mysterious legacy application. With just one a simple pattern you can add a lot of ugly code!

Here are some common symptoms of Lava Flow:

- ❏ Repeated discovery of classes, methods, and variables without a purpose (known as **dead code**)
- ❏ Lack of any documentation or UML artifacts
- ❏ No architect (or too many architects) associated with the application
- ❏ Introduction of new features generates a disproportionate number of bugs

Poltergeists (aka Proliferation of Classes)

A **Poltergeist** is a little class with a little footprint, which does little things and lives for little time periods. The existence of such classes suggests a potentially failed design that requires a lot of simple operations or methods to control the application. The poltergeist classes provide housing for these quick and dirty routines. As with the Blob, practicing the art of design patterns helps keep your code from becoming haunted.

Here are some common symptoms of Poltergeists:

- ❏ Stateless and/or short-life cycle objects
- ❏ Unstable application architectures
- ❏ Classes that sport a single method or property
- ❏ Special-purpose "control" classes

Golden Hammer

The **Golden Hammer** antipattern addresses the problem of applying the same tool or technology to *all* problems. This is surely one of the more common problems that developers suffer from. The name *Golden Hammer* derives from the notion that someone with only a hammer in his toolbox treats every object as a nail. Developers are particularly prone to the golden hammer antipattern when they're new to design patterns, and they are applying them in applications for the first time. It's like the guy who masters Pattern X, and then hammers every problem until it fits within Pattern X.

Here are some common symptoms of the Golden Hammer:

- ❏ The development team's membership appears static
- ❏ The expertise of the team architect is limited to one language or technology
- ❏ All previous applications created by the development team used the same approach

Avoiding Antipatterns

In the ideal software engineering world, an adherence to a rigorous programming discipline and a sound architectural development should be enough to prevent the occurrence of antipatterns in your applications.

However, few of us live in that world! So in reality we need a methodology for identifying and eliminating antipatterns. Code reviews (especially the informal peer-based variety), combined with a little antipattern awareness, usually leads to timely recognition of an antipattern in our midst.

If you want to know more about antipatterns, you may like to know that the authors of the *Antipatterns* book also maintain an informative website at http://www.antipatterns.com/.

Resources and Further Reading

Design Patterns

Design Patterns, Elements of Reusable Object-Oriented Software
Erich Gamma, Richard Helm, Ralph Johnson, John Vlissides
Addison-Wesley, 1994, ISBN 0-201-63361-2

Design Patterns Explained: A New Perspective on Object-Oriented Design
Alan Shalloway, James R. Trott
Addison-Wesley, 2001, 0-201-71594-5

Analysis Patterns: Reusable Object Models
Martin Fowler
Addison-Wesley, 1996, 0-201-89542-0

Asynchronous Programming Design Pattern
http://msdn.microsoft.com/library/en-us/cpguide/html/cpconasynchronousprogramming
designpattern2.asp

MSDN's *Architectural Topics* contains a growing number of pattern discussions in C#. For example:

❑ *Exploring the Factory Design Pattern*
    http://msdn.microsoft.com/library/en-us/dnbda/html/factopattern.asp

❑ *Exploring the Observer Design Pattern*
    http://msdn.microsoft.com/library/en-us/dnbda/html/observerpattern.asp

❑ *Exploring the Singleton Design Pattern*
    http://msdn.microsoft.com/library/en-us/dnbda/html/singletondespatt.asp

For the official website of Smalltalk, the creators of MVC, go to *smalltalk.org*
http://www.smalltalk.org

For Sun's implementation of MVC, see *Model-View-Controller Architecture*
http://java.sun.com/blueprints/patterns/j2ee_patterns/model_view_controller/index.html

Want to design your own design patterns? Try *Seven Habits of Successful Pattern Writers*
John Vlissides
http://hillside.net/patterns/papers/7habits.html

There's an excellent summary of a Store and Forward (SaF) pattern at
http://www.objectarchitects.de/ObjectArchitects/orpatterns/index.htm

There's a helpful listing of other links at
http://www.cetus-links.org/oo_patterns.html

Here are two unofficial "homes" of the patterns community:
http://hillside.net/patterns/
http://c2.com/cgi-bin/wiki/

For design patterns for XML, try *XMLPatterns.com*
http://www.xmlpatterns.com/

Here's a site that gives a treatment of design patterns (and downloadable source) for C# programmers:
http://www.dofactory.com/patterns/patterns.asp

Refactoring

Refactoring: Improving the Design of Existing Code
Martin Fowler, Kent Beck, John Brant, William Opdyke, Don Roberts
Addison-Wesley, 1999, ISBN 0-201-48567-2

Refactoring
Maintained by Martin Fowler (co-author of the *Refactoring* book)
http://www.refactoring.com/

Extreme Programming: Refactor Mercilessly
http://www.extremeprogramming.org/rules/refactor.html

Antipatterns

Antipatterns: Refactoring Software, Architectures, and Projects in Crisis
William J. Brown, Raphael C. Malveau, Hays W. "Skip" McCormick III, Thomas J. Mowbray
Wiley, 1998, ISBN 0-471-19713-0

Anti-Patterns and Patterns in Software Configuration Management
William J. Brown, Hays W. "Skip" McCormick III, Scott W. Thomas
Wiley, 1999, ISBN 0-471-32929-0

The official website of the *Antipatterns* book is at
http://www.antipatterns.com/

Well-known Antipatterns
http://www.mitre.org/support/swee/html/67_mccormick/

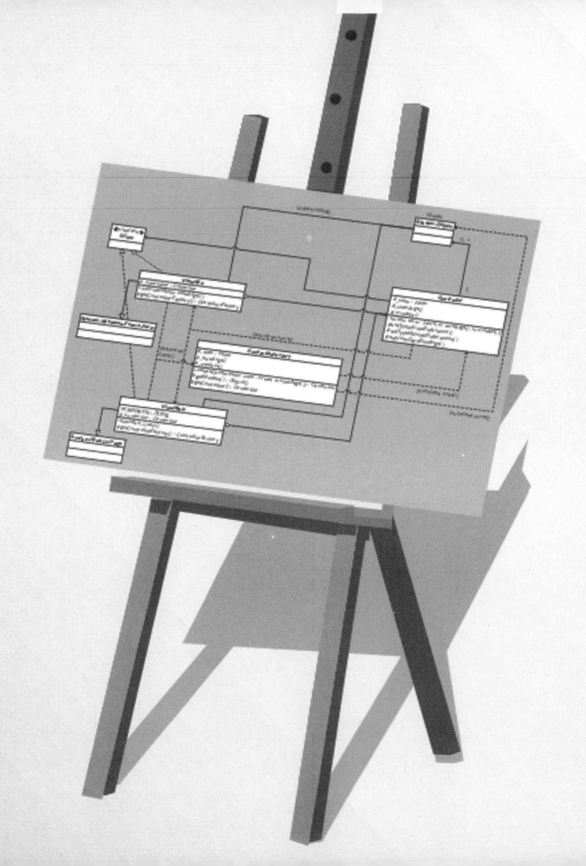

UML Primer

The Unified Modeling Language (UML) can be many things to many different people. Fundamentally, the UML is a defined modeling language that designers, developers and analysts use to express their software designs. The purpose of this chapter is to review some of the fundamentals of the UML, and the most common diagrams you're likely to encounter throughout the rest of this book and in practice, as well as some guidelines for the purpose and general usage of those diagrams.

First and foremost, the UML is a modeling language. It is not necessarily a process or methodology. Rather, it provides a syntax for describing a software application without relying on specific computer languages. In the UML you'll find a series of tools for describing your software applications – their domains and their designs. Since the UML provides so many tools, we can choose what tool is best for a particular situation and group diagrams together as appropriate to best communicate or document our software designs. It is still our responsibility as analysts and developers to make good design and development decisions – the UML merely helps us along toward that end by providing a common, consistent set of tools for expressing our (hopefully) good ideas.

Throughout this appendix we'll review each of the major UML diagrams in a somewhat logical order. That is, starting with diagrams that are most commonly applied in earlier stages of a software development project, we'll progress through logical design diagrams all the way through more physical or deployment-oriented diagrams.

The diagrams we'll cover are:

- ❑ **Use cases**. A use case is a textual and graphical representation of a business process or scenario.

- ❑ **Class diagrams**. A class diagram is an illustration of the various objects that compose a system, generally at one of two different levels of detail.

❑ **Activity diagrams**. An activity diagram is a graphical depiction of the flow of a process from one step to another.

❑ **Interaction diagrams**. An interaction diagram is an illustration of the interaction of objects within a system, particularly focusing on the pattern of passing messages from one object to another. There are two types of interaction diagram: sequence diagrams and collaboration diagrams.

❑ **State diagrams**. A state diagram is a graphical representation of the state of an object throughout its lifetime as events from other objects in the system affect it.

❑ **Physical diagrams**. A physical diagram is an illustration of the physical implementation of a system from a component perspective. There are two types: deployment diagrams and component diagrams.

A Typical Development Process

Although the UML doesn't talk specifically about what particular method to use to develop our software applications, there are some consistent patterns of usage in terms of what diagrams are used at different stages of a development project. This section provides a little insight into how those usage patterns generally emerge. However, let's be clear about something: the UML can be used almost any way you want. The beauty of something like the UML is its generic nature – it can be applied to a wide variety of scenarios and business settings. We'll say more on this topic a little later – for now, let's take a look at a typical software development project and see where the UML diagrams we've already listed are likely to turn up.

Let's say we work for the Acme Software Company and one of our clients has contracted us to design and build a web-based inventory management application. Without knowing much about the particulars of this software project, an experienced developer will be able to predict (with some accuracy) the major stages of this project: requirements development and business analysis, high level and major system component design, detailed or physical design, construction, testing, implementation, and follow-up work like support and maintenance. You probably won't be surprised to hear that the UML can have a role to play at each of these stages in the software project.

Project Stages and UML Tools

We're going to dive into the details of each of these diagrams in the rest of this chapter, but for now let's look at where we might encounter each diagram and how it might be used.

Use Cases

More often than not, the first UML notation you'll encounter as a project unfolds is the **use case**. As we briefly discussed above, use cases are descriptions of a business process or, in other words, they are the description of a particular process in the terms and from the perspective of that process's users and other interacting systems. As you might expect, the employees of Acme Software Company most likely to actually build use cases are business analysts, lead architects or development managers who have experience interacting with clients.

Class Diagrams and Activity Diagrams

It's important to note that at the use case stage, we're not yet thinking in terms of how the system will actually be built or structured. After gathering our requirements and usage data, we then move on to thinking about structure, and it's here that we see the introduction of **class diagrams** and **activity diagrams**. Again, actual usage definitely varies according to the scope of the project, the style of the people leading the project, and other factors, but there is generally a transition from business- or user-oriented diagrams (and techniques like use cases) toward more technical documents like class diagrams and activity diagrams. As we've already noted, class diagrams help express the composition of a system in terms of objects. As we'll see shortly, those objects can be defined in a few different ways – entirely in domain concepts or in more technical, implementation-specific terms.

> **This transition point – from requirements and other domain analysis stages of a project to more technical aspects of a project – is rife with risk. One of the most effective techniques to minimize this risk is** communication. **Proper application of the UML, particularly use cases and high-level class diagrams, can provide a consistent method of communication between analysts, designers and developers.**

More Class and Activity Diagrams, and some Collaboration and Sequence Diagrams

As serious design and development tasks occur, our project is likely to see a pronounced shift toward more technical documentation. This makes sense, of course. Design activities become focused on specific aspects of the project, and the UML diagrams' designers and developers begin to incorporate a more implementation- or physical design-based perspective.

Here we begin to see very detailed **class diagrams** that include attributes and operations (that is, properties, functions and subs in VB.NET parlance), and input and output parameters and return values. We also begin to see detailed **activity diagrams** and our two types of interaction diagrams – the **collaboration** and **sequence diagrams**. We use these diagrams to illustrate how messages flow from one object to another throughout the system. Both require some level of implementation detail to be truly useful.

Deployment and Component Diagrams

As development progresses, a forward-looking designer or developer will start thinking (or worrying!) about deployment and distribution issues. The UML provides **deployment** and **component diagrams** for this purpose. These types of diagram lend themselves to being used at a point in the software project where physical components are known.

Returning to the Use Cases

Finally, before deployment, the project needs to go through a thorough testing phase, and it's at this time that our project can obtain the greatest benefit from the **use cases** we produced at the very beginning. With every use case that was written at the beginning of the project, the development team now has the basis for a ready-made test script. If they were written correctly, the use cases should highlight (in the opinion of users, clients and developers) the important processes or scenarios that the project should have captured. Of course, these are the very same processes and scenarios that a Test or Quality Assurance group should focus on when the time comes to test. Therefore, use cases can be a very useful supplement to normal test cycles.

A Library of Diagrams for the Support Team

Finally, we must remember the process of support and ongoing maintenance for any application we build. UML plays a role here as well. The UML diagrams we produce during a development project will ultimately provide the support staff with an understanding of the software – why it was originally built, how it was built, how it was deployed, and how it works.

Now we have a better idea of when, in general, to expect to see particular aspects of the UML. The next step is to look at each of the diagrams in some more detail. We'll start with use cases.

The Use Case

A **use case** is the definition of a business process or **scenario**. Generally a use case illustrates a series of the logical steps that are necessary to perform some task that is important in the system. Use cases also list all the necessary or important participants in the process. In the UML, these participants are known as **actors** – they may be real people, or machines, or other systems.

A use case can be expressed in text form using a commonly accepted structure, or as a diagram showing the major steps in a process, or both. Properly written, a use case expresses an external view of the given system. That is, it takes the perspective of an outsider looking in without delving into the details of how the system is implemented.

A Sample Use Case

For a good example of a use case, consider an order entry and inventory management application – and in particular the process that a customer undertakes when placing an order. The process is likely to involve several steps – capturing the order information itself, verifying that the inventory is on hand, checking the customer's credit, creating the order and order lines, and confirming the order with the customer.

We also have some idea of the actors involved in this use case – a customer, and (perhaps) an order entry clerk, and (perhaps) some order fulfillment or customer support personnel. And as we've already mentioned, an actor isn't necessarily a person – it could be another application. An actor in a use case can be *any* entity (from outside of the system itself) that participates in the use case.

So now we have all we need to create a sample use case. We can capture the details of this use case in text or in diagrams. For the sake of demonstration, we'll do both.

Presenting a Use Case with Text

Although there are many variations of the following sections of a text-based use case, we can generally break down necessary and useful use case information into the following elements:

Use Case Element	Description
Use Case Number	A numbering or lettering scheme used for unique identification of each use case.
Title	A short descriptive title that indicates the basic purpose of the use case. For example: "Create an Order" or "Add Customer to Database".

Use Case Element	Description
Primary Actor	The main actor (user or another application) who executes the use case. Typically there is one primary actor. If you find that your use case could have more than one primary actor, you might consider breaking it into two or more use cases, or examining whether your two primary actors are really a primary and secondary actor working together.
Secondary Actor	Any other user who can execute a use case. A good example of a secondary actor is a billing department manager. If the primary actor in a use case is a billing clerk, it is reasonable (in theory at least) to expect that that individual's supervisor could also perform their job functions.
Starting Point	The state at which the use case starts. Typically this element in a use case is a short, descriptive paragraph about where the use begins. In an order entry application, a use case starting point might be expressed by a phrase like: "The customer is viewing the Create New Order form."
Ending Point	The state at which the use case ends. In an invoicing application, an appropriate state for a "Create Invoice" use case might read: "The new invoice was saved to the invoice table."
Measurable Result	The result we expect from a use case, and how we can measure it. In some cases the use case ending point and the measurable result might be the same thing. In other cases a measurable result could be expressed as "An order is created" or something equally generic. It is important that the result of a use case means something to the use case (and ultimately to the users and other actors participating in the use case).
Flow of Events	A narrative of everything that occurs between the starting point and ending point in the use case. Sometimes the flow of events can be extraordinarily long and complex. In others, the flow of events is only a few lines long. It depends entirely on the application and the complexity of the application domain. It is worth spending a little extra time detailing the flow of events, because it often has a positive ripple throughout the rest of the development project. Working through the details of an application's workflow early in a development project will help work out or at least identify significant issues early in the project. The danger of going too far here is getting ever-eager developers and designers to focus on how the application will work instead of what it should do.
Alternative Flow of Events	Anything that doesn't occur in the flow of events. Generally this describes exceptional processing, error handling, or other deviation from the flow of events. Since most application development is handling exceptions and alternative flows of events, it is often necessary to take extra time to document these flows. In fact, the more alternative flows could become their own use cases.

As an example, consider the following use case for creating a new order.

Use Case #1 - Create New Order

Primary Actor:
Call Center Staff

Secondary Actor:
Any other call center staff, supervisors or management.

Starting Point:
The primary actor is on the telephone with a customer and has ascertained that the customer wishes to place a new order.

Ending Point:
A new order has been created and the customer is sent a confirmation e-mail.

Measurable Result:
A new order is created including appropriate order lines and available inventory is updated to account for the order items.

Flow of Events:
This use case starts when a new or existing customer places a call to the customer service call center. The call center representative will receive the call and retrieve any customer information that might be available. While speaking on the telephone with the customer, the call center rep will browse the company product catalog answering any questions the customer may have. This might include querying the knowledge base for answers to technical questions. Once all questions have been answered and the call center rep and customer decide what particular product items and quantities should be included in the order, the call center rep will move to the New Order form. On that form the rep can enter all necessary product and order information including product number, quantity, etc.

At this point the customer's order is well defined and available inventory must be checked. The call center rep asks the application to check the inventory on hand for the product items specified on the New Order form. Details about inventory on hand appear within the New Order form and that information is relayed back to the customer on the phone. Finding all the inventory necessary to complete the order is in stock, the call center rep will then check for the latest pricing for each line item in the order and relay a final, bottom line quote to the customer including a calculation of sales tax where applicable and any shipping expenses.

The customer elects to use their credit account already established with the company and informs the call center rep of this wish. The call center rep may have to ask a supervisor to approve the credit request. So the supervisor asks the application to retrieve the customer's credit history and display it in some summarized format. If the supervisor finds that the customer is in good standing and has adequate credit to cover the cost of the order, they approve the request and the process continues. The order is then presented to the call center rep for a final approval, and with the customer's final approval, saves the order and makes it official.

An e-mail is sent to the customer recapping the transaction and providing information about tracking their order through fulfillment and shipping.

Alternative Flows of Events
The customer is a first time purchaser at this particular manufacturer and must be added to the customer service application.

The customer rejects the order summary based on price.

The customer is unsure of the purchase and wishes more time to make a decision. The order and its details must be saved and made available for thirty days.

Inventory is not available in the warehouse, therefore the order is taken but particular order line items are placed on backorder.

Some use case writers would say that this example is overly complicated. There are many things happening in our first use case – inventory is checked, shipping and taxes are being calculated, customer data is being retrieved from a database, the pricing database and corporate knowledge base are being queried, etc. Each of those tasks could easily have been presented in its own use case. We'll get into that in a minute. First, let's take a look at how we'd express this use case graphically.

Presenting a Use Case Diagrammatically

First of all, each of our major steps in the use case will be noted as an oval with a short description. For instance, Calculating Shipping and Tax Expense would look like this:

When we want to show the interaction of an actor with one of our defined steps, the UML uses a simple stick figure (for the actor) and a relationship line between the actor figure and the step itself. To illustrate our call center rep performing a calculation of shipping and tax expenses, we'd use this simple diagram fragment:

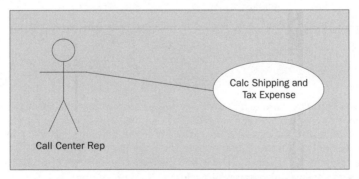

We can see at a glance which actor will be involved with the Calc Shipping and Tax Expense step of the use case.

To build the rest of our use case diagram, we repeatedly apply the same principles we've just seen – covering all of the steps listed in the text version of this use case above. The diagram will look like this:

313

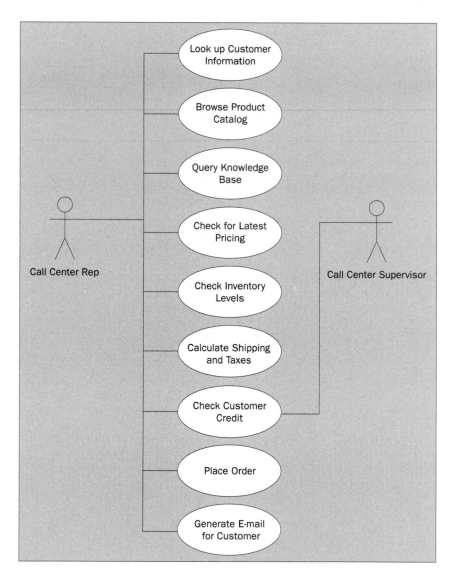

As you can clearly see the use case diagram shows us the steps involved in this use case as well as the involvement or communication between steps and actors. Notice that our primary actor, the Call Center Rep, is most involved in this use case and the Call Center Supervisor really only communicates with one step. Obviously the Call Center Supervisor has to have the ability to do more than just check customer credit and make order approval or denial decisions, but in the context of this use case, as it is written, that's all we're asking our Supervisor to do.

The list of use case steps and communication relationships between the steps and actors in this diagram is certainly useful, but the UML *also* provides a mechanism for organizing and expressing the relationship between use cases. We'll look at that next.

The Extends Relationship

Often when writing use cases, you'll find that some scenarios can benefit by extending the base functionality described in another use case. The UML provides a convenient mechanism for expressing the extension relationship between two use cases – the **extends** keyword. Using «extends» in this case means that one use case is substantially similar to another but defines a more specialized version of the functionality described therein.

To illustrate, let's take a simple example. Sales tax and other withholding taxes are calculated differently all over the world. In the US, for instance, sales tax is generally applied to the listed price of an item and added to the total sales bill. However, in Australia there is a different mechanism for calculating those taxes on goods and services. It happens that the Aussies have a goods and services tax (GST) that is similar to the US sales tax but which defines a different set of items that are exempt from it.

So, let's say we needed to write a use case that includes calculating taxes for an order bound for Australia. We could use the existing Calculate Shipping and Taxes we saw in our previous example and extend that function to be used in a new step called Calculate Australian Shipping and Taxes. The diagram fragment looks like this:

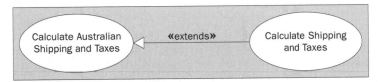

The Includes (or Uses) Relationship

Another commonly used use case relationship is represented by the **includes** or **uses** keyword. It indicates that one use case uses the contents of another use case. Interestingly, this is an object-oriented concept – **reuse** – at work during the analysis phase of an object-oriented software application.

For a simple example, let's say that our actors need the ability to conduct a more lengthy review of a customer than the quick credit review we did in the first use case. Maybe our client asks the Call Center management to perform regularly scheduled, random audits on customers to assess a variety of factors and one step of that audit is a thorough credit and payment history review. We could create a new use case titled Audit Customer Records that would borrow from the Check Customer Credit use case.

Illustrating such a relationship in a use case diagram is rather easy.

Seeing this diagram notation it's clear that the Audit Customer Records use case relies on all or some of the Check Customer Credit use case.

You may find that different UML tools express this relationship a little differently. The diagram fragment above uses the keyword «uses» to indicate the Includes relationship. It was created using Microsoft Visio 2000. Regardless of whether the term «includes» or «uses» is employed, the meaning is the same.

315

Applying Use Cases

We've already discussed the role of use cases early in the requirements development stages of a software project. The benefit of capturing use case information in a standardized format is clear. You and your development team will capture the same information one way or another – with use cases or without them. The employment of a consistent method for capturing and expressing domain information will result in benefits throughout the life of the project.

Writing use cases for projects, then, really isn't much of an issue. It's a good idea that you should try to use it as part of your development methodology. There are a number of talking points – such as the extent to which you write use cases, and the level of detail your use cases contain. There are several schools of thought on the total number of use cases relative to the size of a project. There are also different approaches as to the content of each use case, and how detailed they should be, and so on.

Personally, I've been involved in projects that contained hundreds of use cases. The task of managing such a huge number of use cases becomes cumbersome, and in many instances the use cases themselves morph into implementation-specific descriptions that violate the external view rule every good use case should follow. I've also worked on projects that used only a few use cases, each so broad and abstract in its purpose that they weren't very useful.

So where's the happy middle ground? Well, it depends. The size and complexity of a project obviously plays a role in determining how extensive your use case effort should be. Regardless of size, there are some indicators of what is an appropriate use case topic and what isn't:

❑ If you can identify major processes within a system and the key actors that communicate with those processes, then you have a ready-made list of use case topics.

❑ If you can identify repeating processes or processes that share a large amount of the same work between them, you might be looking at a primary use case and some «extends» relationships.

❑ If your development team or user groups keep coming back to the same discussion topic or slight variations of the same process, then you've probably found another use case topic.

The Class Diagram

The single most common UML diagram is probably the **class diagram**. In fact, the class diagram is not necessarily a UML invention; most object-oriented analysis and design notations and methods use some variation of it.

Class diagrams illustrate the objects that make up a system or a part of a system. Class diagrams can be written from a couple of different perspectives. As tools that help the transition from the analysis and requirements-gathering phases of a project, they can be used to show basic relationships between high-level, abstract business objects. As design progresses into more detailed, software construction issues, class diagrams themselves become more detailed, often including actual implementation-specific objects and their attributes and operations.

> Note that the term "attribute" is object-speak for a VB.NET property, and the term "operation" is another term for function, subroutine, or method. Remember that the UML has to apply to many languages and development environments, so it uses a set of generic terms.

When we think of diagramming business objects and their relationships to one another, we're working at a higher, conceptual level. Thus, a lot of the UML literature refers to these high-level class diagrams as **conceptual class diagrams**. To illustrate the last point, let's take another example from our order entry application to illustrate. From our use cases we clearly know we have a Customer object and an Order object, and probably OrderLine objects as well. We can use a class diagram to illustrate the presence of those objects and their relationships as follows:

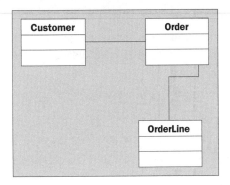

This is a useful tool for indicating that a Customer object is somehow linked to an Order object, which itself is linked somehow to an OrderLine object. Its usefulness ends about there; however, the UML provides all kinds of other useful notations that we can include in our class diagrams to make them very useful. For instance, we have a method for expressing how our objects are associated and how we can traverse the object structure from one object to another. We also have the capability to describe the attributes and operations of each object including details like scope, input parameters and return types, and we have the ability to express how object instances can be grouped and managed my other object instances.

These more detailed notations arise as we continue to move from conceptual relationships between business objects toward actual deployment and physical arrangements of application classes and instances of those classes. As we progress through the following topics, keep in mind where you might expect to see such levels of detail – an early stage conceptual class diagram or a more advanced design stage implementation diagram.

Let's take a look at these topics and a few more of the most common class diagram notations you're likely to encounter.

Associations

One of the first things to notice about our conceptual class diagram that it expresses some relationship between the objects. It's clear there's a relationship because there's a black line from one object to another. It probably makes sense to us as readers of the diagram that a Customer object is related to an Order object, and that the Customer object is not related to the OrderLine object. But to be entirely sure, the UML allows us to describe more precisely *how* these objects are related to one another – using two concepts called **multiplicity** and **navigability**.

Multiplicity

Multiplicity is the expression of the number of instances of a particular object that can exist within a relationship to another object. (Notice the introduction of the word *instance*. That should indicate that as we add more information to our class diagram, we are continuing to progress toward implementation-oriented thinking.) For example, a `Customer` may have zero or more `Orders` ongoing, whilst an `Order` can only exist if it has been automatically generated as a standing order or has been created by a single customer. In other words, it can have only zero or one `Customer` associated with it.

In the UML, the number of instances of one object in a relationship with another object is expressed using the notation *x..y*, where *x* is the lower bound of some range and *y* is the upper bound. The most common ranges on class diagrams are:

- ❑ 1..* means that one or more instances of an object can exist in this relationship.

- ❑ 0..1 means that zero or one instance of an object can exist in this relationship.

- ❑ 0..* means that zero or more instances of an object can exist in this relationship.

- ❑ 1 means that exactly one instance must exist in this relationship.

We show the range by placing it on the line in the diagram that illustrates the association of two objects, as in the following `Customer-Order` class diagram. In many ways, multiplicity is much like relationships between relational database tables and is expressed similarly:

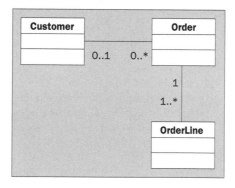

Now that we've added our multiplicity notation, it's clear that our class diagram could contain one instance of the `Customer` object and that each `Customer` object could be associated with an `Order` object, but not necessarily. We can have `Customers` with no `Orders`. It is also clear that if an `Order` exists we must also have at least one `OrderLine` instance associated with it. Our original class diagram is starting to show a bit more detail.

Navigability

Now let's take the other method the UML gives us for expressing associations between objects. Navigability allows us to express how to traverse from one instance of an object to another. In other words, the UML class diagram lets us express the fact that an `Order` instance knows what `Customer` instance it belongs to, but not vice versa. At least at a high level, this capability is reminiscent of data modeling concepts – master-detail relationship and good, normalized database models.

So, let's take our Customer-Order example a step further and add navigability information. In the example below (which still retains its multiplicity details) we can infer that an Order instance is associated with a particular Customer instance and that each OrderLine instance knows what Order it belongs to. Here's the diagram:

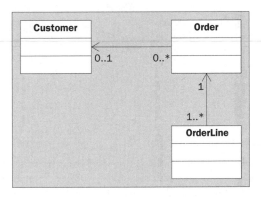

It should make sense that each Order knows to what Customer it belongs and that each Customer doesn't know anything about Order instances. If it's not clear, think about how much Order-specific detail a real world Customer might know – probably very little. It makes more sense that we ask some other object to find us all the Order instances associated with a Customer by giving that other object a CustomerID to work with.

Unidirectional and Bi-directional Associations

Now, take a close look at the relationship between Order and OrderLine. There is something here that doesn't seem proper. Based on what we've learned about navigability, the OrderLine instance knows what Order it's associated with, but the Order won't know anything about its child OrderLine instances (that is, at least as far as this particular design is concerned). That's a problem. Logically, there should be an association that works both ways. Conveniently, there is.

The first type of navigability association we saw is called a **unidirectional association**. It is just what it sounds like – a one-way association. It indicates that one object knows about another object, but not the other way around. What we also need here is an association that goes both ways. In the UML it is, not surprisingly, called a **bi-directional association**. It is used in situations exactly like our Order-OrderLine association. It makes sense that each Order instance is associated with each and every OrderLine instance, and that each OrderLine instance knows all about its Order parent.

We draw bi-directional associations with arrows at both ends of the association line. This diagram now links our Order and OrderLine properly:

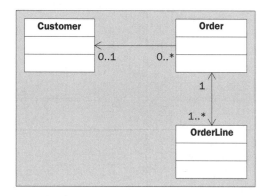

Attributes and Operations

The UML class diagram also illustrates the **attributes** and **operations** of each of our objects. We mentioned earlier that the terms *attribute* and *operation* are fancy object-speak for VB properties, functions, subroutines, and methods. We'll stick with the UML terms for the rest of this chapter. Let's see what they look like in the UML, starting with attributes.

There is a convention within the UML for drawing the boxes that represent individual classes. Our examples so far all follow that convention – each box contains the class name, then a horizontal line, then a list of attributes (listed vertically), then another horizontal line, and finally a list of operations (listed vertically). There is also a convention for how attribute details are written. That convention is:

<Visibility> Name: Type

Where *<Visibility>* is expressed as a symbol:

Symbol	Visibility
–	Private
+	Public
#	Protected

For the Order class, a simple public OrderDate attribute would be written in the UML as:

+ OrderDate: Date

For those of us so inclined, the UML class diagram also has a syntactical provision for including initial or default values. If OrderQuantity will always default to 1 for some reason, we could write that as:

+ OrderQuantity: Integer = 1

Operations are written using a similar structure, except a provision is made for input parameters and a return type of some sort for functions. The structure can be expressed like this:

+ *<Visibility> Name (<input_parameter_list>): return_type*

Here, *<Visibility>* uses the same symbols that we use for attributes; *Name* is the operation name and *return_type* is any valid return data type. If we have no return type then nothing is mentioned. The parameter list is a comma-delimited list of inputs that use the attribute syntax. Often, input parameters are prefixed with in and output parameters are prefixed with out. If our Order object has an AddOrderLine operation that expects a ProductID and Quantity as input and returns a Boolean indicating success or failure, it would be written like this:

+ AddOrderLine (in ProductID: String, in Quantity: Integer): Boolean

A new Order object redrawn with these attributes and operations looks like this:

Order
+OrderID : String   +OrderAmount : Double   +OrderDate : Date   +OrderQuantity : Integer = 1
+AddOrderLine(in ProductID : String, in Quantity : Integer) : Boolean

Aggregation and Composition

Aggregation and **composition** are two concepts that are sometimes difficult to grasp. Both are techniques for describing groups of object instances and their logical organization relative to other object instances. Both are available to the UML class diagram.

Let's consider composition first, because it seems that an understanding of composition helps in the explanation of aggregation.

Composition

We know so far that when two objects A and B depend on one another, they are associated with each other. Continuing with our two objects, we say that A is composed of B if B is a part of A and B's lifetime is tied to A's lifetime.

In the class diagram above, for example, it's relatively easy to deduce that an instance of OrderLine shouldn't exist outside the instance of its parent Order object and that the parent Order instance is more than likely responsible for creating the OrderLine children. This is a classic composition. In the UML class diagram we express that composition as a filled black diamond.

Here's our familiar class diagram illustrating the composite relationship between Order instances and OrderLine instances:

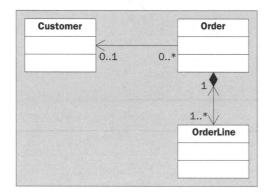

One way to read a class diagram that contains a composite relationship between two objects (at this point we're mainly talking about object instances) is as follows: The Order instance is, among other things, composed of a series of OrderLine instances. As an object reader of this diagram I would surmise that OrderLine instances are probably created, managed and destroyed by the Order instance and that any delete action on an Order instance would automatically require a delete of any associated OrderLine instances. Notice that our navigability and multiplicity settings are still in place.

Aggregation

Composition is relatively straightforward, so what could aggregation be? Well, aggregation is similar to composition, but occurs in cases where the part can belong to many wholes. In other words, a single instance of an object can be used by any number of other object instances to which it is associated. An aggregation relationship is represented by an open diamond.

Our simple Customer-Order-OrderLine example doesn't realistically have aggregation associations, so let's consider a new example. In some organization chart applications, we need to create associations between employees and project teams to which they may be assigned. Let's imagine that we've been asked to build an application that helps a consulting firm manage its projects and project team members. We know that we'll have any number of project team members and we also may have many different project teams, each of which will be populated by one or more team members. Start to see a class diagram and its associations take shape?

A simple class diagram like this could be built using the information in the previous paragraph:

ProjectTeam			TeamMember	
	0..*		0..*	

But what does this diagram not tell us? Since we know some things about project teams, we know a project team potentially consists of many team members and that each team member could possibly be assigned to many project teams. We also know that canceling a project and deleting its related ProjectTeam instance doesn't necessarily mean that we have to delete all of the TeamMember instances assigned to that ProjectTeam. That's aggregation at work. The UML would express all of that information in the same class diagram fragment, but with a single change – the open diamond symbol.

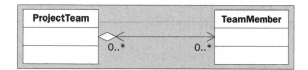

Microsoft Visio adds something useful to the whole composition and aggregation discussion. When creating the diagram above, the property setting on the association line that produces the open diamond is the value of Shared. That's a term that makes a lot of sense. A ProjectTeam instance shares TeamMember instances with other ProjectTeam instances. That's aggregation.

Interfaces

Since this is a book about design patterns, it is more than likely that interface types will be used in some of the case studies. Interfaces are also one of my personal favorite design tools, so we're going to mention the UML class diagram notation for representing interfaces.

We all know that the classes that represent objects can implement interfaces. That gives us developers a lot of design flexibility. As a quick example, consider an Order object that has to serve both web applications and desktop applications. For various reasons there are different attributes and operations required by either platform, but the core functionality of the class is common enough across both platforms that we can write one class that implements two interfaces – IWebOrder and IDesktopOrder.

Illustrating the use of these interfaces in our class diagram is relatively simple. We draw little circles (known as **lollipops**) from our objects:

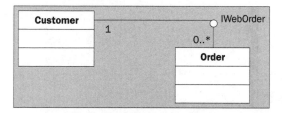

The class diagram that uses the other interface is very similar. Notice the change in the interface lollipop:

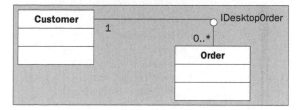

When to use Class Diagrams

Class diagrams are useful at various stages of a development project. Depending on the project stage, class diagrams will contain various levels of detail. During early stage design activities when the basic concepts of an application are being ironed out, class diagrams are ideal for capturing and communicating basic object relationships. Late stage design work may require detailed class diagrams with all the necessary details of attribute names and types and operation names, input and output parameters and visibility.

During detailed design phases, class diagrams provide a consistent mechanism for describing the interfaces each object is likely to support and serves a specification or documentation reference for other developers who may encounter the classes described in the diagram. Class diagrams are also used for post-deployment activities like support and maintenance. Properly written class diagrams will be used long after the original author has moved on to other projects.

The Activity Diagram

An **activity diagram** is an excellent tool for describing a series of activities or discrete tasks completed either by a user, or by a system external to our application, or by some object instance within our system. A UML activity diagram contains many notations and organization techniques to make modeling complex process flows possible.

As an illustration of a simple activity diagram, let's use an abbreviated sequence of activities from the New Order use case we saw earlier in this chapter:

An activity diagram is very useful for expressing the steps required to complete a particular process, even if the details of each step are still relatively unknown. There are a number of other features of activity diagrams that are useful. In particular, their ability to illustrate conditional processes and the flow of logic through those conditions is widely used.

Starting State and Final State

By the way, the blackened circle at the top of the diagram is called the **initial** or **starting state** and the blackened circle with another circle drawn around it is called the **final state**. They are, in effect, the start and stop of an activity diagram. We'll see them again in state diagrams a little later.

Branches

Like many flowcharting notations, activity diagrams have the ability to represent decision steps. In UML parlance, decision steps are called **branches**. The output of decision steps is often dictated by one or more **guard conditions**. In our activity diagram above, we could insert a decision step immediately after the Check for Available Inventory step is complete. Notice the use of bracketed guard conditions:

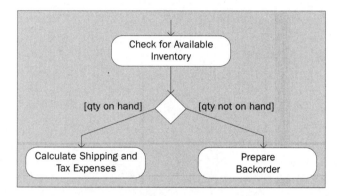

Of course, all the branches will ultimately need to get to the final state, so diagrams like the one above need to be able to merge parallel branches back together. This is also represented by a diamond symbol as in the following example:

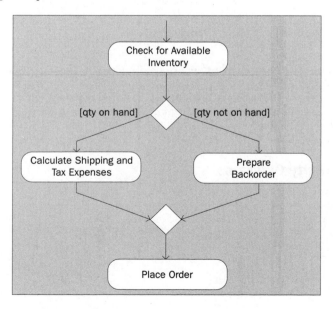

Swimlanes

The UML activity diagram also has the ability to start several process threads in parallel, and bring them back to a single end point at some point later. The start of parallel activity paths starts with a fork symbol and is balanced by its partner, the join. Looking at the New Order example as a whole again, we see that we can perform the Check Customer Credit process in parallel with the other activities we've already identified. However, it could be that the Check Customer Credit process is a time-consuming one, and that we'd rather have the credit review done in the background of our other activities so it's ready when the customer makes their final decision to place an order. The diagram would be drawn like this:

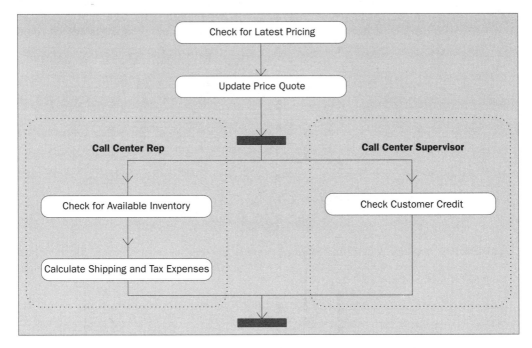

Now we can express parallel process paths rather easily. By adding yet another feature we can use UML activity diagrams to not only illustrate parallel aspects of a process, but also identify who or what is responsible for executing certain steps in a process. This feature is called a **swimlane**. It is just what it sounds like – a lane that is drawn on top of an activity diagram (as in the diagram above). Typically, swimlanes are drawn from the perspective of a user or another system and exist to indicate that the user or system that owns the swimlane has responsibilities to execute whatever activity occurs inside their swimlane.

When to use Activity Diagrams

Knowing when to use activity diagrams is relatively easy – use them whenever you need to document a somewhat detailed process or workflow. Activity diagrams are particularly good at illustrating conditional process flows that might have several outcomes. It is possible to overuse activity diagrams. Given their level of detail and capability for representing all possible outcomes, be careful of thinking you need to document each and every path.

Interaction Diagrams

Up to this point we've seen diagrams and other UML notations designed to help illustrate business processes and the relationships between objects involved in those processes. We've tracked the progression of a typical development project from requirements into detailed, implementation-oriented design as we introduce new UML diagrams. Use cases to class diagrams to activity diagrams loosely parallels the progression of more detail in the design issues we'll encounter as the project moves along.

We've already got a good tool for illustrating the objects in our application – class diagrams. Now, we need to be able to express how those objects are going to talk to each other. We know object relationships (class diagram associations) and we even know the interface each object may have (attributes and operations). **Interaction diagrams** give us the ability to describe how objects communicate, and they actually help describe how objects work together to complete a task or tasks.

There are two types of interaction diagrams – **sequence diagrams** and **collaboration diagrams**. They both illustrate the interaction of objects with one another, but they do so in slightly different ways:

❏ Sequence diagrams show the flow of messages from one object to another in a structured format that very nicely illustrates ordered program flow across all objects.

❏ Collaboration diagrams approach the same illustration goals but from a slightly different diagram format that stresses the conversations between objects and not necessarily the order of those conversations.

One diagram is easily created from the other, so we aren't covering collaboration diagrams here.

The Sequence Diagram

The sequence diagram is one of the most effective tools at illustrating the interaction of a group of objects. During detailed design it may be one of the most important diagrams you could create. It literally illustrates all of the objects involved in a particular scenario, their order of creation, and the order in which one object interacts with the methods and properties of other objects. Also captured in the diagram is a graphic representation of the lifetime of particular objects relative to message calls. At certain points in early design conversations and design reviews, sequence diagrams can be invaluable.

To demonstrate, let's take a new example application – a diary or reminder system. Think of *Microsoft Outlook* or any number of other personal information managers. A user of such an application would want to be able to create tasks and reminders and other schedule-oriented elements. The following sequence diagram illustrates a few simple objects and how they collaborate in the creation of a new task that is configured to remind the user when it's due. Notice how much you can learn about the object structure just from this one simple diagram:

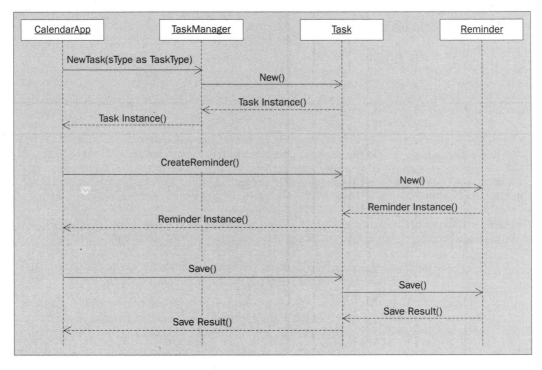

By reviewing this simple diagram it's clear how sequence diagrams focus on illustrating messages sent between objects and how important the order of those messages can be. Notice that all of the objects involved in this particular scenario are arrayed across the top of the diagram. If you read the method calls, it's pretty clear that this scenario involves a TaskManager object, and that this TaskManager object is able to create new Task object instances.

Once created, a Task object knows how to save itself and any Reminder that may be associated with it. The driver in this example is a CalendarApp – probably an interface application of some sort that knows how to display task details. For this diagram, though, the particular implementation of that application is irrelevant. All we need to know is that the application knows how to create a TaskManager.

Lifelines, Requests, and Responses

Extending down vertically from each object is a dashed line. That's the object's **lifeline** – an easy way to illustrate when a particular object is being created and used. A horizontal line, with an arrow drawn from **left to right**, represents a methods call of the object at the right-hand end of the line. The following fragment is the UML sequence diagram technique of representing a TaskManager.NewTask method call. The calling application or object is always on the left and the object that is being activated is on the right:

Messages that flow from **right to left** are typically return messages of some sort, and are denoted with dashed lines. One example is the place in which a `Task` instance is returned from `TaskManager`. Notice that every method call that moves from left to right is answered at some point with a return that travels from right to left. Visually it's easy to spot that exchange.

Object Activation and Self-Calling

This example is relatively simple in terms of the information that it presents to anyone reviewing the diagram, but it is still a powerful representation of the interaction between each of the objects involved in that particular scenario. Like other UML diagrams there are other details that can be expressed in a sequence diagram. Probably the two most common are using wide bars to represent **object activation** – the time that an object is actually working – and the **self-call** message.

By showing object activation, we further enhance the information that we can present graphically by making it clear when an object has been activated and when it has finished doing its work. For example, consider the act of saving the `Task` instance we created. Here's a fragment of that diagram (we've assumed that our object instances have already been created):

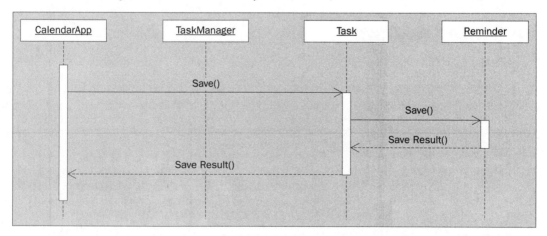

Notice the immediate impact of adding those wide lines to each object lifeline. It is immediately clear how long the object is active and when it's done doing whatever it's been asked to do.

So now, what do you suppose we do when an object calls one of its own methods? That does happen and our sequence diagram fragments above don't really have an obvious technique for illustrating that situation. I mention this only because it is common enough that you will have encountered self-calls in this book and are very likely to encounter them in practice. Since any important self-call should be documented in our diagram if it adds value to the interaction process we're focusing on, we need to include it. The solution is actually rather simple as this diagram fragment illustrates:

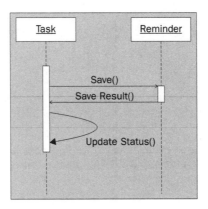

In this example the Task object updates a status of some sort after it asks the Reminder object to save itself. It could be that the status of a particular Task instance is important and the fact that the status is being updated at this point in the sequence has meaning to other developers.

When to use Sequence Diagrams

Any moderately complex set of objects that work together should really have a sequence diagram illustrating their most common or most complex interactions. Sequence diagrams are a highly effective tool when documenting object interactions, and so should be used whenever there are interactions to be documented!

The State Diagram

A **state diagram** does what its name suggests – it illustrates the various states of something (in our case an object) over a period of time. Typically, state diagrams illustrate the states an object can hold throughout its lifetime and how that object may change states when acted upon by outside events. Well, that's nice, but how can something that shows various states of an object be useful? The benefit lies not only in illustrating the various states an object may hold during its lifetime, but the combination of state and all of the external events that force a change in state. After all it's those external events that your application is going to have to respond to.

Let's consider a simple example. In the previous sequence diagram we were working with a set of objects for creating tasks that could have reminders associated with them. The idea was to create a task for someone and at some appropriate, predefined time have a reminder associated with that task appear somewhere. It's the reminder that we'll focus on for our state discussion. Consider that:

❑ When the task is first created and the reminder is first assigned to that task, its state could be said to be *waiting*. That is, the reminder is alive and waiting for a specific time to present itself to the user.

❑ When the time comes for the reminder to be raised to the user, we could say its state is *active* – our term to indicate that the reminder is presently being raised to the user somehow.

❑ Once raised, the user could elect to dismiss the reminder, a state we'd call *complete*, or they could decide that the reminder should be raised at some point in the future, in effect resetting the date and time of the reminder and setting its state back to *waiting*.

Let's create a simple state diagram and see what we can learn about our reminder object.

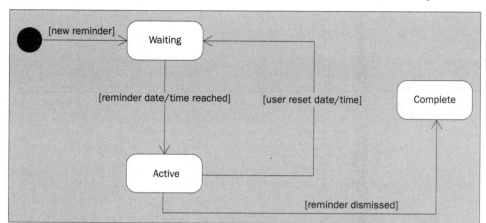

This diagram tells us that to progress from some initial state to Waiting, an event called [new reminder] will affect our system. That event is probably triggered by a user or some other application, sending a request for a new reminder. Once it has been saved, our new reminder simply waits until its predefined date and time is reached. Once the [reminder date/time reached] has occurred, the reminder becomes Active – this is a state that indicates to us that the reminder is actually being presented to a user.

If the user decides they want to be reminded of the same task at some point in the future, that reminder reverts back to its Waiting state, as expressed in the [user reset date/time] event. If, instead, the user decides to dismiss the reminder (that is, to get rid of it and set its status such that it is not raised again) then its state becomes Complete. In this case the external event is the dismissal action of the user.

When to use State Diagrams

If the state of a particular object through its lifetime is particularly complex or the events that might cause an object to change state are extraordinarily interesting, then building a state diagram may be useful. Rarely are state diagrams a common, everyday tool for most developers using the other UML notations. In fact, it is more likely that state diagrams are overused as design overkill.

Physical Diagrams

Since we're all being paid (hopefully) to build and ship software, it's very reasonable that we spend some time actually thinking about the physical implementation of our software and its components. Early in a project it is a good idea to have an idea how you'll move a software application into production. That seems like an obvious statement, but like so many obviously good practices in software development, it easily gets pushed to the side – until the first time you try to get your app ready for a client demo or a conference. Then things really get interesting.

So, the UML gives us a couple of ways for expressing our physical implementation – component and deployment diagrams. **Component diagrams** illustrate physical pieces of code and how they are arranged in relation to one another. **Deployment diagrams** illustrate what the UML literature calls **computational units**, generally a piece of hardware of some sort like a Windows PC or a server.

The Component Diagram

In a component diagram, a piece of code can be an executable, a Windows DLL, a Java package, or just about any other physical manifestation of code (a file, in most cases). Each component is represented by a specific symbol in the diagram and individual components are connected by lines that represent dependencies. Dependencies are a method of indicating that one component is reliant on another component for some reason or another. In our task and reminder object model, we could create a component diagram that wraps our task and reminder objects into one component called Calendar (compiled into the same binary, of course) and illustrate its relationship and dependencies with a UI and a database component:

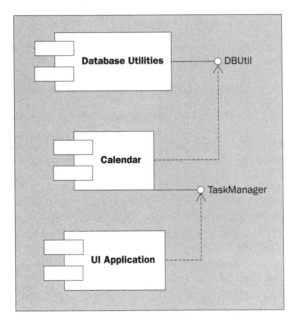

Notice that each component calls the interface exposed by another. It's not necessary to include interfaces in component diagrams. In many cases a single component will expose so many interfaces it would become unwieldy in the diagram to note them all – you'd probably just show the dependencies between components and leave it at that. It is a good idea, however, to think of components and objects in terms of their interfaces, even at a physical level. That's how consumers of our components see them – as a collection of interfaces, literally and figuratively.

The Deployment Diagram

The last UML diagram we'll review in this appendix is generally the last state a software application will hold – a physical deployment. In the UML we have a convenient method of illustrating the pieces of hardware (this is what we earlier called computational units) on which a particular application will run. Deployment diagrams are probably most useful in distributed application design scenarios where an application could easily be spread across machines and those machines are potentially spread around the world. In a simple notation, we'll be able to produce a visually appealing diagram that contains enough detailed deployment information to be useful to a variety of different project roles – techies as well as the planners and managers.

Let's take a look at a client–server application expressed as a deployment diagram. In this case, we've got our calendaring functionality residing on a middle tier server with some kind of UI residing on a Windows PC. Our data layer is any kind of database wrapped up with some standard database components:

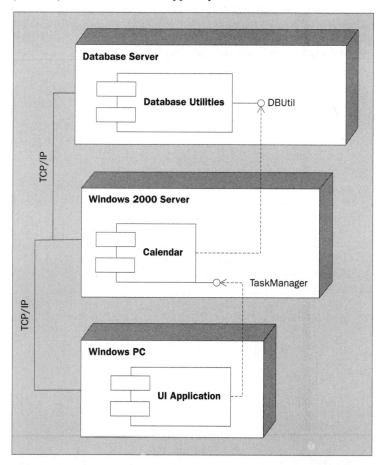

Notice the larger shaded boxes – they are called **nodes**. Each node represents a piece of hardware. In most applications a node will be a PC or server. Also notice what I included with the deployment diagram – our component diagram. I did that to make a point. Deployment diagrams without some link back to the software components that constitute an application are of somewhat limited usefulness. But including deployment diagram details with the same information expressed in a component diagram is very useful. At a glance we know what components are planned to live on which piece of hardware and how those components will relate to one another.

When to use Physical Diagrams

If the application you are designing might reside on multiple machines – as in distributed or client–server applications, it is a very good idea to at least work out some deployment options at early stages in your project work. Deployment and component diagrams are a great way to play through "what-if" scenarios of different physical arrangements and they often times help bring out design issues before you start coding.

Ironically, I've found design reviews that involve deployment diagrams have an interesting psychological effect on development teams. Thinking about and debating the various aspects of physical implementation helps focus team members on the sole purpose of any software project – shipping software. In the early stages of design and development, it is very easy to get lost in the abstract of a software design – how does this class message with this other class, and so on. Personally, that's a trap I often fall into. Sometimes thinking about deployment at early stages tends to shake us out of that less than goal-oriented thinking and back into the right frame of mind.

Summary

We've presented the major UML diagrams in this chapter in a bit of a hurry. You'll find as you read through this book and other literature – for instance, Pierre-Alain Muller's *Instant UML* (ISBN 1-861000-87-1) – that there are other UML diagrams and many variations of the concepts we've just reviewed.

Keep in mind that the most common use of the UML in practice is probably the class diagram, followed by sequence diagrams and maybe use cases, depending on the UML user's role in a software development project – business analyst or developer.

Regardless of what your individual role on a development project happens to be, the material in this appendix should have been enough preparation to turn you into an informed consumer of UML diagrams, and should give you enough information to be able to employ UML basics in your own software development projects.

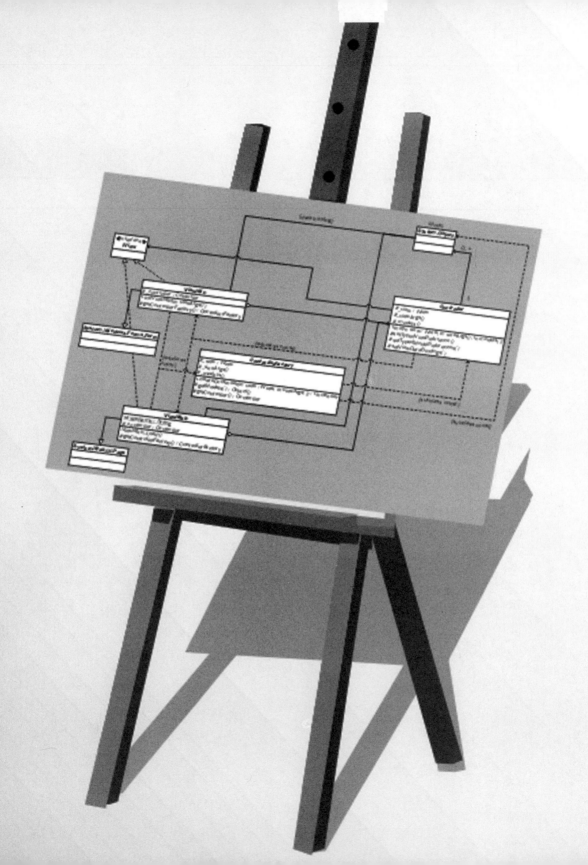

Index

A Guide to the Index

The index is arranged hierarchically, in alphabetical order. Most second-level entries and many third-level entries also occur as first-level entries. This is to ensure that users will find the information they require however they choose to search for it.

Notes

Notes